Sam! Sloan Arch!

P.S.Duval's Steam lith.Press Philad.a

DESIGN FOR A NORMAN VILLA.

SLOAN'S VICTORIAN BUILDINGS

Illustrations of and Floor Plans for 56 Residences & Other Structures

(Originally titled "The Model Architect")

Samuel Sloan

With an Introduction by
Harold N. Cooledge, Jr.

Alumni Professor of Art and Architectural History
College of Architecture, Clemson University

Two Volumes Bound as One

Dover Publications, Inc.
New York

Copyright © 1980 by Dover Publications, Inc.
All rights reserved under Pan American and International Copyright Conventions.

Published in Canada by General Publishing Company, Ltd., 30 Lesmill Road, Don Mills, Toronto, Ontario.
Published in the United Kingdom by Constable and Company, Ltd., 10 Orange Street, London WC2H 7EG.

This Dover edition, first published in 1980, is an unabridged republication of the work originally published by E. S. Jones & Co., Philadelphia, in 1852 under the title *The Model Architect*. The original two-volume work is here bound as one. Plates have been backed up and colored lithographs are reproduced in black and white. An introduction has been written especially for the Dover edition by Professor Harold N. Cooledge, Jr., and a new Contents has been added.

International Standard Book Number: 0-486-24009-6
Library of Congress Catalog Card Number: 80-65627

Manufactured in the United States of America
Dover Publications, Inc.
180 Varick Street
New York, N.Y. 10014

INTRODUCTION

In the summer of 1851, when the Philadelphia publishing house of E. S. Jones & Co. contracted with Samuel Sloan to issue his architectural designs in a series of unbound folios, Sloan had been in private practice for only two years and had assumed the title "Architect" for only a few months. However, between his first independent commission in June of 1849 and the appearance of the first folio in August of 1851, Sloan had become one of the most popular architects of the city. His clients included prominent members of Philadelphia's commercial aristocracy—Biddles, Clothiers, Parrishes and Whartons—and he had acquired powerful friends in both the old Quaker society and among the new industrial millionaires. It is fair to say that Samuel Sloan did not climb to the top of his profession; he began there.

The reasons for his meteoric success lay in the social context of his time. Sloan's career is a classic illustration of Shakespeare's dictum—in which the mid-nineteenth century devoutly believed: "There is a tide in the affairs of men, / Which, taken at the flood, leads on to fortune." Sloan was the right man, at the right time, in the right place.

Sloan was born on March 7, 1815 at Beaver Dam, Honeybrook Township, Chester County, Pennsylvania. In about 1821 he was sent to Lancaster to apprentice with one of his mother's relatives as a carpenter and cabinetmaker. At the same time, Sloan's father moved to Hamilton Village (now part of West Philadelphia) where he was joined by Samuel in 1830. In 1833 Samuel was a carpenter on the construction of part of John Haviland's Eastern State Penitentiary. By 1841, after working on other institutional buildings, he had risen to the post of superintendent of works on Isaac Holden's "new" Department of the Insane of the Pennsylvania Hospital. While working on this building he made the acquaintance of the young Dr. Thomas S. Kirkbride, who became a pioneer in the treatment of insanity in the United States. The doctor befriended Sloan (the two later collaborated on 32 hospitals for the insane organized on the "Kirkbride System") and acted as his patron, encouraging him to study to become an architect.

Sloan was engaged in full architectural practice after 1848. His first large public commission was for the Dela-

ware County courthouse and jail at Media, Pennsylvania, which he won in 1849 in competition with the designs of Thomas U. Walter, later famed for his work on the Capitol building in Washington. More important to his career was the commission he received in 1850 for a villa for Andrew M. Eastwick, a railroad executive. The highly successful result set the young architect in favor with the commercial and industrial elite of Philadelphia. Sloan collaborated with John S. Stewart on the Eastwick house, and in 1852 the two formed a partnership that was, until the panic of 1857, one of the most popular in the nation. Sloan later formed other partnerships, but never regained fully the status held between 1850 and 1860, although he undertook large commissions in his later career. He had moved to Raleigh, North Carolina, where he was supervising construction of the Governor's Mansion and the Insane Hospital in Morganton, when he died on July 19, 1884.

Sloan's practice thrived in that climactic decade, 1850–60, which came at the end of 45 years of optimism and expansion in the United States. These years had begun with Jackson's victory at New Orleans in 1815 and did not end until the threat of civil war overshadowed the nation. In that "Age of Jackson" a determination to success and a fierce conviction of its attainment animated the citizens of the United States, encouraging them to rampant speculation in all areas of national life. That the economic security of the nation was undermined by such speculation seemed to frighten almost no one in an era which economists have called the "period of profitless prosperity." Two financial panics, in 1836 and 1847, did little to dim the inebriate optimism of the speculator, and his apparent success influenced the entire social environment. Speculator values began to be applied to every facet of that environment, including architecture.

There was, however, another side to the national character, a hard-eyed, pragmatic side which was allied with an unusually creative approach to the "mechanical arts." Americans invented things—the elevator, central heating, construction techniques, farm machinery, etc. Not only did these inventions make life easier; they saved that most important commodity, *time*. The maxim "time is money" had an almost religious ring to Americans. No people in all previous history had given time so pecuniary a valuation as did the citizens of the United States in the decade of the 1850s. To save time was both good business and responsible virtue. To waste time was either sinfully improvident or an advertisement of one's financial independence.

In the 1850s Philadelphia, already one of the great mercantile centers of the nation, was rapidly expanding its heavy industry and was engrossed in speculative finance, speculative commerce and speculative building. The new aristocracy of commerce and industry was creating its own fiefs and demesnes, its town mansions, country estates and workers' housing. In the mercantile agora of Market Street and on the financial acropolis of Chestnut Street, its palaces of commerce displayed all the architectural symbols of success.

Philadelphia in the 1850s was also a center of innovation in hospital care and design, was continuing its tradition of prison reform and was a leader in the upgrading of public-school facilities and education. Its benevolent and charitable foundations were among the most active and most forward-looking of any in the nation. But there was a darker side to the city's life. It was terribly overcrowded. The rush of immigrants from Ireland and Continental Europe, which had increased yearly since 1836, had created ethnic ghettos and bred racial conflict. Juvenile gangs terrorized some neighborhoods, pitched battles between fire companies were common and street crime was at an all-time high. There was widespread anti-Black feeling, even some race riots and a few shocking acts of lynch law. In sum, Philadelphia was a vivid city—brash, opportunistic, on the make and sometimes violent; but, withal, vital.

Philadelphia was also one of the nation's centers of architectural book publishing, and its newspapers and periodicals devoted considerable space to reporting architectural affairs. Mention of Sloan's commissions appeared frequently after he was chosen for the Eastwick villa.

It was in this milieu that E. S. Jones & Co. hoped to capitalize on Sloan's sudden rise to prominence when it engaged him for 24 paperbacked folios of his designs. They sold so rapidly that the company at once proposed a hardcover compilation, to be called *The Model Architect*. Sloan was in a position to stipulate how his demonstratedly saleable work was to be presented to the public. He demanded a book which in size, coverage and richness of format was larger and more thorough than any "pattern book" yet published in the United States. Its two folio-sized volumes were profusely illustrated with line drawings and lithographs—even a few three-color plates. It presented building types ranging from low-cost housing to luxurious suburban mansions. There were many plates of cabinet work details and construction together with lists of quantities and estimations of cost. Essays on historic styles, construction methods, materials and landscaping divided the groups of designs. Throughout the book, but especially in its introduction and concluding essay, Sloan set forth his own philosophy of architectural design as it had been formed by the particular environment of the United States.

The Model Architect was a remarkable effort for so young an architect, so shortly in practice. Admittedly many of its designs were derivative, but their adaptation, while nodding in the direction of historic styles, was highly functional for the life-style of mid nineteenth-century Americans of all economic strata. Much of its text was exegesized, but reinterpreted for Sloan's time and place. His essays on construction, materials, siting and mechanical equipment drew upon his personal experience as a carpenter and contractor, and were both practical and imaginative. There was little kowtowing to European precedent. It was a very American book.

In his introduction to the first volume of *The Model Architect*, Sloan gave it as his desire to produce a "matter of fact, business like book." In this he was more successful than could have been predicted, for his "business like" presentations, allied with his understanding use of the visual value symbols of his time, made the work immensely popular. The first volume of the set sold out before the second volume was issued in 1853. All in all, *The Model Architect* went through four legitimate editions (1852, 1860, 1868, 1873) under three publishers, and was twice pirated (once in Philadelphia and once in Boston). Portions of its contents were borrowed—without credit being given—by many subsequent publications, and it is likely that no other work of its kind had so long-lasting an influence upon the development of American vernacular architecture, for it found a national market.

In truth, *The Model Architect* was much more than another "pattern book," for Sloan thought of it, and used it, as a propaganda medium—in part to advertise himself, but also to educate the public as to the demands upon and the responsibilities of an *American* architect. In the "Concluding Remarks" of Volume II, he made this plain:

American works on architecture are few in number, and no works on American architecture have yet been written. Yet there is no country in the world where more houses are projected and built in the course of a year, than our own. . . . It was to supply, in some measure, this deficiency in our national literature, as well as to lend his influence to correcting the prevailing abuses in the noble art, that the author has ventured to turn aside from the daily routine of his profession. It may be that others will follow the example, and we shall soon possess valuable American works on the art of building in our own country.

The Model Architect is still, today, a valuable and relevant work. Although the forms and visual symbols of its architectural designs may seem absurd to architectural generations weaned on the "less is more" philosophy, critical study will show how faithfully those designs reflect the demand and restrictions of Sloan's environment. They are environmental architecture, completely in context, responding not only to the physical parameters of his time and place but also to its metaphysical beliefs. Such response is a lesson that contemporary architects could study with profit.

The essays of *The Model Architect* are well worth the reading time of any present-day architect or architectural educator. The principles they set forth are remarkably "modern." (Some, indeed, are more advanced than we have yet to achieve.) A thoughtful reading of Sloan's opinions on the relation between "form" and "function" is conducive to a greater modesty in those of us who believe that the tenets of contemporary architecture are "all our own invention."

Most important of all, for today's reader, is Sloan's understanding of regionalism—of the size of the United States and the variety of physical and social environments within it. Combined with this is his conviction that, despite its variety, the American way of life is historically unique, demanding unique solutions to its unique requirements. That despite our European origins and our debt to European culture, redactions of European architectural styles cannot, will not ever, be a satisfactory envelope for our lifestyle.

That Sloan did not always—indeed, only seldom— practice what he preached is unimportant. Few of us can, or do, today. What is important is that he believed it, passionately, and that at a critical nexus in our cultural history those beliefs were disseminated to a national public—who remembered, and acted upon, some of them. *The Model Architect* was, thus, a germinal work. Remember, it was published one hundred twenty-seven years ago.

NOTE

In this reprint edition, all the plates have been reduced by 15 percent. Readers should bear this in mind when dealing with the scales given on the plates.

CONTENTS

PREFACE TO THE FIRST VOLUME.

THE present work was undertaken with considerable deference and not without forethought. For some time previous to its commencement the author had been engaged in preparing designs for a large number of country residences to be erected in widely distant places, and was forcibly struck with the great want of information displayed by those concerned in these matters. It is true that much has been written and read on the subject, and a great number of handsomely engraved designs on fine paper have been presented to the public, threatening annihilation to the architect's bill, but no one knows so well as he who has trusted in these promises, the difference between a beautiful picture and a comfortable dwelling. In short such works as have come under notice are quite inadequate to the end proposed. They inculcate very false ideas in the general reader, and give to the builder no new or valuable information. They are much better ornaments for the centre table, than guides to a practical man.

Impressed with these views, the author was led to believe that the production of a "matter of fact" business like book on cottages and country residences was a desideratum. A work that should contain a series of original designs, adapted to every grade of living, from the humblest cottage to the noblest mansion, all accurately delineated to a scale, so that every one might examine for himself and judge of their practicability. He also deemed it requisite that these designs should be complete, comprising both elevations and plans, together with all such details as are usually made out in the form of working drawings, so that the builder might have all parts, both ornamental and constructive, immediately before his eye. In connexion with these, there should be such specifications and bills of quantities as are usually prepared by an architect, and in addition, articles on the various parts of the building that should furnish valuable information to the experienced man and to the learner.

The work thus conceived was determined upon. It was afterwards thought desirable to elevate its character, by adopting such features as would render it interesting and valuable to the general reader and projector, as well as to the artizan. Accordingly, so far as practice would admit, the designs were embellished in various degrees, and the best artists were secured for the engraving. Great care and pains have been expended to make it handsome, interesting and creditable, without detracting in the least from its practical value. Whether this high mark has been reached, the public must judge. It was also thought desirable to issue the work in monthly numbers, containing two complete designs each, thus placing it within the reach of every one. A heavy investment, therefore, was not required at the outset; and the publishers were thus induced to expend more in proportion on each part, than would otherwise have been practicable. This plan too gave the author more time to digest and prepare each design.

The designs thus produced are strictly original. No work had been consulted for hints, but all are such as have either been prepared expressly for the purpose of inserting them here, or have occurred in the regular course of business. It has been a constant endeavour to avoid borrowed features, and if there be any designs which bear a resemblance to others already published or erected, the author is not aware of it; but at the same time he is conscious that it would be almost impossible to exhibit a series of designs, no one of which should be at all similar to any of the thousands which are annually prepared, all having a common object.

For the letter-press the same degree of originality is not claimed. On the contrary, facts have been collected from every available and reliable source. The subjects are such as have been thoroughly studied and written upon long ago, and it would be the height of folly to reject the aid thus proffered. The collation and wording of these facts, however, are entirely our own, and they are accompanied by a large amount of matter never heretofore published; so that there is probably much more originality in these essays than is usually found in works of the kind. They consist principally of a series of articles on the successive operations in the process of building, from the foundation to the finishing, each being described and commented upon. Beside these, there are accounts of the various styles, historical, descriptive, and critical, and other articles on various subjects interesting to all concerned. Each design is also accompanied by full descriptions, and wherever necessary, by specifications; though towards the end these, and the bills of quantities, are discontinued to avoid the constant repetition resulting from their similarity.

It is hoped that the work will not be unacceptable to the public. Every effort has been made to add to its intrinsic value, to give it variety, and to improve its general appearance. Thus far it has been favored with extensive patronage, and until the completion of the next volume no effort will be relaxed to deserve its continuance.

SAMUEL SLOAN, ARCHITECT,

Office, 154 *Walnut Street, Philadelphia.*

INTRODUCTION.

THROUGHOUT the circle of the Fine Arts, none is less indebted to nature than Architecture. Poetry, rhetoricians tell us, is an imitative art, sculpture but copies natural forms of beauty, and the painter's canvass is Nature's mirror. But there is nothing to furnish architectural designs. Trifling decorations may be suggested by many objects around, but the resemblance that a Doric column bears to the human form, or the Gothic style to a bower of trees is a fanciful afterthought, and not the bright preconception which gave them birth. The art stands alone, independent and original. Even the abodes of brute creation have offered no aid, and the caverns of the earth mock by their rugged grandeur our daring aspirations. The architect has drawn entirely from within himself, and given material embodiment to an abstract conception of fitness.

Although so entirely artificial in its origin, architecture nevertheless is completely under the control of nature. Mechanical laws enforce obedience in every structure. The inherent principles of good taste circumscribe design. If the architect violates certain proportions, disregards style, or rejects ornament, then his design, however well executed in other respects, loses all charm and offends every refined judgment. Plans suited to purpose, an appearance in unison with the locality, an adaptation of parts to the whole, and an appropriate use of ornament are all essential to comply with the requisitions of cultivated taste. Thus in every enlightened nation, we find a massive castle erected for defence or confinement, a cottage or villa for a country residence, a palace for a king, and a grand temple or gorgeous Gothic pile for the worship of a God. What artist paints the marble city mansion, surrounded by a pretty rural scene, or a villa, towering upon a mountain cliff, surrounded by jagged rocks? Yet such singular combinations often occur in real life, producing harsh discord.

The erection of these incongruities, however, marks an important step towards refinement. They are the first attempts of a nation to rise above mere utility, and as information is disseminated, and a taste for the Fine Arts cultivated, these will gradually disappear, while beautiful, appropriate and correct designs take precedence. In this, as well as other respects, no people perhaps is advancing so rapidly as our own. A few years ago, when the country was new and the population sparse, we were satisfied with whatever supplied the bare necessities of life, but in the older states resources have rapidly increased, and with them the means of conducing to comfort, and of gratifying that innate love of the beautiful, which has been developed so rapidly, and is diffusing itself among every class. In consequence, everywhere throughout our land, which nature has decorated in such profusion, may be seen springing up ornamental cottages, villas for retired merchants, and summer residences for citizens, all having some pretensions to style and ornament. A few are indeed beautiful, and at once characterize the projector as a man of taste and cultivation, but it is a great pity that many, perhaps the majority, are vain attempts at elegance,—not only destitute of grace in themselves, but are deformities on the fair face of nature.

Still it is a consoling fact, that an effort is being made to throw the charm of beauty around such buildings, for by it we are assured that at no very distant day, Art and Nature will join in decking our land with their beautiful creations. The people are anxious to learn, and as the sources of information increase, so will the principles of good taste be diffused. More elegant buildings will be erected, the mere contemplation of which will conduce to advancement, for every time a man feels the exquisite thrilling sense of beauty, his soul becomes more susceptible to its impressions, more sensible of its presence, and more capable of distinguishing the false from the true. Thus does the national character become infused with refinement.

The public are already aware of the fact, that by a due exercise of taste and judgment a dwelling may be erected, which will combine all comfort and modern convenience with elegance and finished ornament, adding at the same time little or nothing to the cost. It is true also, that thousands of dollars may be expended in decorations, and the result be mere gaudy ostentation, utterly devoid of pleasing effect. The wealthy man may build more extensively, and live in more luxurious splendour than one in moderate circumstances, but he cannot build more tastefully. Even the simple labourer, at no additional expense, may give a highly picturesque effect to his humble home. The painter more frequently copies landscapes surrounding some lowly but beautiful cottage, than those around the lordly mansion.

A man's dwelling at the present day, is not only an index of his wealth, but also of his character. The moment he begins to build, his tact for arrangement, his private feelings, the refinement of his tastes and the peculiarities of his judgment are all laid bare for public inspection and criticism. And the public makes free use of this prerogative. It expects an effort to be made, and forms opinions upon the result. We are beginning to see intellect admired more than wealth or power, and the one who builds a beautiful residence now, is as much respected as were the old Barons with their massive castles and troops of retainers.

But no one can measure how much the charms of home are heightened by adding all the delights of tasteful elegance to the associations which throng its sacred precincts. Around this spot all the thoughts and affections circle. Here is rest. If peace be not here, it will not be found on earth. Then whatever beautifies and adorns home, adds directly to comfort and happiness, nor is there any thing so antagonistic to vice as its alluring delights. Indeed all that is pure in human nature, all the tender affections and gentle endearments of childhood, all the soothing comforts of old age, all that makes memory a blessing, the present delightful, and gives to hope its spur, cluster around that holy place— home.

ARCHITECTURAL STYLE.

UMAN habitations were first erected in compliance with the demands of necessity. When Architecture arose from this position into all the dignity of a Fine Art, it was essential, while supplying these demands, that it should contribute largely to ease and comfort, and also gratify our instinctive love of the beautiful. This love of beauty, however, must not be regarded as the cause of the various styles of architecture. Beauty is universally the same, and the love of it is innate. It was created first, and man then blessed with the perception of it. The same command which gave birth to light gave birth to beauty, and it is as much beyond our control as the rise and set of sun. It is true there are various tastes arising from different degrees of perception of beauty, but primarily their principles are the same. The grade of refinement, or mode of education may determine the purity of taste, or an edict of fashion may for a time distort its features, yet like a twisted branch it will regain its natural position. In consequence of this oneness of the fundamental principles of taste, we find in every part of the globe that refined nations have always built in a style consonant with the object and locality, and have given an expression of uniformity amid variety, of fitness of means to an end, of utility in ornament, and of symmetry in proportions. We must look beyond this for the cause of the characteristic national styles of architecture.

The cause exists in our natural and artificial necessities. These vary with the climate, with national customs and character, and with the advancement of the mechanic arts. Thus in northern latitudes we find the high pointed roof, adapted to throw off the snow which falls in such immense quantities. In warmer regions, no such cause existing, the flat roof is more prevalent. Porches and verandas are not used in the north to the same extent that they are south. In an unsettled country, agitated by civil war or infested by banditti, a massive style is adopted, so that every man's house may be a fortress. The social character of the people, the amount and kind of building material, the number and skill of artizans, all produce effect. These are the impulses which give direction to architectural style.

All styles may be divided into two classes, that derived from the post and lintel, and that derived from the arch. These are sometimes called the horizontal and perpendicular styles, the Grecian being a perfect type of the first, and the Gothic of the second. Frequently both are introduced in the same building, but generally with bad effect. Judging from the remains of the Greeks, they are supposed not to have been acquainted with the arch as an element of building. The Romans were probably the first who employed it, which they did profusely, intermingling it with the Grecian orders; but in the latter part of the dark ages, on account of its ready adaptation, the arched style was used almost exclusively.

We know very little of the domestic architecture of the ancients, but in all their heavy public edifices they have shown themselves to be far more skillful and tasteful architects than the moderns. Their stupendous structures defy the rough touch of time, and even to this day preserve their exquisite beauty. From the Middle Ages we have the elaborate, solemn Gothic, and the massive Norman. From more remote time, the Roman, with its ornate and luxurious magnificence, the Grecian with its chaste and severe simplicity, and the Egyptian with its ponderous and sepulchral grandeur. There are masses of masonry older even than these, but without the high finish essential to a style.

In domestic architecture, however, the moderns have never been surpassed for comfort and convenience. Throughout England and America, all kinds of style in their different adaptations are used, and indeed at the present day there are few countries in which a peculiar national style is exclusively adopted. More generally, those existing are remodelled and mixed in a variety of ways to suit different purposes. Every pure style, however, has features peculiar to itself, and is thus rendered distinct from all others. The proportions, ornaments, or any of the characteristics which thus isolate it, if connected with another, would be utterly discordant, inconsistent, and disagreeable to a cultivated taste. Hence educated men reject this hybrid style, and their residences are generally designed and ornamented correctly. In the course of this work, pure specimens of the various styles will be given, and their history, distinguishing features, and whatever else of interest may be connected with them will be discussed.

AN ITALIAN VILLA.

DESIGN FIRST.

THIS Villa is designed after those which have been prevalent in Italy since the fifteenth century. The style has been introduced into other parts of Europe, into England and America, and so well adapted is it to the wants and tastes of our people, that it is likely to become, if it is not already, one of our most fashionable modes of building. The more wealthy classes have adopted it quite largely for summer residences. It possesses very little of the rural character, and seems much more appropriate for the residence of one accustomed to city life, than for one born and bred in the country. Its location, consequently, should not be in the depths of the forest, but near some frequented highway within a few miles of a city. The grounds around if arranged in smooth lawns, groves, gravelled walks, and finished gardens, would accord well with the general expression of the style. A fountain in front, and a few vases or statues scattered here and there would add to the pleasing effect.

The perspective view, Plate I., gives the general appearance of the building very happily. The gables on either side of the campanile give symmetry to the front, and at the same time, take away that monotony and rigid uniformity, which is likely to result from the nearly rectangular ground plan, and which above all things is to be avoided in country houses.

PERSPECTIVE VIEW.

ITALIAN VILLA.

Design I.

Pl. III.

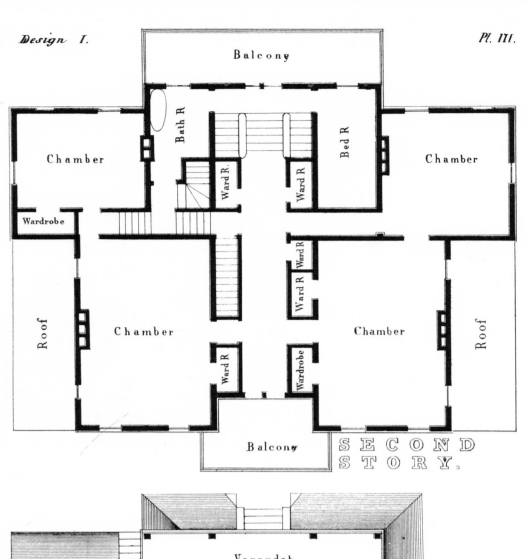

Balcony

Chamber

Bath R

Ward R.

Bed R

Chamber

Wardrobe

Ward R

Roof

Chamber

Ward R

Ward R

Chamber

Roof

Ward R

Wardrobe

Balcony

SECOND STORY.

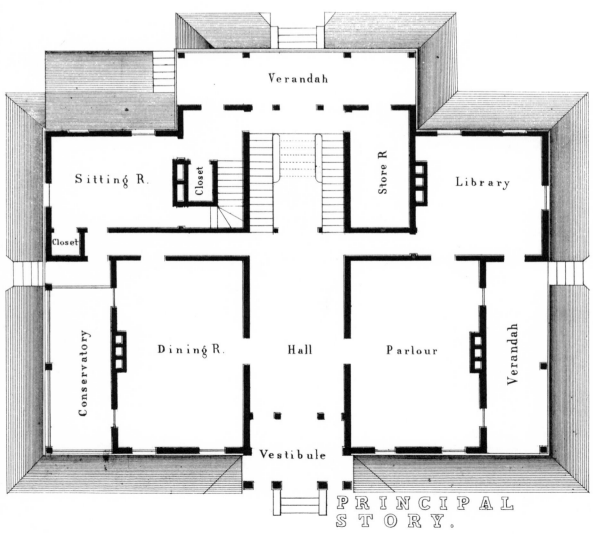

Verandah

Sitting R.

Closet

Store R

Library

Closet

Conservatory

Dining R.

Hall

Parlour

Verandah

Vestibule

PRINCIPAL STORY.

Scale 10 feet to an inch.

GROUND PLANS.

P.S. Duval's steam lith.press Phil.

Fig. 2.

Fig. 3.

Fig. 4.

Fig. 1.

Fig. 5

Scale to door only

¾ inch to a foot.

Scale. One foot to the inch.

DETAILS.

P. S. Duval's Steam lith Press Philad a

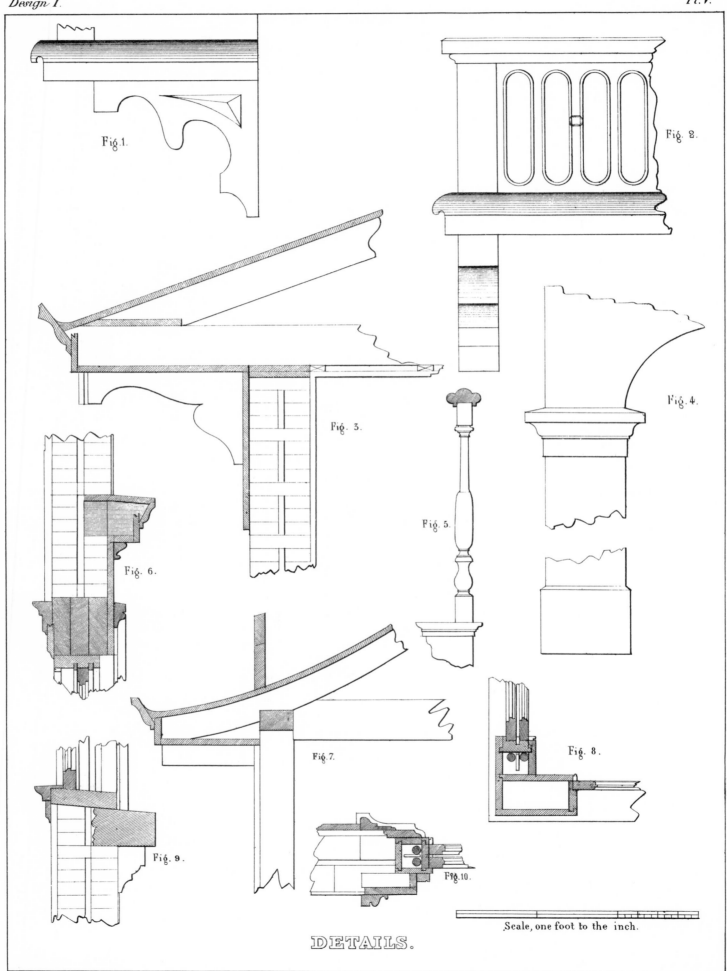

Fig.1.

Fig. 2.

Fig. 3.

Fig. 4.

Fig. 5.

Fig. 6.

Fig. 7.

Fig. 8.

Fig. 9.

Fig.10.

Scale, one foot to the inch.

DETAILS.

P.S.Duval's steam lith press Phila

The campanile itself appears like the centre, around which the other parts of the building are grouped. The porch over the main entrance, the stained glass windows, and the balconies, make it the most ornamental feature, while the verandah on the right, and the conservatory on the left, give the whole an expression of ease and elegance. The windows opening into the verandah may be made to reach the floor, and thus render it accessible from the parlour as well as the library.

Plate II. is a front elevation of the same, giving the proportions correctly, and exhibiting the constructive features of the building more distinctly. Very many of the more prominent details may be taken directly from this plate, without any reference to others.

Plate III. exhibits the plans of the first and second stories. The great conveniences of this compact and delightful arrangement of apartments are here made evident. We see that the building will readily accommodate a family of eight or ten members, servants inclusive. As the kitchen is immediately beneath the room marked Sitting R., it might be more convenient to use this as a dining room, and to use the room opposite the parlour as a sitting room.

Plate IV. consists of details. Fig. 1, exhibits a column of the front porch, with a section through the architrave, frieze and cornice.—Fig. 2, the base of the first and second stories.—Fig. 3, inside doors.—Fig. 4, cornice and cantaliver of the tower.—Fig. 5, section of an inside door, with the dressings.

Plate V. is also detail drawings.—Fig. 1, shows a section of the platform of the tower balcony with bracket.— Fig. 2, front of the same.—Fig. 3, cornice, with cantaliver and section of wall.—Fig. 4, verandah post with capital.— Fig. 5, balusters.—Fig. 6 and 9, section through a window head and sill.—Fig. 7, section of the verandah cornice.—Fig. 8, conservatory post showing the sash.—Fig. 10, window frames with dressings.

All other information necessary to construction may be gathered without difficulty from the following complete

SPECIFICATION

Of the workmanship and materials required in the erection of Design First.

DIMENSIONS.—The entire extent of the front is sixty-two feet, that of the side is forty-one feet together with eleven feet for the projection and verandah in the rear. The first story containing a vestibule, a hall, a double flight of stairs, a dining room, sitting room, parlour, library, store room, private stairs, closets, &c., is to be thirteen feet four inches high to the top of the second floor. The second story containing five chambers, a bath room, eight wardrobe closets, and stairs leading to the tower, is to be ten feet in the clear. The room in the tower is to be nine feet high in the clear. The roof is to pitch six feet. For the divisions and other general dimensions, reference is to be had to the plans on Plate III.

EXCAVATIONS.—The cellar is to extend the entire length and breadth of the building, and to be six feet deep below the line of the yard pavement. The portion under the sitting room, private stairs and entry is to be arranged for a kitchen. There is to be likewise in the rear, an area of the same depth, by five feet wide at the bottom, with a bank sloping upwards and outwards at an angle of sixty degrees. The trenches for foundations in the cellar are to be eight inches deep, and those under the verandahs and conservatory are to be two feet and a half deep. The earth is to be graded around the building from the under side of the water-table to a distance of five feet from the wall. All superfluous earth is to be removed from the grounds, or to such parts thereof as may be directed.

STONE WORK.—All the outside walls of the cellar, and the foundations of the appendages are to be composed of quarry building stone of a good quality. These walls are to be eighteen inches thick, and built as high as the under side of the joists, and all based upon a course of long flat stone, well and solidly laid in mortar. The mortar is to be composed of coarse, sharp sand, and wood burnt lime in such proportions as to insure the strongest cement. All the facings are to be smooth dashed and lime washed.

BRICK WORK.—The superstructure upon the stone wall is to be composed of bricks. It is to be of double thickness, with a hollow space in the centre one and a half inches wide. No soft bricks are to be used in the outer course. The division walls in the cellar are to be of hard brick, and of double thickness, with doorways, &c., as delineated on the plan for basement. All flues are to be formed for gas, warm air, and ventilation, as shown on the plans, and as may be directed during the progress of erection. They are to be pargetted and topped out with smooth brick, as shown upon the elevation. The walls on either side of the hall are to be of brick, one story high, and of double thickness. There is to be a case of brick in the cellar under the hall large enough to receive a furnace sufficient to warm the whole house. The area, the provision cellar and pantry are to be paved with good paving bricks laid in mortar. The area is to have a guard wall fourteen inches high to support the bank, also a gutter to convey water to a cess pool at the end for drainage.

JOISTS, &c.— The joists of the first story are to be of spruce or white oak, three by twelve inches ; those of the second story are to be hemlock of good quality, three by eleven inches ; all to be placed sixteen inches between centres, to be backed, and have one course of herring bone bridging through the centre. The ceiling joists are to be three by five inches, and placed sixteen inches between centres. The joists in the tower are to be three by nine inches, and the same distance apart. The rafters are to be three by five inches, and placed two feet between centres. The studding throughout the partitions is to be three by four inches, those for the doors three by six inches, and all placed sixteen inches between centres. The sleepers in the basement are to be of white oak, three by four inches, and placed twenty inches between centres.

FLOORS.—The floors throughout the interior of the building are to be laid with one inch Carolina heart pine, well worked, well seasoned, firmly nailed to the joists with eight penny nails, and afterwards smoothed off. The front vestibule is to be laid with white pine plank, not over four inches wide or one inch and a half thick, grooved together, and laid with white lead in all the joints.

WINDOWS.—All the windows are to correspond to the elevation and detail drawings. The sash are to be one inch and a half thick, and double hung with the best one and three-quarter inch axle pulleys and patent cord. The sash in the tower and conservatory are to be diamond. The side windows of the parlour, dining room, and second story hall front are to extend to the floor.—The windows of the wings and the rear, are to have close shutters on the first story one inch and a half thick, each shutter to have three panels with suitable mouldings. The corresponding windows in the second story are to have one inch and a half pivot blinds. The shutters to each window are to be in two parts, and all are to be hung with good strap hinges, and secured by ten inch bolts in the first story, and eight inch bolts in the second story. The front windows are to have inside shutters of three folds, with four panels each, and mouldings. They are to be hung in two parts each, and secured in the usual way.

DOORS.—The front doors are to be folding, two inches and a half thick, with four panels in each, and finished by mouldings and fillets. They are to be hung with three four by four inch butts, and secured by an eight inch mortice lock, with a night key, and by two iron plate flush bolts. All the room doors on the first story are to be two inches thick, and contain eight panels each, with mouldings and fillets. They are to be hung with two four by four inch butts, and fastened with four inch mortice locks. All outer doors are to be two inches thick, having a bead butt on the inside, and moulding with fillets on the outside. The room doors in second story and basement are to be one inch and a half thick, with mouldings on both sides, and hung with three and a half inch butts, and secured by three inch mortice locks. All outer doors are to be one inch and a quarter thick, hung with two and a half by three inch butts, and secured by locks wherever necessary.

DRESSINGS.—The parlour, dining room and hall, are to be finished with seven inch pilasters, and a moulding band two inches and a half square. The front windows must have paneled backs. The wash-board is to be seven inches wide, with a two inch and a half sub, and a two inch moulding. The second story is to have five inch pilasters, with a two and a half inch square band. The wash-board is to be six inches wide, with a two and a half inch sub, and a two inch moulding.

CLOSETS.—All the closets and wardrobes throughout the building are to be fitted up and fully shelved. Three in the second story are to have each a set of drawers. The store room also is to be fitted with all necessary shelving.

STAIRS.—The main stairs are to be made of the best heart step boards, one inch and a quarter thick, and put up in the best manner. The newels are to be mahogany, eight inches square, with turned cap and base, and with an octagon shaft. The rail is to be four inches square moulded, also mahogany. The balusters are to be one inch and three quarters in diameter, and turned of maple or other hard wood. The private stairs leading from the basement to the upper room in the tower, are to be made of one inch heart step boards, put together as is usual for such stairs.

VERANDAHS.—The verandahs each are to be constructed in accordance with the drawings. The floors are to be of white pine one inch thick, grooved together with white lead in the joints. The ceiling is to be lined with well seasoned, grooved, quartered and beaded boards, smoothed for painting. The roof of the one on the side is to be curved, of that on the rear to be flat. The roof of the conservatory is also to be curved. The posts, caps, &c., are to be executed as in the detail drawings. The entrance porch is to be constructed according to the drawings, and in the best manner. The sash of the conservatory in the south wing are to be one inch and a half thick, and so constructed as to be readily moved.

ROOFS.—All the roofs are to be sheathed with one inch quartered and grooved boards, firmly nailed to the joists. The cornice is to be constructed according to drawings.

TINNING.—All the roofs are to be overlaid with the best quality one X leaded tin, painted on both sides; the upper side to have two coats. All necessary gutters, and four three-inch conductors to convey the water from the roof, are to be put up and secured to a wall string in the best manner.

ROUGH-CASTING.—All the outside walls are to be rough-cast in the very best manner, by a workman familiar with the business. The materials are to be of the best kind, and the whole laid off in blocks.

PLASTERING.—All the walls and ceiling inside are to be plastered with two coats of brown mortar, and one of white hard finish. The parlour, dining room and hall, are to have a cornice in the angle to girt eighteen inches. Each room and hall is to have a sunken panel on the ceiling three inches deep, with an enriched moulding, also a centre flower three feet six inches in diameter, and one in the hall three feet in diameter. The front rooms and hall of the second story are to have a cornice girting fourteen inches, and all other walls to be plain. The mortar must be composed of clean river sand, and wood burnt lime in proportions to insure strength. The hair mixed with it must be sound, and the lath free from bark.

PAINTING AND GLAZING.—All wood work inside and out is to have three coats of the best white lead paint, and of such tints as the owner may direct. The outside steps are to receive four coats of paint, and be well sanded. All glass is to be of the best quality of American manufacture, well bradded, beaded and back puttied.

HARDWARE.—All hardware necessary to make the building complete in every part must be furnished, and of the best quality of American manufacture. All the door knobs, except those of the kitchen, are to be of porcelain. There are to be seven bells, including that of the front door, placed in such rooms as the owner may wish. All the metal furniture of the front door is to be silver plated.

PLUMBING.—A reservoir of five hundred gallons capacity, strongly made with two inch plank, and lined with lead weighing three pounds to the foot, is to be placed in the loft over the bath room. The bath tub is also to be made of boards, paneled in front, and lined with lead weighing fifteen pounds to the foot. A force pump is placed in the kitchen, with tubes leading to the reservoir, the boiler back of the range, and sink in the kitchen. The bath tub and sink are also to be furnished with a hot water pipe extra strong, and all necessary draw and stop cocks are to be placed upon the different pipes, so that the whole work may be finished in the best manner.

COOKING RANGE.—The kitchen is to be furnished with a medium size range of the best and most improved construction, with a twenty-five gallon boiler attached, and so arranged as to heat the room above and bath room.

FURNACE.—There is to be a furnace in the cellar to warm the whole of the first story except the sitting room, and the second story. The flues to convey the heat to the different rooms are to be tin cased, and furnished with approved registers richly bronzed.

FINALLY.—All the work is to be done in the best workmanlike manner, according to the elevation, plan and detail drawings exhibited on plates II., III., IV. and V., and according to the general intent and meaning of this specification, subject at all times to the decision of an architect.

GENERAL ESTIMATE

OF THE COST IN ERECTING DESIGN FIRST.

The cost of the building will of course vary with the location, with the kind and abundance of material, &c. We suppose it to be situated near a city, where the price of labor, material and transportation is not greater than in this section of the United States. In other parts of the country, a calculation is easily made by comparing costs.

Built of brick, and finished in other respects according to the specification, the total sum will not be *more* than $5,000. If stone be substituted, the sum will be but $4,800. If the size of the building be reduced, so as to accommodate a family of but six or eight persons, servants included, it will diminish the cost to about $4,000. These are estimates in round numbers, but they are calculated from a bill of items, which it was deemed unnecessary to give, and if there is any error, it lies in an excess.

HISTORY OF GOTHIC ARCHITECTURE.

UCH difference of opinion has existed respecting the origin of the Gothic style in Architecture. Many of the best writers on the subject, believe that it was brought from the East. There have been found both in India and Persia, structures of undoubted antiquity, which comprise as a prominent feature the pure Gothic arch. They suppose it to have been brought from thence by the Arabians, and by them carried into Spain, that here the Goths adopted it, who being acquainted with Roman architecture, and mixing its details to some extent with the other, produced the style which has received their name.

Others have believed that the style originated among the Ostrogoths, and was by them introduced into Italy under Theodric, A. D. 484, where it received its finish. Some have imagined the pyramid to be its source; others more poetical have supposed that the general effect of the style was planned by some bright genius in imitation of a grove, and hence the minor ornaments are taken from foliage. The fret work, the groined arches, the pillars in the nave, and the tracery of the windows do bear a distant, but beautiful resemblance to the arcades, and interlacing boughs of a grove.

The true origin of the style, however, is to be found in the corruptions introduced into the Grecian orders by the Romans, which were continued through the Dark Ages, until all trace of the original was lost.

The Lombards who succeeded the Goths in Italy, were thoroughly acquainted with Roman architecture. They were expelled by Charlemagne, and dispersed throughout Europe. In consequence of their different habits, the different material, and an inferior degree of skill in their artizans, they soon made their style of building distinct from the Roman. The arch was found more convenient, and was adopted to the exclusion of the Grecian column. They built more coarsely and more massively.

The Normans on their conversion to Christianity adopted this style, and so improved was it by the zeal of their monks in ecclesiastical architecture, that it became their own. They built with greater finish, enlarged the arches, introduced more of them, added decorative mouldings, and produced magnificent structures, that yet stand to rival modern skill. Their vast conquests soon established these improvements throughout Europe, and after their settlement in England, more attention was given to the art.

Innovations were now gradually introduced. Ornaments were used in greater profusion. The arches were multiplied and stilted. They were brought in close proximity, and finally made to intersect each other, thus producing the pointed arch. This was then exclusively adopted. Perpendicular lines increased in number. The walls were built less massively, and buttresses with pinnacles appeared. More decorations were superadded, and other changes made, until in the latter part of the twelfth century the Gothic style stands confessed and distinct, presenting a most striking contrast to the styles of the ancients.

The Gothic style has never been subjected to rules so strict as its predecessors. There has always been great freedom allowed not only in ornaments but in proportions, and consequently from the time it was first recognized until its abandonment, it was undergoing constant, though very gradual changes; yet such strongly marked features have characterized its different stages of development, that it may readily be subdivided, and its progress thus explained.

The EARLY ENGLISH style prevailed from the latter part of the twelfth until the latter part of the thirteenth century. It has been called the *Lancet Pointed* style from the peculiar form of the windows. These were pointed, long, narrow and without tracery. Towards the first of this period they were placed singly, but afterwards in groups, occasionally combined under one large arch, and the tympanum thus formed was sometimes pierced with a trefoil. The doors were massive with deep jambs, and the Norman zig-zag was replaced by the tooth moulding. The flying buttress was introduced, and a tapering spire superseded the embattlement. There are not a great many original specimens of this style extant. Salisbury Cathedral is perhaps the most perfect, and some parts of Westminster Abbey built thus, are in a good state of preservation.

By an easy transition, we now pass into the DECORATED style, which flourished between the latter part of the thirteenth, and the latter part of the fourteenth centuries. It existed under the reign of Edward I., but chiefly prevailed under those of Edward II. and Edward III., and is considered the perfection of medieval architecture. It was characterized by purity in ornament, with greater freedom and richness in design. The principal feature is the window; it is considerably enlarged, and the arch made obtuse, or with the apex and points of impost at equal distances forming the equilateral arch. The space included in this triangle, or tympanum as it is called, is filled with tracery, sometimes geometrical, but generally flowing in most graceful curves, the mullions branching out with great delicacy and lightness. A peculiar ornament called the ball-flower was used very extensively. The foliage of the capitals was crumpled and carved more naturally. The buttresses were niched, and more elegant general proportions were adopted. There appears to have prevailed during this period a school of art, both in architecture and sculpture, which in beauty of design and finish of execution, surpassed any other since the fall of the Western Empire. The two arts declined together.

The third division is called the PERPENDICULAR or *Florid* style. It flourished from the latter part of the fourteenth century until the Reformation, a period of about one hundred and fifty years. The principal characteristic of this style is also to be found in the window. The arch was much depressed, the mullions, instead of branching into tracery, were continued perpendicularly upwards, and crossed by transoms. Indeed throughout there was a tendency toward vertical lines. There was also a great increase of decoration. Every part of the structure both inside and out was loaded with rich carving, cut with great depth, minuteness and delicacy, but so abundant as to give to the whole a meretricious effect, and hence cause the style to be generally considered a decadency. Highly ornamented paneling, fan tracery for the ceiling, a horizontal hood mould embracing two or more narrow windows, and a high peaked roof elaborately finished, were all introduced at this time. The latter feature is beautifully exemplified in Westminister Hall; and the Chapel of Henry VII., also at Westminister, is a magnificent relic of this age.

About the middle of the sixteenth century the Reformation began, and entirely changed the current of affairs. Architecture among other things was gradually revolutionized. It had been until now, under the protection of the Roman Catholic Church, the zeal of whose dependents was the cause of the present advanced stage of the art. With that liberality which was practised towards everything that would advance their creed, they expended upon these buildings nearly all the monastic revenues, private offerings, and voluntary donations which poured into their coffers. The dignitaries of the church were the architects, and the laity were the workmen, hence the great care and pains expended upon the most minute portions of these venerable fabrics. Domestic architecture of course followed the different styles, but it was in ecclesiastic structures that the whole art was concentrated, and its perfection displayed, nor was there at the time of which we speak any land that could vie with England in the number and magnificence of these edifices. But the time had come when the idolatry of superstition was to give way before a spirit of innovation, which not satisfied with the suppression of monasteries, seemed to retain even against the buildings a prejudice that not only prompted their mutilation or destruction, but opposed itself to a continuance of the style. The revival of classical architecture in Italy about this time, also had a considerable effect in producing what has been called the DEBASED style. The arch was more depressed until almost flat, ornaments were rejected even to plainness, which together with an admixture of Italian details, entirely changed the character of the buildings.

At this time arose Inigo Jones, the architect of White Hall and Surgeon's Hall, also Christopher Wren, Knight, another learned man and accomplished architect, who designed St. Paul's and other famous works. These two were impassioned with the styles then coming into vogue in Italy, and labored hard to reproduce them in England, to the exclusion of that style to which Wren contemptuously gave the name "Gothic." The great fire of 1666, gave the latter ample opportunity for exercising his influence, and this period may be considered as terminating Gothic architecture in England.

On the continent, the Gothic style underwent nearly the same changes that it experienced in England. The Perpendicular style, however, differed in detail somewhat from the Late Gothic in Germany, and the Flamboyant, in France, to which it corresponded in point of time. When the style became extinct in England, it was almost simultaneously abandoned throughout Europe, and the Italian has since been the prevailing mode.

A GOTHIC COTTAGE.

DESIGN SECOND.

Plate VI. gives a perspective view of a Gothic Cottage, the front elevation of which is shown in Plate VII. This beautiful design combines economy with its tasteful appearance ; for if built of brick, and the specification below followed in other respects, it will cost but $2,800, and if stone be substituted, this will be reduced to $2,650. These estimates are carefully calculated, and are certainly not too small. Plate VIII. exhibits the ground plans.

Plate IX. consists of details.—Fig. 1, a verandah post with a section through the cornice.—Fig. 2, crocket course to the preceding.—Fig. 3, post and cornice of the entrance porch.—Fig. 4, inside door.—Fig. 5, a chimney-can.

Plate X. also consists of details.—Fig. 1, shows a window with outside dressings.—Fig. 2, section of inside dressings. —Fig. 3, cornice.—Fig. 4. base.—Fig. 5, section of a window frame.—Fig. 6, Finial.—Fig. 7, section through a conservatory post and sash.

Further remarks are unnecessary, all other important points being explained by the following

SPECIFICATION

Of the workmanship and materials to be used in the erection of Design Second.

GENERAL DIMENSIONS.—The main building is to be twenty by thirty-five feet. Entrance hall is to be fourteen by fifteen feet. The conservatory is to be eleven by twelve feet. The rear building is to be seventeen by twenty-five feet. The whole is to be two stories high ; the first story twelve feet to the top of the second floor, the second story ten feet in the clear, and the roof to have fifteen feet pitch.

ROOMS.—The first floor is to contain a drawing room, library, dining room, hall and kitchen. The second story is to contain five chambers, the entry and bath room. There are also to be two rooms in the loft of the main building.

EXCAVATION.—There is to be beneath the entire extent of the building, an excavation five feet below the yard pavement. The earth therefrom is to be graded around the building to the under side of the water-table, and the surplus earth to be removed to such parts of the grounds as may be directed.

STONE WORK.—All cellar walls are to be composed of quarry building stone of a good quality, and to be eighteen inches thick to the under side of the flooring joists. The foundations of the porch, verandah and conservatory, are to be at least two feet deep. All the above masonry is to be laid in the best mortar, made from good coarse sharp sand and wood burnt lime. All the facings of the walls are to be well dashed and white-washed.

BRICK WORK.—All outside walls and the division wall between the two buildings are to be of coarse hard brick, and to be ten inches thick, with a hollow space in the centre. All flues are to be well pargetted, and topped out above the roof at its apex, finished with an ornamental chimney-can as on the elevation. Also a brick furnace chamber is to be built in the cellar, of a capacity sufficient for the reception of Chilson's No. 4 furnace.

JOISTS, &c.—The floor joists of the first story throughout, and of the second story in the main building are to be three by twelve inches. Those over the dining room, kitchen, and the second story main building are to be three by ten inches. The ceiling joists are to be three by five inches. All are to be well backed, lattice bridged, and placed sixteen inches between centres. The rafters are to be three by eight inch rafter cuts, placed two feet between centres. The ridge piece is to be three by twelve inches, and the wall plate three by ten inches. All the above timber must be good sound seasoned hemlock. All stud partitions are to be formed of three by four inch scantling firmly nailed, and placed sixteen inches between centres ; door studs are to be three by six inches.

STAIRS.—The main stairs in the hall are to be formed of one inch and a quarter heart step boards, put together on strong carriages. The newels are to be black walnut, seven inches square at the base, with an octagon shaft, the rail of the same material and moulded, the balusters of the same, one inch and three quarters square at the base, with a turned shaft. The private stairs are to be continued from the cellar, to the main loft, and put up as is usual for such stairs.

WINDOWS.—All sash are to be one inch and a half thick, hung to casement frames with suitable butts, and secured by plate flush bolts at top and bottom. The glass are all to be diamond shape, except those of the kitchen.

DOORS.—The main entrance door is to be two inches thick, having five panels sunk with mouldings, and hung with four by four inch butts, and secured by an upright mortice lock with night key. The room doors of the first and second stories are to be one inch and a half thick, with mouldings on both sides, hung with three by three inch butts, and secured by a four inch mortice lock. All other doors are to be one inch and a quarter thick, hung with three by three inch butts, and secured by locks where necessary.

DRESSINGS.—The window and door dressings are to be put on as exhibited in the detail drawings, except the kitchen and loft, which will be plain. The wash-board of the first story main building is to be eight inches wide, with a two and a half inch sub, and moulding as referred to in the description of plates. The dining room and second story main building are to have the same without the sub, all others but six inches wide. The cornice and ornaments are to be as shown on the detail drawings. The verandah, porch and conservatory are to be constructed as shown on the elevation, plan, and detail drawings. All roofs are to be sheathed with seasoned boards for slating. All lumber is to be of the best quality, and the carpenter's work is to be executed in a good and workmanlike manner.

ROOFING.—The roof is to be overlaid with the best Susquehanna slate, seven by fourteen inches, laid diamond shape, and secured by four-penny galvanized nails. All necessary tin for the valleys, ridge and hips is to be of a good quality, and painted slate colour.

PLASTERING.—All walls and ceilings are to have two coats of brown mortar, and one of white. The parlor, hall and library are to have a cornice in the angle of the ceiling to girt twelve inches. A centre flower in the parlor is to be three feet diameter, and one in the hall two feet six inches, such as the owner may approve.

PAINTING AND GLAZING.—All interior wood work is to receive three coats of pure white lead paint, mixed with the best linseed oil. The exterior is to receive four coats of paint, and sanded in the best manner. The glass of the first story main building and dining room is to be of the best quality American manufacture, the rest to be second quality. All must be well bradded, beaded and back puttied.

HARDWARE.—All hardware necessary to make the building complete in every part, is to be of a good and approved quality. The knobs in the main building are to be of white porcelain. All others are to be mineral.

FINALLY.—All the work is to be executed in a good and workmanlike manner, after the detail and other drawings, and according to the general intent and meaning of this specification.

ENCAUSTIC TILES.

The Plate No. XI. represents a variety of specimens of Encaustic and Tesselated Flooring Tiles. They are imported, and are for sale by S. A. Harrison, 146 Walnut Street, Philadelphia. We hope to see them introduced very generally in this country, since they are so admirably adapted to our climate. They can be obtained at about one half the price of marble floors, at the same time having a more beautiful effect.

These Tiles are of uniform size and shape, so that they can be fitted together accurately, in laying down the most complicated designs. Being all composed of the same material, variously coloured, they are all of precisely equal hardness, so that floors made with them are not liable to fall into hollows, or become loose in use, which is one of the greatest objections to marble floors that are exposed to much wear. Owing to the great pressure to which these Tiles are subjected, they are quite impervious to moisture. They are of a flinty texture throughout, and to all intents and purposes absolutely imperishable. We hope to see some of our public buildings adopt this beautiful and durable flooring. Tiles have been in use in Europe for many centuries, but through the enterprise and liberality of the Messrs. Minton & Co., of England, a very extensive revival of the use of this beautiful kind of decoration has been attained.

For stores, vestibules, entries, outside verandahs, green houses, churches, and in fact every place where beauty, taste and economy are objects to be attained, there is nothing that can be more suitable than the Encaustic Tiles. We shall in our future number, give a more descriptive account of the use and manufacture of this article, both ancient and modern, which cannot fail to interest all our readers.

PERSPECTIVE VIEW.

Sam! Sloan, Arch!   P. S. Duval's steam lith: Press Philad.ª

ENGLISH GOTHIC STYLE.

Scale ten feet to the inch

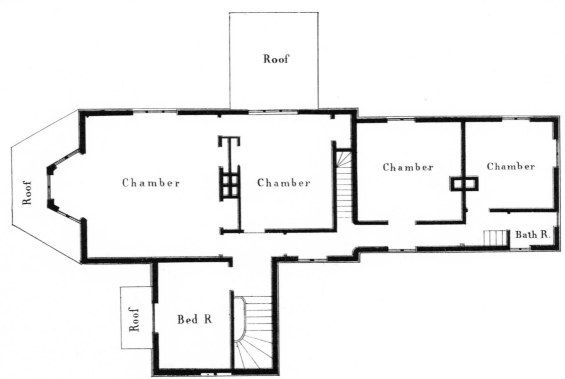

S E C O N D   S T O R Y.

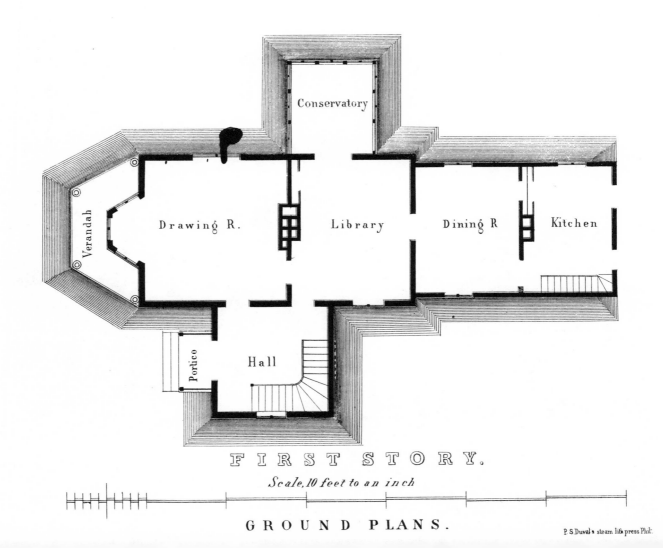

F I R S T   S T O R Y.

Scale, 10 feet to an inch

G R O U N D   P L A N S .

P. S. Duval's steam lith press Phil.

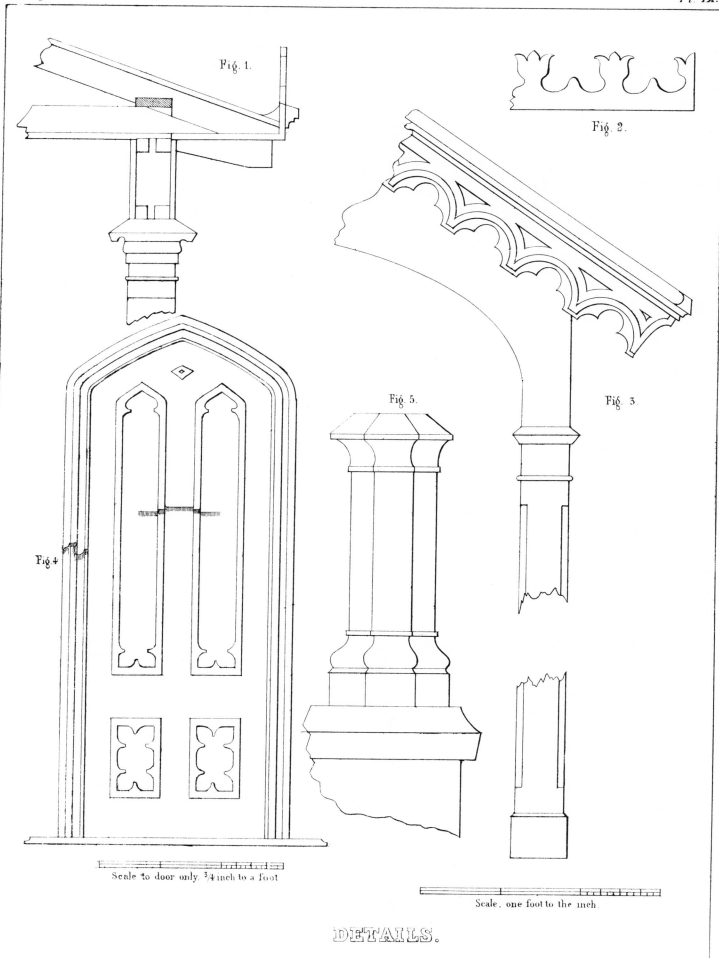

Fig. 1.

Fig. 2.

Fig. 5.

Fig. 3.

Fig. 4.

Scale to door only. 3/4 inch to a foot

Scale, one foot to the inch.

DETAILS.

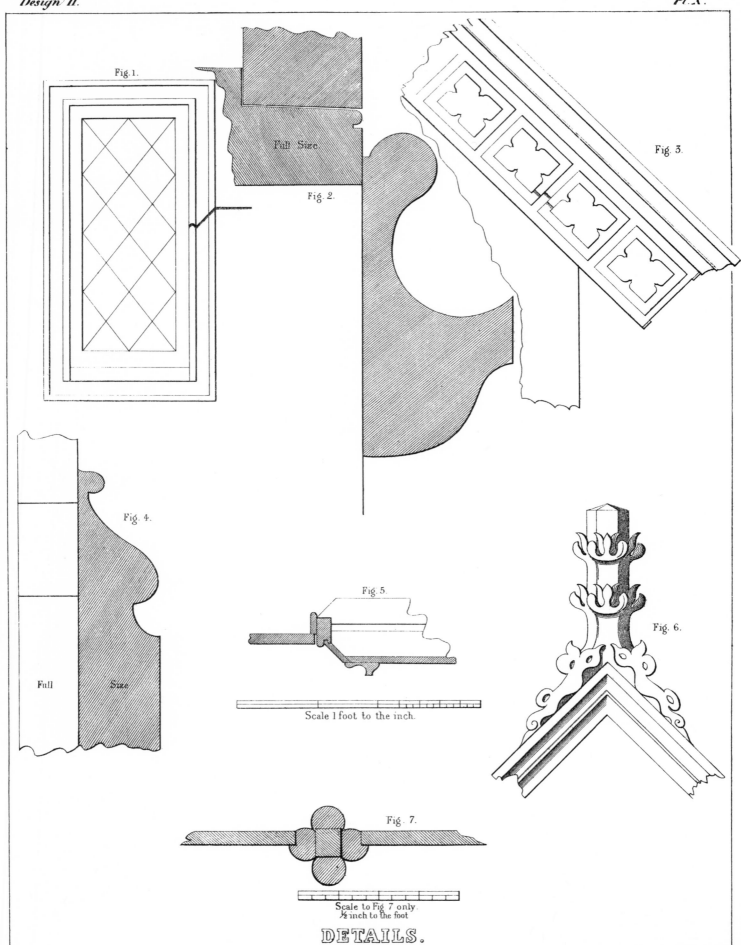

Fig. 1.

Full Size.

Fig. 2.

Fig. 3.

Fig. 4.

Full   Size

Fig. 5.

Scale 1 foot to the inch.

Fig. 6.

Fig. 7.

Scale to Fig 7 only.
½ inch to the foot

DETAILS.

P. S. Duval's Steam lith. Press Philad.ᵃ

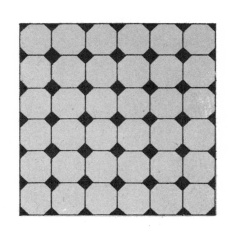

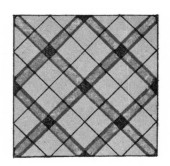

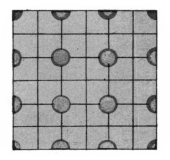

DEBASED GOTHIC.

THIS style has already been referred to as that which prevailed in England during the century immediately succeeding the commencement of the Reformation. The terms Tudor and Elizabethan, have each been used in reference to different stages of its development, but writers on the subject have always disagreed, both in dates and as to the respective characteristics of the two. In using the word Debased, we follow Bloxam, than whom no one is more thoroughly versed in all that appertains to Gothic architecture. The term must not be understood in a bad sense, as depreciating the style, but simply as referring to the fact, that during the time mentioned, i. e., from the last of the Perpendicular style until the total extinction of this species of architecture, there was a constant change being wrought in the principles of the general style, and a rejection of that abundance of exterior ornament which had previously prevailed.

At this time, more attention was given to domestic architecture than had been hitherto. Throughout Old England the nobles seemed to vie with each other in the erection of large and magnificent Manor houses. The splendid reign of Elizabeth most encouraged this, and the decorations from without were apparently transferred to the interior, which was indeed carefully and gorgeously ornamented. Speaking of these buildings, Captain Grose, in his Antiquities of England, says :—"They have a style peculiar to themselves, both in form and finishing; where, though much of the old Gothic is retained, and a great part of the new taste adopted, yet neither predominates; while both thus distinctly blended compose a fantastic species, hardly reducible to any class or name." In fact, this style is far better adapted to domestic purposes than any of those in the same class which preceded it. Pure Gothic architecture is admirably fitted for ecclesiastical purposes, but not for much else; yet when it was shorn to some extent of its long vertical lines, its high pointed windows, and of its elaborate and expensive details, then the irregularity of its outline, the flexibility of its principles, together with the addition of Italian features, gave it all that was desirable for a private mansion.

The Debased style is principally characterized by its comparative plainness. The Tudor arch, as it is called, is much used. It is described from four centres, and is more depressed than its predecessors; so much so, that in some instances it is cut in a single stone, and this placed over the opening like a lintel. Indeed, even this afterwards ceased to be practised, and although some of the circumadjacent details were retained, yet there was no appearance whatever of an arch. This finish was generally confined to windows, and the Roman arched doorway used. The windows, however, especially in the

21

earlier stages, were most frequently composed of three or more openings, with either trefoil or plain pointed heads, covered by a horizontal hood-mould. The octagonal bay-window, which was first introduced in the Perpendicular style, was now made semicircular. Buttresses entirely disappeared, embattlements were freely used, and also porches. The Italian campanile and verandah were frequent in private houses, and in heavier edifices Grecian columns were not uncommon. One after another, the different Gothic features were rejected, until all trace of them was lost.

It is not proper to regard the Debased as a style altogether pure; nevertheless, we must not therefore condemn it entirely, for there have been designs from it which, in grace, elegance and finished decoration, are unsurpassed.

A GOTHIC VILLA.

DESIGN THIRD.

THIS design, as well as the one preceding it, is in the Debased Gothic style. Design second is the earlier of the two, and exhibits many features strongly Gothic. The Tudor flower running along the apex of the high pointed roof, the finial over the gables, some of the windows, the door, and the porch are all decidedly so, and indeed throughout it is much more an "Elizabethan" building than design third. In the latter, the square-headed windows and the tower, which is Italian although finished with a battlemented parapet, show at once that it prevailed subsequent to the other. It has nevertheless retained the Tudor flower, the finial, the steep roof, and the Gothic doorway, forming a most elegant and picturesque building. There is little rural character about the design. It would never do for a farm house, but is evidently fitted for the retiring citizen. This fact at once suggests its locale, and the style in which the grounds should be ornamented.

The side and front elevations are given on Plates XII. and XIII., exhibiting the constructive features of the building in accurate proportion. It is doubtless oftentimes the case that a person, wishing to build, may be much pleased, on the whole, with one of our designs, and would adopt it were it not for some minor feature either in the plan or style of the house unsuited to his peculiar tastes and wants. Alterations, such as he would wish, may frequently be made without injuring the general appearance or the plan; but great care must be exercised in so doing, for they may create an inconsistency in the style, which would afterwards be regretted, or they may, from some little oversight, so affect the plan as to render it impracticable. The best way in such a case, undoubtedly, is to consult the architect, and then no difficulty can obtain. We will, however, from time to time, mention some such changes as may be made consistently. In this design little can be done; yet, perhaps, a porch might be used over the front entrance and the conservatory omitted. The Tudor arch, mentioned above, may be seen over the front door.

Plate XIV. shows the plans of the first and second stories. By these we see that the building will readily accommodate a family of eight or ten persons, servants included, at the same time giving ample space for hall, parlor, spare chamber, library, &c., &c. We cannot omit the opportunity of calling attention to the elegant library herein designed. Any one accustomed to the wants and frequent inconveniences of private libraries will be struck at a glance with the peculiar fitness of this apartment for that purpose.

Plate XVI. Comprises the details. Fig. 1, a section of the tower wall. Fig. 2, a spandrel for the front door. Fig. 3, face of the tower. Fig. 4, principal cornice and section. Fig. 5, design for a conservatory window. Fig. 6, Tudor flower to be placed on the ridge piece. Fig. 7, finial. Fig. 8, buttress for the entrance door. Fig. 9, hood-mould for the windows. Fig. 10, cornice and blocking of the conservatory.

SPECIFICATION

Of the workmanship and materials required in the erection of Design Third.

DIMENSIONS.—The building is to be forty feet nine inches in front, measuring through the tower, by fifty-seven feet six inches flank. It is to be two stories high, the divisions and heights of the stories being made according to the elevations and plans. There are to be three garret rooms, and a room in the tower upon the same level. The tower is to be four stories high.

EXCAVATION.—The cellar is to be throughout the entire extent of the building eight feet deep below the top of the first or principal floor. The foundations of the walls are all to be at least six feet deep below the cellar floor. The earth therefrom is to be graded around the building as the proprietor may direct when the building shall have been completed, and all surplus soil and refuse material is to be removed from the grounds.

MASONRY.—All the outside walls of the building are to be composed of quarry building stone of a good quality. The foundations are all to be laid with large flat stone, well and solidly bedded in mortar. The walls are to be two feet thick to the height of the principal floor, and from thence to the square of the building they are to be one foot four inches thick. The gable ends and facings of the dormer windows are to be one foot two inches thick. The walls of the tower are to be two feet thick from the foundations to the sill course of the third story windows, thence twenty inches thick to the sill course of the fourth story windows, and from thence sixteen inches thick to the square. The cellar doorway under one of the kitchen windows is to be walled on either side with fourteen inch walls to the line of the yard pavement. All the masonry is to be done with mortar composed of good coarse sharp sand and wood-burnt lime, in such proportions as will secure the best and strongest cement. The inner facings of the walls are to be well dashed with the same mortar, and those of the cellar to be afterwards whitewashed.

Of the dressed stone there is to be a sill platform, and one step to the front entrance; also, a sill to the kitchen door, the sizes of which are exhibited on the plans. A moulded water table, eight inches thick and of six inches projection, is to be built in the wall around the building. The above is to be Connecticut brown stone, of a good quality, dressed and set in the best manner.

BRICK WORK.—There is to be built in the cellar a case of nine inch walls and of sufficient capacity for the reception of a furnace suitable to warm the whole building, all flues are to be properly formed for the heated air and gas, and placed as exhibited upon the plans and as may be directed by the proprietor.

JOISTS, &c.—The joists of the first floor are to be three by twelve inch spruce, of a good quality. Those of the second story are to be three by twelve inch hemlock; the third tiers to be three by nine inch hemlock. All are to placed sixteen inches between centres, to be backed and to have one course of bridging through the centre. All trimmers for the flues and stairs must be double thickness. The collar beams are to be one and a half by eight inches, firmly nailed to the rafters, about eight feet above the joists. The rafters are to be eight inches at the foot, of the usual rafter cut, and placed two feet between centres. The cornices are to be as exhibited on the plate.

WINDOWS.—All windows throughout the building are to be in accordance with the plates. The sash of the first and second stories are to be one inch and three quarters thick and double hung. The sash of the lofts and of the third and fourth stories in the tower, are to be one inch and a half thick, and double hung with plastered jambs. The sills are all to be heart pine, and the sub sills to be iron. The windows are all to have moulded heads. The inside shutters of the first and second stories are to be made in two folds with paneled backs and elbow jambs. They are also to be one inch thick, four panels high, moulded, hung and secured in the best manner.

DOORS.—The front doors are to be folding, one inch and three quarters thick, with moulded panels on the face, bead and butt on the inside, hung with four by four best butt hinges, and secured by two iron plate flush bolts, the one at the top being at least three feet long. It is to be further secured by one eight inch mortice upright lock, with a night key which will also open the vestibule door The vestibule door is also to be one inch and three quarters thick, double faced with moulding, hung with four by four inch best butts and secured by a vestibule lock. The doors communicating between the parlor, sitting room, and dining room are to be folding, one inch and three quarters thick, and double faced with moulding. All other doors in the first and second stories are to be one inch and three quarters thick, hung with suitable butts, and double faced. The doors above the second story, and all closet doors, are to be hung with suitable butts and secured by such fastenings as the proprietor may approve.

STAIRS.—The main stairs, extending to the second story, are to be put up in the best manner. The steps are to be one inch and a quarter heart step boards, of the best quality, supported on three strong carriages. The rail is to be four inch moulded, the newel eight inch with a turned cap and base, and an octagon shaft, and the balusters one and three quarter inch turned; all of which is to be mahogany. The private stairs leading from the kitchen and from the second story to the loft, and the stairs in the tower, are to be enclosed and made of heart step boards, in the best manner. The cellar stairs are to be beneath the private stairs.

INSIDE DRESSINGS.—The washboards in the first story are to be twelve inches high including a two and a half inch sub nailed firmly to the floor, and a one and a half inch moulding on the top. The washboards in the second story are to have a smilar finish, but only ten inches in height. Those of the closets, kitchen and loft are to be four and a half inches wide with a one and a half inch moulding on the top.

The window and door dressings, in the first story, are to be seven inches wide and in accordance with the plates. Those of the second story are to be five inches wide, and also according to the plates. Those of the loft and the third and fourth stories in the tower are all to be champhered on the angles of the jambs.

CLOSETS.—All the closets throughout the building must be fitted up and fully shelved, and a dresser in the kitchen is to be finished in such a manner as the proprietor may direct.

PARTITIONS.—All the divisions in the building are to be stud partitions. The studs being three by four inches, except those next the doors, which are to be three by six inches. All are to be placed sixteen inches between centres.

CONSERVATORY.—The conservatory is to be enclosed by diamond sash with Gothic heads, as figured on the plate, double hung by patent cord and axle pullies. The roof is to be flat.

PLASTERING.—All walls and ceilings within the building are to have two coats of brown mortar and one of white. The hall, parlor, sitting-room, and dining-room are to have a cornice in the angle of the ceiling to girt fourteen inches; also, a centre flower in the hall and parlor three feet six inches in diameter, of an approved pattern. The mortar is to be composed of river sand and wood-burnt lime in such proportions as are best. All laths are to be free from bark.

ROUGH-CASTING.—All exterior walls are to be coated with the best mortar, put on in a workmanlike manner, divided in imitation of blocks, and finished with approved tints.

SLATING.—The roof of the main building is to be overlaid with the best purple Welsh slate, laid in four courses of diamond and four courses of square pattern alternately, and fastened with fourpenny nails previously boiled in linseed oil.

PAINTING AND GLAZING.—All wood-work inside and out that it is usual to paint, must have three coats of pure white-lead paint, mixed with good linseed oil, and of such tints as may be directed.

The glass is to be of the best quality of American manufacture. It is to be well bedded, bradded, and back-puttied. That of the conservatory is to be stained in such patterns as may be selected, the cost not exceeding sixty dollars.

TIN WORK.—The conservatory roof and that of the tower and entrance porch, are all to be overlaid with the best one-cross roofing tin, painted on both sides, the upper having two coats. All valleys, ridges, flushings, and gutters are to be tin of the same quality, and all necessary gutters and conductors to convey the water from the roof, are to be put up in a proper manner.

HARDWARE.—All the hardware is to be of a good quality. The locks are all to be of American manufacture. There is to be a bell for the front door with a large sized plated pull, also five other bells in such parts of the house as may be directed. All other hardware necessary to make the building complete is to be furnished.

MANTELS.—There are to be mantels in the parlor, sitting-room, and dining-room, the cost of which shall not be less than ninety dollars. There are to be two in the principal chambers of the second story, the cost of which shall not be less than forty dollars.

RANGE AND FURNACE.—The kitchen is to be furnished with a medium-sized range of the most improved kind. The furnace is to be Chilson's No. 3, with all the necessary dampers, registers, and tin flues sufficient to warm all the first and second stories. The registers are to be of an approved pattern and enameled.

FINALLY.—The contractor is to furnish, at his own cost, all material and workmanship necessary to erect, and complete this building, to the satisfaction of the proprietor, according to the elevations, plans, and details, and the general intent and meaning of this specification.

Saml Sloan, Arch.^t.

P.S.Duval's Steam lith. Press Philad^a

SIDE ELEVATION.

Saml Sloan, Arch.^t.

P.S Duval's Steam lith. Press. Philad^a

GOTHIC VILLA.

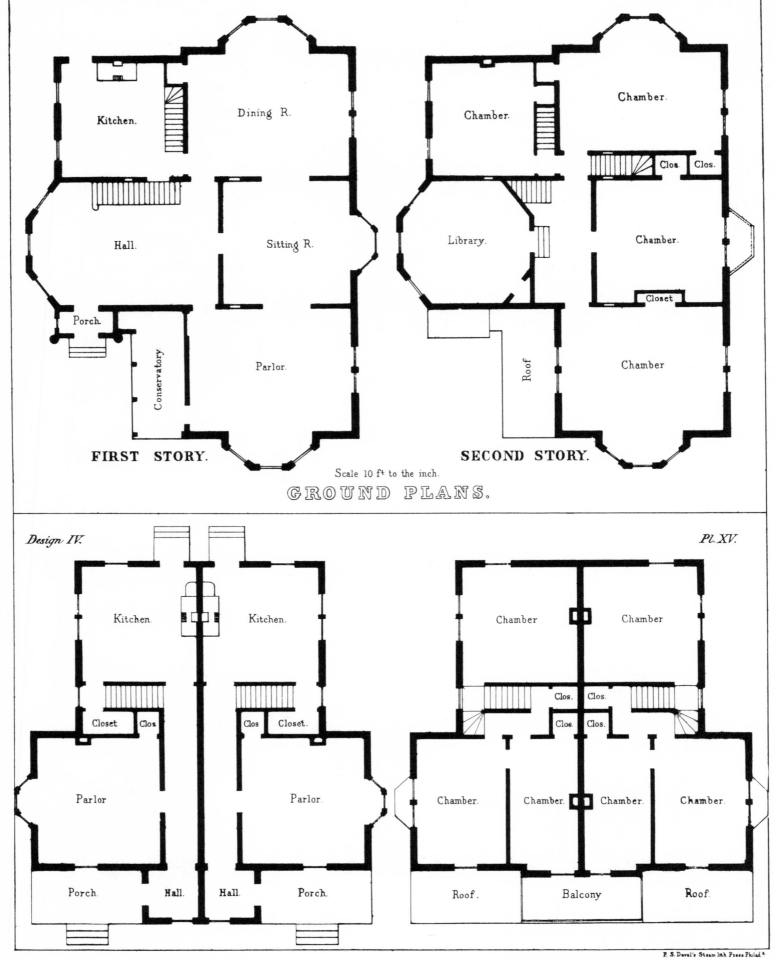

Design III.　　　　　　　　　　　　　　　　　　　　　　　　　　*Pl. XIV.*

Kitchen.

Dining R.

Chamber.

Chamber.

Clos. Clos.

Hall.

Sitting R.

Library.

Chamber.

Closet

Porch.

Conservatory.

Parlor.

Roof

Chamber

FIRST STORY.　　　　　　　　　　**SECOND STORY.**

Scale 10 ft to the inch.

GROUND PLANS.

Design IV.　　　　　　　　　　　　　　　　　　　　　　　　　　*Pl. XV.*

Kitchen.

Kitchen.

Chamber

Chamber

Closet

Clos.

Clos

Closet.

Clos. Clos.

Clos. Clos.

Parlor

Parlor

Chamber.

Chamber.

Chamber.

Chamber.

Porch.

Hall.

Hall.

Porch.

Roof.

Balcony

Roof.

FIRST STORY.　　　　　　　　　　**SECOND STORY.**

P. S. Duval's Steam lith Press Philad.ᵃ

Scale 10 ft to the inch.

GROUND PLANS.

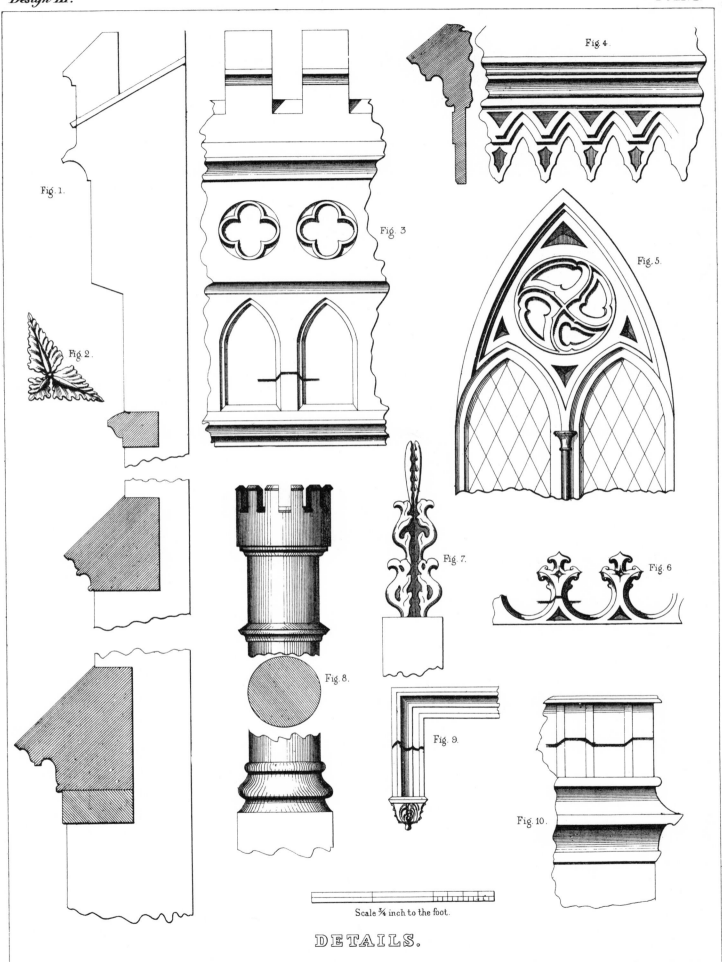

Fig. 1.

Fig. 2.

Fig. 3.

Fig. 4.

Fig. 5.

Fig. 6.

Fig. 7.

Fig. 8.

Fig. 9.

Fig. 10.

Scale ¾ inch to the foot.

DETAILS.

P. S. Duval's Steam lith. Press Philad.ª

ESTIMATE

OF THE COST IN THE ERECTION OF DESIGN THIRD.

WE give below a list, with the prices annexed, of all the materials required for the erection of design third. The sums mentioned comprise not only the cost of the material but also the cost of the work required for preparing, placing, and finishing the same. Thus against the item Brick, we have placed $10.50 per M., which amount includes all other material and all work required in laying, i. e., $10.00 per 1000 "in the wall." All carpenter's and joiner's work, however, is included under the head Workmanship, except the doors, windows, &c., which are generally made by machinery.

The prices are those which prevail in and near Philadelphia, but variations at other places may readily be substituted.

Excavation, 300 yds. @ 20 cts. per yd.	$ 60.00	Window Frames, Inside Shutters, and Sash, - @ $16.00 each, $544.00
Stone, 600 perches @ $2.00 per perch,	1200.00	
Dressed Stone, - - - - -	120.20	
Rough Casting, 743 yds. @ 40 cts. per yd.	297.00	Window Frames and Sash, 21 " 7.00 each, 147.00
Plastering, 1900 " " 20 " " "	380.00	
Slating, 2400 ft. " 12½ " " ft.	300.00	Workmanship, - - - - 675.25
Joists, 4560 " " $12.50 per M.	57.00	Tining, - - - - - 200.00
Rafters, 2280 " " " " "	28.50	Hardware, - - - - - 475.00
Scantling, 5000 " " 12.50 " "	62.50	Furnace and Registers, - - - 125.00
Flooring, 6000 " " 30.00 " "	180.00	Mantels, - - - - - 130.00
Roof sheathing, 2500 " " 12.00 " "	30.00	Painting and Glazing, - - - 430.00
Assorted Lumber, 11000 ft. " 25.00 per "	275.00	Stained Glass, - - - - 60.00
Brick, 18000 ft. " 10.00 " "	180.00	———
Doors, 19, 1¾ in. thick, " 4.25 each,	80.75	2786.25
Doors, 24, 1¼ " " " 2.25 each,	54.00	3304.95
	$3304.95	Total cost of the building, - - - $6091.20

TABLE OF GLASS.

WE are induced to insert here a table in order to obviate the difficulties which so often occur in purchasing glass for buildings. In ordering glass the purchaser knows the size and the number of lights to be used, but is at loss as to the number of boxes required. Every box contains fifty superficial feet of glass; hence by reference to the table the number of boxes required is readily ascertained.

NUMBER OF LIGHTS TO THE 100 FEET.

Sizes.	Lights.	Sizes.	Lights.	Sizes.	Lights.	Sizes.	Lights.	Sizes.	Lights.	Sizes.	Lights.
6 by 8	300	11 by 12	109	13 by 14	79	15 by 15	64	18 by 18	44	24 by 30	20
7 by 9	229	11 by 13	101	13 by 15	74	15 by 16	60	18 by 20	40	24 by 32	19
8 by 10	180	11 by 14	94	13 by 16	69	15 by 18	53	18 by 22	36	25 by 30	19
8 by 11	164	11 by 15	87	13 by 17	65	15 by 20	48	18 by 24	33	26 by 36	15
8 by 12	150	11 by 16	82	13 by 18	61	15 by 21	46	19 by 19	40	28 by 34	15
9 by 10	160	11 by 17	77	13 by 19	58	15 by 22	44	19 by 20	38	30 by 40	12
9 by 11	146	11 by 18	73	13 by 20	55	15 by 24	40	19 by 22	34	31 by 36	13
9 by 12	138	12 by 12	100	13 by 21	53	16 by 16	56	19 by 24	32	31 by 40	12
9 by 13	123	12 by 13	92	13 by 22	50	16 by 17	53	20 by 20	36	31 by 42	12
9 by 14	114	12 by 14	86	13 by 24	46	16 by 18	50	20 by 22	33	32 by 42	10
9 by 16	100	12 by 15	80	14 by 14	73	16 by 20	45	20 by 24	30	32 by 44	10
10 by 10	144	12 by 16	75	14 by 15	68	16 by 21	43	20 by 25	29	33 by 45	10
10 by 12	120	12 by 17	71	14 by 16	64	16 by 22	41	20 by 26	28	34 by 46	9
10 by 13	111	12 by 18	67	14 by 17	60	16 by 24	38	20 by 28	26	30 by 52	9
10 by 14	103	12 by 19	63	14 by 18	57	17 by 17	50	21 by 27	25	32 by 56	8
10 by 15	96	12 by 20	60	14 by 19	54	17 by 18	47	22 by 24	27	33 by 56	8
10 by 16	90	12 by 21	57	14 by 20	51	17 by 20	42	22 by 26	25	36 by 58	7
10 by 17	85	12 by 22	55	14 by 21	49	17 by 22	38	22 by 28	23	38 by 58	7
10 by 18	80	12 by 23	52	14 by 22	47	17 by 24	35	24 by 28	21	40 by 60	6
11 by 11	119	12 by 24	50	14 by 24	43						

LOCATION.

N the succeeding portions of this work, it is our especial purpose to furnish such a series of designs as will gratify all fancies, and illustrate the best styles; and at the same time to demonstrate that, in domestic architecture, good taste and every refined elegance are generally to be found in union with comfort and moderate expenditure. But it must not be forgotten, that the peculiar charm of this species of architecture consists in giving expression to Nature, and in harmonizing the abodes of man with those characters of natural beauty and repose, and sometimes of grandeur, which the arbitrary and restrained conditions of city life do not permit.

It is from oversight in this particular that we meet with so many instances in the vicinity of our large cities, of architectural combinations, pleasing in themselves both as to form and color, but made deformities by being brought into violent contrast with their opposites in nature. We do not look for the Swiss cottage against the flat horizon of a prairie land, nor among the high Alps for the casemented villa of southern France or Italy. However simple or picturesque, however full of grandeur or quiet repose the landscape, its crowning feature ought ever to be the structure, whether humble or stately, that denotes the habitation of man. Both should be in complete harmony and adaptation; for hill-side and plain, grove and river bank, each and all convey a meaning which can never be disregarded without a sacrifice of architectural taste, of propriety, and generally of comfort. Every day's observation reminds us that these suggestions, however obvious, are too often overlooked, and we should therefore fall short of our chief design in this publication, if we did not, from time to time, offer a few pertinent hints on the different localities, both in our vicinity, and in other sections of our diversified country.

There are many such around and near our own city, which properly call our attention first; and which in natural beauty and advantages, as well as in rapid improvement, may fairly challenge the most favored spots in other vicinages. The growing number of country residences in and near such places as Florence, Reverton, and Germantown, is a pleasing indication of the progress of public taste in this region; or, to come nearer home, our charming suburban neighbor Hamilton Village affords a fine instance of natural beauty graced, not banished by art. By some good fortune or better Providence it has enjoyed an almost entire exemption from those invasions of brick and mortar which have so sadly disfigured the fair country in most directions around our city. Its daily chimes are mingled with those which measure our busy hours and ring our city alarms; and though literally " within the sound of Bow-Bells," we know of no country village within a hundred miles of us, which contains so much of rural loveliness and repose, and exhibits in its prevailing features so little cockneyism. These are the spots that in their style of architecture and its accessaries more truly attest the progress of refinement and culture, than the most lavish expenditure upon city mansions.

The grand object of this series is to furnish designs and practical suggestions on the erection and location of rural and suburban residences; and thereby promote the tasteful growth of such places, in the environs of our cities, as have been named; it being the only effectual means of setting limits to a style of building which, if extended much further under the spur of speculation, will in a few years banish natural scenery to points accessible only by the steamboat or railroad.

A DOUBLE COTTAGE.
DESIGN FOURTH.

THIS is a simple design suited either for a village or suburban dwelling. It is intended for small families who desire to live plainly but comfortably. The fact of its being double may give rise to an objection with some, but it certainly has advantages, which a practical man cannot overlook. With the same expense a much more comfortable and handsome building may be erected on this plan, than if each were designed separately; for there is certainly less work and less material required, and hence a difference in cost. Besides this, it is in most cases far from being unpleasant to have agreeable neighbors within ear-shot, more especially if they are another branch of the same family. But these are old sayings, for the thousand double buildings in every direction prove that there are others who think as we do.

Plate XVII. gives the front elevation of the design. The upper story wall of the gable front sets back within twelve inches of the main wall, as is exhibited on the plans, thus making a balcony over the vestibules, surrounded by an iron railing. This balcony might be made to extend over the front porches. The main entrance door is at the end of the porch opening into vestibules in the gable front. All the outside walls and the main division wall are to be built of quarry building stone, and those outside are to be faced with rubble work, ridge-pointed. All other divisions are to be stud partitions. The flues are brick. The main roof is of slate; those of the front porches and bay windows of tin.

The plans of the first and second stories will be found on Plate XV. They show that each of the dwellings will accommodate a family of four or six persons. There are also two commodious garret rooms in the design, which do not appear upon the plans. The back chambers, it will be seen, are several steps below the floor of the second story main building; hence the roof of this part is lower than the main roof. If it were desired to extend this plan, there might be a basement kitchen under the back-room, which would then be used for a dining room. A back verandah also might be placed in an angle of the kitchen and parlor walls.

We give no plate of details in connexion with this design, because, being plain and simple, they may be readily taken from the elevation. Nor was it deemed necessary to prepare a specification. Any contractor with our specifications of other buildings and the descriptions herein contained before him, can easily write out a complete specification for this.

The cost of this cottage in this vicinity, where stone can be procured and delivered for a dollar a perch, built according to the plates and general description, with a cellar throughout its entire extent, and finished handsomely in all parts not described, will be about $2200.00, or $1100.00 for each dwelling. If brick, at six dollars a thousand, be substituted for stone, and rough-cast, it will increase the cost about $200.00 on the whole.

ITALIAN RESIDENCES.
DESIGN FIFTH.

THIS building is designed for suburban residences. It is in the Italian style which prevails so extensively in our cities. The general appearance of it displays finely that half-town and half-country expression so essential to handsome suburban dwellings. The main entrance appears beneath the side porches on the front elevation Plate XVIII. The bay windows on front, and observatory, are highly ornamental features, and could not be omitted without doing violence to the tasteful appearance of the building.

The plans of the first and second stories are exhibited on Plate XIX. Each dwelling will accommodate a family of eight or ten persons. A very convenient back porch might be placed in the angle of the dining-room and kitchen walls.

Plate XX. consists of details. Fig. 1, bracket and cornice of the main roof. Fig. 2, cornice of side porches. Fig. 3, cornice of the bay windows. Fig. 4, base of the bay windows. Fig. 5, bracket and cornice of the observatory. Fig. 6, posts and bracket of the side porches. Fig. 7, corbel of the second story windows.

We give no specification under this design for similar reasons to those given in the previous article, but we annex a general description, by the aid of which, a specification may readily be prepared.

The entire extent of the front, including the wings, is forty-two feet. That of the side is forty-eight feet. The building is two and a half stories high; the first story being twelve feet eight inches to the top of the second floor; the second story being eleven feet four inches to top of the third floor; and the half story being eight feet in the clear. The main roof is to pitch four feet. The observatory is fifteen feet square and eight feet high in the clear. The cellar, throughout the entire extent of the building, is to be six feet six inches deep. The dimensions of the different apartments may be taken from the plans. The outside walls are of stone covered with mastic, which is divided into blocks and tinted to represent brown stone. The angles of the front projection have quoins of Connecticut brown stone with the edges bevelled, and a water table of the same is built around in the wall. The windows are all casemented, and have inside shutters to the first and second stories, in two folds to each jamb, and are hung with the usual back flaps. The outside and principal room doors of the first and second story, are one and three-fouths of an inch thick with two and a half inch mouldings and fillets. All other doors are one inch and a quarter thick and moulded on one side. All glass, in the first story front and sides, is the best American crown glass, the rest may be of an inferior quality. The roof is overlaid with the best quality of leaded tin. The wood of the interior has three coats of paint. The exterior has four coats and is sanded.

The cost of the whole building will be between $2400.00 and $2800.00 if erected in accordance with the elevation, plans, details, and the above general description.

Pl. XVII.

Sam.l Sloan, Arch.t

P.S Duval's Steam lith: Press. Philad.a

DOUBLE COTTAGE.

Pl. XVIII.

Sam.l Sloan, Arch.t

P.S Duval's Steam lith Press, Philad.a

ITALIAN RESIDENCES.

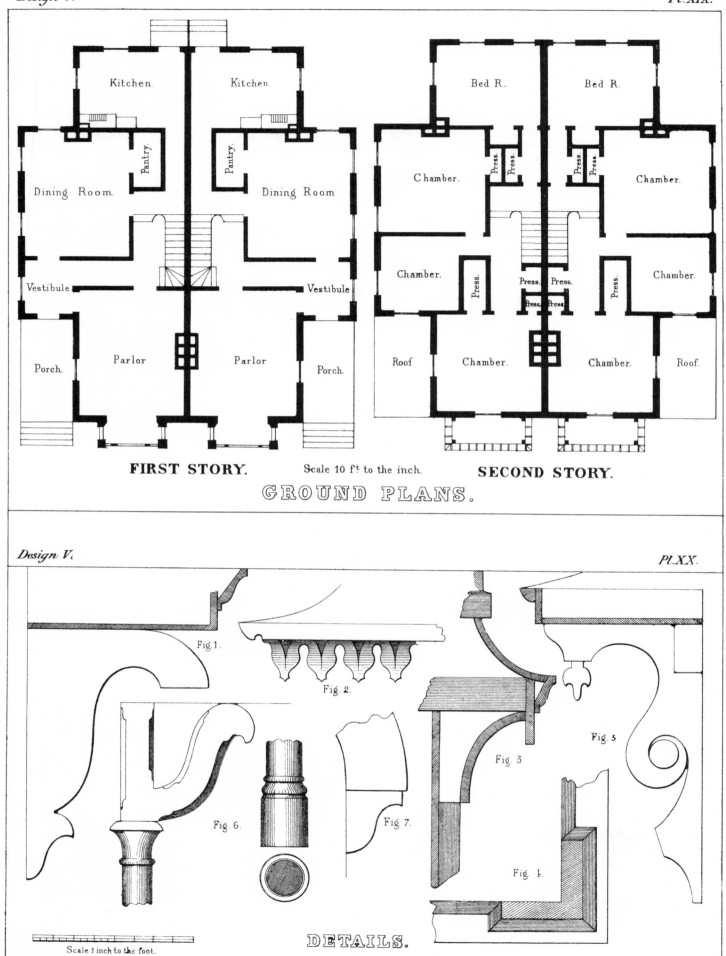

Kitchen.   Kitchen.

Pantry.   Pantry.

Dining Room.   Dining Room

Vestibule   Vestibule

Porch.   Parlor   Parlor   Porch.

Bed R.   Bed R.

Chamber.   Press. Press.   Chamber.

Chamber.   Press.   Press. Press.   Press.   Chamber.

Press. Press.

Roof   Chamber.   Chamber.   Roof

FIRST STORY.   Scale 10 f.t to the inch.   **SECOND STORY.**

GROUND PLANS.

Fig. 1.

Fig. 2.

Fig. 3

Fig. 5

Fig. 6.   Fig. 7.

Fig. 4.

Scale 1 inch to the foot.

DETAILS.

P. S. Duval's Steam lith. Press Philad.a

ITALIAN ARCHITECTURE.

THE Goths who inundated Italy and swept away the last vestiges of Roman strength, sought also to destroy and obliterate all remaining traces of the grandeur, pomp, and refinement of the empire, as exhibited in its mighty works. Magnificent temples and palaces were razed to the ground, and the greater the work, the more sure was it of destruction. But these "architects of ruin" could not annihilate. "The rude heaps that had been cities, clad the ground with history," and have been the eager study of all succeeding ages. When the state of society became somewhat more calm, the materials of these structures, which lay in vast confusion, formed, so to speak, artificial quarries, from which new cities were built. It is easy to imagine what incongruous combinations must consequently have arisen. The different orders were mixed, and highly sculptured ornaments were placed in close connection with coarse, rough work; and hence the manner of building at this time cannot justly claim to be a style in architecture. But this could not long exist among a people of whom natural good taste is a characteristic, and accordingly we find many buildings of an early date that commanded the admiration of Michael Angelo.

The present national style cannot be said to have existed earlier than the fifteenth century. At this time the writings of Vitruvius, having been discovered in manuscript, were published, and thoroughly studied. He was a Roman architect, who flourished under the reign of Augustus, and wrote his work about the time of the Christian era. It contains a complete and excellent, but oftentimes obscure account of both Grecian and Roman architecture. To this we are indebted for the most of our knowledge of the art in ancient times, and for the great change which has been wrought in it throughout the enlightened world. Brunelleschi was one of the first who studied so enthusiastically this work and the relics of past ages. He remained in Rome a long time, measuring and minutely examining her noble remains, and did much to restore the knowledge of the art and diffuse a taste more correct. In the year 1407, he offered to the assembly of architects and engineers, at Florence, his design for the erection of a dome on the cathedral of St. Maria del Fiore, and was hissed from the hall for his pains. He subsequently, however, was appointed as the architect, and the design was completed. Other domes were erected in every direction, until that of St. Peter's, by Michael Angelo, set all competition at defiance. Between these two great men there flourished many architects, composing the "Cinquecento School," all of whom labored with a devotion and zeal that speedily perfected the art. It may be well remarked, that these men were not only architects, but sculptors, painters, musicians, and even poets. They seem to have studied the fine arts *en masse*, and

29

many mastered them all.   Their refined taste is yet reflected from Italian architecture, for since then there has been little or no change in the principles of the style, variations occurring only in details.

Alberti, one of these architects of the fifteenth century, wrote a work on the subject, which was afterwards followed by the works of Serlio and Palladio, all of which were, upon their publication, translated into French, German, Dutch, and English.   As a result of this, a radical change soon began to show itself throughout Europe.   In England the suppression of monasteries had prepared the way, and there were several architects who labored for the introduction of the new style.   Inigo Jones, though not the first, was one of the greatest reformers.   He spent some years in Italy, studying under the patronage of the Earl of Pembroke, and was afterwards appointed Royal Architect.   The illustrious Sir Christopher Wren, who has been called the greatest of all architects, completed the change, which may be regarded as established throughout the cities not only of England, but of all Europe, soon after the middle of the seventeenth century.   It has since universally prevailed.

The deep veneration which has always existed for antiquity, would certainly cause the moderns to imitate in every particular the ancient models, were it possible; but these models, though specimens of exalted taste, and suited to their times, are utterly inadequate to supply our wants, and illy accord with our customs.   In public buildings we sometimes see them reproduced with a creditable finish and seeming appropriateness, but for domestic purposes they are altogether insufficient.   The arts of construction too, are much improved, and give us great advantages.   In unwearied patient labor, careful finish and tasteful skill, the ancients are unsurpassed, but in manual dexterity, tools, machinery, and adaptation of material, we excel.   Among other things, the introduction of glass has made a great difference.   The excavations at Pompeii prove that it was used latterly, to some extent, by the Romans, but we know that Nero gave a vast sum for a pair of drinking glasses; hence it could not have been used as a material for windows to any great extent.   Its place was supplied by thin canvass, or a highly transparent mineral, which they called speculum.   After the art of manufacturing glass became better known, it gave the window, unlike its former position, a prominent place in architectural designs.

Setting aside, however, these minor differences, it is utterly impracticable for the moderns to build on the magnificent scale which the Roman style demands.   Among that people, every villa was a palace, built from the extorted revenues of large provinces, and on one of their public edifices an amount was expended that would build for us a handsome city.   In short, the construction of society is, ever since has been, and we hope ever will be, totally different.   The Italian architects followed as nearly as possible the footsteps of antiquity, but for these reasons they varied considerably from the standard.   Ever since, the difference has been gradually increasing, and their peculiar combinations being altogether abandoned, we only retain general principles and ornamental details.

Before giving the characteristics of this style, it is well to mention the distinction which exists between the mode of building in the city and in the country.   Exterior architectural ornaments in the city are generally confined to a rectangular front, while in the country, where all sides are exposed, much more attention must be paid to general effect. But without attempting to define the obvious difference which obtains between the two, we will confine all future remarks, as the nature of our work demands, to isolated buildings.

Most generally, Italian villas have an irregular outline from every point of view. The predominant figure is the rectangle, but many being introduced and so disposed as to break in upon each other, the irregular outline is formed without difficulty. The angular effect is relieved by the semi-circular arch which is freely used. Great license is also permitted in the ground plans, thus admitting almost every possible arrangement of apartments. This results probably from the fact that the buildings are generally erected on uneven ground. A most prominent and almost universal feature is the square tower, or, as it has been latterly called, the campanile. Properly, the campanile is a bell tower, built nigh a church, but detached from it, as the leaning tower at Pisa. The term is now frequently used as applied above. Pliny, in describing Roman villas, speaks of a tower which had in its upper story a dining room, so that guests, while gratifying their appetites, might feast also their eyes on fine views around. In modern times such a use of the campanile is unknown, but so universally is it introduced, that we look for it in every Italian landscape. It overlooks all parts of the house, and has balconies, and other ornamental features, which give it grace and finish. The principal entrance is generally in its first story, which also often affords a good position for the main stairway. It differs from a steeple, or an ordinary observatory, in having at least one of its sides visible from eaves to base. The roof, both of the campanile and main building, is never steep. In Italy it is generally composed of tiles, which form a beautiful and permanent roof. Tin is used more with us, and is so arranged as to have nearly the same effect. It has been stated that gables do not occur, but this is incorrect: we simply cite Raphael's villa, in the Borghese Gardens. Hip roofs are, however, common. In all cases the eaves are heavy and projecting, being supported by brackets and cantalivers of various patterns. The chimneys are prominent, and serve to give greater variety to the outline. The windows are made double, or treble, and, together with the doors, have either square or arched beads, according to the importance of their position. Bay-windows are frequent. All window and door dressings are made very heavy, and, indeed, throughout there is a tendency rather to boldness than minute decoration. Heavy arcades, porches with large square pillars, verandahs, balconies, antæ, pilasters, quoins, rustic work, and string courses, all often occur. In consequence of the great abundance and variety of the best material in Italy, the walls always present a finished appearance, accompanied by great stability. The best are built of dressed stone; but rough-casting is quite common. Buttresses are often placed against the basement when it is high, which die into the wall just beneath the water-table.

The character of this style is far from being rural, but is genuinely picturesque. The irregularity of the ground plans and vertical outline, and the great freedom allowed in general design, give considerable room for the exercise of taste. In Italy, the surface of the country is greatly diversified by hills and valleys, and advantage is taken of this in erecting the villas so as to command landscapes. The brow of a steep hill is a frequent location, and adds much to the fine, bold effect of the buildings. In such situations, terraces are much used. The style is, however, by no means incompatible with a level country, but in that case the design is more regular and symmetrical. The adjacent grounds should be kept in a finished state. Statuary, vases, fountains, and other such accessaries are in entire accordance with the style.

Country residences in the Italian style are becoming more and more popular, both here and in the old world. Its great pliability of design, its facile adaptation to our wants and habits, together with its finished, elegant, and picturesque appearance, give it precedence over every other. It speaks of the inhabitant as a man of wealth, who wishes in a quiet way to enjoy his wealth. It speaks of him as a person of educated and refined tastes, who can appreciate the beautiful both in art and nature; who, accustomed to all the ease and luxury of a city life, is now enjoying the more pure and elevating pleasures of the country.

AN ITALIAN VILLA.

DESIGN SIXTH.

THIS presents another Villa in the Italian style, quite regular and symmetrical in plan, and therefore best adapted to a level situation. The whole appearance of the building is broad, heavy and spreading. If desirable, this expression may be added to by making the eaves of the tower, house and verandah, still more projecting. In its details, it presents many features referred to in the preceding article; but, although true to its origin, it is not an elaborate specimen of the style. It was designed rather as a family mansion, and we are convinced will make a complete, comfortable dwelling.

Plate XXI., the Perspective View, explains our meaning. The broad verandah encircling the house is a graceful and convenient, though expensive appendage. It would be more highly appreciated in a warmer climate than this, but even here our hot summers make it grateful. Comfortable summer residences are never without a verandah. Plate XXII. is a front elevation of the same building.

Plate XXIII. exhibits the floor plans. The house will accommodate a family of ten, servants included. The part of the verandah in the rear may be omitted, and a back porch be placed in the angle formed by the kitchen wall and end of the hall. The flues from the chambers on the right are to be overdrawn so as to meet and issue from the roof at a point corresponding to the one on the other side.

Plate XXIV. consists of details. Fig. 1 is a front view of the Balcony. Fig. 2, side view of the same. Fig. 3, bracket and section of tower cornice. Fig. 4, verandah post. Fig. 5, front door. Fig. 6, bracket and section of main cornice.

The main walls are of brick, rough-cast and laid off in blocks. The foundations are, however, of quarry building stone, as high as the joists of the first floor. This includes the foundations of the verandah, as high as the base course; from thence brick to the floor. The sill course around the tower, the base course, the outside door sills, and the front steps, are all of dressed stone. The main division walls on either side of the hall are of brick as high as the joists of the second story.

Saml Sloan, Arch.^t   P.S. Duval's Steam lith: Press. Philad.^a

PERSPECTIVE VIEW.

Saml Sloan, Arch.^t   P.S. Duval's Steam lith Press. Philad.^a

ITALIAN VILLA.

Pl. XXIII.

Chamber

Chamber

Cl.

Cl.

Chamber

Chamber

Cl.

Cl.

W.Closet

Stairs

Bath Room

Servant's R.

Bed Room

Balcony

SECOND STORY.

GROUND PLANS.

Drawing Room

Hall

Cl.

Cl.

Privy

Private stairs

Kitchen

Pantry

Dining Room

Parlor

Vestibule

Verandah

FIRST STORY.

Scale 10 feet to the inch.

60'.

P. S. Duval's steam lith press Ph.

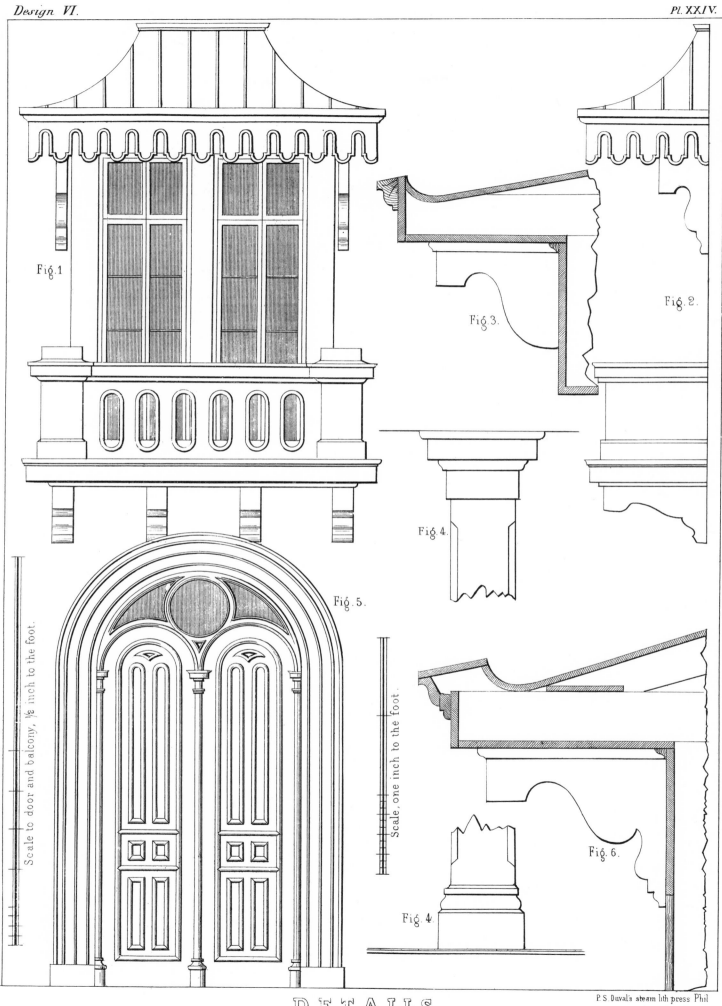

Fig.1.

Fig.2.

Fig.3.

Fig.4.

Fig.5.

Fig.4.

Fig.6.

Scale to door and balcony, ½ inch to the foot.

Scale, one inch to the foot.

D E T A I L S .

P.S. Duval's steam lith press Phil

All others are stud partitions. The house is designed to be warmed by a furnace; and for its reception a case, six by eight feet, with double walls of single thickness, four inches apart, is built of hard brick in the cellar.

The outside doors are one inch and three quarters thick, the inside room doors are an inch and a half thick, double-faced, and the closet doors are an inch thick, single-faced. The stairs are of heart pine boards, on three strong carriages; the rail and newel are of mahogany, and the balusters are of maple turned.

The plastering is executed in the best manner, with handsome cornices in the dining room, drawing room, hall and parlor. The drawing room has two centre flowers, the hall and parlor one each.

The roofs are entirely of tin. The central part of that over the main building is flat. All the flues are cased with tin.

The remainder of the building, in its details, is entirely similar to Design First, and hence requires neither further description nor specification. An estimate is given below, which furnishes all other necessary information.

ESTIMATE

OF THE COST IN THE ERECTION OF DESIGN SIXTH.

THE following bill of items is prepared on the same plan as the preceding.

Excavation, 350 yds. @ 20 cts. per yd. -	$ 70.00
Stone, 75 perches @ $2.00 per perch, - -	150.00
Dressed Stone, - - - - - -	175.00
Brick, 130,000 @ $10.00 per M. - -	1300.00
Rough Casting, 670 yds. @ 40 cts. per yd. -	268.00
Plastering, 1800 yds. " 20 " " " -	360.00
Floor Joists, 4800 ft. @ $12.50 per M. -	60.00
Ceiling Joists, 1500 ft. " " " " -	18.75
Rafters, 1700 ft. " " " " -	21.25
Scantling, 4500 ft. " " " " -	56.25
Flooring, 6500 ft. " $30.00 " " -	195.00
Sheathing, 2200 ft. " $12.00 " " -	26.40
Assorted Lumber, 11400 ft. " $25.00 " " -	285.00
Workmanship, - - - - - -	600.00
Window Frames, and } 4 @ $20.00 each, - Sash in Tower, }	80.00
	$3665.65

Window Frames, } Inside Shutters, } 15 @ $22.50 each, - - and Sash, }	337.50
Window Frames, } Outside Shutters, } 12 @ $15.50 " - - and Sash, }	186.00
Doors, 17, 1¾ in. thick, @ $4.25 " - -	72.25
Doors, 25, 1½ " " " $2.75 " - -	68.75
Tinning, - - - - - - -	675.00
Furnace and registers, - - - - -	175.00
Mantles, 8, - - - - - - -	200.00
Hardware, - - - - - -	440.00
Painting and Glazing, - - - - -	400.00
	2554.50
	3665.65
	$6220.15

THE ARCHITECT.

ESIGNING a house is no easy matter. Such abilities, indeed, are required to do it well, that it has become a business, a profession, an art. Men who have devoted their lives to it are, notwithstanding, continually making blunders; then what are we to expect from him who endeavors to build, while destitute of taste, experience, and knowledge of construction? If those who have long studied and practised the art sometimes fail, perhaps he that knows nothing about it might do well to pause before he acts independently. When a pleasing design, with all its concomitants, is found, whose source is good authority, it may be adopted without hesitation; but when a building adapted to some peculiar notions is desired, the only safe course is to communicate these to some experienced Architect, who will elaborate them.

A good Architect must possess just taste, more especially if he aspire to any originality. The existing models are so numerous and so complete as sometimes to require but little tact in adapting them to modern use, but such servile imitation is unworthy of an intelligent man, and of the genius of our age. On the other hand, it is not best to throw away entirely the accumulated knowledge and beautiful designs of the past, and start out nude again to collect. There is between these extremes a course to which taste and reason point; but to pursue this course aright a keen sense of discrimination is necessary. The Architect must also have been, and must be, a hard student and a strong original thinker. Not one whose memory is overloaded with facts, but to whom every fact has added strength; whose mind is expanded by each, and does not again contract, if he chance to forget it. Such an one may throw off the shackles of the past, and yet feel its influence. In his hands the art will advance, but with others it either stands still or retrogrades.

But there is a vast fund of practical knowledge required. The Architect must have a thorough appreciation of the wants of society. He must be well versed in all the arts of construction. There is no necessity for him to possess manual dexterity, but he must be a good judge of masonry, carpentry, and their kindred. He must be acquainted with all the varieties of the best material, and their prices, together with the prices of all kinds of labor. He must also be familiar with all modern improvements which add to the comforts of living.

This is a mere glance at the proper attainments of an Architect. It was said of Wren, that, "since the time of Archimedes, there scarcely ever has met, in one man, in so great a perfection, such a mechanical hand and so philosophical a mind." Besides possessing an eminently practical character, he was named by Newton first among the great geometricians of the age.

When the projector has communicated his wishes to an Architect, the first step taken is to form the ground plan of the design. For a small one story house this is easy, but when there are several stories they must be made to correspond. The arrangements for heating, ventilation, and the admission of light, also create difficulties. After these have been successfully overcome, the next thing is to adopt a style. In doing this, both the peculiarities of the plan, the locality, and the purpose of the building, have to be taken into consideration. Then the elevation must be sketched. Much taste and knowledge are required in this. All the general features and minute decorations must be carefully designed and arranged, so as at once to be true to the style, and form a graceful, well proportioned whole. He finally prepares a specification and bill of the cost of each thing concerned in the building, the sum of which gives the general estimate. From now until the completion of the building he holds himself in readiness to give any information to the contractor, and acts as a referee between him and the proprietor. From time to time during its progress, he gives, on examination, certificates to the contractor of the completion of certain parts of the work according to contract, without which the latter cannot properly draw upon the owner. This is the usual arrangement. The Architect's bill is proportioned to the cost of the building, generally about three per cent. on the whole.

There is one abuse in particular to which the Architect is subject, and that is, after a design has passed from his hands, the projector sometimes makes changes in it without his consent, and even without consulting him. Luckily this self-conceited ignorance is often punished by the result. An intelligent man will employ an Architect who is his superior in matters connected with building, and having done so, will always deferentially advise with him upon any changes or additions he may wish to make. Besides regarding his own good in this, he remembers that an observer of a handsome building as often asks the name of the Architect as he does that of the owner, and if there is any thing bad in the design, the Architect gets the credit of it. He will avoid, therefore, doing any thing which may materially injure the other in reputation and business.

AN ELIZABETHAN VILLA.

DESIGN SEVENTH.

THIS Villa is in the style which we have technically termed Debased Gothic. We have however subscribed it Elizabethan, because it is more popularly understood as such. It corresponds to the old manor-houses erected during Elizabeth's reign, many of which are yet extant. This is more regular than most of the originals, the plan being rectangular, but the convenience and compactness of it are thereby promoted.

Plate XXV. gives the general appearance of the building in perspective. Plate XXVI. is the front elevation, drawn in correct proportion to a scale of ten feet to the inch.   The battlemented verandah and conservatory, the bay-windows, and the finials, give it a pleasing appearance to lovers of the unique.   Hammer-dressed stone would be the most appropriate, but an expensive material for the outside walls.

PLATE XXVII. exhibits the floor plans.   The house will accommodate a family of six or eight persons.   It is large and roomy, giving ample space for a family of this size, and might comfortably receive a larger one.

Plate XXVIII. consists of details.   Fig. 1, verandah cornice and posts.   Fig. 2, enlarged section of the verandah cornice.   Fig. 3, section of the cornice of the building.   Fig. 4, finial.   Fig. 5, front-door.   Fig. 6, chimney-can.   Fig. 7, horizontal section of the bay-windows.   Fig. 8, section of the sill of the bay-windows.

We give no specification for this design, but annex a general description, which occupies less room, and is sufficient for all practical purposes.   Many things will be mentioned which do not belong essentially to the design, but which must be stated, in order that the building may be clearly understood, and an estimate of its cost correctly made.

The front is forty-four feet, and the side thirty-six feet in extent.   Beside the two stories there are attic rooms, and a cellar, which is eight feet deep below the first floor.   The trenches for the walls and piers in the cellar must be at least six inches deep, and those for the foundation of the verandah and conservatory two feet six inches deep.

The walls in the cellar, up to the joists of the first floor, and the foundation walls of the conservatory and verandah, are all of good quarry building stone, well laid in the best mortar.   All other walls are of brick.   Those of the first story are thirteen inches thick, and those of the second nine inches, both with a hollow space in the centre, two inches wide, and bonded at every seventh course by alternate headers.   All flues are of brick, and overdrawn where necessary, to the peak of the roof.   The mortar for all the work is to be composed of the best fresh lime and clean river sand.

The joists of the first story are three by twelve inch spruce, those of the second three by eleven inches, and those of the attic three by ten inches; the two last are hemlock, and all are placed sixteen inches between centres, backed and herring-bone bridged.   The rafters are three by five inches, and placed two feet between centres.   The studs for partitions are all three by four inches, except those next the doors, which are three by six inches.   The inner floors are all of Carolina heart pine, one inch thick.   That of the verandah is of white pine boards, one inch and a quarter thick, four inches wide, tongued and grooved, and laid with white lead in the joints.   There are four twin windows in the rear, corresponding to the front bay-windows.   The others are single.   All are to have panneled inside shutters.   The sash are diamond, one inch and three quarters thick, and hung as casements.   The front doors are two inches thick.   All room doors are one inch and three quarters thick, and double-faced.   The closet doors are one inch and a quarter thick, and single-faced.   The washboard of the hall, parlor and dining room, is eight inches wide, with a sub and moulding.   All others are but six inches.   The window and door dressings are heavy, with handsome mouldings.   The stairs are of heart pine, on three strong carriages, with a mahogany newel and rail, and turned maple balusters.

All plastering is executed in the best manner, with handsome cornices and centre flowers in the parlor, hall and dining room.   All the exterior walls are rough-cast, tinted and laid off in blocks.   All wood work is to receive three coats of the best paint.   The glass of the first story and second story front is the best American crown, the rest may be inferior.   The roof is of slate.   The gutters, vallies, flats, flushings, verandah and bay-window roofs, are of the best one cross leaded tin, painted on both sides, the upper side receiving two coats.   The hot-air flues are of the best two cross tin.

The cost of this building as described, will be $6250.00.   If stone at a dollar a perch be substituted, it will be $6000.00. If the conservatory be omitted it will reduce this about $500.00.

Saml Sloan, Arch.^t   P.S. Duval's Steam lith. Press, Philad.^a

PERSPECTIVE   VIEW.

Saml Sloan, Arch.^t   P.S. Duval's Steam lith. Press, Philad.^a

ELIZABETHAN   VILLA.

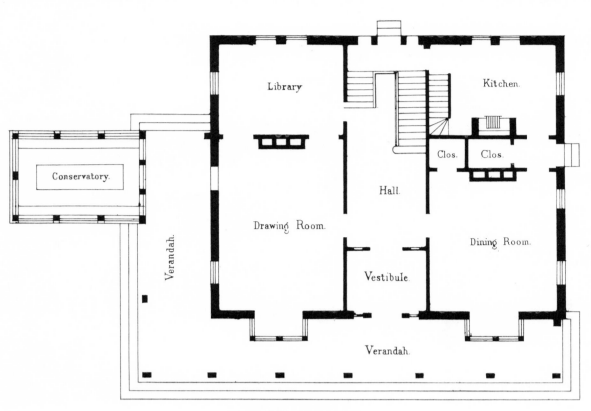

Library

Kitchen.

Clos. Clos.

Conservatory.

Hall.

Verandah.

Drawing Room.

Dining Room.

Vestibule.

Verandah.

FIRST STORY.

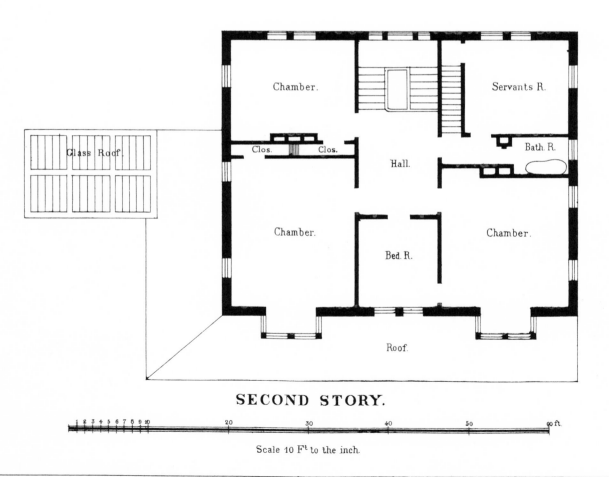

Chamber.

Servants R.

Glass Roof.

Clos. Clos.

Bath. R.

Hall.

Chamber.

Chamber.

Bed. R.

Roof.

SECOND STORY.

1 2 3 4 5 6 7 8 9 10   20   30   40   50   60 ft.

Scale 10 Ft to the inch.

P. S. Duval's Steam lith Press Philad ª

GROUND PLANS.

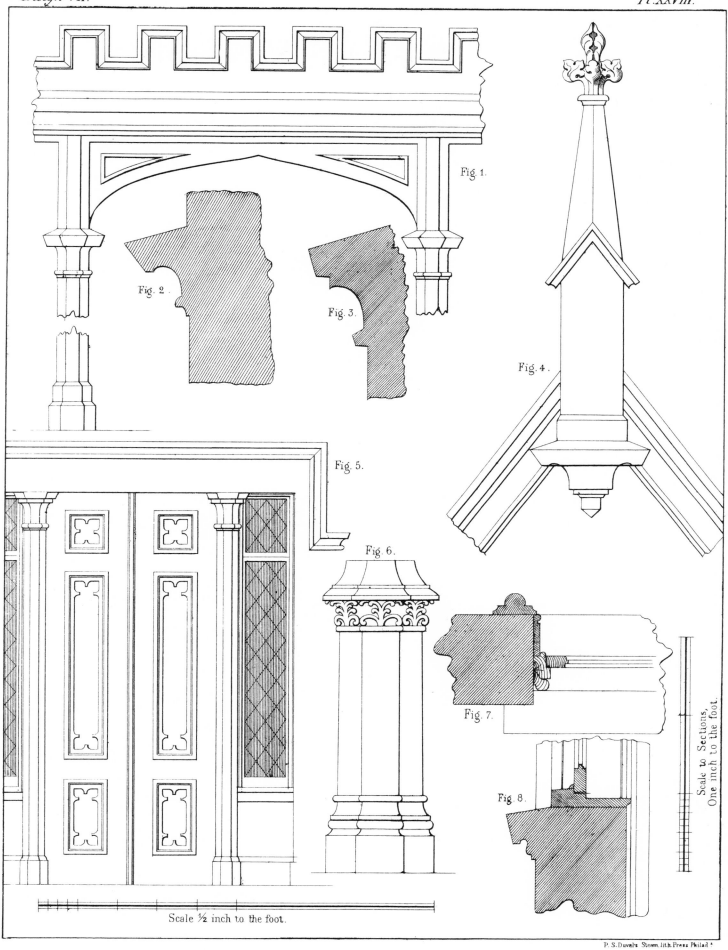

Fig. 1.

Fig. 2.

Fig. 3.

Fig. 4.

Fig. 5.

Fig. 6.

Fig. 7.

Fig. 8.

Scale to Sections,
One inch to the foot.

Scale ½ inch to the foot.

P. S. Duval's Steam lith. Press Philad.ᵃ

DETAILS.

ARCHITECTURAL DRAWINGS.

HE number of drawings which are required by the builder varies of course with the extent and finish of the building. For the most simple houses two are sufficient, a Ground Plan and Elevation. For very elaborate buildings many more of different kinds are necessary, which require great labor and skill in their execution. Of these, which are usually called working drawings, the Ground Plans properly come first. They consist of the plans not only of the ground floor, but of the different stories, attic and cellar, and would therefore more properly be called floor plans, though the other term has been sanctioned by custom. Only such are drawn as in the case may be necessary. They exhibit the situation of the walls and partitions, and the relative positions of the doors, windows, flues, stairs, porches, &c. The whole being drawn in accurate proportion to a scale, usually laid down on the drawing for convenient reference, the exact dimensions of each part are ascertained by applying the compasses. We sometimes see introduced into architectural works Isometric drawings. These suppose the subject to be viewed from above, and are drawn in perspective. A horizontal section of a building, made just above the window sills is occasionally exhibited in this way, but is of very little practical value, since measurements cannot be taken from it, and only serves to inform the unpractised eye.

The next drawings are those of the Elevations. One is sometimes sufficient, but often four have to be made, one of each front of the building. These elevations are drawn in what is called geometric projection. Each point of the front drawn is supposed to be projected perpendicularly upon a vertical plane situated immediately behind it; or, in other words, the front is supposed to be viewed from an infinite distance in which all the lines of sight are parallel. The variations caused by the light and shade are retained, and serve to show the irregularities of the surface. These drawings are also made to a scale, and accurate measurements may be taken from them. The general effect, however, is very different from that which exists in nature. Two objects are often exhibited on the same elevation, which cannot really be seen from the same point of view, and the more irregular the design the greater is the deviation from the true appearance. The object in elevation drawings is not so much to present a view of the building as to furnish the workman with a chart from which to take dimensions and ascertain the relative position of parts. An elevation of a vertical section of the building is sometimes drawn, and is valuable for exhibiting constructive features and internal arrangements.

The general appearance of the building is sometimes exhibited in a Perspective view. This drawing is the most difficult in execution, it depending on more complicate geometrical rules than the others. It represents the building exactly as it appears in nature from a given point of view, and is drawn more for the information of the projector than the use of the workman, since it affords no measurements whatever.

Other drawings are generally the details of different parts of the building. These are on a large scale, showing the manner of construction and minute ornaments which cannot be exhibited upon the general drawings; such as the framing of floors, partitions and roofs, for the carpenter; sections of door and window frames and mouldings, for the joiner; the patterns of the various iron work, for the founder; decorative details of columns, entablatures, cornices, flowers, leaves, scrolls, brackets, finials, &c., for the carver. These drawings are either sections or geometrical projections. They are more numerous than any other, and are in constant requisition from the commencement until the completion of the work.

As has been said, a correct and finished execution of these working drawings is a matter of no small difficulty. A good draughtsman, in addition to a correct eye and the readiness attained only by practice, must be thoroughly versed in the principles of geometric projection, perspective, and chiascuro, or light and shade, without which he will work at random and his drawings will be incomprehensible. No one except the experienced can conceive how great a change may sometimes be wrought in a drawing by a single line or a simple shadow. The greatest care is requisite that there may be no falsity. The engraved drawings in this work illustrate these remarks. No pains are spared to make them correct, and that a complete set may accompany each design.

AN ITALIAN RESIDENCE.
DESIGN EIGHTH.

THIS is a genuine Italian building. Its high finish gives it the character of a suburban rather than a country dwelling, and indeed throughout it is much more elaborate than any preceding design. It is without the frequent campanile, whose place is somewhat supplied by the front pediment. The simplicity of the outlines is relieved by the ornamental details.

The front elevation is exhibited on Plate XXIX. We will here make a reference to a remark in the preceding article. It may be observed that the roof of the building in this elevation is entirely visible, which takes away somewhat from the graceful appearance of the façade, by making the wings appear too near the eaves of the body of the building. This, were the real building before us, would not appear. An observer would have to be at a considerable distance to see the roof at all. Thus the remark is illustrated that an elevation drawing may give a very false idea of the real building, and therefore cannot be taken as a criterion in every respect, but simply as a chart for the workman. This elevation is drawn to a scale of ten feet to the inch.

One elevation only of this design is given. That of the right wing would display a window on the side of the main entrance hall, with two immediately above it in the second and third stories. Also four single windows in the end of the wing; the two beneath the verandah reaching the floor. The octagonal projection of the body of the building in the rear would come into view with its windows, and roof hipped somewhat in the manner of the front in Design First, only much more flat. The dressings of this elevation are more plain than those of the front.

Plate XXXI. of the ground plans exhibits the octagonal projection mentioned. A verandah encircling this would be a pleasant appendage. The entrance hall in the first story might be enlarged by continuing the wall, which separates the kitchen and stairs, across the end of the dining room. This would make the entrance more free to the parlor from the hall, and make the stairway more open and airy, besides bringing the partition immediately below the one in the second story. The alteration, however, would diminish the size of the dining room, and alter its shape.

It would probably be quite as convenient to use the Dining Room as a sitting room, the Kitchen as a dining room and the Wash-House as the kitchen. The end of the hall beneath the turn of the stairs might be partitioned off, and with the window and a door opening into the kitchen, would form an excellent pantry. The door of the wash-house would perhaps be more convenient in the rear. In the second story the size of the closet over the stairs might be diminished so as to avoid the blank window, and thus give additional light in the passage. The plan of the third story corresponds exactly to that of the second story main building. This house is evidently very roomy. A family of ten would by no means find it too small. If the servants be included in this number there will be apartments for a library and spare chamber.

Plate XXXII. consists of Details. Fig. 1 shows the cornice and brackets of the wings. Fig. 2, section of the cornice and wall. Fig. 3, part of the front pediment. Fig. 4, section of the same. Fig. 5, front door. Fig. 6, crowning ornament of the pediment. Fig. 7, front porch. Fig. 8, section of the same. Fig. 9, chimney-can.

Plate XXXIII. is also of Details. Fig. 1 is the third story balcony. Fig. 2, section of the same, showing the bracket. Fig. 3, second story windows. Fig. 4, first story windows. Fig. 5, section of the same, showing the bracket. Fig. 6, newel and baluster of the stairs. Figs. 7 and 8, sections of the window frames.

The entire front of the building, including the verandah and wash-house, is sixty-six feet. The depth, measuring through the Dining Room and the porch, is forty-two feet six inches. The divisions and their dimensions are all figured on the floor plans. The first story is thirteen feet four inches high to the top of the second floor. The second story is twelve feet to the top of the third floor in the main building, and the third story is ten feet in the clear. The cellar throughout the entire extent of the main building and wings, is eight feet deep in the clear, and the trenches for foundations are at least eight inches below the cellar floor, the earth therefrom being graded around the building as may be requisite to embellish the grounds.

The walls of the cellar, as high as the joists of the first floor and the foundations of the verandah and wash-house, are all of quarry building stone; that of the foundations is large and flat, solidly bedded in the mortar. The facings are all smoothly dashed, and afterwards whitewashed. The mortar for this masonry is composed of good coarse sharp sand and fresh wood-burnt lime. The outside walls of the superstructure are composed of bricks, and are thirteen inches thick; no soft brick being placed within four inches of the exterior surface of the walls. The inner walls of the main building are nine inches thick. All other divisions are stud partitions. The front corners of the main building have each a pilaster projecting four inches from the wall. The flues are located as exhibited on the plate of plans. They are well pargetted and surmounted with the chimney-can exhibited on the plate of details. A case of brick is built in the cellar for a furnace. All this brick-work is done with good firm mortar. The bricks of the exterior are three eighths of an inch distant from each other, and the mortar removed from between them at least half an inch deep.

The joists of the first floor are three by eleven inches, and of spruce pine throughout. Those of the second and third stories are of the same dimensions, of hemlock. Those of the second story wings are three by ten, and also of hemlock. All are placed sixteen inches between centres, and have a course of bridging through the middle of each room. The studs for partitions are three by four inches, and are also placed sixteen inches between centres. The rafters are three by five inches, and placed two feet between centres; they are sheathed with quartered and well seasoned boards, for a metal covering.

The floors are all of one inch Carolina heart pine, well worked and well seasoned. The stairs are put up on three carriages, with one inch and a quarter heart step boards, having one and three quarter inch balusters, a newel and moulded rail, all of mahogany. The newel, balusters and brackets are richly carved as on the plate of details. Other stairs are in the usual style; those to the cellar are under the main stairs, or may lead from the wash-house.

The windows of the front correspond with the elevation. Those of the first story are enriched with terra-cotta brackets and head-piece. Those of the second and third stories all are arched and have a finish like to those on the front. The windows of the first story sides and rear, and those of the verandah reaching the floor, have square heads, but are more plainly dressed than the front. They are twin or single, as delineated on the ground plans. The sash are all double, hung with axle pullies and patent cord, and all of the first and second stories have inside double shutters, one inch thick, in two folds of two panels each, with fillets and mouldings. All glass is the best American, well bedded and back-puttied.

The doors on the front are two inches thick, with fillets and mouldings on one side and bead and butt on the other. The side lights have inside shutters. The dressings correspond with the plate. All the room doors in the first and second stories are one inch and three quarters thick, with moulding and fillets. Those in the third story, and all closet doors, are one inch and a quarter thick, with moulding and fillets on one side. All the one and three quarter inch doors are hung with four by four inch butts and secured with four inch mortice locks. The front doors have an eight inch upright mortice lock, and are further secured with bolts. The closet doors also have locks. The knobs of the first and second stories are all of porcelain.

The front porch, verandah and balconies are all partly exhibited on the plates of details. The floors are of one inch and a quarter white pine, quartered and grooved, the joints being well coated with white lead. The whole of the wood-work, inside and out, has three coats of pure white-lead paint, that of the exterior having an additional coat, tinted and sanded so as to represent stone.

The walls and ceilings throughout have two coats of brown mortar and one of white hard finish. The Parlor, Dining Room and Hall have each a moulded cornice girting twelve inches, with a centre flower in the Parlor three feet six inches in diameter, one in the Dining Room three feet, and one in the Hall two feet six inches. The exterior is all to be rough-cast in the very best manner, tinted and laid off in blocks.

The roofs of the building and its appendages, all having concealed gutters, are overlaid with the best one cross leaded tin, well painted on both sides, the upper side receiving two coats. This tin is drawn over slats laid from the apex of the roof to the eaves, two feet between centres, as exhibited on the elevation. There are four three inch conductors necessary to convey the water from the roof.

All the materials used in the above work are of the very best quality, and in all respects not herein described the work is executed in the best style.

The cost of this building, according to the present rates of material and workmanship, would be about $5,200.

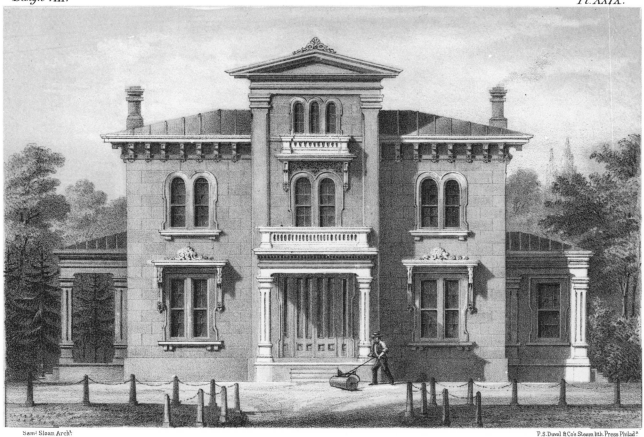

Sam.¹ Sloan Arch.ᵗ   P.S.Duval & Co's Steam lith.Press Philad.ᵃ

ITALIAN RESIDENCE.

Sam.¹ Sloan Arch.ᵗ   P.S.Duval & Co's Steam lith.Press Philad.ᵃ

ORNAMENTAL VILLA.

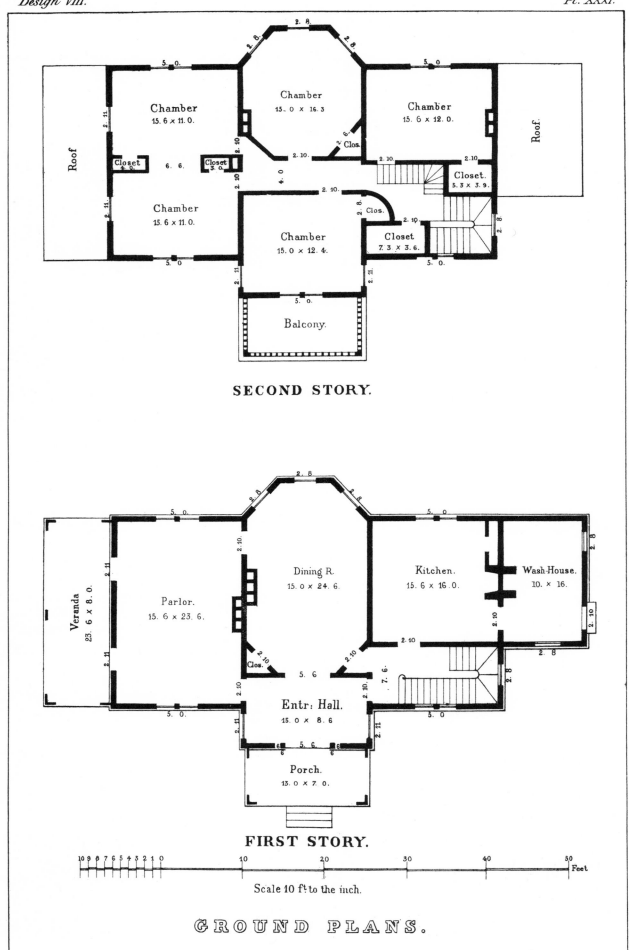

SECOND STORY.

- Chamber 15. 6 × 11. 0.
- Chamber 15. 0 × 16. 3
- Chamber 15. 6 × 12. 0.
- Roof
- Roof
- Closet 4. 0.
- Closet 3. 0.
- Clos.
- Closet 5. 3 × 3. 9.
- Chamber 15. 6 × 11. 0.
- Chamber 15. 0 × 12. 4.
- Clos.
- Closet 7. 3 × 3. 6.
- Balcony.

FIRST STORY.

- Parlor. 15. 6 × 23. 6.
- Dining R. 15. 0 × 24. 6.
- Kitchen. 15. 6 × 16. 0.
- Wash-House. 10. × 16.
- Veranda 23. 6 × 8. 0.
- Clos.
- Entr: Hall. 15. 0 × 8. 6
- Porch. 13. 0 × 7. 0.

Scale 10 f.t to the inch.

GROUND PLANS.

P. S. Duval's Steam lith. Press Philad.ª

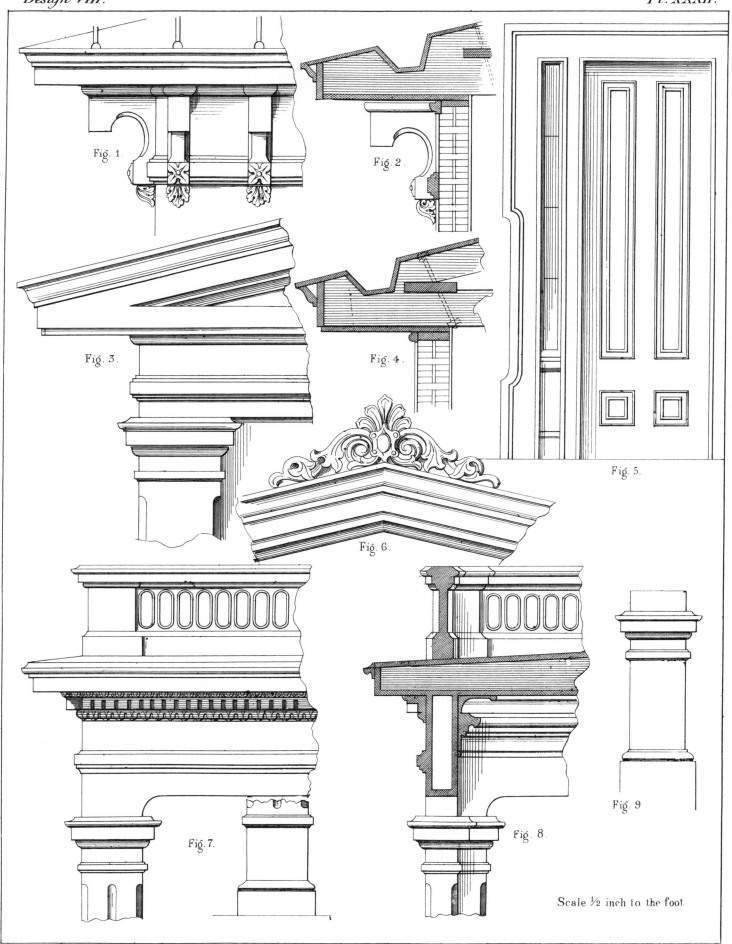

Fig. 1.

Fig. 2.

Fig. 3.

Fig. 4.

Fig. 5.

Fig. 6.

Fig. 7.

Fig. 8.

Fig. 9.

Scale ½ inch to the foot

DETAILS.

Fig. 1.

Fig. 2.

Fig. 3.

Fig. 4.

Fig. 5.

Fig. 6.

Scale to Fig.ˢ 7 & 8
one inch to the foot.

Fig. 7.

Fig. 8.

Scale, ½ inch to the foot.

DETAILS.

AN ORNAMENTAL VILLA.

DESIGN NINTH.

WE present on Plate XXX. the perspective view of an Ornamental Villa. The enriched appearance of this design is due almost entirely to the balconies, brackets and other ornaments about the eaves. The style of these is Swiss, and it therefore might be named, a villa ornamented in the Swiss style. It has long been acknowledged that there is nothing more beautifully picturesque than this kind of decoration, when well arranged. It has an elegant and highly finished, though it may be a somewhat meretricious effect. The building is evidently not a rural cottage, nor would it do for a farm house; nevertheless a retired situation best accords with its expression. This indeed is characteristic of the Swiss style, or any thing approaching thereto, that it is best adapted to a wild and mountainous, or at least a hilly locality. A high position, affording a view of the building from the distant landscape, is always desirable.

There is one great objection to it, however. The ornamental appendages are expensive. But it is to be hoped that the time is, or is coming, when such near-sighted utilitarianism will give way to more liberal views of life, and that he who builds for himself a home, will aim beyond mere physical comfort.

Plate XXXIV. presents an elevation of the side which is partially exhibited in the perspective view. On this we have the conservatory displayed, which is the chief ornamental feature of the elevation. It has above a large balcony, approached from the second story. The roof in both elevations is so arranged as to destroy a monotonous effect, but its real appearance must not be judged the same as that here presented. As there is a cellar beneath the building, square windows, barred, might be introduced beneath the lower balconies, to give light and air.

Plate XXXV. is the Front Elevation. It is well to observe that the brackets of the balconies, those under the porch and the very projecting eaves, are all of various patterns suited to their positions. Those of the eaves are clustered against each pilaster. The side porch appears only on this elevation, but is of simple design. Both of the elevations are drawn to a scale of twelve feet to the inch.

On Plate XXXVI. are the Ground Plans. This house, as a glance makes evident, is large, but not designed for a large family. It would accommodate six or seven persons readily, yet, planned as it is for luxurious livers, it would be none too large for only four or five. The Hall receives its light principally from the cupola above. The flues are arranged either for grates or for a furnace in the cellar. A ventilating flue from the water closets might be encased in the wall. The side porch may be extended to any desirable length, and an outside cellar door made beneath it. All the divisions of the first story, and those corresponding in the second, are of brick.

Plate XXXVII. is of Details. Fig. 1 is the front porch, balcony and window above. Fig. 2, section of the porch cornice. Fig. 3, front balconies and windows of the wings. Fig. 4, section of the upper balcony in fig. 3, showing the bracket. Fig. 5, section of the lower balcony in fig. 3, showing the bracket.

Plate XXXVIII., also of Details, shows, in Fig. 1, the crowning and other ornaments of the front gable. Fig. 2, section of the same, showing the gable bracket. Fig. 3, bracket of the eaves. Fig. 4, cupola. Fig. 5, section of the same, showing the exterior and interior brackets. Fig. 6, chimney-can. Fig. 7, cornice, &c., of the conservatory.

S P E C I F I C A T I O N

Of the workmanship and materials to be employed in the erection of Design Ninth.

EXCAVATION.—The cellar is to extend beneath the entire building, and be nine feet deep from the level of the principal floor. Dig all the trenches for the foundations at least ten inches below the cellar floor, and deeper if necessary to secure a good foundation. Cut away and fill up with earth around the building to the intended line of ground level, ramming the same quite hard, and provide for all necessary drains, cess-pools, dwarf-walls or other such work required by the plans, or directed by the architect.

MASONRY.—Construct the lower walls of stone as follows,—nine feet ten inches ,in height and twenty-two inches thick, the foundations of the divisions eighteen inches thick and ten inches in height, and compose all of the best material, as hereinafter set forth. Flush the whole in mortar of the best approved compound of sharp sand and well burnt lime. If the material be of an absorbent quality the whole must be grouted every two feet.

BRICK-WORK.—All the exterior walls, from the level of the first floor to the roof, are to be constructed of well burnt and approved brick, and are to be fourteen and a half inches thick, with a hollow space in the centre one inch and a quarter broad, the inner course being four inches and one fourth thick, and those without being eight inches and a half thick. The division walls in the cellar, as high as the first floor, must also be of sound and well constructed brick-work, thirteen inches thick, corresponding in position to the divisions in the plan of the first story. All openings in these walls are to be arched. The principal divisions of the first and second stories, corresponding with the plans, are to be of brick-work nine inches thick. All flues, for thoroughly warming and ventilating the building, are to be placed as on the plans and as may be directed during the progress of the work. Those for gas must in no case be less than nine by thirteen inches, and be so arranged that stove pipes can be passed into them from each of the principal rooms. They are to be pargetted and surmounted with a chimney-can. This brick-work must be done with mortar compounded of the best clean river sand and well burnt lime. The mortar is to be removed from between the exterior bricks to the depth of half an inch.

CARPENTER-WORK.—Place all joists, studs and rafters sixteen inches between centres. The joists of the first floor are to be three by eleven inch spruce pine. Those of the second floor are to be of hemlock, three by twelve inches. A course of herring-bone bridging is to run through the middle of each tier. The ceiling joists are to be two by ten inches and also bridged. The rafters are to be three by six inches. The wall plates at the eaves and on the gables are to be three by nine inches. The ridge piece is to be three by twelve inches, and the whole roof must be framed according to working drawings, to be provided for the purpose, and furnished with all bolts, straps, spikes, lathing and other material necessary to finish and prepare the same for the slater.

FLOORS.—The floors throughout the interior are to be of the best Carolina heart pine boards, one inch thick, and not over four inches wide when tongued and grooved. They must be well seasoned, well worked, firmly nailed to the joists and afterwards smoothed off. The floors of the balconies and porches are to be of white pine board, two inches and a half wide, tongued and grooved and with white lead in all the joints. The underside of all the balconies must be ceiled with sound half inch planed and grooved boards.

STAIRS.—Place all stairs on three strong carriages and make the steps of one inch and a quarter heart boards. The risers must be of pine one inch thick, grooved and glued to the steps. The newel of the main flight is to be eight inches in diameter and richly carved. The balusters must be turned and not less than two and a quarter inches in diameter. The rail is to be moulded, and in size two and a quarter by four and a half inches. The rail and balusters of the gallery are to be like to those of the main stairway, all being of the best mahogany. The newel of the private stairs is to be six inches in diameter, and the balusters one inch and three quarters turned. The rail must be moulded and be two by three and three quarter inches.

DRESSINGS.—The brackets for the projecting eaves, gables, balconies, &c., are to be constructed in accordance with the form shown on the plates of details, and must be well secured to the soffits of the roof, &c., with spikes, and also to the walls before rough-casting. The cupola, face of the eaves, verge board, dressings of the gables, balconies, porches, conservatory and window dressings, must all be constructed as set forth on the plates of details. The wash-boards throughout the principal rooms of the first and second stories, vestibule, lobbies, halls and gallery, must be one inch and a quarter thick with a one and three quarter by four inch sub, and a moulding on top two inches and a quarter high, the whole, including the sub and moulding, being fourteen inches broad. All other wash-boards are to be eight inches broad, with a moulding on top. The inside dressings of the windows and doors must be of high finish, as may be directed.

DOORS.—All the principal doors in the first story must be two inches thick, with eight inch stiles and bottom rail fourteen inches wide. The panels are to have rich mouldings on both sides, with carved flowers in the centre of each. The kitchen, conservatory, store room and closet doors are to be one inch and three quarters thick, with plain mouldings two inches and a quarter wide. The principal room doors in the second story must be one inch and three quarters thick, with seven inch stiles and bottom rails twelve inches wide. They are to have two and a half inch mouldings on both sides. The doors of the bath room and closets are to be one inch and a half thick, with mouldings on one side.

WINDOWS.—The windows are to correspond with the elevation and detail plates. The sash in the first story are to be one inch and three quarters thick, and those of the second story are to be one inch and a half thick. Each window is to have inside shutters, panelled and one inch thick, with four folds to each jamb. The inside dressings of all the doors and windows are to correspond with those of the exterior, except the head piece, which is to be more rich. The windows of the kitchen and minor apartments are to have four inch mouldings inside. Provide lintels eight inches deep over each opening in the wall, nine inches longer than the breadth of the opening beneath.

CLOSETS.—The closets throughout must be fully and neatly shelved, or have clothes hooks, as may be directed. Provide a dresser in the kitchen of most approved construction.

PLASTERING.—Lath all stud partitions and ceilings for plastering. Give all walls and ceilings throughout the interior of the building two coats of brown mortar and one of white hard finish. Place a centre flower in the parlor five feet in diameter, one in the dining room four feet in diameter, and one in the vestibule three feet and a half in diameter. The cornice in each of these rooms is to girt seventeen inches. There is to be a cornice in the lobby, hall, library and the two principal chambers, girting nine inches. Lath and plaster the external soffits of the projecting eaves and the ceilings of the porches, and tint the same as may be desired. The whole external brick-work is to be rough-cast in the very best manner, and hard finished for painting and sanding, by a workman familiar with the business.

SLATING.—The roof is to be overlaid with the best domestic slate, of small size, secured with oiled nails, two to each slate. This slating must be made tight to the house and pointed underneath with strong hair mortar, to exclude better the driving rain and snow.

TINNING.—The hip ridges, vallies, flushings and gutters, are to be laid with good leaded tin, prepared for the purpose. All the projecting window heads and porch roofs are to be covered with the same. Provide four tin conductors, extending from the gutters to the ground, with shoes, eave pipes, &c., all put up securely and painted. All hot air flues must be lined with two cross tin.

PLUMBING.—Place a reservoir in the loft over the bath room, lined with sheet lead three pounds to the foot, and supplied by a force pump. Provide and arrange all necessary lead pipes for conveying the water from the reservoir to the bath room, to the water closets, to the sink and range in the kitchen, and to wash-basins in the two principal chambers. The bath tub and sink are to be of enamelled iron, and to be supplied with additional pipes for warm water from a boiler in the kitchen. A hot and cold shower bath is to be placed over the tub. The stop-cocks in the chambers are to be silver plated. All others are to be bronzed. China bowls must be provided for the chambers and water closets. All pipes are to be five eighths of an inch, extra strong, and every thing must be furnished, put up and completed.

PAINTING, &c..—All tin-work on the roofs is to be painted on both sides, the upper side receiving two coats corresponding in color with the slate. Paint and sand the exterior walls in the best style. Paint all exterior wood-work with four coats, tinted and worked in imitation of old oak. Paint all interior wood-work with three coats of pure white-lead, mixed with the best linseed oil, all joints and holes having been puttied and the knots properly subdued. The newels, balusters and rails of the stairways and gallery are to have four coats of varnish. The sash are all to be glazed with the best American crown glass, well bedded, bradded and back puttied. The window over the stairway is to be stained glass of a selected pattern.

HARDWARE.—Provide four by five inch silver plated butt hinges for the doors of the lobby and vestibule. The front doors are to be furthermore furnished with an eight inch, upright, mortice, rebate lock, with a night key and porcelain furniture ornamented, the cost of the lock being not less than fourteen dollars. Provide the rest of the above doors with mortice locks having porcelain knobs, the cost of each not being less than six dollars and a half. The principal doors in the second story are to have four by four inch plated butt hinges, and locks with porcelain furniture, not costing less than five dollars each. All other doors must be hung with suitable butts and secured by locks with mineral knobs at three dollars each. All windows are to be double hung with axle pullies and patent cord. Provide one dozen double and one dozen single brass clothes hooks and place them in the bath room and closets as may be directed. Procure two and a half cwt. of iron anchors, bolts, &c., to be used in the framing of the floors and roofs where necessary. Place in the kitchen a bell connected with a porcelain pull in the front door, the cost of the whole complete not being less than five dollars and a half. Place six other bells in the kitchen, with pulls in the principal rooms, as may be directed. Place four mantles, of enamelled iron, in the four principal rooms, the cost of each not being less than thirty dollars.

DEAFENING.—The second story floor is to be deafened by placing cleats on the joists. These must be then floored over and filled with mortar flush to the edge of the joists.

TILES.—The vestibule, lobby and hall are to be paved with plain tiles, No. 25 pattern, buff and black. In the hall place an octagon centre piece, of encaustic tiles, three colors, covering twelve square feet.

FINALLY.—Complete the whole of the above work in the best and most workmanlike manner, according to the working drawings and the general intent and meaning of this specification, subject at all times to the direction and decision of the owner or his superintendent.

A FULL ESTIMATE

OF THE COST IN ERECTING DESIGN NINTH.

THIS estimate is intended to comprise nearly all the minutiæ of the building, each thing being of the very best quality and set at the market cash price for the same. It will be perceived that the amount is greatly increased by expensive decorations, which, if desirable, could be omitted or reduced, and thus considerably diminish the cost.

Excavation, 741 yds. @ 20 cts. per yd.	$148.20
Stone, 112 perches, quarry measurement, @ 90 cts. per perch,	100.80
Laying the same, including sand and lime, @ $1.25 per perch,	140.00
Brick, $118,000, delivered at $6.00 per M.	708.00
Lime and sand @ 90 cts. per M. brick,	106.20
Laying the same at @ $3.00 per M. brick,	354.00
Rough-casting, including all material, 790 yds. @ 45 cts.	355.50
Plastering, 2665 yds. @ 25 cts.	666.25
Centre flower in the parlor,	18.00
Centre flower in the dining room,	13.00
Centre flower in the vestibule,	9.00
Cornice girting 17 in. 216 ft. @ 17 cts.	36.72
Cornice girting 9 in. 400 ft. @ 9 cts.	36.00
Tiles for flooring, 468 ft. laid @ 42 cts.	196.56
Centre piece in hall, 12 ft. @ $1.25,	15.00
Scaffolding, 4000 ft. @ $12.00 per M.	48.00
Joists of spruce pine, 7500 ft. @ $17.00 per M.	127.50
Joists of hemlock, 7500 ft. @ $12.50 per M.	93.75
Joists for ceilings, 3100 ft. @ $12.50 per M.	38.75
Rafters, &c., for roof, 4800 ft. @ $12.50 per M.	60.00
Slating lath, 4350 ft. (in length) @ $5.00 per M.	21.75
Studs, 3 by 4 in. 5500 ft. @ $12.50 per M.	68.75
Studs next the doors, 3 by 8 in. 1000 ft.	12.00
Flooring boards, 6150 ft. @ $33.00 per M.	202.95
Main stairway, both workmanship and material,	160.00
Private stairway, " . "	120.00
Front door according to plate,	26.00
Doors 2 inches thick, 8 @ $7.50,	60.00
Doors 1¾ inches thick, 16 @ $5.25,	84.00
Doors 1½ inches thick, 8 @ $4.75,	38.00
Windows, triple and twin, 14, the frames, sash, inside shutters and outside dressings delivered @ $35.50 to each window,	497.00
Windows, single, 10, frames, sash, &c., delivered @ $19.00,	190.00
Brackets of eaves over conservatory, 4 @ $5.25,	21.00
Brackets of the other eaves, 35 @ $5.00,	175.00
Brackets of gables and balconies, 37 @ $4.00,	148.00
Assorted lumber, 14500 ft. @ $28.00 per M.	406.00
Workmanship not stated above, 860 days @ $1.75,	1505.00
Carver's bill, including cost of material,	128.00
Slating, 3000 ft. @ 10 cts.	300.00
Tinning,	165.00
Painting and graining and sanding the exterior,	280.00
	$7879.68

Painting within and glazing, including material,	$450.00
Stained glass for window, 32 ft. @ $1.00,	32.00
Mortice lock for front door,	14.00
Mortice locks, 5 @ $6.50,	32.50
Mortice locks in the second story, 5 @ 5.00,	25.00
Locks of other doors, 22 @ $3.00,	66.00
Butts, silver plated, 9 pair, 4 by 5 in. @ $5.50,	49.50
Butts, silver plated, 4 pair, 4 by 4 in. @ $4.50,	18.00
Iron butts, 6 pair, 3½ by 4 in. @ 16 cts.	.96
Iron butts, 4 pair, 3½ by 3½ in. @ 15 cts.	.60
Iron butts, 12 pair, 2 by 3 in. @ 8 cts.	.96
Back flaps for shutters, 24 doz. pair, @ 45 cts.	10.80
Butts for shutters, 10 doz. pair, 2 by 3 in. @ 70 cts.	7.00
Front door bell and furniture,	5.50
Bells inside and fixtures, 6 @ $3.00,	18.00
Axle pullies, 4 doz. 1¾ in. @ 50 cts.	2.00
Sash cord, 18 lb. @ 31¼ cts.	5.62½
Sash lifts, 4 doz. @ 50 cts.	2.00
Brass clothes hooks, double, 1 doz.	1.50
Brass clothes hooks, single, 1 doz.	.62½
Mantles, 4 @ $30.00 each,	120.00
Wrought iron work, 2½ cwt. @ $10.00,	25.00
Nails and spikes, 21 kegs @ $4.50,	94.50
Lightning rod of twisted wire, 80 ft. @ 15 cts.	12.00
Platinum point for the same,	4.00
Lining the reservoir with lead,	34.00
Force pump,	30.00
Bath tub and sink,	29.50
Shower bath over the tub, with brass shower,	17.00
China bowls in the chambers, 2 @ $3.00,	6.00
Plated stop-cocks to the same, 4 @ $5.00,	20.00
Stop-cocks elsewhere, 7 @ $2.50,	17.50
Lead pipe, 210 ft. @ 20 cts.	42.00
Fitting up the whole complete,	45.00
Water closets, 2, with soil-pipe, 17 ft. @ 70 cts.	161.90
Ventilators, 6, Dr. Arnott's self-acting, @ $3.00	18.00
Furnace, Chilson's No. 4, including setting,	140.00
Register for the parlor, plated, 11 by 16 in.	17.50
Register for the dining room, black, 11 by 16 in.	7.50
Register for the hall, octagon, polished,	16.00
Register for the library, black, 11 by 12 in.	4.00
Registers in 2d story, 5, black, 9 by 14 in. @ $4.75,	23.75
Cooking range, &c., complete and set,	125.00
	1752.72
	7879.68
	$9632.40

Sam.! Sloan Arch.!

P. S. Duval & Co's Steam lith. Press Philad.ª

FRONT ELEVATION.

Sam.! Sloan Arch.!

P. S. Duval & Co's Steam lith. Press Philad.ª

SIDE ELEVATION.

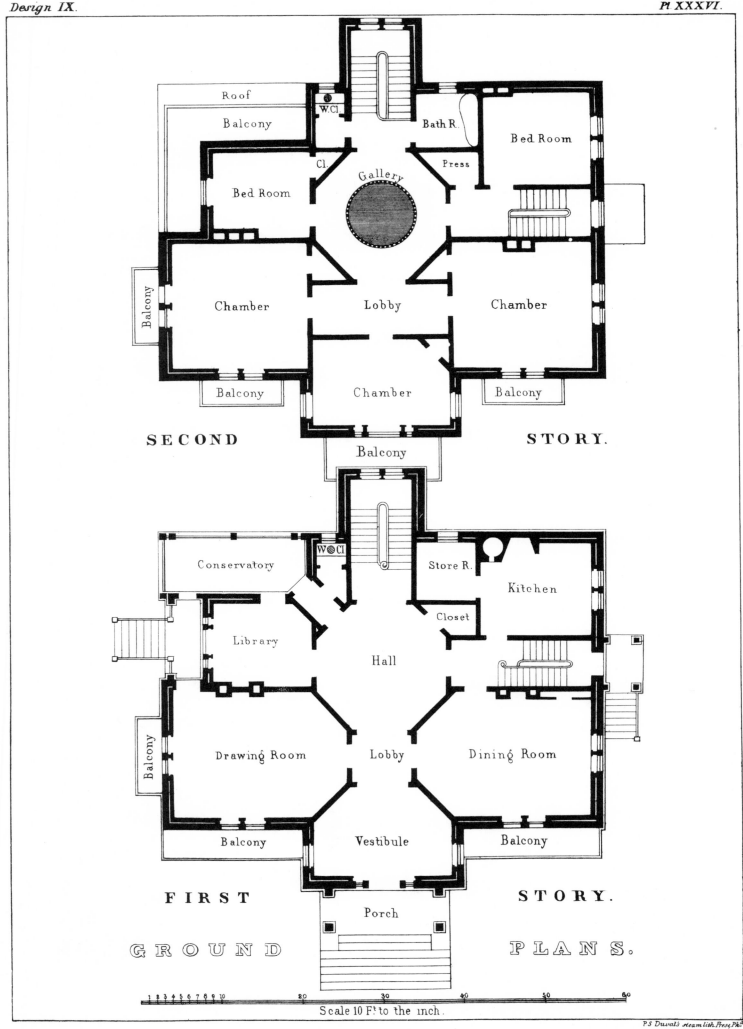

Roof

Balcony

W.Cl.

Bath R.

Bed Room

Cl.

Press

Gallery

Bed Room

Balcony

Chamber

Lobby

Chamber

Balcony

Balcony

Balcony

Chamber

Balcony

SECOND

STORY.

Balcony

Conservatory

W Cl

Store R.

Kitchen

Library

Closet

Hall

Balcony

Drawing Room

Lobby

Dining Room

Balcony

Balcony

Vestibule

Balcony

FIRST

STORY.

Porch

GROUND PLANS.

1 2 3 4 5 6 7 8 9 10   20   30   40   50   60

Scale 10 Ft to the inch.

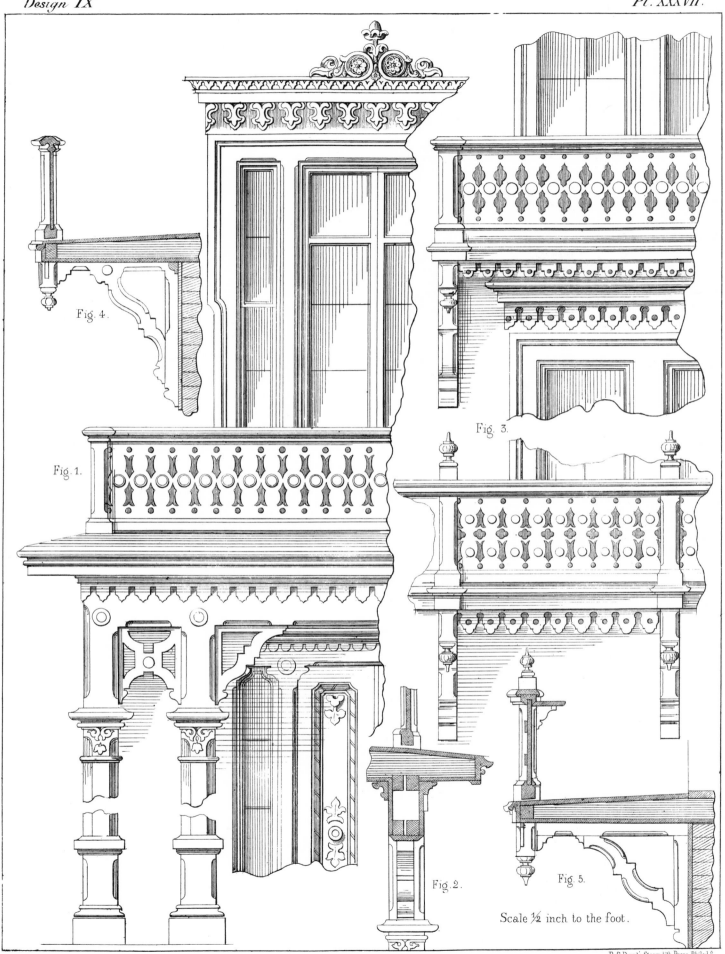

Fig. 4.

Fig. 3.

Fig. 1.

Fig. 2.

Fig. 5.

Scale ½ inch to the foot.

DETAILS.

Fig. 1.

Fig. 2.

Fig. 3.

Fig. 4.

Fig. 5.

Fig. 6.

Fig. 7.

Scale ½ inch to the foot.

DETAILS.

NORMAN ARCHITECTURE.

ORMAN Architecture was the precursor of the Gothic, and its origin may be traced to the buildings of the northern barbaric hordes who over-ran Italy. With the fall of the Roman Empire, as was remarked in a previous article, Architecture suffered a great depression, and has not since returned to its former position. When Italy became independent again of foreign power, and the works of Vitruvius were discovered, then old principles were resumed and the labor of perfecting was carried on with vigor; but until that time, even in Italy, barbarous modes prevailed. The Goths, who retained supremacy there during nearly a century, did nothing for the advancement of the art. They used the materials of overthrown temples, attaching highly sculptured ornaments to the rude massive walls of their castles and palaces, thus producing harsh contrasts and falsity of expression that exclude their mode from the domain of art.

The Lombards succeeded the Goths in northern Italy, and founded a kingdom which lasted for two centuries. In building they used new materials and exhibited much taste and skill, combined with considerable originality. They were influenced doubtless by the buildings of the Goths and the remains of the destroyed empire; but their edifices were very rough, and being constructed principally for the purposes of defence, had immense massive walls from six to nine feet thick. In the year A. D. 590, Theodolina, queen of the Lombards, embraced the Catholic faith and endowed several ecclesiastical establishments, and in constructing buildings for their reception, a higher order of art was attempted. The massive walls were retained, but the windows were more frequent, larger, and arched at the top. The influence of the monuments around is perceptible in the production of these very creditable edifices.

Charlemagne expelled the Lombards, and in the year 800 ceded the government of Italy to the Pope. The Lombards were scattered throughout Europe for a time, and communicated their knowledge of Architecture to the more barbarous tribes in France and Germany. These, feeling the need of military fortifications, erected buildings for the purpose, in imitation of the Lombardic manner.

During the ninth century the Normans settled in the north of France, a province having been granted them by Charles the Simple. They soon afterwards embraced the Christian religion and began to erect edifices for its conduct. Their superior energy of character and their zeal for the new religion, caused them readily to surpass their cotemporaries in the art. The ecclesiastics labored night and day, both as architects and artificers, and the monasteries exceeded even the castles of the nobles in magnificence. All their buildings were upon a more elegant and grander scale than those in the Lombard style, and finally differed from them materially in general design, ornament and execution. The massive proportions were disused, and the walls diminished in thickness were built to a greater height. Their edifices nevertheless appeared cumberously heavy, but they ceased not to improve in this and other respects until the style gradually changed to the Gothic, and although these improvements were every where diffused, yet on the continent the mode was never distinguished by any particular name, but was termed, with that which preceded it, the Lombard style.

William, Duke of Normandy, afterwards self-styled the Conqueror, invaded England in the year 1066, and having become possessed of the throne, sought to secure his conquest by building castles in various places. Among these was the tower of London which served both as a stronghold and palace. He also gave every encouragement in his power to the depressed church. Under his auspices it increased rapidly in power and wealth. Cathedrals, abbeys and other such buildings went up in all directions, each endeavoring to excel its neighbor, until every little town had something of which to boast and be proud. Thus the Norman soon supplanted the Anglo-Saxon style which formerly prevailed in the island. When the government became more settled, such impregnable fortresses as their castles were not requisite, and more attention began to be paid to comfort. The advance of the style was now characterized by greater lightness in construction and delicacy in details. The windows were increased both in size and number, and the carvings were more profuse and less rudely executed.

The unsurpassed skill in adapting mathematical principles which characterized the mediæval architects may be attributed almost entirely to the labors of the society of Free Masons, whose origin as a guild is lost in obscurity, but who at this time were gathering knowledge and strength. They roved in bands from place to place wherever there was a castle or church to build, and by their intercommunication, secrecy and united action soon monopolized the erection of all large edifices. In the twelfth century they were granted great privileges by the Pope, and to their scientific skill we owe those grand monuments of that and succeeding ages. The ramifications of this powerful fraternity extend throughout the world, but it has long since ceased the practice of Architecture, and we have great cause to regret that so many of their records, which would be of practical value in the art, have been destroyed.

About the middle of the twelfth century a radical change began to exhibit itself in Architecture. The transition was easy but decided, and as has been before remarked, at the close of the century the style had so changed as to receive a new name, the Gothic. The Norman style prevailed in England for about a hundred and fifty years. On the continent it merged into the Gothic about the same time as in England, but having existed earlier, it may be said to have prevailed there under a different name for about a century more. During this time it was continually undergoing gradual changes and improvements.

Norman buildings were principally of two kinds, those for religious service and those for the purpose of defence, both being used as habitations. The castles were erected in provinces or districts with huts of poor construction, the homes of the peasantry, scattered around. The chief man of the province with his retainers occupied the castle, to which all repaired in times of danger. Ecclesiastical edifices were sometimes simply for worship, but generally they were also the dwellings of the ecclesiastics, hospitals for the afflicted, the refuge of the oppressed, and sufficiently strong to be put in a state of defence when necessary. The plan of the churches was peculiar and every where the same. It was taken from that of the Roman Basilicæ, or halls of justice, many of which were used by the early Christians as places of worship, and found so convenient for the purpose, that the plan was universally adopted. When the service of the church began to require more space, a transept was added which gave the plan the form of a Latin cross, the upper part of which, so to speak, always laid towards the east and was called the chancel, the western portion, being the main body of the building, was called the nave, and the southern portion of the transept was the choir. The form of other buildings, and that of the castles, was subject to no particular rule. They were oftentimes surrounded by a heavy wall and had watch-towers, strongholds and dungeons.

The walls of the buildings were of immense thickness. The outer courses were mostly constructed of ashlar-work or "clene hewen stone," as it is termed in the old contracts and the intermediate space filled with grouted rubble-work. Sometimes this rubble-work was used for the outer courses, the buttresses and angles only being of ashlar-work, and in all cases the joints were very wide. Buttresses were not introduced until the wall was so diminished in thickness as to render them necessary to resist the lateral thrust of the arches. They were so flat as to resemble pilasters, and either ran into the corbel-table, thus presenting the appearance of panelling, or finished into the wall just beneath the cornice. The embattled parapet which surmounts the walls of many towers is supposed to be of subsequent construction, but is certainly a fine addition. Heavy string courses are common, both plain and moulded.

The tower of this style is either round or angular. In very large churches it was erected on the intersection of the nave and transept, but in others it either occupied the angles formed by the intersection, or the western corners of the edifice. In other buildings it had no particular position, but was generally placed at an angle of the walls, which it always overlooked. It was frequently surmounted by a conical roof of wood or tiles, with overhanging eaves, which form was afterwards elongated and became the spire. Of the roof of the main building we can say nothing, no specimens being extant.

The principles of the arch were well understood by the Normans. Beneath their buildings were found extensive crypts and vaults, both barrel and groined, whose stability has shown them to be of excellent construction. All doors and windows were headed with an arch, which was stilted when the style approached its term. The openings had above them the semi-circular hood-mould, resting on ornamented corbels. No part of the structure received so much attention as the portals. Occasionally porches were used, and always the doors were deeply recessed in the wall. In the latter stage of the style they were elaborately enriched with mouldings of various patterns, and the archivault was composed of numerous ribs. Whatever of sculpture adorned the building was generally placed on or near the doorway. The tympanum was often decorated with rudely executed bas-relief, generally symbolical or grotesque. In this work there was no effort at high finish, a striking bold effect being only desired. The windows were long, narrow and decorated with mouldings. They were placed either singly or in pairs, and were sometimes ranged in arcades. In these arcades we may occasionally see the intersecting arches from which the pointed arch of the early Gothic was derived. There is a fine instance of this in the Croyland Abbey Church, Lincolnshire, where a range of pointed arches occurs immediately below such an arcade.

The mouldings of the Norman style are peculiar and characteristic. The most frequent is the chevron, or zig-zag, from which nearly all others and the tooth-moulding of the early Gothic originated. There are besides this the embattled, the double cone, the alternate billet, the lozenge and others. The running mouldings and arch ribs were of various patterns. The cornices, doors, windows and piers only received these ornaments.

The piers on which these arches rested were at first made heavy, and plain, but as the style advanced they were more finished and ornamented. The body of the pillar was generally square with a cylindrical shaft placed against each side. The corners of the square continued formed the groin, and the shaft also continued formed the arch. Occasionally it was composed entirely of clustered shafts, which at the doorways were embedded in the jams and so arranged as to be continuations of the arch ribs. The cap just beneath the point of impost was either plain or richly sculptured with foliage or other fanciful designs, and the base was formed of moulded bands much resembling those of the classic orders.

The Normans in their partially civilized state knew but little of the comforts of living, and although they took great pride in their buildings, yet the peaceful arts did not occupy much of their attention. They supplied by manual skill, patience and perseverance, all mechanical deficiencies, and the expression of the style is in general very bold, great strength being combined with vast and ponderous magnificence.

Of the adaptation of the Norman style to modern purposes a word may be said. For all public buildings, such as Capitols, Departments, Court-Houses, Prisons, Military Establishments, &c., where something beyond mere brick and mortar is desirable, the style stands without a rival, and for Collegiate Institutions and Libraries it is better adapted than any other with which we are acquainted. For Churches it is only surpassed by the Gothic, whose lofty and impressive grandeur seems to claim this as its peculiar province. In adapting the classic orders to our purposes, it is almost impossible to retain that purity which is their greatest charm, but we may produce buildings in the mediæval styles, which, with entire truthfulness, will combine harmony of expression and purpose. The great pliability of design which belongs to these styles, gives them advantages over every other, for they admit almost any arrangement, and hence, need not be servile imitations such as the classic orders require. An elaboration of these views may be found in the " Hints on Public Architecture," where the accomplished author has given extended and popular illustrations of this subject. For dwellings, this style is only adapted to those on a large scale. Its heavy, bold, and rich expression would be lost in a building of small size, but for an extensive villa it presents most admirable features. The design here given speaks to the point.

Pl. XXXIX.

Design X.

Saml Sloan Arch^t

A NORMAN VILLA.

P S Duval's Steam lith Press Philad^a

Pl. XL.

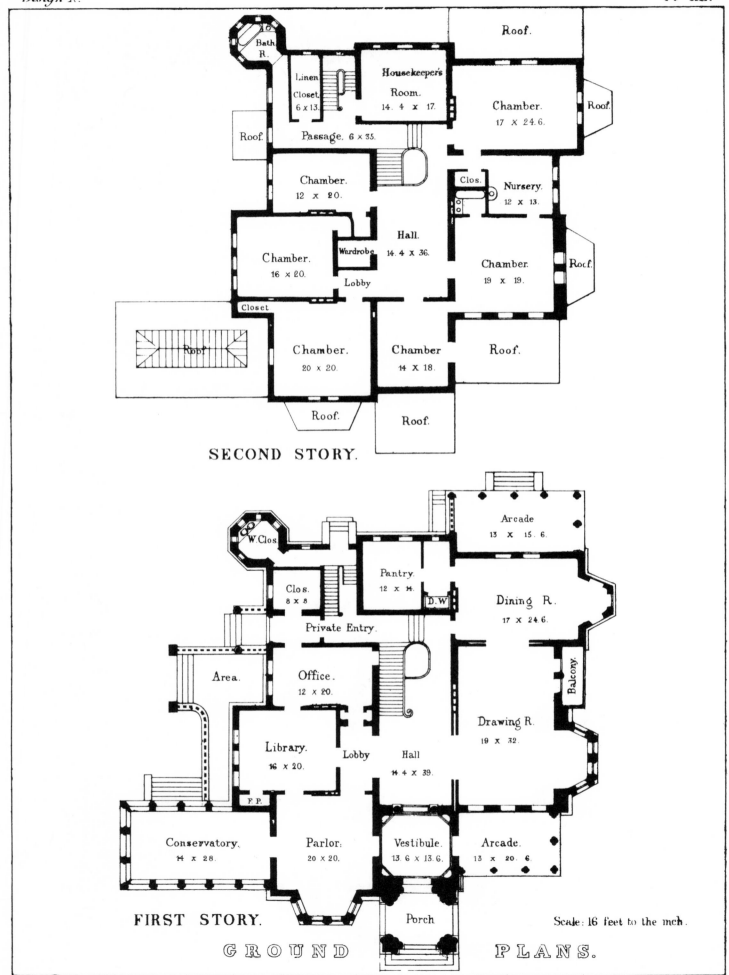

Roof.

Bath R.

Linen Closet. 6 x 13.

Housekeeper's Room. 14. 4 x 17.

Chamber. 17 X 24.6.

Roof.

Roof.

Passage. 6 x 35.

Chamber. 12 x 20.

Clos.

Nursery. 12 x 13.

Chamber. 16 x 20.

Wardrobe

Hall. 14. 4 X 36.

Chamber. 19 x 19.

Roof.

Lobby

Closet

Roof.

Chamber. 20 x 20.

Chamber. 14 X 18.

Roof.

Roof.

Roof.

SECOND STORY.

Arcade 13 X 15. 6.

W. Clos.

Clos. 8 X 8.

Pantry. 12 X 14.

D.W

Dining R. 17 x 24.6.

Private Entry.

Area.

Office. 12 X 20.

Balcony.

Drawing R. 19 X 32.

Library. 16 x 20.

Lobby

Hall 14. 4 x 39.

F. P.

Conservatory. 14 x 28.

Parlor. 20 X 20.

Vestibule. 13. 6 X 13. 6.

Arcade. 13 x 20. 6.

FIRST STORY.

Porch

Scale: 16 feet to the inch.

GROUND PLANS.

P. S. Duval's Steam lith Press Philad.ª

Fig. 1.

Fig. 2.

Scale ½ inch to the foot.

Fig. 3.

Fig. 4.

Fig. 5.

DETAILS.

Fig 1.

Fig. 2.

Fig. 3.

Fig. 4.

Scale ½ inch to the foot.

DETAILS.

A NORMAN VILLA.

DESIGN TENTH.

THIS Villa was designed originally for A. M. Eastwick, Esq., and is now nearly completed at a cost of about thirty thousand dollars. The interior decorations are of the richest description, and make it the most elegant residence perhaps in this section of country. Plate XXXIX. presents a perspective view of the design, the front elevation of which composes the frontispiece of this volume. The side and rear elevations will be found plates on XLIII. and XLIV., and all are drawn to a scale of one-sixteenth of an inch to the foot.

Plate XL. is the ground plans of the first and second story, with the dimensions of the different apartments laid down. The points marked F. P. and D. W. are the positions of the fire-proof closet and the dumb-waiter. In the second story the bath room communicating with the principal chamber to the right, is made with a half partition so as to admit light from above. In both bath rooms and the nursery, wash-bowls are to be arranged.

Plate XLV. exhibits the plans for the basement and attic stories. In the front bed-room of the latter are the stairs leading to the upper stories of the tower. In the passage leading to this room is a circular glass plate fixed in the floor for giving light to the hall below, received from the sky-light in the roof above. The furring-off is shown in the different chambers.

Plate XLI. is of details. Fig. 1, outside dressings of the twin windows of the chambers over the parlor and drawing room. Fig. 2, outside dressings of the side window of the chamber over the dining room. Fig. 3, bay window of the parlor and drawing room. Fig. 4, bay window of the dining room. Fig. 5, window sills, &c.

Plate XLII. is of details. Fig. 1, finial of the front porch. Fig. 2, front porch and front door beneath. Fig. 3, cornice cap, post and base of the arcades. Fig. 4, cap of the front porch enlarged.

Plate XLVI. is also of details. Fig. 1, balcony over the front porch. Fig. 2, side view of the same showing the bracket. Fig. 3, chimney, gable cornice and corbel. Fig. 4, cornice of the tower. Fig. 5, section of the front porch post. Fig. 6, design for an interior corbel. Figs. 7 and 8, designs for interior caps. Fig. 9, finial of the tower.

SPECIFICATION

Of the workmanship and materials to be used in the erection of a Norman Villa, designed for A. M. Eastwick, Esq., Bartram's Gardens, on the west bank of the Schuylkill, near Philadelphia.

EXCAVATION.—The cellar is to be, throughout the entire extent of the building, including all appendages, ten feet deep below the level of the principal floor. The trenches for foundations are to be at least eight inches deep below the cellar bottom. Excavate also all areas, drains, cess-pools, &c., required by the plans, and a well beneath the octagonal tower to the water gravel. The earth from the said excavations is to be graded around the building as high as the intended line of ground level and rammed quite hard. All superfluous earth is to be removed from the grounds, or be placed where the owner may direct.

MASONRY.—All the exterior walls of the basement story are to be composed of quarry building stone of the best quality. The foundations are to be of large flat stone, well and solidly bedded in mortar. The walls must be well flushed in mortar of the best and most approved compound of sharp sand and well burnt lime, and grouted every two feet if the material used be of an absorbent quality.

The foundations of the main tower are to be three feet thick to the level of the cellar floor and from thence two feet nine inches thick to the first tier of the joists. The foundations of the octagon tower are to be two feet six inches thick to the level of the cellar floor, and from thence two feet three inches thick to the first tier of joists. The foundations of the exterior

49

walls of the building are to be two feet three inches thick to the level of the cellar floor, and from thence two feet thick to the first tier of joists. The foundations of the conservatory, the arcades and the areas, are to be two feet thick to the level of the cellar floor, and from thence twenty inches thick. The foundations of the front porch must be of sufficient thickness to receive the granite plinths for the clustered columns.

CUT-STONE.—The steps and plinths of the front porch, the steps, sills and plinths at the side, the sill of the kitchen door, the steps and sill of the rear entrance, the base-course and water-table around the building, are all to be of the best Connecticut granite, neatly tooled and completed as set forth in the working drawings which describe minutely the form and mode of finishing.

BRICK-WORK.—All the walls of the superstructure are to be composed of the best burnt bricks. The exterior course is to be of hard brick, no soft brick coming within four inches of the face of the wall, and the mortar is to be removed from all the exterior joints at least half an inch deep from the surface. The walls of the first and second story of the main tower are to be eighteen inches thick and the wall above thirteen inches thick. The walls of the first story of the octagon tower are to be eighteen inches thick, and the remainder thirteen inches. The walls of these towers must be grouted every fifth course. The exterior walls of the buildings are to be fourteen inches thick to the roof, with a hollow space one inch and a half wide, in the middle between the inner four inch course and the body of the wall, the two being tied together by making every fifth a heading course.

All the divisions in the basement, which according to the plan exceed nine inches in thickness, are to be thirteen inches thick and composed entirely of the best hard bricks, well laid. In the apartments marked "cellar," the walls are to be flushed with white mortar, and the walls of the others are to be faced for plastering. The division walls in the first and second stories are also to be of good brick-work nine inches thick. All bond timber, lintels, &c., throughout the building are to be properly bedded in mortar. The principal openings of the interior are to have arched heads. The openings for the bay-windows are to have strong lintels with arches concealed in the wall above. Construct a fire-proof closet in the library according to the usual method, with a soap-stone head and sill, and iron doors.

In the furnace cellars, two cases located as on the plan are to be bricked up with two walls each of single thickness, with a hollow space, four inches wide between. The sizes of these cases are delineated on the plan.

The flues for heating and ventilating the building must be arranged in such a manner and in such places as is required by the plans, or as may be hereafter directed. They are to be of brick, and those for the escape of gas must be well pargetted and topped out as shown in the detail drawings.

A culvert for drainage, eighteen inches in diameter, is to be constructed of brick below the cellar depths extending to the nearest point of the river. All necessary brick-work for the construction of other drains, cess-pools, is to be performed as the owner may desire. The sides of the well beneath the tower must be walled with one course of hard brick.

The mortar for all the above work must be the best and most approved compound of clean sharp river sand and well burnt fresh lime, in such proportions as will insure the strongest and most durable cement.

CARPENTER-WORK.—In the basement story the passage, store room, laundry, kitchen, servants' hall and tool room are to have floor joists three by six inches of white oak, firmly bedded in good concrete composed of stone chips and gravel mortar. The joists of the principal floor are all to be three by twelve inches, of spruce pine. Those of the second and attic floors are to be three by ten inches, and of hemlock. All are to be placed sixteen inches between centres, to have one course of herring-bone bridging through the centre of each tier, and are to have three-fourths of an inch crown.

The wall plates at the foot of the roof, and those for the gable timbers to rest upon, are to be three by nine inches, and to project two inches from the face of the wall. All bond timbers and lintels are to be provided when and where required of sizes suited to their purposes.

The rafters for the roof are to be of the usual cut and three by eight inches, those in the vallies being three by ten inches, and those for the flat over the hall three by nine inches. All are to be placed sixteen inches between centres and to be closely sheathed. The whole of this roof is to be framed according to the working drawings provided for the purpose. Provide all necessary bolts, straps, spikes and other material necessary to complete the work for the slater. The rafters for the roofs of the arcades, conservatory and other flats, are to be mere continuations of the floor joists, prepared for tinning. The roof of the main tower is to be of strong plank, properly curved, firmly secured to the wall plates, sheathed and covered with the best cedar shingles in diamond pattern. Each side of this roof is to have a dormer window as on the elevations. All other dormer windows are also to be constructed according to the elevations.

All requisite studs for partitions are to be three by four inches except those next doors, which must be three by six inches. Provide all necessary furring-out from the rafters to the floor, for the sides of the attic rooms, wherever delineated upon the plans, with studs three by four inches. Place all studs sixteen inches between centres.

OUTSIDE DRESSINGS.—The cornices of the eaves and gables are all to be constructed as set forth on the elevations and other working drawings which exhibit their peculiar form and mode of finishing. Reference is to be made to these drawings for the completion of the porches, arcades, conservatory, doorways and all other outside dressings. The carved work is of wood painted and sanded. The clustered columns of the front porch and arcades, and those of the bay-windows and conservatory are of heart pine turned and placed as exhibited by the drawings.

FLOORS.—The floors in the basement and principal story are to be composed of boards four inches broad, when laid, and one inch and a fourth thick. Those of the second and third stories are of the same width, and one inch thick. All are to be of the best Carolina heart pine, mill-worked, well seasoned, firmly nailed to the joists and afterwards smoothed off. The attic floor need not extend beyond the furring out. The floors of the second and third stories are to be deafened by nailing cleats to the joists four inches from the edge, flooring them over and filling the space with mortar flush to the edge of the joists. The floors of the arcades, &c., are to composed of white pine boards, one inch and a quarter by four inches. They must be well laid with white-lead in all the joints. The ceilings of the same are to be lined with half inch white pine boards, quartered, grooved, leaded and neatly smoothed off for painting.

STAIRS.—The main stairs are to be of one and a quarter inch heart step boards of yellow pine, best quality, with one and a quarter inch white pine risers, placed upon four three by twelve inch bearers of hemlock. The newel is to be ten inches at the base, with a richly carved shaft, the balusters are to be three inches at the base, and also richly carved, the rail is to be two and a half by five inch moulded, and all are to be of black walnut. The private stairs leading from the basement to the attic, are to have turned balusters and newel of a smaller size, but in all other respects they are to be similar to the main stairway. The whole of the work must be executed in a firm and workmanlike manner.

DOORS.—The front entrance doors are to be of double thickness, making two inches and a half in all, put together with two inch screws. They are to be paneled, moulded and richly ornamented, as shown by the drawings. They must be hung with five by five inch silver plated butts, the joints being bushed with steel. The lock is to be eight inch, upright, mortice rebate, with ornamented porcelain furniture and night key. The doors are to be further secured by two iron plate flush bolts with porcelain knobs, the one at the bottom being ten inches long, and the one at the top three feet six inches. The door opening into the parlor from the vestibule, is to be two inches thick, and finished like to the front doors, except that the butts are to be four by five inch and the lock four inch. Provide also two sets of sliding doors for the openings from the drawing-room to the hall and to the dining room. They are to be two inches and a half thick, constructed, finished, and in the same manner as the front doors. All are to have arched heads.

All other room doors throughout the first story are to be two inches thick and the closet doors are to be one inch and a half thick. They are all to have arched heads and must be paneled and moulded, with ornaments in the panels. The room doors are to be hung with four by four inch silver plated butts and secured by locks with ornamented porcelain furniture. The closet doors are to be hung with three by four inch plated butts, and secured with three and a half inch locks with porcelain knobs. The doors throughout the second story are to be entirely similar to those in the first story, except that they have plain butts and are without the panel ornaments. The room doors in the attic story are to be one inch and a half thick, the closet doors are to be one inch and a quarter thick, and all are to be otherwise similar to those in the second story, except that the panels are to have no mouldings.

The entrance doors to the kitchen must be two inches thick and hinged with four by four inch butts and secured with a six inch mortice lock, and two six inch iron plate flush bolts. The other room doors throughout the basement are to be one inch and a half thick, hung with three and a half by three and a half inch butts, and secured by suitable locks. All closet doors must have locks and be finished similar to those in the attic.

WINDOWS.—All windows are to have arched heads and must be finished according to the working drawings. Provide inside shutters to those of the basement, first and second stories, made in the requisite folds, one inch thick, paneled, moulded and otherwise finished in the best manner. All sash, except those of the dormer windows and octagon tower, are to be one inch and three quarters thick, and double hung with axle pullies and patent cord. Those of the conservatory are to have one sash each, so arranged as to descend into the basement. The sash of its roof are to be arranged as to open easily with cord and pullies.

INSIDE DRESSINGS, &c.—The skirting of the parlor, hall, drawing room and dining room must be fourteen inches wide, including the sub and moulding. That of the other rooms in the first story and of those in the second story, are to be twelve inches wide and of a similar finish, and all other skirting must be seven inches wide, including a one and a half inch moulding. All other dressings are to accord with the drawings.

There is to be a plank reservoir, strongly bolted, and of 1500 gals. capacity, placed in the square tower near the ceiling of the fourth story; also one similar in the third story of the octagon story, having a capacity of 800 gals. The reservoirs referred to are in Mr. Eastwick's house, made of boiler iron, strongly riveted and painted.

The closets are all to be fitted up with shelves, hooks, &c., as may be directed. There must be a dumb waiter arranged at the point marked on the plans D. W., with cords, pullies and weights, so as to move readily between the basement and first story.

PLASTERING.—All walls and ceilings of the building are to receive two coats of brown mortar, and one of white hard finish. All studding is to have lath free from bark securely nailed. There is to be a cornice in the vestibule, hall, parlor, library, drawing room, dining room and principal chambers, executed and finished according to sectional detail drawings provided for the purpose. There are to be centre pieces in the same rooms of the first story of an agreed size and pattern.

ROUGH-CASTING.—All the exterior walls must be well brushed, to remove dust and loose mortar, previous to rough-casting, and be kept well saturated with water during the progress of the work. The materials are to be of the very best quality, the sand being well-washed before using. The whole is to be laid off into blocks, tinted to represent stone.

SLATING.—All the roof of the building except the flats is to be overlaid in diamond pattern with the best purple Welsh slate of a large size. Each slate is to be secured with two copper nails, and the whole pointed beneath with strong hair mortar, to exclude the driving rain and snow.

TINNING.—All flues for heated air are to be cased in tin. All flats, vallies, flushings, and the roofs of the octagon tower, arcades, and bay windows, must be overlaid with the best one-cross roofing tin, painted on both sides, the upper receiving two coats. Provide also all necessary gutters, conductors, &c., of the best tin.

LIGHTNING-RODS.—There is to be a lightning rod placed against the main tower. It must descend at least six feet below the surface, be properly secured to the wall, ascend at least six feet above the roof of the tower, and finish with a platinum point, costing not less than four dollars.

TILES.—The vestibule, kitchen and conservatory are to be floored with English tiles; the pattern of the first being red buff and black with a centre of encaustic tiles in five colors; that of the second being red and black; and that of the third being black and buff.

BELLS, &c.—There are to be twelve bells with wire pulls and six speaking tubes arranged in such parts of the building as the owner may direct. The bell pull of the front door must be of ornamented porcelain.

MANTLES.—There must be a mantle placed in the drawing-room at a cost not less than $150, one in the parlor and dining room at $100 each, one in the library at $50, one in the office at $30, and two in the principal chambers at $40 each. The patterns are to be selected by the owner.

PAINTING AND GLAZING.—All the wood-work of the interior that it is usual to paint, must have two coats of pure white-lead mixed with linseed oil, tinted as may be directed. The rail, &c., of the stairs is to have four coats of the best varnish. All exterior wood-work, except the floors, must either be painted and grained in imitation of oak, or in imitation of stone, and sanded as may be directed.

All the sash are to be glazed with the best American glass, well bedded, bradded and back puttied.

PLUMBING.—The reservoirs supplied by force pumps are to be lined with sheet lead weighing three lbs. to the square foot, and the bath tubs with lead weighing five lbs. Arrange water-closets in the first three stories of the octagon tower, with china bowls and a soil pipe connecting with the well beneath. Provide china wash basons in each of the bath rooms and in each of the principal chambers. The above must be supplied with water from the reservoirs by pipes extra strong. All necessary waste pipes must also be provided. Water must also be conveyed to the sink and range in the kitchen, and conveyed from the boiler thence wherever required. All necessary stop-cocks must be provided, those in the chambers being silver plated. The whole must be executed in the best manner and every thing furnished to make it complete.

COOKING RANGE.—A large sized cooking-range must be placed in the kitchen, with water back and a circulating boiler attached. It must be of the best and most approved construction.

FURNACE, &c.—Place one of Fox's and one of Chilson's No. 5 furnaces in the cases prepared in the cellar. The register in the drawing room is to be ten by sixteen inches, that in the hall nine by fourteen inches, those in the parlor, library and office, eight by twelve inches, and that in the dining room nine by fourteen inches. There are to be eight in the second story eight by twelve inches each. Those in the drawing room, dining room, hall and parlor, must be silver-plated, all others must be enameled.

FINALLY.—All the above work must be executed and completed in the best workmanlike manner, according to the general intent and meaning of this specification, and in all parts, not herein described, according to the working drawings; the work being subject at all times to the decision of the Architect.

DESIGN FOR A CEILING.

UPON a following plate we present a design for a ceiling. It may be executed either in stucco or fresco, but in the latter case the principal panels must be retained in order to aid the effect of the painting. The details of this design together with an extended account of this kind of decoration will be given in another part of the work. The proportions are four by six.

Pl. XLIII.

Sam.! Sloan, Arch.!   P. S. Duval's Steam lith. Press Philad.ᵃ

REAR ELEVATION.

 Pl. XLIV.

Sam.! Sloan, Arch.!   P. S. Duval's Steam lith. Press Philad.ᵃ

SIDE ELEVATION.

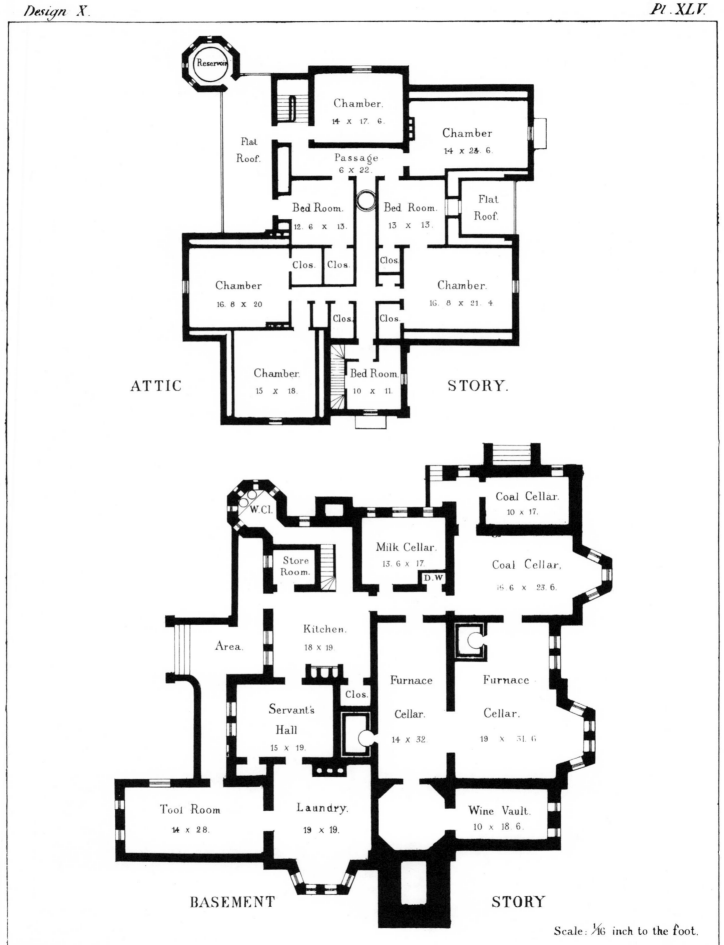

Reservoir

Flat
Roof.

Chamber.
14 x 17. 6.

Chamber
14 x 24. 6.

Passage
6 x 22.

Bed Room.
12. 6 x 13.

Bed Room.
13 x 13.

Flat
Roof.

Chamber
16. 8 x 20

Clos.   Clos.

Clos.

Chamber.
16. 8 x 21. 4

Clos.   Clos.

Chamber.
15 x 18

Bed Room.
10 x 11.

ATTIC   STORY.

W. Cl.

Coal Cellar.
10 x 17.

Store
Room.

Milk Cellar.
13. 6 x 17.

D. W

Coal Cellar.
16. 6 x 23. 6.

Area.

Kitchen.
18 x 19.

Clos.

Furnace

Cellar.
14 x 32.

Furnace

Cellar.
19 x 51. 6

Servant's
Hall
15 x 19.

Tool Room
14 x 28.

Laundry.
19 x 19.

Wine Vault.
10 x 18. 6.

BASEMENT   STORY

Scale: 1/16 inch to the foot.

GROUND PLANS.

Fig. 1.

Fig. 2.

Fig. 8.

Fig. 3.

Fig. 7.

Fig. 6.

Scale of Fig.ˢ 6. 7. 8. 9.
one inch to the foot.

Fig. 9.

Fig. 5.

Fig. 4.

Scale ½ inch to the foot.

DETAILS.

Pl. XLVII

Des.d by Sam.l Sloan, Arch.t

P S Duval s steam lith press Phil a

DESIGN FOR A CEILING.

THE CONTRACT.

THE working drawings, specification, and bill of quantities, are examined by the contractor, who then makes his estimate and bids for the work. The successful bidder enters into a formal contract with the projector who, as a general thing, submits to him the whole work and pays for it by instalments. This is the usual and best arrangement for such buildings as are herein described, but sometimes parts of the work are performed under separate contracts. For very large buildings, such as heavy public works, many other arrangements are necessary, but we refer only to such as are within our limits. The minutiæ of an agreement are varied by different circumstances, and being innumerable, we cannot comprise them here. We simply insert a usual form of contract, drawn up by a member of the Philadelphia bar, which may be relied upon for its accuracy. The italicised words must be changed in using.

ARTICLES OF AGREEMENT made this, the *first day of December*, Anno Domini, one thousand eight hundred and *fifty-one*, by and between RICHARD ROE, of *the city of Philadelphia and State of Pennsylvania, Merchant*, of the first part, and JOHN DOE, of the *city of Camden and State of New Jersey, Builder*, of the second part, as follows, viz :—

The said party of the second part, for and in consideration of the covenants and agreements hereinafter mentioned, doth for himself, his executors, administrators and assigns, covenant, promise and agree to and with the said party of the first part, his executors, administrators and assigns, that he the said JOHN DOE, shall and will, within the space of *nine calendar months* next ensuing the date hereof, to wit: on or before *the first day of September*, Anno Domini, one thousand eight hundred and *fifty-two*, in good and workmanlike manner, and according to the best of his art and skill, well and substantially erect, build, set up, and deliver to the said party of the first part, or his legally authorized agent, free and discharged of all claims, liens, and charges whatsoever, or cause to be erected, built, set up, finished and delivered as abovementioned, on a lot or piece of ground, situate and being, (here insert the description as contained in the deed, and designate the part of the lot the house is to occupy,) one house, messuage or tenement, according to the plan, draft or scheme, with specifications annexed, made, drawn, and furnished by SAMUEL SLOAN, Architect, the contents whereof are as follows, viz:—(here insert the plans, &c., or refer to them by numbers or letters, and affix them to these articles, as in case of difficulty under the contract, they alone can decide.) And the said party of the second part further agrees, for himself, his executors, administrators and assigns, to furnish, at his own proper cost and charge, all the materials which may be requisite for the construction of the aforesaid house, messuage or tenement, according to the plans and specifications aforesaid ; and to ensure on his part the performance of this part of these presents, it is further agreed, that JOHN WHITEACRE, of the city of Philadelphia, Carpenter, be and the same is hereby appointed superintendent, who shall have power to inspect, and accept or reject any work done, or materials it may be proposed to use in or about the con-struction of the house aforesaid, and whose decision shall be final and conclusive, as between these parties.

And the said RICHARD ROE, the party of the first part, as aforesaid, in consideration of the above premises, doth for himself, his executors, administrators and assigns, covenant, promise and agree, well and truly to pay, or cause to be paid unto the said party of the second part, his executors, administrators or assigns, the sum of *Eight Thousand Dollars*, good and lawful money of the coin of the United States, in three several payments, in manner following, to wit :—

On the first day of *March*, Anno Domini, one thousand eight hundred and *fifty-two*, or as soon thereafter as the walls shall have been completed, the sum of *Two Thousand* Dollars.

On the first day of *April*, Anno Domini, one thousand eight hundred and *fifty-two*, or as soon thereafter as the floors shall have been laid, the partitions set, lathed and scratch coated, the sum of *Three Thousand* Dollars.

On the first day of *September*, Anno Domini, one thousand eight hundred and *fifty-two*, or as soon thereafter as the building aforesaid, shall have been delivered as aforesaid, the sum of *Three Thousand* Dollars.

And it is further agreed between the aforesaid parties, that all alterations of the annexed plan and specifications, by which the costs of building may be either increased or diminished, shall be endorsed on these articles, and signed by the parties, before they shall be deemed binding on either party.

And for the performance of all and every the articles and agreements abovementioned, the said RICHARD ROE and JOHN DOE, do hereby severally bind themselves, their executors, administrators and assigns, each to the other, in the penal sum of *Ten Thousand Dollars*, good and lawful money as aforesaid, firmly by these presents.

In witness whereof, the said parties have hereunto set their hands and seals, the day and year aforesaid.

RICHARD ROE,   *******
                    * SEAL. *
                    ****

SIGNED AND SEALED

IN THE PRESENCE OF

SAMUEL WILLIAMS,

THOMAS RICHARDS.

JOHN DOE.   *******
                    * SEAL. *
                    ****

For the faithful performance of all and singular the covenants, agreements and promises, contained in the above arti-cles, on the part of JOHN DOE, the party of the second part aforesaid, we do hereby jointly and severally bind ourselves, our executors, administrators and assigns, to the aforesaid RICHARD ROE, his executors, administrators or assigns.

Witness our hands and seals, the day and year aforesaid.

JAMES SMITH,   *******
                     * SEAL. *
                     ****

SIGNED AND SEALED

IN THE PRESENCE OF

SAMUEL WILLIAMS,

THOMAS RICHARDS.

RICHARD JONES.   *******
                     * SEAL. *
                     ****

The above contract is complete, and may readily be adapted to suit circumstances. Great care, how-ever, must be exercised in making alterations or additions, as a false expression might render the whole whole invalid. In the appointment of a superintendent or referee, other articles must be signed by him and the parties, binding him for a consideration to the faithful discharge of his obligations. Most fre-quently this appointment is superfluous, the work being inspected by the owner in person. It is only in case the work be at a distance or so extensive as to require constant attendance, that the owner need make the transfer. If there are any reservations made by either party, they should be endorsed upon the articles of agreement. The security of the party of the first part is in the same form as that given, the names of the parties being reversed. When the work is complete, it is essential that the owner receive a release "of all claims, liens, or charges whatsoever," signed by each and every person who either may have furnished material for the building, or who may have done any labor in its erection; otherwise, after the business between himself and the contractor be finally closed, he may be compelled to liquidate claims which the other has failed to discharge.

The business of entering into and fulfilling such a contract is by no means easy, and inexcusable carelessness in this is the cause of innumerable lawsuits. By using the above form, and exercising judgment and care in its adaptation, no difficulty need be apprehended.

A PLAIN AND ORNAMENTED VILLA.
DESIGN ELEVENTH.

Two front elevations of this design are presented on plates XLVIII. and XLIX. They are spoken of as the same design, because their breadth, depth, and general features are similar, and the same floor plans are used for both. The first of these elevations is quite plain, being almost destitute of ornament, but at the same time so finished as to avoid a barren appearance. The second on the other hand is highly ornamented, and a half story higher than the first, thus giving a commodious garret, the circular windows of which may be seen over those of the second story. The observatory of this elevation is covered, and might be arranged without a floor, so as to give additional light and ventilation to the garret rooms. The garret or loft is approached in each by a flight of stairs, over those leading to the second story. The cellar door is beneath the main stairway, and the windows are on the sides of the building. The elevations are drawn in a scale of ten feet to the inch. The design is best adapted to a village or suburban dwelling.. We have presented the extremes of plainness and decoration, so that any desirable medium may be attained.

On plate L. are the floor plans of the design. The house is intended to be warmed either by stoves or by a furnace beneath the hall. The flues for heated air are in the cross partitions, and the gas flues are at the sides of the building, giving a sufficient breadth of projection for mantles. The recess in the dining room, next the vestibule, is a convenient situation for a sideboard. The parlor and library are separated by sliding doors. It would be as well, perhaps, to reverse the steps and have them begin against the rear wall, thus presenting a better appearance from the hall. A convenient back porch might be placed in the rear or at the side of the kitchen, which might be built two stories high, and thus give an additional chamber. The two windows of the first and second story, in the rear of the stairway, serve to admit more light to the passage below and the hall above, but might be dispensed with.

Plate LI. is of details. Fig. 1, is the cornice, eave ornaments, &c., of the ornamented front. Fig. 2, details of the porch and front door. Fig. 3, section of the same. Fig. 4, front window, with a section beside it of double size. Fig. *a*, section of the architrave of the front door. Fig. *b*, section of the front door lintel Fig *c*, section of the door rail.

Plate LII. also consists of details. Fig. 1, observatory of the ornamented front. Fig. 2, section of the same. Fig. 3, observatory of the plain front. Fig. 4, cornice of the same. Fig. 5, section of the cornice. Fig. 6, details of the front porch. Figs. 7, 8, and 9, a design for a mantel.

The first story of this design is twelve feet and eight inches from floor to floor, and the second story is ten feet in the clear. The cellar, throughout the entire extent of the main building, is eight feet deep in the clear, and the trenches for the foundations are at least six inches deep below the cellar bottom, and those for the porch and kitchen are two feet deep.

The walls of the cellar are eighteen inches thick, and those of the first and second stories are sixteen inches thick. The foundations of the kitchen and porch are also sixteen inches thick. All are composed of good quarry building stone and the best mortar. The foundation course is large flat stone solidly bedded in mortar. All facings are smooth-dashed, and those of the cellar lime-washed. All gas flues are of brick well pargetted. There are two cross walls of brick in the cellar, immediately beneath the main partitions above, having arched openings.

The kitchen is framed and closely boarded, for painting and sanding, to appear like the walls of the main building. It also might be built of stone or of brick, but this would increase the cost of the whole.

The joists of the first floor are three by twelve inches, of spruce pine. Those of the second are three by eleven inches, of hemlock. Those of the third are three by ten inches, and also of hemlock. Those of the porch floor are three by nine inches, and those of the ceiling are three by five inches. All are placed sixteen inches between centres. The side rafters are three by five inches, and the hip rafters, with the framing rafters at the corners, are three by ten inches. They are placed two feet between centres, and are closely sheathed for tin. The wall plates and the ridge piece are three by twelve inches. The doors and windows are to have lintels six by six inches, extending nine inches into the walls.

The floors within are of Carolina heart pine, and that of the porch is of white pine, laid with white lead in the joints. The washboard of the first story main building is eight inches wide, with a three inch sub and two inch moulding, that of the second is six inches wide, with a sub and moulding, and that of the kitchen is four inches wide, with plain moulding.

The window frames of the main building are all similar in construction, having sash one inch and a half thick, double hung. Those of the first story have paneled shutters, and those above have pivot blinds, both being one inch and a half thick, and hung with strong hooks and straps. The front doors are two inches thick, and all other doors below are one inch and three-quarters thick, except the closet doors, which are one inch and a half thick. The room doors of the second story are one inch and a half, and those of the closets are one inch and a quarter thick. All knobs in the first story are of white porcelain, and those in the second are mineral. The window and door dressings in the first story are six inch diminished pilasters, with a two and a half inch moulded band. The windows above have plastered jambs.

Beside the usual plastering, the parlor, hall, library and dining room have appropriate cornices and centre flowers. All the exterior of the main building is to be rough-cast, tinted and pointed. The roofs of the main building, porch and kitchen are tin, painted on both sides, the upper receiving two coats. In all other respects the house is handsomely and completely finished, with various modern improvements.

The cost of the building, with the plain front, as estimated from a bill of items, would be about $2500; the cost of the other would be $3400.

A PLAIN VILLA.

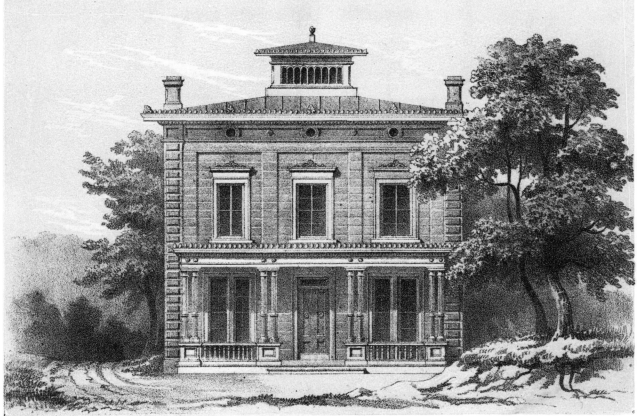

Sam.¹ Sloan Arch.ᵗ　　　　　　　　　　　　　　　　P. S. Duval's Steam lith

THE SAME ORNAMENTED.

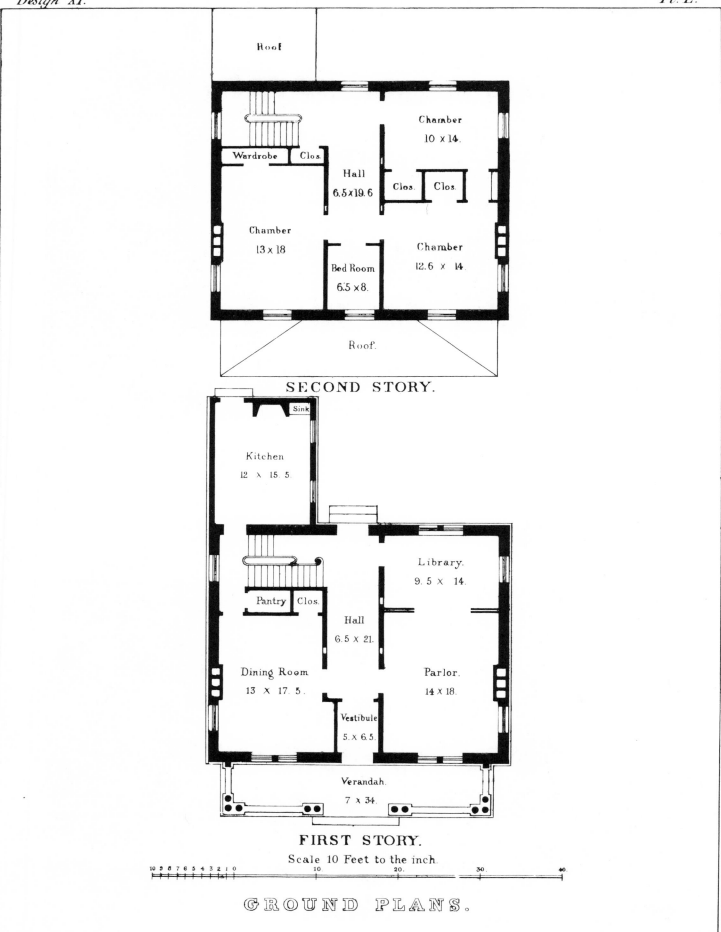

Roof

Chamber
10 × 14.

Wardrobe   Clos.

Hall
6.5 × 19.6

Clos.   Clos.

Chamber
13 × 18

Bed Room
6.5 × 8.

Chamber
12.6 × 14.

Roof.

SECOND STORY.

Sink

Kitchen
12 × 15. 5.

Library.
9. 5 × 14.

Pantry   Clos.

Hall
6.5 × 21.

Dining Room
13 × 17. 5.

Parlor.
14 × 18.

Vestibule
5 × 6.5.

Verandah.
7 × 34.

FIRST STORY.

Scale 10 Feet to the inch.

10 9 8 7 6 5 4 3 2 1 0   10.   20.   30.   40.

G R O U N D   P L A N S.

P. S. Duval's Steam lith. Press Philad.ª

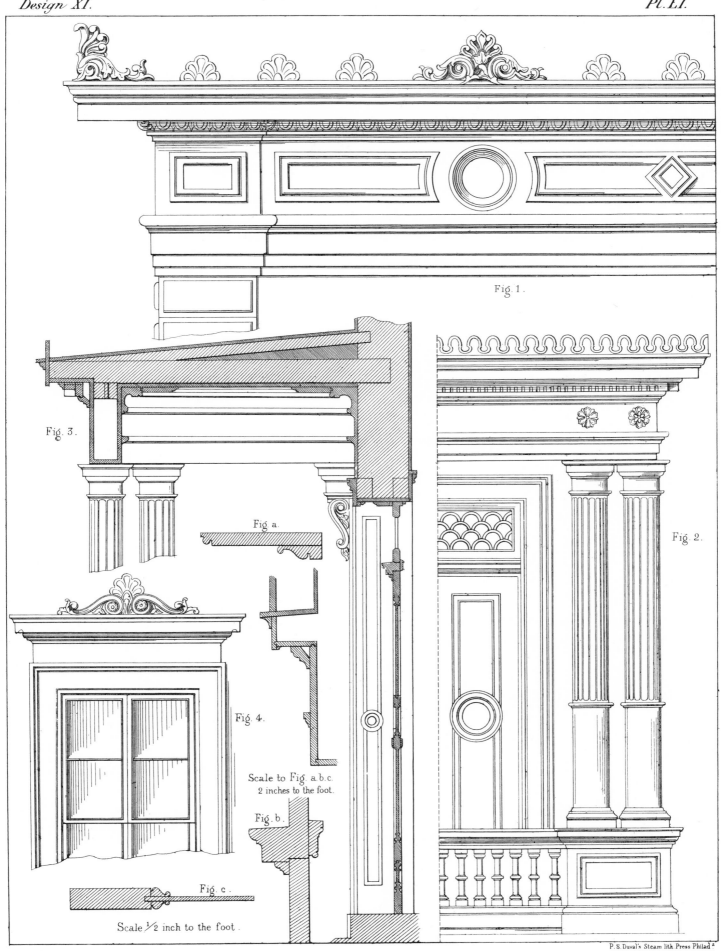

Fig. 1.

Fig. 3.

Fig a.

Fig. 2.

Fig. 4.

Scale to Fig. a.b.c.
2 inches to the foot.

Fig. b.

Fig. c.

Scale ½ inch to the foot.

DETAILS.

Fig. 1.

Fig. 2.

Fig. 3.

Fig. 4.

Fig. 5.

Fig. 6.

Fig. 7.

Fig. 8.

Fig. 9.

Scale for Figs. 7. 8. & 9, one inch to the foot.

Scale ½ inch to the foot.

P. S. Duval's Steam lith. Press Philadª

DETAILS.

THE EXCAVATIONS.

A CELLAR well lighted and ventilated is a great convenience in any dwelling. It is sometimes finished as a basement story, and contains the kitchen, laundry, and store rooms. Outhouses are often used for these purposes, but even then, in this climate, a cellar is almost indispensible. At the present day dwellings are warmed by heated air, it being found the cheapest, as well as the most salubrious method, and the furnace for this purpose cannot be well placed elsewhere. The various apartments serve for the storage of fuel and vegetables, which are here secure from the effects of dampness and frost. Besides this, it brings the foundations upon deep, firm ground, and thus enhances the stability of the building. Many advantages may be obtained by building upon a declivity, and the excavation, for reasons mentioned hereafter, should always be, if possible, throughout the entire extent of the foundation.

The greatest objection to cellars, or basement stories, is the damp to which they are usually subject. It is best to examine well the contour and nature of the grounds before excavating, to avoid earth constantly wet, and springs, which are a source of great trouble when once opened. Unless there be some such extraordinary cause, there need be no dampness whatever. The cellar walls may be so constructed or coated as to be quite impervious. This object may be attained more perfectly by also laying the pavement in hydraulic cement, or, if the cellar be floored, the sleepers should be bedded in concrete, thus preserving them from moisture and rot, which is at once disagreeable and unwholesome.

In preparing trenches for the foundations much care is requisite. If the building be without a cellar, they should be so deep that the bottom will not be subject to the contraction and expansion caused by variations of temperature. But there are two things which, in all cases, are especially to be provided against,—the unequal settling of the superstructure, and the lateral escape of the support. It cannot be too much impressed upon the mind, that the object is not so much to prevent settling as that it may be uniform throughout the structure. If this last be the case then no evil consequences can ensue, but if this settling, which it is impossible wholly to prevent, be irregular, then the walls of the building will inevitably crack, and present those fissures, which impair both the beauty and the stability of the building. Hence the bottom of the trenches should be in the same stratum throughout, and the ground should be well examined before building, to see that it is a uniform and firm bed, or else it is impossible to avoid bad results. The bottom of the trenches should also be on the same level, if practicable, for when the contour of the ground requires it to be 'benched out,' the unequal yielding cannot so certainly be prevented. It must also be kept in mind that not only does the support generally yield, but the walls themselves settle more or less. In the walls, the most settling occurs where there are the greatest number of mortar joints, and hence although the prime support may be perfectly firm, yet an irregular surface, giving the walls different heights, may cause them to crack. It is for this reason that the cellar had better be throughout the building, for otherwise the foundations will rest on different levels.

As might be supposed, the best support for a foundation is a bed of rock, but this is only the case where it has a level surface, either natural or artificial. The difficulty of obtaining a perfectly level bed of rock, and the expense of leveling it render this support infrequent; yet we cannot see why good concrete, composed of coarse gravel and a little lime, which when once set is entirely incompressible, might not be used for reducing all irregularities of surface, and form an excellent support for building. But, taking all things into consideration, perhaps the best support for a foundation is a uniform bed of compact gravel. Such a bed yields very little, and is not liable to be affected by air or moisture, and hence the excavation should be continued to such an one if it be attainable. Sand, which is incompressible would be equally good, were it not so easily affected by water, and therefore cannot be used with safety. Clay is very bad, as it escapes laterally, and is subject to great contraction and expansion. We sometimes meet in excavating a bed of shale, which, when first uncovered, is as hard as stone, but after a little exposure runs into sludge. This must be avoided if possible, but when it cannot, care must be taken to expose it but little, by covering it at once with concrete, and building immediately. Good firm earth forms an excellent support, but as it yields considerably it must be built on with care. By a judicious use of concrete, a good foundation may be secured in almost any situation, and it is an excellent practice to build the foundations as high as the first tier of joists, and let them remain in this state for a season before erecting the superstructure. They then have time to become firmly fixed, and any failing may be remedied before the other walls are erected.

The only other excavations of importance which are usually made about a dwelling, are for the conveyance and reception of refuse matter. The accumulation of filth about even the most cleanly dwelling, if there be no systematic and effectual plan for its removal, is such as to be not only in the highest degree unpleasant but also noxious. The usual way is to construct the privy distinct, at a short distance from the house, and to throw the offal of the kitchen into a vessel for subsequent removal, or to allow it to pass off in a surface gutter. In building with the modern improvements, however, the water-closet is generally placed within doors, over a well, into which the offal is also allowed to pass. The well, in this case, should always be excavated to the water gravel, which to a great extent, absorbs and carries off its contents. There are, however, many objections to this plan as experience has shown, and a little reflection will suggest. A much better way is to convey all offal through pipes to an underground drain, which conducts to a stream, cess-pool, or well. If a stream be near of sufficient size, it forms a ready and effectual means of removal. But sewage of every description is a most excellent manure. It is of the greatest importance to a farmer, or to those who cultivate even small gardens, and hence should be preserved for the purpose. To effect this, it may be received in a cess-pool at a distance from the house, or better in a well, for the open pool is an unsightly, offensive and unwholesome object, but a well is not so when covered over deeply by soil. The well in this case also should be excavated to the water gravel, that the liquids may be absorbed. If, however, the manure be of the highest importance, as it would be to a farmer, the cess-pool lined with clay is perhaps better, for then the liquids evaporate, and the soluble matter, which is the most valuable, is retained.

It is important that the drain for the conduction of this refuse matter should be well constructed. The point of discharge at the foot should be carefully finished, and the head should have a good syphon, or other trap, which will allow of the free entrance of any matter, and at the same time prevent the escape of noisome gases. This drain should in all cases have a continuous fall of one inch in forty or fifty, so that the water may not remain in it, but descend with sufficient impetuosity to bear along all solid matter, and thereby prevent choking, by keeping the drain well washed. It should not be so small as to detain solid matter, nor again so large as to make a shallow stream, for then, in consequence of increased friction the stream is sluggish. A diameter of from four to six inches is amply sufficient to drain any ordinary dwelling. When other material can be obtained, it is not well to use bricks in the construction of a drain, for their roughness adds greatly to the friction of the descending matter, and in consequence of their permeability the earth adjacent becomes damp and offensive. The best and cheapest drains are made of earthenware pipes, glazed inside, which at once lessens the friction and renders them impermeable. They are in short pieces with socket joints, or of a conical shape, so as to fit each other, and are put together with a little cement. It is evident that any bends in such drains are to be avoided if possible. Altogether, this subject is one of the greatest consideration in the erection of a cleanly and comfortable dwelling, but does not, we think, always receive that attention which its importance demands.

A DESIGN FOR A COTTAGE.
DESIGN TWELFTH.

ON Plate LIII. is presented the front elevation of a Cottage more simple and cheap than any preceding one. It is of frame work, vertically weather-boarded, the joints being cleated with narrow strips. Plate LIV. is numbered as the same design, because of its similarity in general features, and because the proportions are such that the same floor plan would apply to either. It is, however, without an attic floor, which the one above has, and in general is cheaper and plainer than the other. They are both in a scale of ten feet to the inch.

Plate LV. exhibits two sets of ground plans, which may be used interchangably for either of the accompanying elevations, the one on the right being the most simple. The other has a back building two stories high, thus rendering it necessary to light the hall up stairs by means of the front window. The stairs to the attic are immediately over the main stairway. The house may be warmed either by stoves or a furnace.

On Plate LVI. are the details. Fig. 1, finial and cornice, with a section of the gable in plate LIII. Fig. 2, Tudor flower. Fig. 3, section of the same. Fig. 4, cornice and eave ornament. Fig. 5, section of the same. Fig. 6, details of the front porch and door. Fig. 7, section of the door. Fig. 8, details of the front window. Fig. 9, gable window on plate LIV. Fig. 10, section of the same. Fig. 11, dormer window. Fig. 12, section of the same. Fig. 13, porch.

In the subjoined description reference is made to plate LIV. in connection with the smaller floor plan, for which also the cost is estimated in the bill of items. There is a cellar under the main building five feet deep from the natural surface of the ground. The cellar walls are of stone, sixteen inches thick and eight feet high, to the top of the first tier of joists. The joists of the first floor are three by twelve inches, those of the second three by ten inches, and placed sixteen inches between centres. The ridge piece is three by twelve inches, and the rafters are eight inches at the foot, of the usual rafter cut, and placed two feet between centres. The main sills are six by six inches, the corner posts and girts are three by eight inches, the plates are three by six inches, the studding and braces are three by four inches and sixteen inches between centres. The weather-boarding is all uniformly eleven inches wide, grooved together and the joints cleated, the cleats being narrow beveled strips terminating in pointed arched heads, as on the elevation. The whole exterior is painted with three coats of good paint in any desirable tint, then sanded and afterwards repainted. Otherwise, the house is finished in a plain and substantial manner, the usual arrangements in respect to construction being adopted throughout.

A FULL ESTIMATE

OF THE COST IN ERECTING DESIGN TWELFTH.

THIS estimate is made for the smallest elevation, in connection with the smallest plan of the two given above. The difference of cost between this and the other elevation and plan, would be about $550.

Excavation, 200 yds. @ 20 cts. - -	$40.00
Stone, 91 perches @ $2.00, lime and sand included,	182.00
Plastering, 850 yds. @ 18 cts., including material,	153.00
Slate, 2000 superficial feet @ 72 cts. - - -	1440.00
Chimney-cans, 2 @ $5.00, - - - - -	10.00
Joists, 4800 feet @ $12.50 per M. - - -	60.00
Rafters, 2000 feet @ $12.50 per M. - - -	25.00
Studding, 7500 feet @ $12.50 per M. - - -	93.75
Framing timber (white pine), 2100 ft. @ $18 per M.	37.80
Sheathing boards, 2000 feet @ $9.00 per M. -	18.00
Flooring boards, 2300 feet @ $27.00 per M. -	62.10
Mather boards, 5000 feet @ $27.00 per M. - -	135.00
Carpenter work, 220 days @ $2.00, - - -	440.00
Window frames, 14, with sash and inside shutters, delivered at the building @ $12.00, -	168.00
Window frames &c., for kitchen, 2, @ $10.00, -	20.00
	2884.65

Doors 1¾ inches thick, 5, delivered @ $3.25, -	16.25
Doors 1½ inches thick, 11, delivered @ $2.25, -	24.75
Doors 1¼ inches thick, 4, delivered @ $2.00, -	8.00
Assorted lumber, 4200 feet @ $25.00 per M. -	105.00
Stairs, including all material, - - -	90.00
Front porch, including all material, - - -	85.00
Back, including all material, - - -	35.00
Tin, for gutters and conductors, - - -	30.00
Painting and glazing, - - - -	160.00
Hardware, including locks, &c., &c., - - -	136.00
	690.00
	2884.65
Total, - - - - - -	3574.65
Difference between the elevations, &c., -	550.00
	4124.65

Sam.¹ Sloan Arch.ᵗ   P.S.Duval's Steam lith press Ph.

DESIGN FOR A COTTAGE.

Sam.¹ Sloan Arch.ᵗ   P.S.Duval's Steam lith press Ph.

DESIGN FOR A COTTAGE.

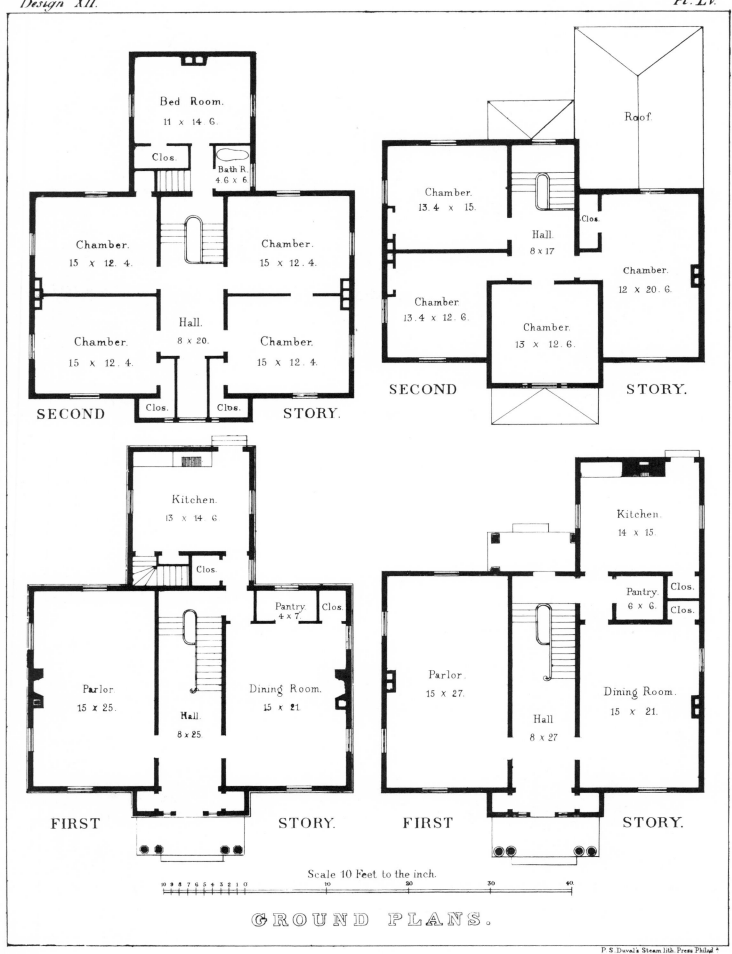

Bed Room.
11 x 14. 6.

Clos.

Bath R.
4. 6 x 6.

Chamber.
15 x 12. 4.

Chamber.
15 x 12. 4.

Hall.
8 x 20.

Chamber.
15 x 12. 4.

Chamber.
15 x 12. 4.

Clos.

Clos.

SECOND   STORY.

Roof.

Chamber.
13. 4 x 15.

Hall.
8 x 17

Clos.

Chamber.
12 x 20. 6.

Chamber.
13. 4 x 12. 6.

Chamber.
13 x 12. 6.

SECOND   STORY.

Kitchen.
13 x 14. 6

Clos.

Pantry.
4 x 7

Clos.

Parlor.
15 x 25.

Hall.
8 x 25.

Dining Room.
15 x 21.

FIRST   STORY.

Kitchen.
14 x 15.

Pantry.
6 x 6.

Clos.

Clos.

Parlor.
15 x 27.

Hall
8 x 27

Dining Room.
15 x 21.

FIRST   STORY.

Scale 10 Feet to the inch.

10 9 8 7 6 5 4 3 2 1 0   10   20   30   40.

GROUND PLANS.

P. S. Duval's Steam lith. Press Philad.ª

Fig. 1.

Fig. 2.

Fig. 3.

Fig. 4.

Fig. 5.

Fig. 6.

Fig. 7.

Fig. 8.

Fig. 9.

Fig. 10.

Fig. 11.

Fig. 12.

Fig. 13.

Scale ½ inch to the foot.

DETAILS.

THE FOUNDATION.

AFTER preparing the excavations, the next step towards building is to lay the foundation. By this term all the walls as high as the first tier of joists, are included. It must be remembered that in this series of articles no more is treated of than the nature of our work requires. To go beyond this would lead into discussion of points unessential in the erection of country dwellings. Should we attempt, for instance, to give a complete treatise upon foundations, it would lead to a long dissertation, including an account of the various methods pursued in laying the foundations of such vast structures as prisons and forts, and also of such as are erected in marshy ground or in water, such as light-houses, bridges and docks. We should have to discuss the various topics connected with pile-driving, coffer-dams, caissons, pierre perdue and the like. All this would be quite foreign to our purpose and require much more space than we have apportioned to the subject. Let it be understood then, that we wish merely to give a concise yet comprehensive view of the foundations requisite for such buildings as are described in this work; yet even within these limits, we fear our space will not permit an entire investigation of the subject.

In the article upon excavations mention was made of concrete as a valuable aid in procuring good foundations. Little attention has been given to concrete in this country, at least for such small structures as dwelling houses. It is composed of stone chips or coarse gravel mixed with lime while hot from slacking. Sometimes the lime is mixed in the caustic state with the stone or gravel and water then poured upon it. This practice is strongly reprobated by the most experienced, who insist that it is far better for the lime to be brought to a thick paste before using. It may also be made into a mortar by mixing with it a small quantity of sand. In any case marble chips combined with hydraulic lime, are the best materials that can be used. When hydraulic lime is used in combination, instead of the ordinary lime, the mass is usually termed béton.

When concrete is placed in its position it should be rammed until the mortar begins to flush out at the top. This then, allowed to dry, is incompressible and firm, and gradually becomes converted into an artificial stone. It is evident that this concrete or béton can only be used when it has a support at the sides. It has often been used to fill between inner and outer courses of stone where the walls are of great thickness. It frequently may be advantageously placed at the bottom of the foundation trenches, thus producing a firm and uniform bearing surface. Concrete may be regarded as a sort of imperfect rubble work, and its value consists in becoming quickly 'set,' and its ready self-adaptation to an uneven surface. It is not a new method but was well understood by the accomplished architects of the middle ages, and was in use among the Romans.

The material best adapted for the foundation wall is granite. Its durability, solidity and firmness is superior to any other, and if laid in good mortar, of which we are to speak in a future article, it will last for centuries. Bricks in contact with moist earth are liable to disintegration and are therefore unsafe, so that of whatever material the superstructure be built, whether of wood, brick, stone or marble, it is best to have the foundation of good quarry granite.

Hewn stone is the best, since but little mortar is required, and in consequence of its flat surfaces the whole weight of each course, bears upon that immediately beneath, without even a tendency to lateral pressure.   The stone which splits from the quarry in cubical blocks is less expensive and equally good. But when neither can be obtained, an excellent foundation may be formed of rubble work.   The greatest advantage of the other consists in having fewer and smaller mortar joints, and hence yielding less to the superincumbent weight.   If, however, the foundation is to be of rubble work, stones should be selected having at least two surfaces parallel, which when laid horizontally form an excellent firm wall.   This precaution is essential, because stones of an irregular shape tend to wedge into the course beneath, and only the cementing qualities of the mortar preserve the wall from being destroyed.   We refer more particularly here to such parts of the wall as are above ground or constitute the cellar walls.   Another precaution may be suggested.   Masons, in order to have the face of the wall look well, are apt to lay the largest stones on the exposed side.   This side then, in setting, yields less than the other, and hence the wall leans or is weakened by cracks.   In a previous article we mentioned that it is a good practice to allow the foundations to remain exposed for a season before erecting the superstructure.   This is especially true in the case of rubble work, thereby giving it a fair opportunity of becoming fixed.

But whatever be the character of the others, the first course should be laid with broad flat stone, the largest that can be procured.   By this means any slight irregularity in the nature of the bearing stratum, may be avoided, and we more certainly secure that uniformity of settling which is so desirable.   It is for this that concrete or béton is recommended.   Before setting it yields freely and adapts itself to the surface of the bearing stratum, and afterwards it may be regarded as one large stone.   It also presses laterally and thus distributes the weight more.   To this end, where the earth is firm and not liable to the action of water, a layer of sand at the bottom of the foundation trench is also recommended.

Where the ground is treacherous, we must resort to some expedient to throw the weight of the building upon a deep firm stratum.   This may be done by driving piles at short distances from each other, and by springing arches in the walls, from one to the other.   The plan is also recommended, under certain circumstances, of boring holes at different points and refilling them with sand for the support of the arches. Such expedients require a great deal of care and skill, and are only requisite in extreme cases, seldom being necessary for dwellings.

A much more important matter, is the footing. To produce this we lay the first course much broader than the intended thickness of the wall, and gradually narrow each succeeding course until the requisite thickness is attained. By this means we give the wall greater strength in resisting any lateral force which may bear against it, such as the wind, and hence it is of importance in the erection of towers. But a much more essential advantage is gained thereby, in distributing the weight over a greater surface of the bearing stratum. The walls of St. Paul's Cathedral, in London, are to this day uninjured and firm, although they are erected on a bed of clay, only from ten to twenty feet thick, overlying a quick-sand. The most important points in the construction of footings are to build them of the largest blocks, and to keep the back joints as far from the exterior as possible. It is also desirable to give as little projection to the footing courses as may be essential to the end in view, otherwise a very slight lateral force may crack them entirely from the face of the main wall, and disastrous consequences ensue.

It may appear that we give to this subject more attention than its importance demands, and recommend practices which are unnecessary. When we reflect, however, on the desirableness of a firm foundation, we are forced to believe that too much care and skill cannot be exercised in its construction. How often are buildings, which were intended to last for years, found cracked from top to bottom, and how often do we hear of walls actually tumbling and crushing the workmen, or it may be, if later, the inmates of the building. The vast majority of these accidents, if properly inquired into, may be traced to a defect and consequent movement in the foundation. Thus are those unsightly and dangerous fissures produced, or it may be, the wall is slightly moved from its perpendicular, and hence either falls itself or yields to an otherwise ineffective lateral force. In Great Britain and throughout Europe much more attention is paid to this subject than here, and this is one principal reason why buildings there so far surpass ours in durability. When building, why not build well; why not erect such a dwelling, that fifty years hence it will still be valuable property and not an incumbrance? In even twenty or thirty years many of our houses become superannuated and crazy, while those in the old world remain, valuable legacies to posterity and interesting exemplars of their times. We Americans are not ashamed that we have nothing now venerable in years, but we may fear that our descendants will have cause so to be, and have few buildings to point out, saying, this is the work of our fathers.

A COTTAGE.

DESIGN THIRTEENTH.

ON Plate LVIII. is presented the perspective view of a cottage, the front elevation of which is on the left side of the plate above. We have before incidentally remarked upon the ease with which every man may make his home pleasant, not only by its internal convenience, but by its tasteful appearance. It is usually considered necessary, in order to build in good taste, that a variety of ornaments should be stuck on here and there, even when they may be entirely unessential in the construction of the building. The expense attending this, has usually deterred those having a limited amount from even attempting to give their buildings a handsome appearance. But we beg leave to state, that this general opinion is a very great mistake, and are happy in believing that it is becoming less prevalent. We must remember that the first element of architectural beauty, is graceful proportion. Even the plainest house will please, or at least cannot displease, when its proportions are good; but when they are not, nothing can save it from just censure. Ornaments we may divide into two classes. Features which belong essentially to the building, and are made ornamental by giving them shape and finish, such as the chimney tops, shingles, the ends of the rafters, brackets, and we may mention in this design the cleats of the weather-boarding. To make these contribute to the appearance of a building, but little expense is necessary. The other class of ornaments are those which are not essential to the building, but which suggest at once to the mind a need which they appear to supply. In this class we may include a great many brackets, which apparently yield support to parts which do not really require it of them. Either of these two classes of ornaments may be enriched by mouldings or carvings which every where must thus be made subordinate.

By using good proportions, and the first class of ornaments, we may display great taste in a building, and make it please the eye much, without additional expense. Hence we hold fast to the opinion, that there can be no reason for putting up those bold, bare and flat houses, which unfortunately are everywhere. We have endeavored to express in this design the above thoughts, and venture to say that the same room and conveniences could not be obtained by the same methods of construction at less expense. The cost of the building finished throughout, would be about two thousand dollars.

On left side of Plate LIX. are the ground plans of this design. Both the plans and elevations are in a scale of sixteen feet to the inch. The house is quite large and roomy although apparently small, which is because of the reduced scale, and will accommodate a family of ten persons, including the servants. It is designed to be warmed by grates, but in a cold climate a furnace would be preferable. It may be observed that there is no furring-out marked upon the plan for the attic floor. This was omitted because the elevation is so designed that the outside wall extends two feet above this floor. As the attic rooms however are quite large the outside walls might be reduced and the furring-out easily arranged.

Plate LX. consists of details. Fig. 1, is a chimney-can. Fig. 2, is the gable window. Fig. 3, a section of the same. Fig. 4, the finial and eave ornament of the gable showing a section of the cornice. Fig. 5, ornament of the drip eaves. Fig. 6, front porch. Fig. 7, section of the same. Fig. 8, vestibule bay window. Fig. 9, section of the same. This plate also exhibits a side elevation of the design. It may be remarked that the strong contrast of white and black lines in this gives it a harsher appearance than it would have in nature.

SPECIFICATION

Of the labor and materials to be used in the erection of Design Thirteenth.

GENERAL DESCRIPTION.—The first story is to contain a parlor fourteen by twenty-four feet in the clear, a hall seven by twenty-four feet, a vestibule seven by eleven feet, a dining room eighteen by eighteen feet, and a kitchen twelve by eighteen feet, having a closet between it and the dining room two feet and six inches deep. The second story will contain three chambers, one fourteen by twenty-four feet, one eighteen by eighteen feet and one twelve by eighteen feet, besides a bed room seven by fourteen feet. The attic story will contain three chambers, one fourteen by twenty four feet, one eighteen by twenty four feet and one fifteen by eighteen feet. For the relative position of these rooms reference must be had to the plans. The first story is to be twelve feet eight inches from the first to the top of the second floor. The second floor is to be ten feet to the top of the attic floor, the attic rooms are to be seven feet and six inches in the clear, and the roof is to have twenty feet pitch. There is to be a porch on the front eight feet wide by thirteen feet long, and one on the rear seven by twenty-two feet.

EXCAVATIONS.—The cellar is to be, throughout the entire extent of the building, five feet deep from the surface of the ground, the earth therefrom being graded around the building as hereafter directed. The trenches for the foundation walls are to be at least six inches below the bottom of the cellar. The trenches for the porch foundations are to be of sufficient depth to secure them from the effects of frost.

MASONRY.—All the walls of the cellar must be composed of quarry building stone of a good quality. Those of the first course must be large and flat and solidly bedded in mortar. These walls are to be sixteen inches thick throughout, and eight feet six inches high from the cellar bottom. The mortar for this masonry must be composed of good coarse sharp sand and fresh wood-burnt lime in just proportions. All facings are to be smoothly dashed and afterwards lime washed.

BRICK WORK.—There are to be two stacks of flues emanating from the cellar, extending beyond the roof and surmounted with terra cotta chimney-cans, such as are exhibited on the plate of details. Each stack is to contain two flues nine by thirteen inches, well pargetted within and constructed of good sound brick laid in strong mortar. Their positions must be taken from the ground plans. All piers or cross walls in the cellar, for the support of the joists, must be constructed of sound brick and their facings smooth dashed.

FRAMING, &c.—The sills of the outside and division walls are to be six by six inch Norway pine. The corner posts and girts are to be four by eight inches and the plates are to be four by six inches, all of white pine. The intermediate braces and studding, and the studding throughout the partitions, are to be three by four inches, and placed sixteen inches between centres. The whole is to be well framed and pinned as is usual for such buildings. The exterior is to have hemlock laths one and a fourth by three inches, nailed in horizontally flush with the face of the studding, and three feet between centres, to which the weatherboards are to be secured. The joists of the first floor are to be three by twelve inches, those of the second are to be three by eleven inches, and those of the attic are to be three by nine inches, all of hemlock, and placed sixteen inches between centres. The trimmers for the flues and stairs are to be double thickness. The joists are all to be backed and are to have a course of herring bone bridged through the centre. The rafters are to be eight inches at the foot, of the usual rafter cut, and placed two feet between centres. The ridge pole is to be three by twelve inches, and the collar beams one and a half by six inches, strongly nailed to the rafters.

The exterior of the building is to be boarded vertically with one inch boards, of a uniform width to each front, from ten to thirteen inches, grooved together and cleated as exhibited on the plate of details. The rafters are to be lathed with hemlock strips, which must be overlaid with white pine shingles of a good quality, laid in courses of eight inches each in a diamond pattern. Each shingle is to be secured with two eight penny nails.

FLOORS.—All the flooring is to be a good quality heart pine flooring boards, well worked, well seasoned and firmly nailed to the joists, with the joints afterwards shot. Those in the porches are to be of white pine boards, quite narrow and laid with white lead in the joints.

STAIRS.—The stairs are to be made with heart pine step boards of a good quality. They are to have one and three quarter inch turned balusters, a six inch turned mahogany newel and a cherry rail, all put together in the best and most workmanlike manner.

WINDOWS.—The windows are all to have one inch and a half sash, and are to be double hung with axle pullies and patent cord. Those of the first and second stories are to have inside shutters, hung and secured in the usual manner. They are to be in three folds and are to part in the centre, each division having two panels neatly moulded on the face and with bead and butt on the inside. They are to fold into the soffits of the jambs.

DOORS.—The front door is to be one inch and three quarters thick, having panels with bead and butt on the inside and moulding with fillets on the outside. It is to be hung with four by four inch butts and secured by a seven inch upright mortice lock with porcelain mountings. The parlor, dining room, vestibule and back doors are to be one inch and a half thick, hung with three and a half inch butts and secured by four inch mortice locks. All other doors in the first story and the five principal doors of the second story are to be secured by three inch mortice locks, but otherwise are similar to the rest.   All other doors are to be one inch and a quarter thick, hung with three by three inch butts and secured as may be directed.   All doors are to have panels and, except those in the kitchen and attic, must be moulded.

The closets are all to be fitted up and shelved wherever it may be required and the kitchen is to be furnished with a dresser fitted up with drawers, shelves, paneled doors, &c., as is usual.

DRESSINGS.—All the outside window and door dressings, the cornices, architraves and finials, are to be constructed as set forth by the details.   The window and door dressings of the parlor, hall and dining room are to be six and a half inch architraves, with mouldings.   Those of the second story are to be five inches wide, and those of the attic and kitchen are to be three inches wide.   The wash-board of the parlor, dining room and hall is to be twelve inches high, including the moulding and a two and a half inch sub.   That of the second story is to be ten inches wide with a moulding and those of the attic and kitchen are to be four inches wide with a bead on the top.

TINNING.—The roofs of the porches and of the bay-window and all the gutters of the main roof are to be of the best one cross leaded roofing tin, painted on both sides, the upper receiving two coats.   There must be provided three three inch conductors of the same material to convey the water from the roof to the ground.

PLASTERING.—All the walls and ceilings throughout the building are to have two coats of brown mortar and one of white.   The parlor and vestibule is to have a cornice girting twelve inches and the parlor is to have in addition a centre piece three feet in diameter.   The plastering is to be done with mortar composed of good clean river sand and fresh wood burnt lime in the best proportions.   All laths are to be sound and free from bark.

PAINTING AND GLAZING.—All the woodwork of the interior that it is usual to paint must have three coats of pure white lead, mixed with the best linseed oil.   The exterior is to be painted with four coats of Silver's patent fire proof paint in a brown tint.   The stair rail, newel and balusters are to have four coats of varnish.   The sash are to be glazed with the best American glass, well bedded, bradded and back puttied.

FINALLY.—The contractor is to furnish at his own cost all the material and workmanship necessary to finish and complete this building, according to the true intent and meaning of the plans and other drawings, and of this specification, and also to the satisfaction of his employer.

A COTTAGE.

DESIGN FOURTEENTH.

IT is evident at a glance that this design, the front elevation of which is presented on the right of Plate LVII. possesses many points of similarity to the one which precedes it.   Although the internal arrangement of apartments is totally different, yet we have adopted the same methods of construction and in a general way the same style for the dressings and finish.   We have now presented three consecutive designs for houses whose sides are framed and vertically boarded. Frame houses are much preferred in many parts of our country, chiefly on account of their local cheapness, for in some places we find them outnumbering those of brick or stone, ten to one.   The cost being equal, a brick house is much to be preferred but the other may be equally comfortable.   Of this we shall have occasion to speak in future.

It has been the almost universal custom to place the boards on frame houses horizontally, making them to overlap each other so as to turn off the rain.   There are many objections to this, not the least being the very disagreeable effect produced upon the eye, by a multitude of parallel lines, especially in the sun-light.   The same objection does not seem to apply to vertical lines with equal force, and consequently they are preferable.   Care must be taken however in these last to exclude driving rain. If the joints, before the cleats are put on, be made tight, we more certainly secure this end, but by nailing the cleats closely and using paint freely the liability may be avoided.

Sam! Sloan Arch!   P. S. Duval's Steam Lith. Press Philad.ᵃ

COTTAGES.

Sam! Sloan Arch!   P. S. Duvals Steam lith. Press Philad.ᵃ

PERSPECTIVE VIEW.

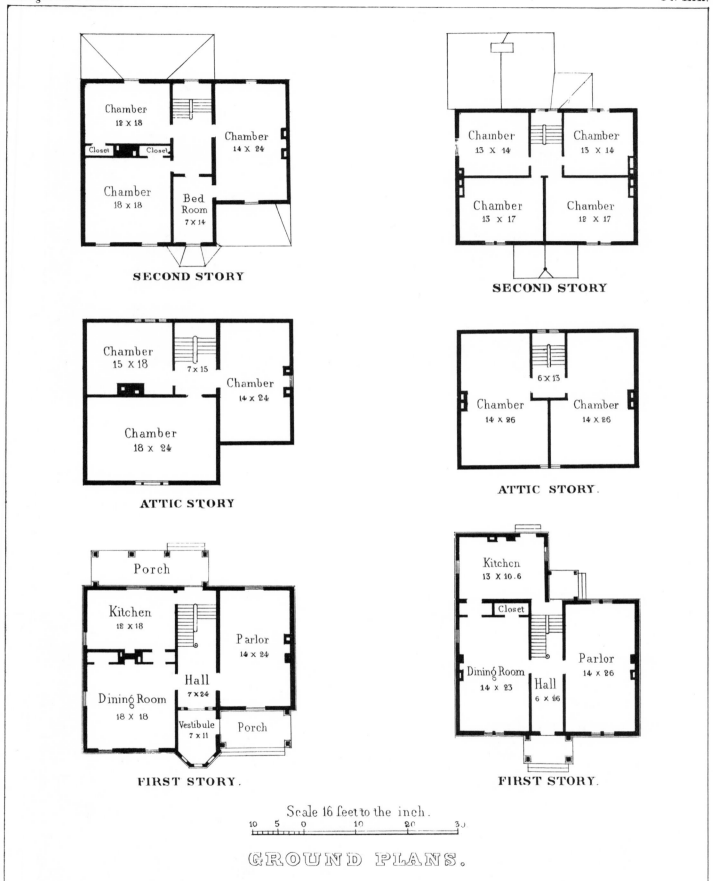

Chamber
12 X 18

Closet   Closet

Chamber
14 X 24

Chamber
18 X 18

Bed
Room
7 X 14

SECOND STORY

Chamber
13 X 14

Chamber
13 X 14

Chamber
13 X 17

Chamber
12 X 17

SECOND STORY

Chamber
15 X 18

7 X 15

Chamber
14 X 24

Chamber
18 X 24

ATTIC STORY

6 X 13

Chamber
14 X 26

Chamber
14 X 26

ATTIC STORY.

Porch

Kitchen
12 X 18

Parlor
14 X 24

Dining Room
18 X 18

Hall
7 X 24

Vestibule
7 X 11

Porch

FIRST STORY.

Kitchen
13 X 10.6

Closet

Dining Room
14 X 23

Hall
6 X 26

Parlor
14 X 26

FIRST STORY.

Scale 16 feet to the inch.
10   5   0   10   20   30

GROUND PLANS.

P. S. Duval's Steam lith press Phil.

Fig. 1.

Fig. 2.

Fig. 3.

Fig. 4.

Fig. 5.

Fig. 6.

Fig. 7.

Fig. 8.

Fig. 9.

Side Elevation

Scale 16 f.t to the inch.

Scale ½ inch to the foot.

DETAILS.

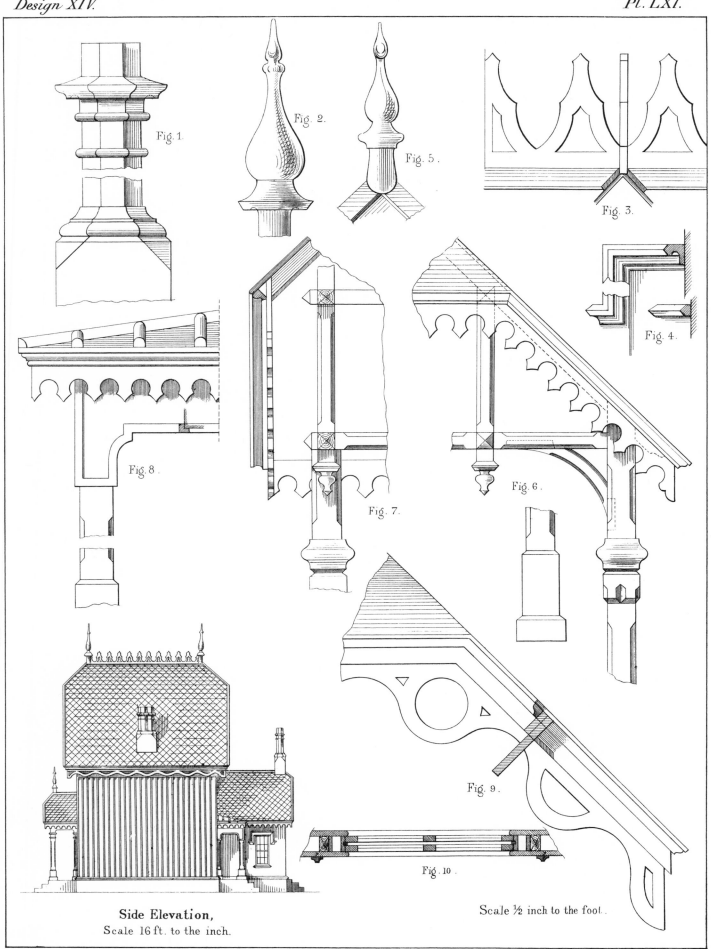

Fig. 1.

Fig. 2.

Fig. 5.

Fig. 3.

Fig. 4.

Fig. 8.

Fig. 7.

Fig. 6.

Fig. 9.

Fig. 10.

Side Elevation,
Scale 16 ft. to the inch.

Scale ½ inch to the foot.

P. S. Duval's Steam lith Press Philad.ª

DETAILS.

On the right side of Plate LIX. are the ground plans of this design. It is also a good sized house, the scale being but one inch to sixteen feet. It is smaller, however, than the preceding design, and consequently less expensive. The porches too, being smaller, diminish the cost. The accommodations are about the same as those of the other, the only difference being in the size of the rooms, for we have on the second floor, as in the other design, four chambers. Two of these are thirteen by fourteen feet and the other two thirteen by seventeen feet. There is however on this floor in the other design a small bed-room and an additional chamber on the attic floor. It will be observed that in both designs the kitchen and dining room communicate by double doors. We regard this as essential to the pleasantness of a dining room in order to shut off more effectually the odors always attendant upon culinary operations.

On Plate LXI. are the details of this design. Fig. 1, a chimney-can. Fig. 2, the finial of the roof. Fig. 3, the Tudor flower with a section. Fig. 4, the hood-mould and sill of the windows. Fig. 5, the finial of the front porch. Fig. 6, a front view of the porch showing the framing and post. Fig. 7, section of the same along the peak, side view. Fig. 8, back porch. Fig. 9, eave ornament and cornice. Fig. 10, a section of the twin windows. Upon this plate also is presented a side elevation of the design.

The aforementioned similarity between the two designs renders it unnecessary that we should give a specification for this. That of the other with very few alterations may be substituted. In it we have specified the best style of finishing suited to the general design. Were this surpassed, incongruities would arise and there would be too much ornament or finish for the basis. On the other hand, however, we may detract from this finish very materially without destroying the completeness of the design or violating good taste, and at the same time diminish the cost. Were this building to be finished according to the specification the cost would be about seventeen or eighteen hundred dollars.

A SMALL VILLA.
DESIGN FIFTEENTH.

THIS is comparatively a small building, the principal room on the first floor being but fourteen by fifteen feet. It is best suited to a warm climate, for the open hall with the staircase in it would make a delightfully cool sitting room. The front elevation is exhibited on Plate LXII. and the side elevation on Plate LXIII. There is very little pretension in its appearance, but it possesses an air of neatness. The ornaments are few and simple, and at the same time present many bold features. It is by no means rural in its character, but would seem to indicate a degree of cultivation in its occupants, or rather, we should say, it seems to indicate that they have a greater acquaintance with the busy world than country folks generally possess.

On Plate LXIV. are the ground plans of this design. The porch and pantry, placed on opposite sides of the hall, give symmetry to the design. The apartment marked 'living room' is intended to be used both as a sitting and dining room, and in cold weather as a parlor also. As was before intimated, the hall will admirably serve this latter purpose during the summer months. The window in the kitchen is designed to open to the floor, thus giving a means of egress. The stairs to the cellar are beneath the hall.   The flues are to be overdrawn so as to issue from the point in the roof indicated on the elevations.   The building will accommodate a family of four or five with the servant included.

On Plate LXV. are the details.   Fig. 1 is the front gable.   Fig. 2, a section of the same, showing the bracket.   Fig. 3, the gable window.   Fig. 4, a vertical section of the same.   Fig. 5, a horizontal section of the same.   Fig. 6, the cornice and post of the porch.   Fig. 7, the window beneath the balcony.   Fig. 8, side view of the balcony.   Fig. 9, the circular window of the gable.   Fig. 10, a section of the same.   Fig. 11, the chimney-can.

We deem it unnecessary, in this case also, to give a specification, in consequence of its great similarity to preceding designs.   We may, however, mention that it is intended to have brick walls, rough-cast without the pointing.   The roof is of tin.   If it be desirable to build on this plan, but at less expense, the house may be framed and the studs lathed without and then rough-cast.   The appearance in this case would be the same, the only difference being in the permanency of the building.   Instead of lathing, we might closely board the outside, having the joints tongued and grooved.   This, then, painted and sanded, would look about as well and be much stronger than if it were lathed.   In view of this latter case the plates of details have been arranged.   The cost, if built of brick, would be $1200, if boarded, $1050.

A PLAIN DWELLING.
DESIGN SIXTEENTH.

On the upper portion of Plate LXIV. are the ground plans of this design.   It is quite simple and requires no explanation.   In every building the greatest sources of expense, perhaps, are the doors and windows, and wherever they can be dispensed with the expense is accordingly diminished.   In the parlor of this plan the rear window might very well be left out.   It looks immediately into the back yard, and cannot be needed for any other purpose than that of lighting and ventilating the room, which object is sufficiently attained by the other two as the room is small.   The same remark may be applied to the corresponding window in the chamber above.   One window would be amply sufficient for the kitchen and one for the bed room above.   Two were introduced in each that the intermediate spaces might be equal.   This is not, however, of very great importance.

The front elevation of this design is on Plate LXVI., together with the details.   Fig. 1 is the balustrade on the roof. Fig. 2, the post cap of the same.   Fig. 3, the end of the chimney stack.   Fig. 4, a front window.   Fig. 5, the cornice and posts of the front porch.   Fig. 6, the cornice of the building.

The roof of this building is to be of tin, and the walls are to be framed, closely boarded, painted and sanded in the way suggested for the previous design.   There is, it will be perceived, a front porch exhibited on the elevation which is not laid down on the plans.   With this porch, an end view of which is also given, the cost of the house would be about $1450.

Saml Sloan Arch.^t

A SMALL VILLA.

Saml Sloan Arch.^t   P. S. Duval's Steam lith. Press Philad.^a

SIDE ELEVATION.

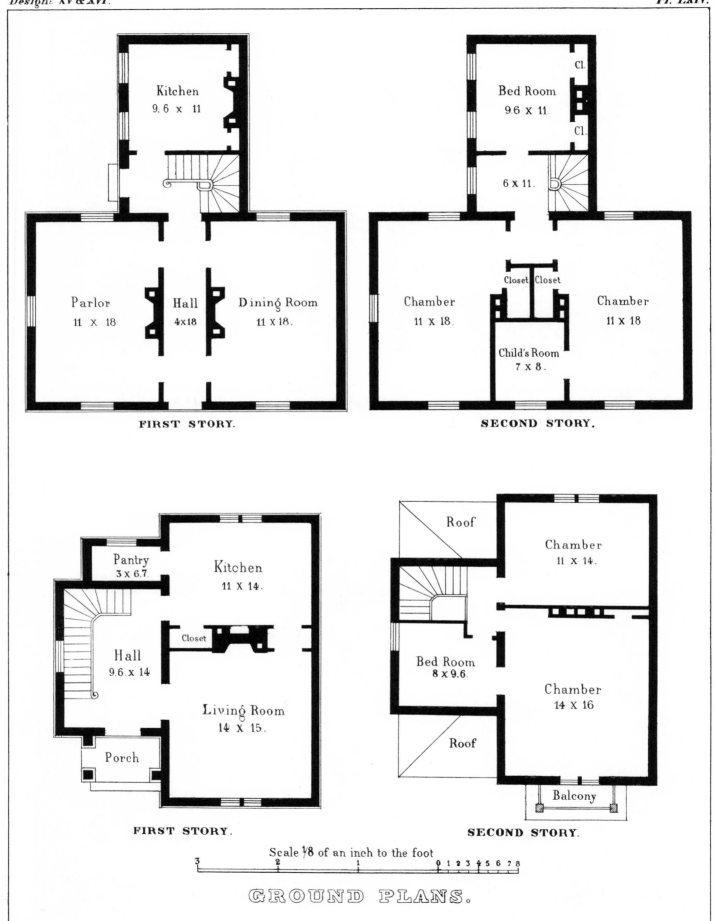

Kitchen
9.6 x 11

Parlor
11 x 18

Hall
4 x 18

Dining Room
11 x 18.

FIRST STORY.

Cl.

Bed Room
9.6 x 11

Cl.

6 x 11.

Closet Closet

Chamber
11 x 18.

Chamber
11 x 18

Child's Room
7 x 8.

SECOND STORY.

Pantry
3 x 6.7.

Kitchen
11 x 14.

Closet

Hall
9.6 x 14

Living Room
14 x 15.

Porch

FIRST STORY.

Roof

Chamber
11 x 14.

Bed Room
8 x 9.6.

Chamber
14 x 16

Roof

Balcony

SECOND STORY.

Scale ⅛ of an inch to the foot

3   2   1   0 1 2 3 4 5 6 7 8

GROUND PLANS.

P. S. Duval's Steam lith. Press Ph.

Sam! Sloan Arch!   P. S. Duval's Steam Lith Press Phil

DETAILS.

Fig.1

Fig.3

Fig. 5.

Scale ½ inch to the foot.

Fig. 4.

Fig. 2.

Fig. 6.

Scale, ⅛ of an inch to the foot.

FRONT ELEVATION

DETAILS.

SCHOOL-HOUSES.

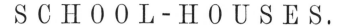

NTIL recently little attention has been given to the subject of School-houses. Throughout the length and breadth of the country our 'practical' people have for some time past condescended to bestow a few rude touches of architectural art upon their buildings. First, upon the principal public buildings, inasmuch as the additional expense was not immediately felt, and also because their dignity and importance seemed to demand it. Next, pride and the love of comfort materially added to the conveniences and improved the appearance of dwellings. Last, as though least, the School-house begins to exhibit traces of having received some of the attention which is its due. It would be curious to inquire into the cause of this neglect; but at present we have only to do with the fact, which we may venture to say lives in the memory of every one when he thinks of his school-boy days, unless perchance he was so highly favored as to be sent to some aristocratic select school. But we who were not thus favored well remember the dilapidated building, with only one room, standing on the cheapest lot in the neighborhood, and perhaps without any enclosure. We know how hot it was in summer, how damp in wet weather, how cold in winter, with the wind pouring in chill streams through innumerable crevices; or it may be that a red stove kept the close room hot, and the air, breathed over and over again, became putrid and disgusting. But chiefly we remember when perched on the high, hard, backless bench how we would long for the hour of letting out, with what delight we would escape from the pseudo penitentiary, what little pleasure Monday morning brought, and how each day intervening the vacation was carefully numbered. There is in an old spelling book this sentence, "Boys hate study," and once we thought that nothing indeed could be more true; but now we know that it was not so much the study that excited dislike as its unpleasant associations.

But these facts and their causes, though with us as household words, have not until lately found their way into print. The Genius of Improvement at last reached the School-house and found great room for exercise. There is now lying before us the results of systematic and official inquiry into the state of the schools throughout New England and the Middle States, giving testimony to their bad condition. They are the reports of various committees of examination, which, when published, at once brought to public view the undesirable state of things. Some of the details are shocking and almost incredible. We have no space for these, but can introduce only a few facts which were perhaps general. In the report to the Legislature of New York by the Hon. Samuel Young, we find the following:

"One-third only of the whole number of School-houses visited, were found in good repair; another third in ordinary and comfortable condition, only in this respect—in other words, barely sufficient for the convenience and accommodation of teachers and pupils; while the remainder, consisting of three thousand three hundred and nineteen, were to all intents and purposes unfit for the reception of man or beast."

The report of Hon. Horace Mann, secretary of the Board of Education in Massachusetts, for 1846, says—

"For years the condition of this class of edifices, throughout the State, had been growing worse and worse." "In 1837, not one-third part of the Public School-houses, in Massachusetts, would have been considered tenantable by any decent family, out of the Poor-house or in it." Again: "At the time referred to, the School-houses in Massachusetts were an opprobrium to the State; and if there be any one who thinks this expression too strong, he may satisfy himself of its correctness by inspecting some of the few specimens of them which still remain."

The First Annual Report of the Secretary of the Board of Commissioners of Common Schools in Connecticut, for 1838–39, contains the following:

"I will say generally that the location of the School-house, instead of being retired, shaded, healthy, attractive, is in some cases decidedly unhealthy, exposed freely to the sun and storm, and nearly all on one or more public streets, where the passing of objects, the noise and the dust, are a perpetual annoyance to teacher and scholar—that no play-ground is afforded for the scholar, except the highway—that the size is too small for even the *average* attendance of the scholars— that not one in a hundred has any other provision for a constant supply of that indispensable element of health and life, pure air, except the rents and crevices which time and wanton mischief have made—that the seats and desks are not, in a majority of cases, adapted to children of different sizes and ages, but on the other hand are calculated to induce physical deformity and ill health, and not a few instances (I state this on the authority of physicians who were professionally ac- quainted with the cases,) have actually resulted in this—and that in the mode of warming the rooms, sufficient regard is not had either to the comfort and health of the scholar, or to economy."

We cannot insert more, though there is an abundance. The School-houses of Pennsylvania and those, generally, throughout the South and West were, if possible, worse. Although there is, as before stated, a decided movement for the better, still this state of things is by no means as yet extinct. The "old field school" is still kept in a log hut, and has benches made of timber slabs. The site generally selected for the School-house is that wanted for nothing else. In the country, it is seated in the wild woods, without enclosure and without any other clearing than the highway which runs immediately before the door. In villages, it is either in some back alley or in a hollow. The building itself is seldom better than the barns within sight. It is often a mere log hut having of course but one room, and that without a ceiling. More generally it is a frame building, as plain as possible, destitute of window shutters and always having broken glass. The winds rock it to and fro, and the cracked plastering, the innumerable chinks and various ingenious carvings of the boys, give evidence of its dilapidated condition. The school-room is either so small and crowded as to be uncomfortable, or so large as to be comfortless. It is often so low that an ordi- nary man may touch the ceiling; thus in Rhode Island, the height of over two hundred school-rooms averaged less than eight feet. Sometimes it has a stove and sometimes an open fire-place, we cannot say is warmed by either, for the wind whistling through the cracks forbids. In this, however, we do injustice to many where the stove is kept shut, until the air is almost enough to stifle a Hottentot. None are ever provided with means of artificial ventilation by which the air may be kept uniform in purity and temperature, but when it becomes so impure and so contaminated with smoke as to be positively insupportable, the window is raised, and in pour colds and consumption.

Public attention has happily at last been aroused. Horace Mann says, that there was one argument used by the advocates of reform with irresistible effect. The meeting of the voters on the question of erecting a new School-house was called in the old one. " Cold winds, whistling through crannies and chinks and broken windows, told with merciless effect upon the opponents. The ardor of opposition was cooled by snow-blasts rushing up through the floor. Pain-imparting seats made it impossible for the objectors to listen patiently even to arguments on their own side, and it was obvious that the tears they shed were less attributable to any wrongs they feared than to the volumes of smoke which belched out with every gust of wind from broken funnels and chimneys. Such was the case in some houses. In others, opposite evils prevailed; and the heat, and stifling air, and nauseating effluvia were such as a grown man has hardly been compelled to live in, since the time of Jonah." Such arguments were indeed cogent, and we now see their effect in the many comfortable and convenient School-houses newly built or building around us. But the stone has just struck the water, and the circles are not yet spread. In the principal cities and towns only does reform exist, but as information is disseminated through the press, and as models are presented, so much the more rapidly and widely will improvement extend.

A word may be said as to what School-houses should be. The best situation in a village is not on the principal street, nor on the most worthless lot to be had, but in some quiet, respectable neighborhood where there is little or no stir out of doors to distract the attention of the inmates. The building should always be enclosed with a yard large enough for a playground, and be surrounded by shade trees. In the country there should be no more trees around than are necessary for a pleasant shade, and in all cases it should have a high, dry and healthy site, protected by a hill-side or a grove of evergreens from the bleak north winds.

The building, if the means at hand will not allow of its being made attractive, should certainly not be repulsive in its external appearance. The internal arrangement and conveniences of course are of the first consideration, but every effort should be made to give it as much architectural effect as possible. Without detailing the results of this, we may say generally that it reacts as a public benefit; it makes going to school more pleasant, and every tasteful moulding, every carving impresses the mind, and is in itself a schoolmaster. Of the interior the same holds true, and it should therefore be finished in the most tasteful manner possible. It is a notorious fact, that in Europe valuable statuary and paintings may be exposed unguarded to public gaze, and they will never be touched. There nothing is carelessly injured. It is equally notorious that Americans deface everything they can reach with a knife or pencil point. Where is this learned but at School? There is not one School-house in a thousand that is not covered with marks and carvings, oftentimes so obscene as to have a polluting effect on the susceptible minds of children. This is best avoided by giving every thing the highest finish, for the mind naturally shrinks from injuring that which is beautiful and produced by labor and pains-taking, and then, too, if the injury is done, it becomes a more punishable offence.

A school-room should never be less than twelve feet high, it should have about as much vacant as occupied space on the floor and should be well lighted. There should be other apartments for the purpose of entry, for the stairway and for the deposit of loose clothing. The furniture should always be conveniently designed and arranged. Every possible attention should be paid to the comfort of both teachers and scholars. If both sexes are taught in the same building, they should be separated by being in different stories or apartments, there should be different places for entry and distinct conveniences throughout.

It may be thought entirely superfluous to say that the construction of the building should be sound in every part. On the evening of April 28th, 1851, the ceiling of the Southwest School-house in this city, fell bodily to the floor. We were called upon to examine it, and found that the ceiling joists had been attached to the beams by tenpenny nails, in such a way that the mere weight of the plastering, laths and joists brought the whole down. Had the fall occurred during school-hours, in all human probability, seventy little children would have been crushed to death. On examining further the building, the wall was found to have so separated, the facing from the body, in consequence of its not being well bonded, that it barely gave sufficient support to the floors and roof. The terrible calamity which occurred in the School-house on Greenwich Avenue, New York, on the 20th of Nov. 1851, is still fresh in painful recollection, and would not have occurred had the stairway been properly designed and the bannisters been constructed with a proper degree of strength. A panic, that strange cloud of ignorant fear which overshadows the reason and leaves only instinct and the body active, came upon the children. They crowded on the stairway, the bannisters broke, and for some time a living stream poured over the brink, down the well, and dashed itself on the stone floor, piling up a mass of quivering flesh and bones. We need mention no more than this one horrible affair to show the necessity of careful attention to construction, and the folly of those who build with the least possible expense of labor and material.

The best methods of warming a School-house are those which apply to other buildings. We have no space to discuss this point now, but in a future article will speak of it at large. The great desideratum is to secure a large and steady influx of moderately heated air, which in large rooms is best done by means of a cellar furnace. Stoves may be so constructed and managed as to attain the same end very effectually. But ventilation is a point of equally great importance and has received heretofore little or no attention. So long as open fire-places were used the chimney acted to this end, but now when our best constructed rooms are made almost air tight, it must be otherwise provided for. In three hours the air in the largest of our school-rooms, with its ordinary complement of scholars, would become so vitiated as to be utterly unfit

Sam.ᵗ Sloan, Arch.ᵗ   P.S Duval's Steam lith. Press. Phil.ᵃ

FRONT ELEVATION.

Sam.ᵗ Sloan, Arch.ᵗ   P.S. Duval's Steam lith. Press Ph.

SCHOOL HOUSE.

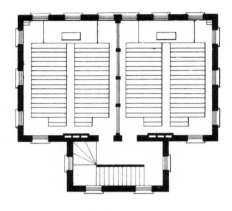

SECOND STORY.

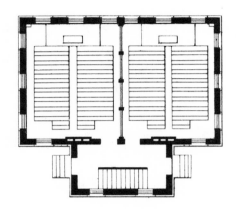

FIRST STORY.

DESIGN ENLARGED.

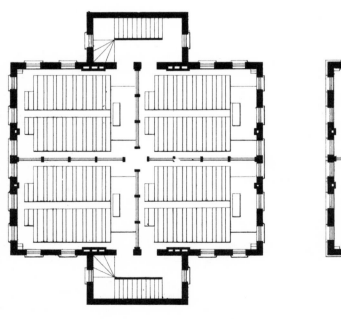

SECOND STORY.

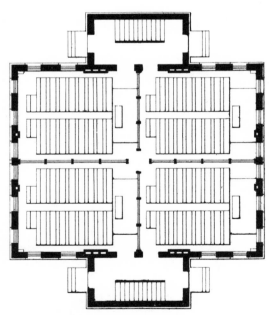

FIRST STORY.

Scale 16 feet to the inch.

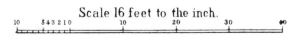

GROUND PLANS.

P. S. Duval's Steam lith Press. Philada.

Fig. 1.

Fig. 2.

Fig. 3.

Fig. 4.

Fig. 5.

Fig. 6.

Scale, ½ inch to the foot.

P.S.Duval's Steam lith.press. Philad ª

DETAILS.

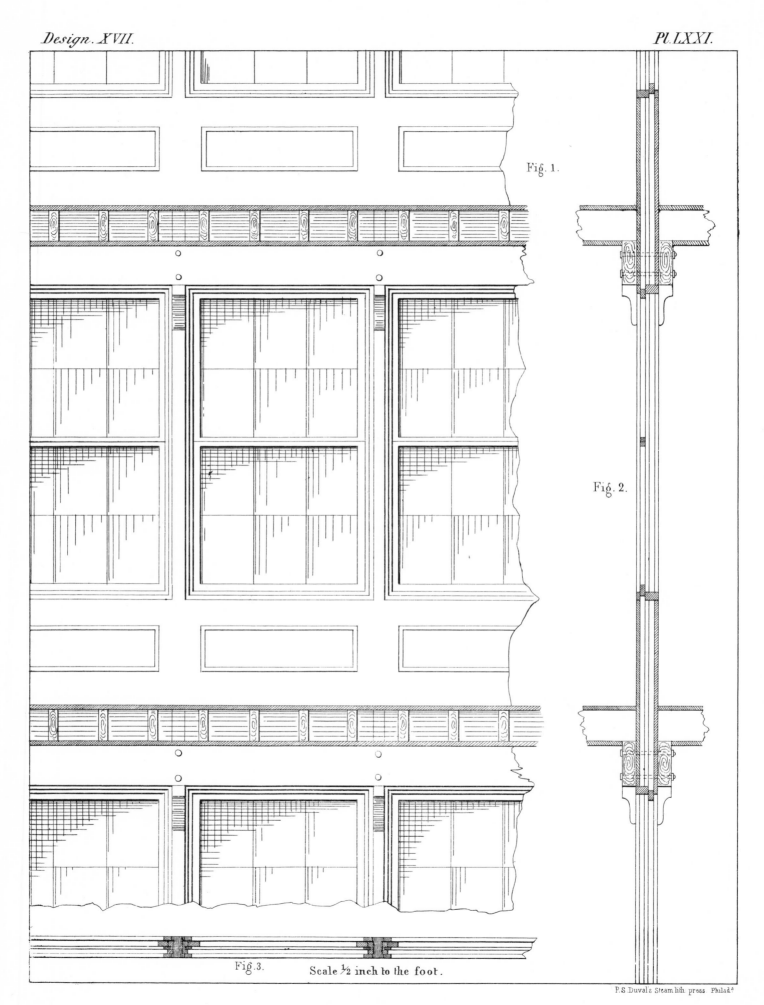

Fig. 1.

Fig. 2.

Fig. 3.　　Scale ½ inch to the foot.

DETAILS.

for the purposes of respiration. This is no guess work, but a fact calculated upon scientific principles. The effect, where this even partially occurs, is to stupify the brain and produce a total disinclination to physical or mental labor, too certainly planting disease. Plans for ventilation will also be discussed in future.

It is hardly necessary to urge further the improvement of School-houses. Probably we will give hereafter, in another form, an extension of our views on this subject, but at present enough has been said to show its importance. When we reflect on the plastic and susceptible nature of the youthful mind and body, the tenacity with which in after years it retains early impressions and influences, how desirable it appears that we should surround this stage of life with the most pleasant and healthful associations. Should the School-house be a place of both mental and physical torture? It is indeed too frequently so, our most painful recollections being oftentimes connected with it. Certainly we should desire our children to pass the few years they are subject to us, the naturally pleasantest portion of life, as happily as possible; but in the usual condition of things, no wonder they grow up with an utter dislike to mental labor, since connected with it they have been accustomed to such circumstances as would degrade and break the spirit of a man, and the influence of which it requires all the buoyancy of youth to resist.

A SCHOOL-HOUSE.
DESIGN SEVENTEENTH.

In the latter part of the year 1850, the Board of Controllers of the Public Schools in the city and county of Philadelphia, made a public proposal for designs for School-houses. They subsequently fixed upon those offered by the author, and since that time have been busily engaged in erecting buildings on these plans. Up to this time the arrangements for the accomodation of the various schools have been indifferent, and in some cases decidedly bad. Oftentimes they have been kept in rented buildings, erected for other purposes entirely, in one of which, during January, 1852, the ceiling fell, fortunately during the night, but had it fallen in school hours the disastrous consequences would have been equally great with those mentioned in the previous article, in connexion with a similar accident. In another of these rented buildings a school of over one hundred children has been kept in a room destitute of ventilating apparatus, and having only one dark narrow stairway as a means of egress. These defects in the system the Board have taken most prompt and energetic measures to remedy, and have now determined to erect new buildings wherever there is any need.

The design which was adopted as aforementioned, we now lay before our readers. An elevation and perspective suited to the plan are exhibited on Plates LXVII. and LXVIII., the ornaments of which are taken from the Norman style.

The most important feature, however, is the mode of partitioning; this may be seen on Plate LXIX. of ground plans, and on the second plate of details. It consists of dividing the building into the requisite number of school-rooms by means of glass partitions, which are so arranged, (see the specification,) that the whole story may be thrown into one room, and thus the various divisions of the school may be taught separately or together, as desired. Each apartment is intended to accomodate about sixty scholars.   On the upper part of the plate are the plans to which the specification refers, and below we exhibit plans of the same design, doubled in size.   In this the rooms communicate through the opening in the centre by means of four glass doors.   The means of egress in both are ample.   The cost of the buildings on the first plan is $4000, of the second $7000

On plate LXX. are the details of the outside.   Fig. 1, the belfry.   Fig. 2, the cornice, corbel course and eave bracket. Fig. 3, is the pediment bracket.   Fig. 4, corbel course of the eaves.   Fig. 5, window.   Fig. 6, section of the window.

Plate LXXI. shows the construction of the partitions.   Fig. 1, is a front view, drawn as if for a three story building, and shows a section of the floors.   Fig. 2 is a vertical section.   Fig. 3, a horizontal section.

SPECIFICATION

Of the workmanship and materials to be used in the construction of a new School-house, situate, &c.

GENERAL DIMENSIONS.—The building is to be forty-two feet six inches front, by twenty-five feet six inches deep, and two stories high.   The vestibule is to be externally twenty-four by ten feet six inches, and the roof is to have four feet pitch.   The first story is to be thirteen feet one inch and a half to the top of the second story floor, and the second story is to be twelve feet in the clear.   All other dimensions must be taken from the accompanying drawings.

EXCAVATION.—The cellar must be, throughout the entire extent of the building, seven feet deep below the underside of the first floor joists.   The trenches for the foundation must be at least one foot deep below the cellar bottom.   The earth from the cellar is to be graded about the premises as may be directed.

MASONRY.—The foundations or cellar walls, as high as the first tier of joists, are to be two feet thick.   The walls above, as high as the second tier of joists, are to be twenty two inches thick, and to the third tier or square of the building are to be eighteen inches thick, and those of the tympanums are to be sixteen inches thick.   All these walls are to be built of good quarry building stone, the first course of the foundations is to be of large flat stone well, and solidly bedded in mortar.   The mortar must all be composed of good coarse sharp sand and wood burnt lime, in such proportions as will ensure a good cement.   All facings are to be smooth dashed with the same material and those of the cellar are to be lime-washed.

CUT STONE.—A base course of the best hewn stone is to extend around the building two feet eight inches high, projecting two inches from the face of the wall, with a wash on the top.   The two outer door sills are to be four feet two inches long, one foot six inches wide and eight inches high.   There is to be a platform step to each, four feet eight inches long by two feet six inches wide, and two steps of the same length and one foot tread; each rise is to be eight inches high.   All the above is to be blue marble, clear of all defects and chamfered where necessary.

BRICK WORK.—There are to be three piers in the cellar, built of brick eighteen inches square, of height sufficient to give support to the girders, and situate immediately beneath the partition posts.   The warm air and gas flues are also to be constructed of sound brick, well pargetted within.   The gas flues must be topped out with sound brick at least three feet above the roof.   There is also to be a case of brick work built in the cellar, having two four inch walls, four inches apart, for the reception of a furnace.   The cold air ducts are to be constructed of bricks under ground, communicating with the external air at the nearest accessible point.

CARPENTER WORK.—The joists of the first story are to be three by twelve inches, spruce pine of good quality, placed sixteen inches between centres, and well backed with one inch crown, each tier having two courses of herring bone bridging through the centre.   These joists are to be supported by two girders fixed across the building, six by twelve inches each, and placed six inches apart.   These girders are to rest upon the brick piers built for the purpose in the cellar to the proper height.   They are to be bolted together with three quarter inch iron bolts, two over each pier, passing through the ends of iron posts, placed over the piers to support the partition, and are to rest upon iron brackets cast on the posts beneath. The joists of the second story are to be of the same dimensions, backed, bridged, &c., as last mentioned, but of hemlock and placed twelve inches between centres.   The girders are to be entirely similar to those below, bolted in the same way. The ceiling joists of the second story are to be of hemlock, two by ten inches, bridged and placed sixteen inches between centres.   They also will rest upon girders bolted and placed similar to those below, which are, however, but four by twelve inches.   The posts of the second story, which are of wood, and in position and size correspond with the iron posts of the first story, must extend to the roof and be framed into the ridge piece in front of the belfry, and into the rafter opposite on the rear.   The rafters of the roof are to be three by five inches, placed two feet between centres, strongly framed and put together in the most substantial manner.   These rafters are to be overlaid with hemlock board, free from knots, firmly nailed to the rafters and otherwise prepared for metal.   The floors are to be one inch and a quarter heart pine boards, well seasoned, well worked, tongued and grooved, and firmly nailed to the joists, the joints being afterwards shot.

STAIRS.—The steps are to be composed of one inch and a quarter heart pine step boards, four feet six inches long, each step having eight inches rise and eleven inches tread. They are to be enclosed by a partition formed of one and a half inch boards, grooved, quartered and beaded. There is to be a wall rail secured to the partition in the usual way. The opening in the second floor is to be surrounded by a strong rail, closed beneath to correspond with the wainscoting, and not less than four feet from the floor. There are to be stairs to the cellar, beneath the main stairs, put together in the usual manner, and also a step ladder to the loft.

DOORS.—The outside doors are to be one inch and three quarters thick, each having six panels with bead and butt, and being hung with three four by four inch butts, and secured by seven inch upright mortice locks. The frames are to correspond with those of the windows, the tympanum of the arch being glazed. The inside doors are to be one inch and a half thick, having six panels with bead and butt, and being hung with three and a half by three and a half inch butts, and secured by four inch mortice knob latches. The cellar door outside is to be beneath one of the windows as may be directed, the opening being three feet six inches broad by four feet out, having a stone head and sill and eight inch cheeks. The door is to be in two parts, strongly put together with wrought tenpenny nails, and to have white lead in all the joints. They are to be one inch and a quarter thick with three battens, each six inches wide, hinged with hooks and straps and secured by a hasp and padlock.

WINDOWS.—All are to be alike in construction. The sash are to be one inch and a half thick and double hung with axle pullies and patent cord. There are to be shutters within having two folds to each jam, and cut half way up opposite the meeting rails of the sash. These shutters are to be hung with back flap hinges, and are to fold into soffits formed in the jambs for their reception. They are to be one inch and a quarter thick, with two panels to each division, the stiles not being over one inch and three fourths in width. The frames are to be reveal with clean heart pine sills. The cellar windows are to have sash hinged to a narrow frame and secured with a small bolt. Each opening is to have three iron bars without, built in the wall. There is also to be a circular window, as shown on the front elevation, having a pivot sash, to light the loft.

PARTITION.—The partition is to be constructed as shown upon the detail drawings. The sash are to be one inch and a half thick, and hung to balance each other, with patent cord passing over one pair of axle pullies to each window, so that as the lower sash descends the upper one will ascend. The wainscoting will receive the lower sash and the upper will pass into the wainscoting above. There are to be three iron posts in the first story, and three wooden ones in the second, corresponding in appearance, to give support to the sash and girders.

DRESSINGS.—The dressings to the doors and windows are to be an architrave and moulding, in all eight inches wide. That of the windows is to be furred out at the jambs, giving sufficient space for the blinds. Outside there is to be a hood-mould over each opening, and a sill beneath, both of wood. All the rooms are to be wainscoted to the height of the window sills, properly secured, neatly capped and otherwise corresponding with the lower part of the partition exhibited on the plate. The wall next the stairs is to have wainscoting passing up the entire distance of the stairway. In each vestibule there are to be at least two hundred and fifty clothes hooks secured to wall strips, as may be directed. The cornice brackets, &c., are to be constructed according to the drawings. The belfry is to be put together strongly of light materials, for the reception of the bell, placed at the junction of the roofs, and finished as detailed on the plates.

VENTIDUCTS.—Each room is to have a wooden ventiduct placed in the angle diagonally from the warm air flues, made of thoroughly seasoned lumber, nine by fourteen inches outside, smooth on all sides and grooved together with white lead in joints, so as to be perfectly air tight. Each duct is to have two openings equal to its capacity, one near the floor and the other near the ceiling. The first will have a tight door, hinged below to drop inwards, and the one at the ceiling will revolve and be so arranged as to be moved at pleasure by means of a cord. These ducts are all to connect immediately under the apex of the rear pediment, with one equal in capacity to all the four; this is to pass up to the roof and there be surmounted with one of Emerson's patent ejecting ventilators, of fifteen inch calibre.

PLASTERING, &c.—All the walls and ceilings are to have two coats of brown mortar and one of white hard finish. The mortar must be composed of good clean sharp sand and wood burnt lime, in such proportions as will insure firm smooth plaster. The laths must be sound and free from bark.

The exterior of the building is to be rough cast in the best and most approved manner, of such a tint as may be directed, and laid off in blocks, so as to appear like dressed stone.

DEAFENING.—The second floor must be deafened by nailing cleats to the sides of the joists, and then flooring them so that the surface of the floor will be three inches below the top of the joists. This space must be filled with coarse mortar.

PAINTING AND GLAZING.—All wood work within and without must have three coats of pure lead paint, mixed with the best linseed oil. The wainscoting throughout must be tinted and grained to represent old oak, and have two coats of varnish, so also the doors and door and window frames externally. The hood-moulds and sills must be tinted and sanded to represent stone. The cornice brackets and cupola must be of an approved tint.

All sash must be glazed with the best American glass, well bedded, bradded and back puttied.

IRON WORK.—The iron posts in the first story supporting the glass partitions, are to be three by six inches, including the flanges.   The bolts for the girders are all to be made of three-quarter inch round iron.   A lightning rod is to be placed against the cupola, extending at least four feet above its highest point and terminating in a platinum point, the cost of which must not be less than four dollars.   The lower part of the rod is to be welded to an iron bar one inch and a half square, which must be driven into the earth at least four feet.   Provide all other iron work necessary to complete the building in a satisfactory manner.

TIN WORK.—The roof is to be overlaid with the best quality one cross leaded roofing tin, painted on both sides, the upper receiving two coats.   Provide of the same material all necessary gutters and conductors to convey the water to the ground.   The conductors must be three inches in diameter, with shoes and spout stones, and secured to the wall in a substantial manner.

FURNACE.—The building is to be warmed by one of Chilson's No. 5 furnaces, properly set in the brick case prepared for its reception in the cellar.   The registers throughout are to be ten by fourteen inches, and the whole arrangement is to be completed in accordance with the latest improvements.

FINALLY.—The contractor is to furnish at his own cost and expense all the materials and workmanship necessary to complete the building in all its parts as above described, in accordance with the plans and details and to the satisfaction of the Board of Controllers.

AN ORIENTAL VILLA.
DESIGN EIGHTEENTH.

THE style of building which has prevailed among the most civilized nations of the East, and which was introduced by the Moors into Spain differs essentially from any other species of architecture.   The horse-shoe arch and the minaret are the two most prominent distinguishing features, but throughout the whole style of finishing and the character of the embellishments are materially distinct, and it therefore possesses just claims to be considered a style in architecture.   Every one whose judgment and taste may be considered as authority in these matters, speaks of this eastern style as beautiful, but the immense quantity of carving required in order to give it full effect, prevents it from being used to any great extent by us.

On Plate LXXII. we present the front elevation of a building which is ornamented with some of the characteristics of this style, and the plate below exhibits the rear elevation of the same building.   It would be sheer folly to introduce the original pure style into this country, for no wise man will sacrifice his comfort in order to secure consistency in the appearance of his house with those which have been built in other countries, in other climates, and perhaps for other purposes by people with different customs.   Our style of living is totally unlike that in the East, and were we to build just such houses as they have, we would certainly part with comfort.   This last is of the first importance.   Let every one arrange his dwelling so as to secure the greatest amount of convenience, and then exercise his judgment in decoration. We hold that, in a manner, each building is an independent being, and if it be consistent with itself both internally and externally, and as to its purpose, then no fault can be found with it on that score.   Many buildings similar to the one here given have been erected in this country and command universal admiration.   The best location would be on the banks of some of our noble streams, the Mississippi or the Hudson.

The ground plans of the design are exhibited on plate LXXIV.   The drawing room and dining room communicate with the ante-room by wide sliding doors, so that on occasion the three may be thrown into one.   The front part of this ante-room might be partitioned off so as to give a vestibule.   In connexion with the library a fire-proof closet is arranged for the reception of valuable papers, books, plate, &c.   The whole house is designed to be warmed by a cellar furnace,

Saml Sloan, Arch.^t   P.S.Duval's Steam lith: Press Phila.^a

ORIENTAL VILLA.

Saml Sloan Arch.^t   P. S.Duval's Steam lith Press Ph.^a

REAR ELEVATION.

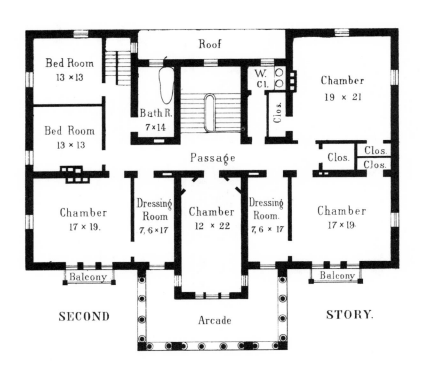

Bed Room
13 × 13

Bed Room
13 × 13

Roof

Bath R.
7 × 14

W.
Cl.

Clos.

Chamber
19 × 21

Clos.

Clos.
Clos.

Passage

Chamber
17 × 19.

Dressing
Room
7, 6 × 17

Chamber
12 × 22

Dressing
Room.
7, 6 × 17

Chamber
17 × 19.

Balcony

Balcony

SECOND   Arcade   **STORY.**

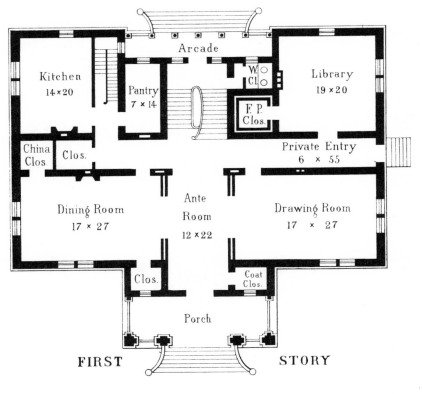

Arcade

Kitchen
14 × 20

Pantry
7 × 14

W.
Cl.

Library
19 × 20

F. P.
Clos.

China
Clos.

Clos.

Private Entry
6 × 55

Dining Room
17 × 27

Ante
Room
12 × 22

Drawing Room
17 × 27

Clos.

Coat
Clos.

Porch

FIRST   **STORY**

Scale 16 feet to the inch.

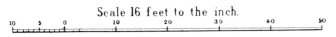

10   5   0   10   20   30   40   50

GROUND PLANS.

Fig. 1.

Fig. 2.

Fig. 4.

Fig. 3.

Scale ½ inch to the foot.

Sam.ᵗ Sloan Arch.ᵗ   P. S. Duval's Steam lith. Press Philad.ᵃ

DETAILS.

Fig. 1.

Fig. 2.

Fig. 3.

Fig. 4.

Fig. 5.

Fig. 6.

Fig. 7.

Fig. 8.

Scale: ½ inch to the foot.

Sam.ᵗ Sloan, Arch.ᵗ   P. S. Duval's Steam Lith. Press Philad.ᵃ

DETAILS.

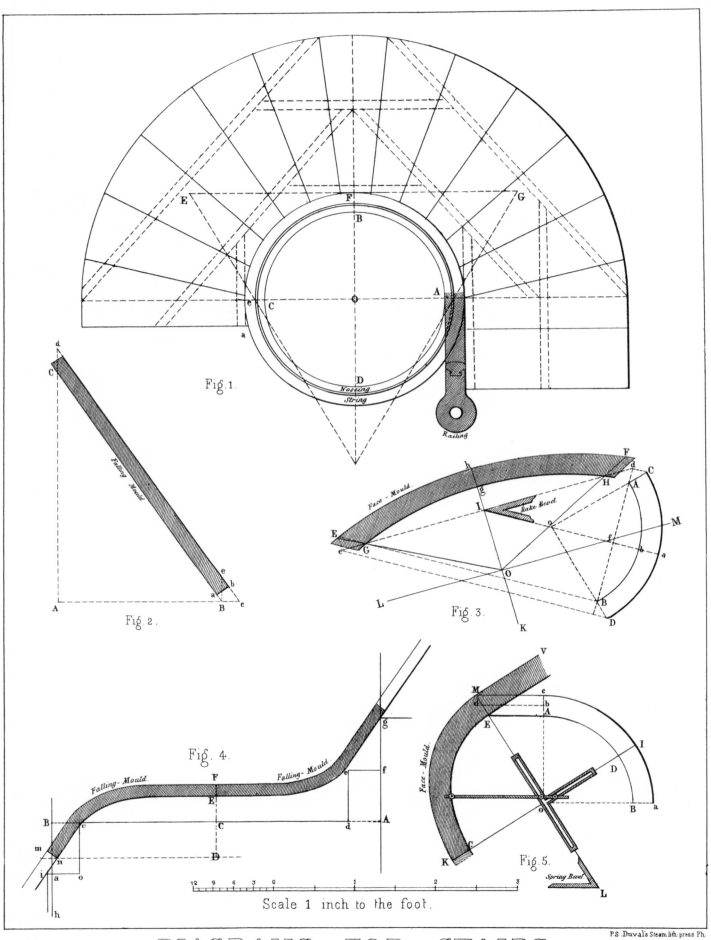

Fig. 1.

Noseing
String

Railing

Fig. 2.

Falling Mould

Fig. 3.

Face - Mould

Rake Bevel

Fig. 4.

Falling - Mould

Falling - Mould

Fig. 5.

Face - Mould

Spring Bevel

12 9 6 3 0   1   2   3

Scale 1 inch to the foot.

P.S. Duval's Steam lith: press Ph.

DIAGRAMS FOR STAIRS.

and the position of the gas flues and warm air flues are exhibited.   There are also rooms in the attic lighted by round windows which may be seen beneath the cornice on the front elevation.

Plate LXXV. consists of details.   Fig. 1 is the outside dressings of the front windows of the wings.   Fig. 2, the porch front.   Fig. 3, section of the pillar.   Fig. 4, side view of the wing balcony.

Plate LXXVI. is also of details.   Fig. 1, minaret on the corner.   Fig. 2, cornice, brackets and windows of the tower. Fig. 3, section of the same.   Fig. 4, cupola of the tower.   Fig. 5, section of the same.   Fig. 6, minaret of the front porch.   Fig. 7, main cornice, brackets, &c.   Fig. 8, paneling.   More minute description of this building is unnecessary.

CIRCULAR STAIRS.

UPON the plate facing this page will be found diagrams for planning a geometrical stairway, and for obtaining the moulds by which to cut out the hand-rail.   They were furnished for our work by John S. Basehore, Esq., stair-builder of this city, and undoubtedly comprise the simplest and most complete method now in use, being far superior, as practice has shown, to the old cord-line method.   They are called trammel drawings, because that instrument is used to draw the sections of ellipses.   The following concise explanation of the diagrams may be useful to aid in comprehending them.

In preparing to build a stairway we must first draw a vertical projection, as in Fig. 1.   This is quite a small stairway, but sufficient for our purpose.   The framing of the carriages is shown by the dotted lines.

To obtain the falling mould for that part of the hand-rail which lies between A and B, Fig. 1, or B and C, we take the distance AB on the inner side of the string, by the stretch-out, and have AB=FG.   Now in Fig. 2, we draw AB equal to FG, Fig. 1, and on the perpendicular (Fig. 2) we take AC equal to the sum of the heights of the risers between the points A and B, Fig. 1.   Join B and C, Fig. 2, and take a b equal to the thickness of the rail, and draw c b d.   Erect the perpendicular B e and draw a b so that its centre will lie in B e.   Also let the centre of the other butt lie in C d.

The face mould for the same part of the rail is obtained as follows.   Draw the quadrant o A b B, Fig. 3, with a radius equal to OA, Fig. 1, and take AC equal to the width of the rail, and draw CaD.   Draw AB and erect the perpendiculars D e, BG, a o and C d.   Take BG equal to AC, Fig. 2, and through G and d draw e d.   At the point I where a o meets e d erect IK perpendicular to e d.   Take IO equal to o f, and draw LM perpendicular to IK.   These lines, IK and LM, are the trammel lines.   Take Ig equal to f b, and g h equal to b a.   Fix the trammel on the lines IK and LM, and then describe GgH.   Draw eE perpendicular to e d, and also draw OE and OF.   Again with the trammel describe EhF.   This gives us EFGH, the face mould.   This is laid upon a plank as thick as the width of the rail, and marked.   Then the rake bevel shown in the figure is applied at the point G to get the corresponding point on the other side, when the mould is again set and marked.   After this is cut from the plank the falling mould is applied to the edge, and the piece again marked and cut, thus giving the exact shape of the rail.   The overwood, from which the butt is cut, is also shewn.

To obtain the falling mould for that portion of the rail which lies between C and D, Fig. 1, and that between D and A in ascending a second flight beginning over the second step of this, take the whole stretch-out, EG, Fig. 1, and lay it down from A to B, Fig. 4.   Let fall the perpendicular Bh, and take cB equal to a e in Fig. 1.   Now draw the steps c o i and d e f g, and extend Ag.   Through the point C in the middle of the line AB, draw the perpendicular FD, and take EC equal to ½ e d.   Draw now gEi.   Take EF equal to the thickness of the rail, and through F draw a line parallel to gEi. The centres of the extreme butts will lie in Bh and Ag respectively.   Draw Dn parallel to AB through the point n.

It now only remains to obtain the corresponding face mould.   Draw the quadrant oADB, Fig. 5, similar to oAbB in Fig. 3.   Make Ac equal the width of the rail, and draw cIa.   From the point b midway between c and A, draw b d equal to DE on Fig. 4, and parallel to o a.   Through d and o draw the trammel line ML, and perpendicular to this through o draw the other, IK.   Let oK=oI, and oC=oD.   Draw also Mc and AE parallel to d b.   Now place the trammel as exhibited on the lines, and draw EC and KM.   Then is KMEC the face mould.   The strip beyond ME must remain attached to the mould.   The edge MV is ranged with the edge of the plank, and the mould marked. This edge must then be beveled with the spring bevel whose lower side is parallel to o a.   The edge MV is placed against the beveled edge on the other side, the mould marked and the piece cut out.

THE MORTAR.

IT will doubtless be a matter of surprise to some that this subject should receive an extended notice, although really it is of the highest importance. Unfortunately, however, it is one of the points in which little or no care is exercised, and the master mason usually builds with mortar prepared either by a careless apprentice or an ignorant laborer. He never thinks of the permanence of his work, unless it be surrounded by extraordinary destructive agents, but if the finished structure stands, he and his employer are satisfied. But in the present day, when our walls are built so thin and lofty and are often veneered upon the outside with slabs of marble or granite, a mortar should be used that will bind the mass together, and make the whole as one stone, otherwise premature decay will continue to crumble our dwellings, and our cities and villages, as indeed is now the case, will require rebuilding every few years. It is time that all interested should be aroused to attend to this matter, more neglected perhaps than any of the many neglected processes connected with erection of ordinary buildings. There have been a few treatises on mortars published by those whose position has interested and enabled them to experiment extensively, but the little light admitted by these researches seems to show that we are almost void of any knowledge of the subject. What we shall say is mainly derived from such sources, and combined with a little practical knowledge acquired by observation, may serve to awaken inquiry in the minds of some who have as yet treated longer and more complete essays with indifference.

Mortar may be described in a general way as a compound of various substances capable of entering into a chemical combination that indurates the mass, attaching it at the same time to the building materials, and thus binding them firmly and lastingly together. One of these ingredients is sand, of which little need be said, but that little is important. It consists essentially of silica or quartz, the purer the better except in the case of arénes, the foreign matter in which is of a nature to increase its value. Sea-sand, when none other is accessible, must be thoroughly washed in order to free it from the salt with which it is impregnated, and indeed in all cases the sand should be washed and sifted. River-sand when well selected will answer every purpose, but pit-sand, when economically obtained, is preferable. The former is generally cleanest, but the grains composing it are apt to be rounded in their passage down the stream, and it consequently contains fine powder, the result of the abrasion, which must be avoided. The grains of pit-sand never having been subjected to such action are sharp and angular, and therefore, as will hereafter appear, are much better fitted in this respect for the purposes of the builder.

The other essential and most important ingredient of mortar is lime. The limestone yielding it is found native, and contains in addition a certain amount of carbonic acid chemically combined, thus forming a carbonate of lime. Before the lime is fit for use this acid must be expelled by calcination in kilns, which is always accompanied by a loss of weight to the amount of about forty-five per cent., which includes also the water. A high degree of heat is requisite to disengage the carbonic acid, and the whole process is one requiring experience and care. The smaller the pieces of limestone are the less is the time required, the disengagement of the acid being greatly aided also by having them moist when placed in the kiln, but still a good red heat must be maintained for several hours, varying in number according to circumstances. This heat too must gradually be augmented, since the last remaining portions of the acid are most difficult of expulsion. It requires no small amount of skill to know how much heat to apply, and when to stop the process. Some of the best limestones if over heated are rendered useless or "killed," and often the calcination must be stopped before all the acid is expelled. With the rich limestones an almost inexplicable case obtains. If a certain portion of the acid be retained the lime is excellent; if the burning cease at the point when all the acid is expelled the lime is almost useless, and if it be continued for a certain time beyond this point the lime is again excellent, except that it is apt to swell in setting. Unfortunately, so little is certainly known that we cannot yet give definite directions on the calcination of limestones, although it is as important as any other point connected with our general subject; but as Mr. Burnell, who is perhaps the most recent and best authority, says :—" At present our best guide is experience, and a kilnsman who has watched the action of his own kiln for years knows more upon the subject than the first theoretician in the world."

The lime thus obtained is by no means chemically pure, but always contains a variable quantity of clay, which consists of alumina and silex together with certain other substances in such small quantities however, that they may be disregarded. But the result is materially affected by the proportion of alumina and silex which may exist in the lime. The varieties thus produced will be spoken of as lime, hydraulic lime and cement. Villeneuve thus classifies them and says :—" The calcination of the carbonate of lime containing from one to six per cent. of clay produces ordinary lime ; if the quantity of the clay be greater (equal to from six to twenty-three per cent.) the lime is suitable to be made into hydraulic mortar. Beyond twenty-three to twenty-seven per cent. of clay the result of the calcination of the calcareous compound is termed cement. Practical experience has shown that between lime suitable for hydraulic purposes, and cements a line of demarcation exists in the form of the lime containing about twenty-three to twenty-eight per cent. of clay. This combination neither slacks into powder when wetted with water, nor does it cohere permanently when mixed with water and beaten together." But this can only be regarded as a general statement which may fail in practice, and hence the selection of a limestone should rest mainly on experiment. Vicat, whose extensive and valuable researches gave the first impulse to enquiry on the subject, says :— " The physical characters which serve to distinguish calcareous compounds fail to give any certain indication of the qualities of the lime they contain. Even chemical analysis is but an approximate mode of investigating them. Experience by actual trial ought to be the builder's only guide." We may remark in passing that the limestones of the United States are very generally characterized by containing a large amount of magnesia which seems to unfit most of them for building purposes.

Before the mortar is compounded the lime must be slacked. It is a well known property of caustic lime to combine powerfully with water, forming what is technically termed the hydrate of lime, or in common parlance, slacked lime. This action is accompanied by the evolution of considerable heat, and the lumps decrepitate into powder to a greater or less extent, after which the whole will be found to have increased in weight according to the quantity of water combined. The rich limes should always be slacked by gradually adding water and allowing them to remain wet, for these limes will retain their plastic state beneath the water, until the effect is thoroughly accomplished. We are told the Romans had a law that the lime should not be used until it had laid in a moist state for three years. This it was supposed would give ample time for the most minute particles to become hydrated.

The case however is different with the hydraulic limes, and the better their quality the more imperfect will be the comminution of the lumps. It is therefore essential, we may say, that they should be brought to a state of fine division before slacking, either by pounding them, or much better, when the magnitude of the work justifies the expense, by grinding them in a mill. Another reason why this should be done is that very soon after slacking the hydraulic lime begins to set, and hence everything which facilitates the rapidity of mixture and use adds to its value. After being ground it should be slacked by sprinkling with water and working the paste until the slacking be thorough and complete, which is important, since limes swell in slacking and will therefore disintegrate the mortar if not fully hydrated.

We have remarked that the limes containing from six to twenty-three per cent. of clay are suitable for hydraulic mortars. The great superiority of these has led to their artificial production by mixing various foreign substances with the rich limes. It was ascertained that the Roman artizans in preparing their mortar, which at this day is more firm than the building stones, mixed with their lime a volcanic substance called puozzolano. Subsequently the same material was discovered in Germany, where it is called trass, in France and in Scotland, and has been used with wonderful success. It consists chiefly of alumina and silex, mixed with a small proportion of lime and highly magnetic oxide of iron. When introduced into the mortar it communicates the property of setting with great rapidity even under water, and of retaining a firmness and cohesive power for ages, after the manner of natural hydraulic mortar.

Some clays after a moderate calcination are found to possess the same properties to a very considerable extent when not subjected to the action of sea water. Their composition is nearly the same as that of the puozzolanos, but the components are hydrated and this water must be driven off by the calcination. Mr. Burnell thinks that the lime and clay should be calcined together so that a more intimate mixture may be secured, thereby favoring chemical action. Experiment at present is the only way to test the goodness of the clay and the degree of calcination. The Romans often used pounded bricks or tiles, and the slag and scoriæ from iron furnaces are also excellent ingredients. They must previously be reduced to a powder, and only those are fit for the purpose which will dissolve or become gelatinous under the action of muriatic acid. Ashes of various kinds have also been successfully tried, but before mixture they must be freed from the alkalies by washing.

Experience has shown that the best plan in preparing mortar is first to bring the lime to the consistence of a smooth and uniform paste before adding the components. The sand must be gradually intermixed and the whole thoroughly worked together. This is a point usually but little attended to, but nevertheless is of great importance. The more the mortar is worked the more sand will it take, and the greater will be its durability. The old Romans, Vitruvius says, had a proverb that mortar should be moistened with the sweat of the brow. It may be proper to observe that in the case of hydraulic mortar this working must be done with many hands since it is requisite that it should be placed in position as soon as possible. As to the proportionate quantity of the sand to the lime, again we cannot be definite, so much does it depend on the various qualities of the latter; we may state, however, that the rich limes require a larger quantity than the hydraulic. Vicat thinks it better to err in a deficiency than an excess of lime in mortar made from the rich limes, and vice versa with that from hydraulic limes. According to Vitruvius, the Romans prescribed three parts of coarse sand to one of lime; and according to Pliny, four of the former to one of the latter. In compounding the artificially hydraulic limes, such proportions must be used as experiment shows to be best. Except where both are calcined together the clay, burnt and powdered, must be mixed with the lime after slacking and before the sand is introduced.

The setting frequently alluded to is an imperfect crystallization by which the whole becomes converted into an indurated crystalline mass. The result is greatly aided by the sharp angles of the sand grains which afford nuclei for this crystallization, and are points of attachment by which the whole is firmly bound together. On this principle, also, the mortar adheres to the stone or brick of which the wall is constructed. In the ordinary mortars, those composed of rich lime and sand, the crystalline portion is carbonate of lime, and hence if all the carbonic acid be expelled in the calcination it must be reabsorbed from the air before the setting can take place. This is a slow process. The mortar may become somewhat dry in the course of a few days and possess a slight cohesive power, but it may require years in order to become thoroughly indurated. There have been cases where walls a hundred and fifty years old were found to contain on the interior mortar as soft and fresh as the day it was laid. This justifies the French proverb that mortar of a hundred years is still young, and shows the importance of using, where it is possible, those mortars that do not depend on the absorption of carbonic acid for induration.

Such is the case with hydraulic mortars both artificial and natural. They set in a few hours after being prepared; hence we must believe, and indeed subsequent analysis shows that the crystalline substance is not carbonate of lime, but some other chemical compound of the several ingredients. Upon the nature of this, however, chemists are not as yet fully prepared to pronounce.

The hydraulic mortars have engaged most of our attention, because of them little is practically known, and they certainly are of the first importance. The name hydraulic is given them because of their property of setting under water, and heretofore they have been used almost exclusively for marine and other hydraulic works. It is highly important, however, that we should possess and put into practice the means of giving greater durability and security to our ordinary buildings, and there is no reason why the hydraulic mortars should not be used to this end. They act equally well, if not better, in air, and with skill can doubtless be made so economically that the difference in expense is no ground of preference for ordinary mortars. It is only necessary that the experiment be made a few times. Success is certain, and will be the greatest, the most valuable advance in modern construction. Of cements little has been said, since they are rather disconnected with the peculiar views which we wished to inculcate. It is nevertheless gratifying to know that their composition and properties are being thoroughly examined, and the recent experiments at the World's Exhibition show that little is left to be desired in the accomplishment of the purposes to which they are particularly adapted.

A VILLAGE CHURCH.

DESIGN NINETEENTH.

THIS is the first design for a church introduced into our work. It is after the Romanesque style, but nevertheless retains the general outline and plan usual in this country as being the best adapted to our present form of worship. We have given it a most compact arrangement, but at the same time have been quite free in exterior ornament. There is a medium to be observed here. We view with natural displeasure any parsimony that may exhibit itself in the house of God, and at the same time dislike great attention to physical comfort, or lavish expenditure in decoration as shewing too much regard merely to the place of worship. The building should possess dignity, nobleness, grace, and be free from every trace of gaudiness. The interior should be comfortable but not luxurious, and should be fitted entirely to the form of worship. Any one may see that to meet all these requisitions is no easy matter.

The apartments of the present design as was remarked, have been compactly but we hope conveniently arranged. Reference to the floor plans, Plate LXXIX. will explain this arrangement. The lecture room is placed in the basement. Around three sides of the building an area extends as deep as this floor, by which we avoid any great elevation of the body of the building. A gallery is placed in the church on small iron pillars, and is attained by means of two stairways. From it we ascend the tower. These stairways are on either side of the tower, the base of which constitutes the principal vestibule or lobby.

Pl. LXXVII.

Sam.l Sloan Arch.t

P.S. Duval's Steam lith. Press. Phila.d

A VILLAGE CHURCH.

Pl. LXXVIII.

Sam.l Sloan Arch.t

P.S. Duval's Steam lith. Press. Philad.

FRONT ELEVATION.

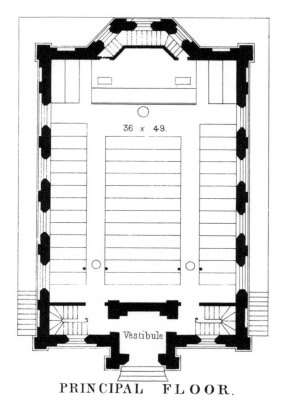

PRINCIPAL FLOOR.

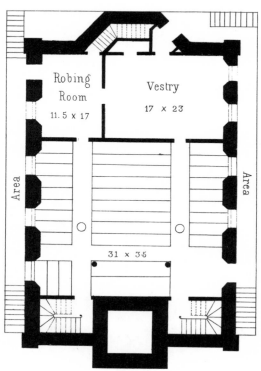

BASEMENT.

Scale 16 Feet to the inch.

GROUND PLANS.

Sam.ᷤ Sloan Arch.ᷤ

P.S. Duval's Steam lith. Press. Philad.ᷤ

Fig. 1.

Fig. 2.

Fig. 3.

Fig. 6.

Fig. 7.

Fig. 4.

Fig. 5.

Scale ½ inch to the foot.

DETAILS.

Fig. 1.

Fig. 2.

Fig. 3.

Fig. 5.

Fig. 6.

Fig. 7.

Fig. 4.

Scale, ½ inch to the foot.

DETAILS.

Plate LXXX. consists of details. Fig. 1, elevation of a side of the tower. Fig. 2, finial of the tower. Fig. 3, window of the tower. Fig. 4, section of the octagonal part of the tower. Fig. 5, section of Fig. 3. Fig. 6, finial of the tower buttress. Fig. 7, finial of the corner.

Plate LXXXI. is also of details. Fig. 1, the cornice and corbel course of the front. Fig. 2, section through the line a b. Fig. 3, front door. Fig. 4, section of the front door. Fig. 5, moulding of the triangular panels. Fig. 6, round window of the tower. Fig. 7, section of the window.

The building is forty-three feet front by sixty feet deep; it has a recess on the rear four feet deep, and the tower projects forward four feet. From the basement floor to the main floor, which is three feet above the natural surface, is ten feet, and from thence to the ceiling twenty-two feet. The walls are of brick, on a stone foundation as high as the basement floor, and are two feet thick to the second floor, and from thence eighteen inches to the square of the building. The panels on the outside walls are three inches deep, and those on the buttresses are two inches. The walls of the tower are two feet six inches to the first floor, and from thence two feet thick to the square. The octagonal portion is entirely constructed of wood, and crowned with a spire and finial. It is proposed to enclose the spire with the best purple slate, in an ornamental pattern. All the exterior walls are to be rough-cast, and afterwards coated with Silver's plastic paint. The basement contains a lecture room, a vestry or school room and a robing room, which last has stairs in the recess leading to the pulpit. The lecture room also has stairs leading beneath the gallery stairs to the principal floor. The dimensions of these rooms and of the body of the church are marked upon the plans. The seats on the principal floor including the gallery would comfortably accommodate three hundred persons.

For warming this building we would recommend a Chilson furnace, No. 6, which is the most effectual and durable that has come under our notice. This furnace should be located under the basement floor near the tower, and will require an excavation of about seven feet in the clear. The furnace chamber should be about eight feet square, and constructed of two four inch walls with a four inch space between. The cold air must be introduced through an underground duct, in size about twelve by thirty-six inches in the clear. The sides and bottom may be of brick and the covering of flag stones. This duct must communicate with the external atmosphere at the nearest accessible point, and be protected at the opening with an iron grating. Of the four warm air flues which emanate from the crown of the chamber, one will lead to the intersection of the division walls in the basement, so that it may communicate with the robing room, vestry, lecture room, or the main room above. Of the others one will communicate with the lecture room, and the other two with the room above. By this arrangement any apartment may be completely warmed.

To thoroughly ventilate this building ventiducts should be placed in the wall on each side of the pulpit. Likewise in the second and third piers. Each of these ducts should be at least nine by sixteen inches in the clear, made air-tight, and smooth on the inside. Each must extend from the floor to the apex of the roof, at which point they are connected into one, equal in capacity to all the others, extending a few inches above the roof, and neatly capped with one of Emerson's twenty-four inch ejecting ventilators. The ducts referred to must have valves at the floor and ceiling which can be opened and closed as the temperature of the room may require.

The cost of the design here presented, with such specifications and details as we would provide, finished in the best manner within and without, would be about four thousand eight hundred dollars.

ITALIAN VILLA.

DESIGN TWENTIETH.

PLATE LXXXII. presents the front elevation of an Italian Villa, the perspective of which is exhibited on the plate below. There is nothing peculiar in this design to call forth extended remark. Its prominent features are bold, and the details are plain and simple. The situation best suited to its character is as represented in the midst of a park, with a fine command of prospect and surrounded by a variety of shrubbery and trees. It may be placed in a very secluded position and yet harmonize strictly with objects around. Still we must remember that the character of the style is not rural, but requires surrounding evidences of art and taste to give it consistency.

Plate LXXXIV. exhibits the various floor plans. The one beneath is of the basement story which contains, as may be seen, both dining room and kitchen. This arrangement possesses many superior conveniences, but is much more extensively used in England than in this country. The furnace by which the whole building is warmed is placed in the middle of the basement and within a double brick case. It is in a position where it cannot incommode, and in an apartment that could be used for nothing else, since it cannot be lighted.

On the first floor to which we ascend by the stairs beneath the hall stairs, there are five apartments. The dotted lines in the porch shew the general outline of a pattern of flooring tiles. Indeed it would be well to floor the hall with either tiles or marble, it being the most permanent as well as the most beautiful style in use. The windows of the parlor, drawing room, and library opening into the verandahs are designed to reach the floor.

The second story contains six chambers, and will readily accommodate a family of eight including the servants. Above the central stairway is placed a sky-light to light the upper hall. The narrow stairway leads to the apartment in the tower. The roofs above the verandahs might well be arranged as balconies, in which case there might be additional windows in the central back chamber leading out on them.

Plate LXXXV. exhibits the details. Fig. 1, is the chimney-top. Fig. 2, side view of the same. Fig. 3, section of the gable shewing the cornice and bracket. Fig. 4, cornice of the eaves. Fig. 5, cornice of the tower. Fig. 6, railing of the entrance. Fig. 7, section of the same. Fig. 8, Finial of the tower. Fig. 9, side butment of the same.

The basement story of this design is ten feet high in the clear. The first story is twelve feet eight inches from floor to floor, and the second story is eleven feet in the clear. The walls of the basement as high as the first tier of joists are of stone, and eighteen inches thick. All other walls are of brick, and sixteen inches thick. The two principal division walls are also of brick, but all others are stud partitions. The main roof and that of the verandahs and tower are all to be of tin ribbed in the manner represented on the front elevation and details. The front porch is to be entirely open with a groined vault above, and the front door also is to have an arched head. The whole of the outside wall is to rough-cast in the best manner, and all outside wood-work except the door and window frames is to be painted in the same tint as the rough-casting, and sanded. All the windows throughout are to have inside shutters. In all other respects the building is to be finished in the same way as similar buildings heretofore described.

84

Sam.ᵈ Sloan Arch.ᵗ

P.S. Duval's Steam lith: Press. Philadᵃ

FRONT ELEVATION.

Sam.ᵈ Sloan Arch.ᵗ

P.S. Duval's Steam lith: Press. Philadᵃ

ITALIAN VILLA.

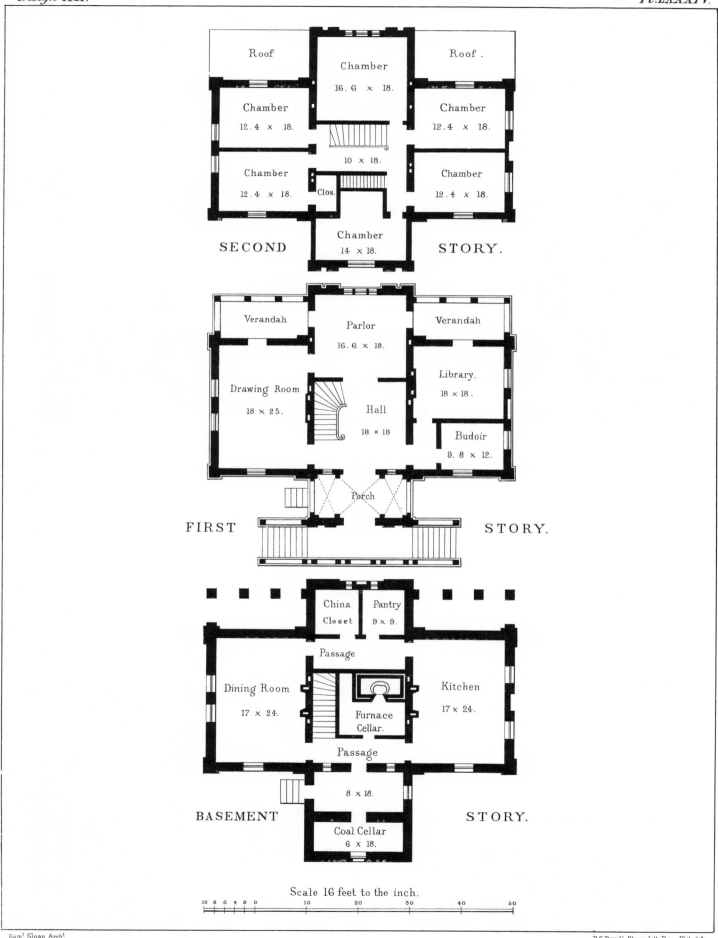

Roof

Chamber
16. 6 × 18.

Roof .

Chamber
12. 4 × 18.

Chamber
12. 4 × 18.

10 × 18.

Chamber
12. 4 × 18.

Clos.

Chamber
12. 4 × 18.

SECOND

Chamber
14 × 18.

STORY.

Verandah

Parlor
16. 6 × 18.

Verandah

Drawing Room
18 × 25.

Hall
18 × 18

Library.
18 × 18 .

Budoir
9. 8 × 12.

FIRST

Porch

STORY.

China
Closet

Pantry
9 × 9.

Passage

Dining Room
17 × 24.

Furnace
Cellar.

Kitchen
17 × 24.

Passage

8 × 18.

BASEMENT

STORY.

Coal Cellar
6 × 18.

Scale 16 feet to the inch.

10 8 6 4 2 0   10   20   30   40   50

Sam! Sloan Arch!.   P.S.Duval's Steam Lith.Press Philad.ª

GROUND PLANS.

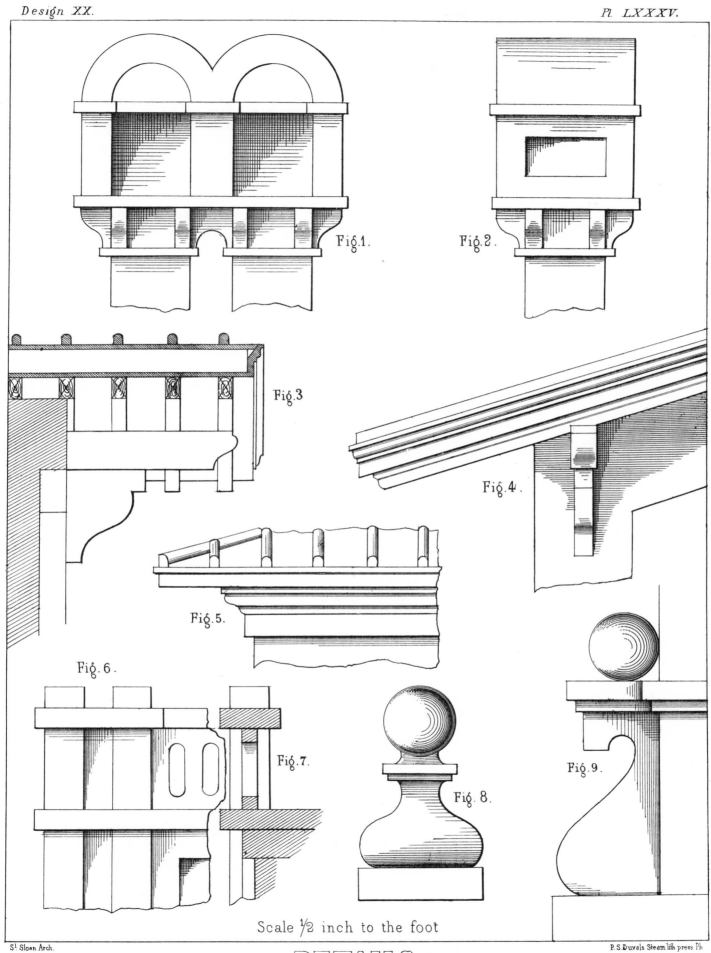

Fig. 1.

Fig. 2.

Fig. 3

Fig. 4.

Fig. 5.

Fig. 6.

Fig. 7.

Fig. 8.

Fig. 9.

Scale ½ inch to the foot

DETAILS.

S.ᵗ Sloan Arch.

P. S. Duvals Steam lith press Ph

MASONRY.

THE next point to which our attention must be directed, in reviewing the process of building, is the wall. It may be constructed of various materials, as stone, brick, or wood, each of which requires a separate consideration. The masonry of the ancients is yet unsurpassed. It is superior to that of modern times, not only in its exquisite finish, but also in strength and solidity, and in the gigantic size of its parts. We are accustomed to consider our age as far beyond any preceding one in the possession and use of mechanical power. Perhaps it is so; but the fact only increases our wonder when examining ancient works, and forces us into the belief that they were executed by an unheard of amount of toil, patience and expense. In old Egyptian architecture, particularly, it is not uncommon to find masonry composed of stones from twenty-five to thirty feet long, elevated to great heights, and evidently brought from great distances. In the great temple at Baalbec, built by the Romans, "about twenty feet from the ground, there are three stones, which alone occupy one hundred and eighty-two feet nine inches in length, by about twelve feet thick; two are sixty feet, and the third sixty-two feet nine inches in length." There are other great works which also seem to rival the might of Nature, and will, in all probability, stand until some convulsion occurs great enough to level the mountains. The masonry of the Egyptians was often highly finished, but the Greeks and Romans bear off the palm in this. Their walls were always elegant, the surface joints fitting with the utmost nicety, and the facings often being ornamented with bas reliefs

There were various methods which the ancients adopted in putting their masonry together, and those in present use are quite similar. Vitruvius designates them as the "opus incertum," or rubble work, the "isodomum," in which the courses were of equal heights, the "pseudisodomum," in which the heights were unequal, and the "emplectum," or ashlar-work. There was, besides, the "opus reticulatum," so called from its network appearance, the joints running diagonally, and the stones often having the shape of a rhombus or lozenge. This is usually considered a handsome wall, but is certainly weak, depending entirely on the cohesion of the mortar, and hence is undesirable.

The material used by the Greeks and Romans was principally marble, the best of which abounds in that part of the continent, and all their heaviest works were executed without mortar, as was also the case with the Egyptians. The mere weight of the masonry was sufficient to give it stability, but sometimes joggles and bonds of bronze were used. The common thickness of Grecian walls was seven or eight feet, but those of the Acropolis of Pharsalia are fifteen feet and a half thick. Sometimes each course was a single row of blocks, but where the walls were of great thickness, as the Acropolis, the "emplectron" was used. Roman walls were generally lighter.

The masonry of the mediæval architects differed essentially from that which preceded it. They used almost universally granite or sandstone, and latterly built their walls quite light. Breadth is a characteristic of classical architecture, and height of mediæval architecture. During the age of the latter there seem to have been no powerful engines for raising weights, for in one building, foundation stones which "would resist the efforts of many men to lift," were believed to have been placed by a miracle. All the stones were generally such as one or two men could carry up a scaffold; and having discarded the heavy cornice, they were thus enabled to attain towering heights. The Normans, however, built very thick walls, filling the space between the outer and inner courses with rubble, rag masonry, or concrete. In the earlier times, the whole was of rubble or rag masonry, often, if not always, plastered without and within. The mediæval architects never gave so high a finish to their masonry and sculptured work as the Greeks and Romans, probably only because their style did not require, nor their material admit of it; but never, before nor since, has constructive masonry attained such perfection. The practice of the pointed arch belonged exclusively to the fraternity of freemasons, and the rules and principles which governed their labor were kept secret, and have been lost to them and to us. Even with the specimens before our eyes we are unable to fathom many of these principles, so that one of the greatest of modern architects, when viewing the arches, vaulting and tracery of one of these specimens, remarked that, so far from being able to construct another such, he could not tell even how to lay the first stone.

There are many other remains of ancient masonry scattered over the globe, which are interesting from their size and antiquity. We may instance Armenian masonry, which has joints fitted with the nicest art; the walls at Tiryns and Mycenæ, alluded to by Homer, and Stonehenge, the work of the Druids. In this country remains of ancient and excellent masonry have been found, the origin and object of which are unknown. A description of some of these has been published by the Smithsonian Institution.

The materials used in masonry at the present day may be classified as the granites, the sandstones and the limestones. Granite is an igneous rock, composed of grains of quartz, mica and feldspar, which having been partially fused, give to the mass a granular structure, whence its name. It is found in large quantities, having different degrees of hardness, and the various proportions of its components give it a great variety of color, though most usually it is gray. There is a species of granite termed by the mineralogists syenite, which contains in addition hornblende, and this is found to be the most durable. Granite is the strongest and most lasting material, but it is most suitable for a plain wall, both because of the difficulty in working it, and also because the effect of light and shadow is almost lost where its color is gray. The Quincy and Quarryville granites are perhaps the most celebrated in this country.

Sandstone is a less durable, but a much cheaper material. It is supposed to be an aqueous formation, the sand grains being cemented together by carbonate of lime and oxide of iron. In it also there is a considerable variety of color, and indeed nothing can compare, for rich and highly finished work, with the brown sandstone, such as that obtained from Connecticut and New Jersey. Many sandstones are totally unfit for building, since after a short exposure they begin to decay. The public buildings at Washington are a lamentable instance of this fact.

Magnesian limestone was used in Gothic structures to some extent, and in St. Paul's at London, in all of which buildings the ornaments have until now retained their sharpness. It is believed that those specimens are best in which the quantities of lime and magnesia are most nearly equal. Marble seems best adapted to the classic orders. It is too glaring for a country house, and we may point to Grace church, N. Y., as an expensive instance of its inaptitude to the Gothic style.

There is one material which we wish we could dwell on at length, the serpentine rock, such as is found in Chester county, Pa. Nothing can be better for a certain class of cottages, its greenish hue giving it a rural expression of the most pleasing kind. The walls already built of it promise to last well, and we would recommend it, wherever it can be obtained, as a most excellent material, and more easily worked than any other, since it is soft when first quarried and hardens on exposure.

In constructive masonry mention may be made first of the rag work found in Norman buildings. The stones are flat, not often larger than a brick, and are laid horizontally. If the mortar be good, it makes an excellent wall, but is most useful for filling in. Herring-bone work differs from this in the stones being somewhat larger and laid aslant so that, with pieces of different lengths, we may obtain a smooth upper surface for the succeeding course by giving them different inclinations. The Normans sometimes used this externally for ornament, and it is found also in Roman work, but does not make a very good wall. Rubble or random work, the "incertum" of the Romans, consists in the use of stones irregular in shape and size, just as they come from the quarry, and fitting them together as well as possible in the wall, laying the largest near the foundation. This makes an excellent and handsome wall, especially for Gothic cottages. We have once before mentioned that the strength of this masonry depends greatly upon the quality of the mortar. Care must be taken by the mason to avoid this dependence wherever it is practicable, which he may do by laying the stones as flat as may be consistent with good appearance. Rubble is the cheapest masonry, excepting rag work, and answers excellently for filling in or backing, in which case the flatter the stones are the better.

Many granites split from the quarry in blocks with parallel surfaces, which have the same direction as the laminæ of the mica grains. Thus we are often enabled to obtain it in nearly the most desirable shape without the expense of dressing. A wall of these blocks is the best that can be made of undressed stone, and under the name of coursed work we may include with it masonry of dressed stone. The former is much more rural, and is therefore, as a general thing, better adapted for buildings in the country.

The last kind of masonry we need mention is that usually termed ashlar work. The outer course or facing of the wall is composed of dressed stone, and the backing is of different construction. The most important point in this work is to use quick setting mortar, else the greater number of joints within may cause the wall to lean or crack in setting. It is hardly necessary to add, that in every species of masonry much attention must be given to the bonding. To enter upon this part of the subject would lead us beyond our limits, hence we can merely press its importance. The succeeding article will furnish some suggestions on the matter. The higher branches of the mason's art will be treated of hereafter.

The greatest objection to stone walls for country houses is the dampness to which they are liable. There are several methods which have been adopted to obviate this, the chief of which is to fasten strips to the wall within, to which laths are nailed for plastering. Thus the dampness cannot reach the interior, and the stratum of air between the plaster and the wall renders the apartments more easily warmed. The dampness which arises from the capillarity of the stone or mortar may be prevented by building in the wall near the ground, a course of clay slate, which is nearly impervious; this should be done in all cases. We cannot see why a first coat of asphalted plaster throughout the interior would not completely prevent dampness. Something of the kind must always be adopted, both for the walls and floor of a basement story.

There are many ways of giving variety to the appearance of stone walls which have not been mentioned. For instance, we have seen stone chips laid in all the surface joints and giving a very pretty effect to the exterior. We will not, however, delay longer on the subject, but close with the remark that, to our taste, stone walls are preferable to all others, because of their strength and durability, their naturalness, and their handsome, bold and truthful expression.

A SUBURBAN RESIDENCE.

DESIGN TWENTY-FIRST.

PLATES LXXVI. and LXXXVII. present the front elevation and a perspective view of a three-storied country mansion. Its style is such as to give it the suburban character already referred to, and is equally adapted to an open country, or a park. The building is roofed with tin, and the walls are of brick, stuccoed or rough cast, without pointing.

Plate LXXXVIII. presents the floor plans of this design. There is a cellar under the back-building, having stairs under the private stairway, and also a furnace cellar beneath the hall communicating with the former, and having stairs under the main stairway. The principal division walls are of brick, as high as the floor of the third story. The plan of this story corresponds to that of the second story, main building; the whole thus affording ample accommodation for a family of eight or ten, including the servants.

Plate LXXXIX. is of Details. Fig. 1. Details of the front door and balcony above. Fig. 2. Section of the balcony. Fig. 3. Chimney top and section. Fig. 4. Sill of the second story front window. Fig. 5. Cornice of the back building.

Plate XC. is also of Details. Fig. 1. Cornice and third story front window. Fig. 2. Profile of the bracket. Fig. 3. Ornament on the pediment. Fig. 4. Details of the verandahs. Fig. 5. First story front window. Fig. 6. Section of the same.

Sam.ˡ Sloan Arch.ᵗ   P.S. Duval & Co Steam lith.press.Ph.

FRONT ELEVATION.

Sam.ˡ Sloan Arch.ᵗ   P.S. Duval's & Co Steam lith.press.Ph.

A SUBURBAN RESIDENCE.

Pl. LXXXVIII.

Design XXI.

SECOND FLOOR.

Roof

Chamber
15 × 16.

Chamber
15 × 16

Roof

Chamber
18 × 19

Bath R
7 × 9

Hall
9 × 36,5

Balcony

Chamber
16 × 18.

Chamber
14 × 16

Roof

PRINCIPAL FLOOR.

Verandah

Laundry
11 × 18

Kitchen
18 × 19

Drawing Room
16 × 16

16 × 16

Hall
9 × 27

Vestibule
9 × 9.5

Dining Room
16 × 19.5

Office
14 × 16

Verandah

GROUND PLANS.

Scale 16 feet to the inch.

50 40 30 20 10 5 4 3 2 1 0

Fig. 1.

Fig. 2.

Fig. 3.

Fig. 5.

Fig. 4.

Scale ½ inch to the foot.

Sam¹ Sloan Arch¹   P. S. Duval & Co's Steam lith Press Philad ª

DETAILS.

Fig. 1.

Fig. 2.

Fig. 3.

Fig. 4.

Fig. 5.

Fig. 6.

Scale ½ inch to the foot.

Sam.¹ Sloan Arch.ᵗ

P. S. Duval & Co's Steam lith. Press, Philad.ᵃ

DETAILS.

BRICK WORK.

UR every day acquaintance with the art of brick-making makes us familiar to a great extent, with its details. There is scarcely a member of the public, who has not at some time, if not often, seen the whole process, which, from its simplicity, is intelligible to any mind. It is almost always conducted in the open air, where every casual passer-by may inspect each operation, and the interest which all, at some period of life, have in building, also tends to excite curiosity. Nevertheless, however simple the grosser points may seem, the art is still capable of much improvement, and to produce our best bricks, a considerable degree of skill is requisite, resulting from care and long experience.

Good bricks must be sound and hard; they must be uniform in size, shape and color; and the manufacture must be so managed, that they may not warp or be otherwise injured. Their hardness, soundness, and uniformity of color depends mostly on the quality of the clay used. Alumina is the principal ingredient in all brick earth, but the purest clay, the great mass of which consists of this substance, will shrink and crack in drying, and warp in firing. To obviate this result, sand is mixed with the clay when it does not already exist in sufficient quantity. When these two substances alone, exist together, we have a fire clay suitable for making crucibles, glass-house pots, furnace-bricks, and like articles. From the expensiveness of these we may justly infer the difficulty of obtaining the compound; and it is the truth, that there is nearly always a greater or less amount of foreign matter intermingled. The presence of lime which acts as a flux often renders the clay useless, because of its liability to fusion. If oxide of iron be present, it also renders the clay fusible at a furnace heat, if the silica and alumina are in nearly equal proportion; hence, as oxide of iron almost always exists, care must be taken to have a considerably less quantity of sand than clay. It is this oxide of iron which gives the red color to nearly all our building bricks, and the white ones, which are sometimes used for filling in, are comparatively free from it and are generally much harder, though sometimes this absence of color results from over-burning.

Brick clay must be thoroughly worked in a pug mill before moulding, to increase its tenacity and secure a uniform mixture of its ingredients. When moulded, the bricks must be dried gradually, and uniformly, and the heat of the kiln must be well regulated into a slow and steady increase and decrease of intensity, or the bricks will crack and warp. "Sound and well burnt bricks are of a clear and steady color, and when struck together, will ring with a clear metallic sound. Deficiency in either of these points indicates inferiority."

The pressed bricks which give the smooth and finished appearance to our city fronts, are made by machinery and burnt in kilns built for the purpose, and not in the ordinary open stack. There has been no machine as yet invented that will make bricks so cheap as the old manual plan, which has been practised from time immemorial. It is one of those arts which has been nearly stationary ever since the time of the flood, and is the first of the series that ends in the manufacture of fine porcelain.

The shape of bricks is of considerable importance. That in present universal use, the Flemish brick, is perhaps, the best. There have been many attempts to improve it by giving such a shape as will facilitate the bonding, and thereby add security to the wall, but as yet none other has been generally adopted. In England hollow bricks are used to some extent, and their advantages are such as would warrant introduction into this country. They are at least one-third lighter than the ordinary bricks, and the difference of strength is small. Their size and shape is the same as the ordinary Flemish brick, but they differ in having a hole from end to end, which gives the qualities of a tube. As the size of bricks is unimportant so that they be thoroughly burnt, and easily handled, this latter kind might be made much larger, and would then present a better appearance in the wall. We are not satisfied, however, that their resistance to a crushing force is sufficient; it certainly cannot equal that of the ordinary bricks; still they might be used with advantage over lintels.

Walls are built with much less thickness now than formerly, and in fact a false economy so influences our builders, that as a general thing, they are made much too thin. They are named according to the number of bricks used in the breadth of each course; thus we have a wall one brick thick, a brick and a half, two bricks, and so on; corresponding respectively to an eight inch, a twelve inch, and a sixteen inch wall. They are best made heavy at the base, and carried up lighter and lighter, the diminution occurring at each tier of joists. Partition walls seldom need be made more than one brick thick, unless they have to support heavy weights, such as girders. Hollow walls are coming into very general use, especially for country mansions, and are certainly a great improvement. They are much lighter than ordinary walls, requiring only about one-third the number of bricks, and are sufficiently strong. They prevent dampness, completely, and render the building more easily warmed. To describe the various methods of constructing them, would require considerable space and are generally understood by bricklayers; we therefore merely recommend them in all cases where they are practicable.

In speaking of bonding we may premise that those bricks laid lengthwise in the wall are called stretchers, and those laid across are called headers. For solid walls there are two principal kinds of bonding, the Flemish and the English. In the Flemish bond the stretchers and headers alternate in each course, and the headers in the succeeding course are laid on the middle of the stretchers in the course below. In the English bond the courses are alternately of headers and stretchers, and so arranged as to break joints throughout. It is generally conceded that the Flemish bond is the most agreeable to the eye, and nearly all of our old brick buildings are thus built, but there is no doubt at the same time, that the English bond makes much the strongest wall, and hence, wherever a wall is to be rough-cast, this bond should always be adopted.   It is more necessary to urge this because of late years, much of the strength of walls has been sacrificed to appearance.   Brick facings are now made almost entirely of stretchers, every seventh or tenth course being of headers, and sometimes there are no headers in the face of the wall whatever.   This is a bad practice, but is somewhat compensated by the use of iron strap bonding, which consists in laying pieces of hoop iron in the mortar joints and gives effectual security.   We must, however, reprobate the entire use of stretchers on the face of the wall, and cannot admit the plea of appearance, for to one acquainted with the subject, and he only can properly judge, it carries with it a sense of insecurity utterly inconsistent with agreeable appearance.

Another point must be attended to in laying bricks, which is not to carry up one portion of a wall more rapidly than another, otherwise, owing to an inequality of settlement, it will inevitably sustain fractures. Again, if the building be conducted in very dry weather, the bricks should be wetted, as they are laid, or the moisture of the mortar will be rapidly absorbed by them before it can properly adhere.

The practice of introducing concealed arches for the purpose of distributing the weight more equally, is a good one, when exercised with judgment.   Inverted arches may be turned from pier to pier beneath openings, but care must be taken that the corner be a sufficient abutment, or in settling it may be pushed outwards below.   Over long lintels, arches are often turned to advantage, and the only difficulty in their free use, is owing to their unyielding nature, which may create an inequality of settlement, and thus most certainly cause fractures.

Bricks are frequently and advantageously used for backing in ashlar work, but it requires a skillful workman to build a secure wall of this character.   We consider too, this mode of building at variance with good taste, for it is a deception, and the attempt to deceive is altogether repugnant to feelings of pleasure which might otherwise arise.   Sun-dried bricks are used occasionally for filling in a brick wall, and sometimes the entire wall is built of them, but only when economy is of primary importance.

Modern architects have for a long time shown a great disrespect for brick walls; why, it is difficult to determine.   The public have acted very differently, and urged by motives of economy, have built the principal part of our cities and towns of this cheap and durable material.   Architects have been compelled to acquiesce, but always exhibit a great desire to hide the bricks with plaster, and have not, till very lately, made any attempts to give architectural effect to this legitimate and excellent material.   Chiefly on account of its prevailing color, we do not think brick work well adapted to country houses, but for city architecture it is entirely proper, and recent attempts show conclusively, that it is susceptible of a high degree of embellishment peculiar to itself.   There is no doubt but the prejudice must give way.

No art is more ancient than brick-making, if we except the art of Tubal Cain.   The tower of Babel, so much of it as was built, was of bricks, and there are some very curious records of the art as practiced by Egypt.   Beside the scripture account, we have some of their characteristic pictures, which exhibit the whole process, both for burnt and unburnt bricks, and evidently tend to confirm that account.   From them, the art spread throughout the East, and was practised to some extent by the Grecians.   From these the Romans received it and carried it to a perfection never since attained.   The shape of their bricks generally differs from ours.   They were seldom more than an inch and a half thick, and varied in size, the smallest being about seven inches square.   Many specimens of Roman brick work are yet extant, showing at once the excellence of the work and the durability of the material, though they chiefly owe their continued existence to the quality of the mortar.   Generally the wall was stuccoed, but there are some ornamental walls of bricks beautifully designed and finished.   From Italy the art spread northward, and was carried by the Romans themselves into Britain.   In some Gothic structures bricks were used, and they are found in old Saxon buildings which are believed to have been erected either during or immediately succeeding the presence of Roman power.   There is no doubt but that the peculiarities of the Norman style originated in the use of bricks.   Their characteristic mouldings, the zig-zag, the alternate billet, the lozenge and others, have all been found constructed of bricks.   Since then bricks have been adopted only for plain walls, except in some cases where they were rudely sculptured after being laid, but we have, as before intimated, reason to hope that this branch of practical architecture will soon be greatly improved.

A COTTAGE.

DESIGN TWENTY-SECOND.

Plates XCI. and XCII. exhibit the front and side elevations of a comparatively plain country dwelling whose unostentatious simple appearance as well as internal arrangements, give it every requisite for a gentleman's farm house.   The roof is designed to be slate and the walls brick or stone, rough cast without pointing.

Plate XCIII. comprises the ground plans.   There should be a cellar beneath the whole building, having stairs under the private stairway, and also an outside cellar door and stairs in the rear.   The accommodations are sufficient for a family of six or eight persons, and the cost of the building would be about $3800.00.

Plate XCIV. is of Details.   Fig. 1. Drip ornament of the gable eaves.   Fig. 2. Oriel window.   Fig. 3. Section of the same. Fig. 4.   Hood mould of the front gable first-story window.   Fig. 5. Details of the verandah.   Fig. 6.   Section of the verandah.

SUMMER HOUSES.

DESIGN TWENTY-THIRD.

On plate XCV. will be found a design for four summer houses, two in the Oriental style, and well adapted to the Villa, design XVIII.   It is needless to remark upon them further as they speak for themselves.

Sam.¹ Sloan. Arch.¹

P.S. Duval's & Co Steam lith press. Ph.

FRONT ELEVATION.

Sam.¹ Sloan. Arch.¹

P.S. Duval's & Co Steam lith; press. Phil.

A COTTAGE.

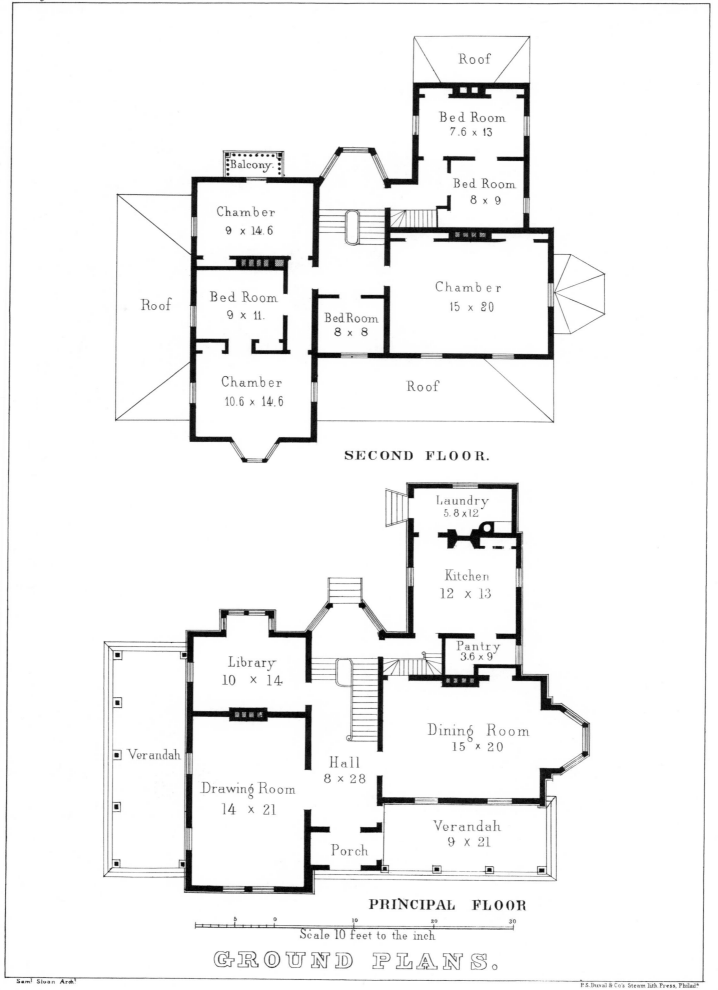

Roof

Bed Room
7.6 × 13

Balcony.

Bed Room
8 × 9

Chamber
9 × 14.6

Roof

Bed Room
9 × 11.

Chamber
15 × 20

Bed Room
8 × 8

Chamber
10.6 × 14.6

Roof

SECOND FLOOR.

Laundry
5.8 × 12

Kitchen
12 × 13

Library
10 × 14

Pantry
3.6 × 9

Verandah

Dining Room
15 × 20

Hall
8 × 28

Drawing Room
14 × 21

Verandah
9 × 21

Porch

PRINCIPAL FLOOR

5   0   10   20   30

Scale 10 feet to the inch

GROUND PLANS.

Saml Sloan Arch^t   P. S. Duval & Co's Steam lith. Press, Philad^a.

Fig. 4.

Fig. 1.

Fig. 6.

Fig. 2.

Fig. 5.

Fig. 3.

Scale ½ inch to the foot

Sam! Sloan Arch!

P.S. Duval & Son Steam lith Press Philad!

DETAILS.

Scale 4 feet to the inch

Sam! Sloan Arch!

P. S. Duval & Co's Steam lith Press Philad!

SUMMER HOUSES.

TIMBER.

HO has not looked upon the mighty forests of America with admiration? Mighty not only in their extent and density, but in the greatness of each member. Admirable too in their almost infinite variety of flowering and fruit bearing exogens bounded by the pines of the North and the palms of the South. In Europe, the teeming population have long been thinning the noble ranks of trees, but here, though they have shrunk from the approach of civilization like frost-work from the breath, yet their vast extent is undiminished, and they still retain their primitive luxuriance and grandeur. The rapid and monstrous growth of our necessities has produced a proportionate increase in the demand on these sons of the soil. We lose in every forest felled, a volume of eloquence and beauty. What landscape is complete without majestic woods, and what more elevates the thought than to contemplate such handiwork of Nature? Touched with their superior power to humble yet expand the soul, our lyric poet says :—

> "The groves were God's first temples. Ere man learned
> To hew the shaft, and lay the architrave,
> And spread the roof above them,—ere he framed
> The lofty vault to gather and roll back
> The sound of anthems,—in the darkling wood,
> Amidst the cool and silence, he knelt down
> And offered to the Mightiest solemn thanks
> And supplication."

We can never see Nature's architecture destroyed without feeling a regret. When the axe with resounding stroke descends again and again on the sturdy trunk, and the noble tree with its wide spreading top of branches and leaves, with all its vivified machinery for growth and reproduction, sways, reels, and falls in crashing thunder down, we are forced to relieve our painful impression by considering the necessity of the act, but still feel as if evil has been done that good may come. A healthy mind abhors needless destruction of life, of beauty, of utility, or the undoing of whatever cannot be at once identically restored. These thoughts may seem somewhat irrelevant to the practical subject in hand, but there have been few protesting voices raised against the wanton waste of our trees. Viewing these immense forests at a glance, one would be inclined to laugh at the idea of their exhaustion, but it must be remembered, that the greater portion of them is useless for timber, and that only a small

(93)

portion of the valuable part is accessible.   Still we do not contemplate exhaustion, but an advanced cost may readily be conceived that will render it impossible for every poor man to have a home.   The inroads upon our invaluable live oak have already so far diminished its quantity that the Government has found it necessary to interfere and encourage the planting of acorns, in order to prevent its entire extinction.   The Cinchona nitida of South America, which species furnished much the best bark of commerce described in the Materia Medica, has become totally extinct, because of this reckless treatment.   No power, however, can induce a careful and judicious management of our forests, for our countrymen in their indivi- dual action, always will show a total disregard for posterity so long as families are unsettled, and estates so liable to disruption.   In Europe, the laws of primogeniture have done much to preserve the forests and encourage the cultivation of timber, but we are happy, nevertheless, in the entire absence of this system.

It has already been remarked that only a small part of our great forests can be used for timber.   An insufficiency of size or an inferior quality of wood, will render any species useless.   The most important of those not thus disqualified, are here briefly described.

Forests of Pine, Spruce and the other species belonging to the same family (*Coniferæ*) abound in every section of the United States, and furnish by far the greatest amount of timber.   Of these, the pine exists in much the largest quantity, and together they more than double in extent all other useful trees.   The general qualities of the wood which they furnish are very similar, and owing to its abundance, the timber can generally be obtained at a much less rate than any other material.   The ease with which it is worked, and its lightness, tend much to lessen this cost and enhance its value.   The grain is smooth and firm, and the body of the tree is quite free from knots, the branches putting forth only near the extreme top.   The great length of the trunk from this point to the ground, its strength, lightness and durability, in which last it at least equals many of the oaks, form a combination of good qualities possessed by none other.   They fit it admi- rably for building, and therefore it is used in vast quantity.   Indeed, except in cities where brick and stone are required, about nine-tenths of our buildings are constructed entirely of it, and even where other material is used for the wall, the rafters, girders, joists, floors and dressings of every description, are almost always of these woods.   We may mention that the value of the trees, especially the pine extends much further. Immense quantities are used in this country for ship-building, and the exportation of the timber for this and other purposes forms a most important branch of our commerce.   There are many other uses which render these trees invaluable.   From a species of pine all the resin is obtained which furnishes the important products, spirits of turpentine, rosin, tar, and pitch; and besides, the wood is much prized as fuel either when reduced to charcoal, or by using the knots and other highly resinous parts wherever much flame is required, as in brickmaking, or on steamboats.

There are many species of pine, but only a few serve the purpose of the carpenter and joiner; the Southern Yellow or Pitch pine (*Pinus palustris*) being in this respect, perhaps, as well as in others, the most important.   It first occurs in the southern part of Virginia, and from thence extends along the entire coast of the ocean and gulf, not reaching inland more than a hundred and fifty miles.   It is termed at the North the Southern Carolina, or red pine, and at the South, the yellow or pitch pine, but the proper name, according to Michaux, probably our best authority, is the long leaved pine, the length of the leaves being about a foot, which characterizes the species; we have adopted the other name, however, because it makes more special reference to the qualities of the timber.   This tree attains the height of eighty feet, and often is from sixteen to eighteen inches in diameter, for two-thirds of that distance, the foliage in the larger trees not occurring within sixty feet of the base.   It has, however, from an inch and a half to two inches of useless sap-wood, which is the newly formed wood next the bark.   In deep and dry, though not rich mould, this tree attains its greatest size, but on the sea coast, where a shallow soil overlays sand, it is smaller, more branching, and contains a greater amount of resin.   In the first case it is called the yellow pine, and in the latter, the pitch pine.   Regarding its resin alone, for this tree yields very nearly the whole of that article in trade, it is the most important of the species, but at the same time its wood is the firmest and most durable of all the pines.   On this account preference is given to it before any other in naval architecture, especially the variety called red pine, the wood of which acquires that hue from the nature of the soil.   The carpenters of the North have it in great demand for all parts of the building, especially for floors and step-boards, since it suffers comparatively little in wear, and but for its higher price they would use it exclusively.   At the South, within its localities, the wood work of all buildings is constructed entirely of this material.   The remarkable durability of the wood results chiefly from its pores being filled with resin, and it is besides strong, firm, smooth, even grained, and under varnish, has a rich yellow appearance.   These qualities would seem to fit it admirably for the joiner, and the only objections are, its liability to shrink both longitudinally and laterally, especially in the soft grain; and the effect of the summer heat in causing the resin to exude and discolor the paint.   The white pine (*P. strobus*) is next in importance, and is more extensively used in this region than any other.   The tree is the largest of the species, excepting the Rocky Mountain pine, for it sometimes reaches the height of a hundred and eighty feet by six in diameter, and contains only about a half inch of sap-wood.   Hence boards can be obtained from it of great length and width, but owing to the rapid diminution of the trunk towards the top, it does not furnish timber as large in proportion to its size as other species.   It is found in immense quantities from New York northward throughout the Canadas, and also along the Allegheny mountains.   It is still quite abundant, though disappearing fast, on the head waters of the Delaware, whence it is floated to supply the towns on the shore.   Much is brought down the Susquehannah, and it is also floated down the Ohio and Mississippi, even as far as New Orleans.   Large quantities are exported from Maine and the shores of Lake Champlain. The qualities and uses of the wood are too familiar to require much detail.   It is very durable when well protected from the weather, light, free from knots, smooth, and more easily worked than any other wood, and hence, although liable to swell with moisture, is a favorite with the carver and joiner.   In carpentry it should not be used extensively, not being very strong, but for joinery it is excellent, when not exposed to humidity, though owing to its softness and weakness, a slight blow is often sufficient to destroy or deface the best work. This tree is very valuable in furnishing masts, yards and other parts of vessels. Large quantities are used for packing boxes and a thousand other things, in which a light and easily worked material is required. The true Yellow pine (*P. mitis*) is more valuable than any other in the Middle States, where it chiefly abounds. It is also called the yellow spruce, and in Georgia, the short leaved pine. It has a diminishing trunk fifty or sixty feet in height, with a diameter of fifteen or eighteen inches, but at the South it grows much larger though more sparingly. The sap wood, which speedily decays, is about two or two and a half inches in depth. A vast quantity of the timber is used in the dock-yards of the Middle States for all parts of the ship, and it is exported to some extent. We quote Michaux :—" The heart is fine grained and moderately resinous being compact without great weight. Long experience has proved its excellence and durability. In the northern Middle States and Virginia, nine-tenths of the houses are built entirely of wood, and the floors, the casings of the doors and wainscots, the sashes of the windows, etc., are made of this species as more solid and durable than any other indigenous wood." This last was true when written, but we may regret that its place with the joiner is now so much occupied by the cheaper and softer, although in itself excellent white pine. Poor soils furnish a fine, smooth, and compact wood that cannot be surpassed. For joists, girders, and all heavy framing, it is next in value to the long leaved or southern yellow pine, and in this region is used very extensively for these parts of the building. There is another species occurring principally in the Atlantic States, which deserves mention, this is the Pitch pine (*P. rigida.*) It grows to some extent throughout the United States in meagre soil, and abounds on the Allegheny mountains in Pennsylvania and Virginia. The height of the tree is about thirty-five or forty feet by twelve or fifteen inches in diameter, but in swamps it grows much larger; the wood in the latter case, however, being nearly all sap, is therefore useless. The better sort have numerous branches, the timber is knotty but compact, heavy, full of resin, and resists rot better than any other, excepting the southern pitch pine. The Red Canadian pine (*P. rubra*) receives its name from the clear red color of the bark, and is widely distributed throughout the Canadas and Maine. The tree is quite large, and yields broad, heavy, resinous, compact, and durable planks, fifty feet long, which are chiefly used in ship-building, and large quantities are exported for this purpose.

There are several other genera of this family which may be mentioned collectively; the first of these, is the Spruce, (*Abies,*) the same as the fir in Europe, which is distinguished from the pine in classification, by having no sheath around the base of the leaves. The Black or Double spruce, (*A. nigra*) naturally belongs to cold regions, having in this latitude only a stunted growth. The Black Mountain in South Carolina, is covered with it, the dark hue of the leaves having a gloomy appearance. Sometimes it is called red spruce, from the color of the wood. The tree is seventy or eighty feet high by fifteen or twenty inches in diameter, and suffers a regular diminution from the base to the top. The wood is strong, light, and elastic, being tougher than white pine but more liable to crack. It is exported from Maine to most of the northern ports, where it is used for all parts of the frame, and is generally considered much better than hemlock spruce. The Hemlock spruce (*A. Canadensis*) is common from Hudson's bay, southward throughout Vermont, and on the Alleghanies. The tree is seventy or eighty feet high, and has a uniform diameter of six or nine feet for two-thirds of its height. The wood is as durable as any other when guarded, but decays rapidly when exposed. The fibre makes frequent circuits of the stock, the grain is therefore irregular and coarse; the wood is firmer than white pine, gives a better hold to nails, and is esteemed for its rigidity. There is another member of this series, very valuable in the South and South-west, where it abounds, the Cypress (*Taxodium distichum.*) It grows mostly in swamps and marshy ground, and hence is generally difficult of access; nevertheless, all the wooden houses in New Orleans and around, are built of it almost entirely. The wood is lighter, and much more durable than pine; strong, elastic, fine-grained, and possesses the property of long resisting the heat and moisture of that climate. On account of these qualities it is especially esteemed for shingles, and large quantities are exported to the North. They will last, if cut in the winter, forty years. The White Cedar, (*Cupressus thyoides,*) which makes excellent joiner's work, is also highly valued for shingles, being considered in many points much better than the cypress, and therefore commanding a higher price. It is much more durable and secure from worms than white pine, shingles of which will last not more than fifteen or twenty years. The American Larch would be our most valuable tree did it exist in sufficient quantity, inasmuch as it is better in every respect than any pine.

The Oak (*Quercus*) is the only other genus which is comparatively of great importance to us in house-building. For this purpose, it is in some respects inferior to pine, and in others superior. Being less plentiful and less easily worked, it is not so cheap; and this, together with the weight and inferior size of the timber, prevent its exclusive use. There is, however, no other wood so strong, firm, and durable, none which in all respects, repays so well the first cost. It is justly esteemed in the better sort of joinery. A material which may be exposed in fine work, always makes a better and more pleasant impression on the spectator than any paint can give; hence our furniture is so seldom painted, and indeed, the mere fact that the material has cost more, and the work has required more labor and skill, adds to this impression. We have no indigenous wood, unless it be the curled maple, superior in these respects to oak. In all ornamental work it has a beautiful rich appearance, which increases with age. This tree is not valuable in building houses alone. It is of the greatest national importance for ship-building, and thousands are hewn for this purpose every year. But it would be impossible within these limits even to name the almost infinite variety of uses to which it is applied. The different species of oak are widely distributed over the northern temperate zone, to which it is almost exclusively confined.

The European Oak (*Q. robor*) is a species of which unfortunately, we are not possessed, though its eminent qualities render its introduction very desirable, and we need only remark that it surpasses in every respect, all other oaks, unless it be our live oak, which in a few points excels. This species, the Live Oak,

(Q. *virens*,) furnishes the finest timber in the world for strength and durability when not exposed to changes of wet and dry. The tree, however, is not very large, it being difficult to obtain a stick of timber thirty feet long by a foot square, but the irregular growth of its wide spreading top, furnishes many knees for ships, and it is on this account invaluable. It is found from the lower part of Virginia all along the southern coasts in a narrow strip only twenty or twenty-five miles wide, thus seeming to require the sea air. It is this oak that our Government has endeavored to protect from practical annihilation in consequence of large exportation, home consumption, and clearance of lands valuable for cotton; but these and its slow growth, have already produced a great advance in price. Because of this, it is little used in building, although strong, firm, compact, fine-grained, smooth, durable and better in every respect than any other of our oaks. The White Oak, (*Q. alba*,) so called from the light colored bark and wood, is generally considered a variety of the European Oak. This species is at present the most important, and because of its great size, best adapted to building purposes. It is the largest of the genus, often being six feet in diameter, by seventy-five or eighty feet high. It is found in all parts of the United States, but there are only a few localities where it sufficiently abounds to render it of great service. Throughout the Middle States it grows in large quantities, and is used extensively. In ship building it is of the highest national importance, being next in value to the live oak, and the wood is applied to an infinite variety of other purposes. Whenever the price permits, it is much used in the frame work of houses, and is invaluable in such parts of the building as are exposed to alternate moisture and dryness, since it supports these admirably. In joinery it makes excellent work, though somewhat liable to shrink, warp, and crack, and when varnished or polished, has a rich elegant appearance, well adapted for furniture. The wood is strong, neither breaking or splitting easily, hard, fine-grained, and smooth, of the greatest durability, and not very difficult to work. The other oaks are not so important, and may be briefly noted. The Post Oak is abundant south of latitude 40° and is usually considered near akin to the white oak, though its comparatively small size, prevents extensive use. The wood has a finer texture, more strength and durability, but is not so elastic. The Black oak is abundant in the Middle States and southward. The tree is ninety feet high by four in diameter. Its wood is reddish, coarse, and has large empty pores, but is strong and durable, and frequently substituted for white oak, which, in some places, is much more expensive. Immense quantities of the red oak barrel staves are made from this tree, and the bark is valuable in both tanning and dyeing.

There are many other valuable indigenous trees, among which the Black Walnut (*Juglans nigra*) is chief. It is found throughout the United States in considerable quantity. The tree attains the height of sixty or seventy feet by three or four in diameter, and furnishes a wood the sap of which decays quickly, but the heart is sound, durable, light and smooth, though splitting easily. It has a rich, dark hue, which is prized in joinery and for furniture, but the wood being quite soft the least blow cracks the varnish and leaves its mark. There is no wood, however, more beautiful for these purposes than that kind of the Red

SIDE ELEVATION.

Sam! Sloan Arch!.   P.S.Duval & Co's Steam lith.Press.l'hi!.

AN OLD ENGLISH COTTAGE.

Pl. XCVIII.

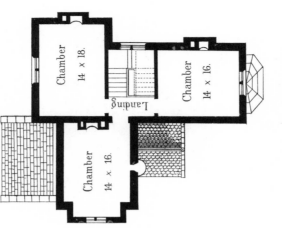

Chamber
14 × 18.

Chamber
14 × 16.

Chamber
14 × 16.

Landing

SECOND FLOOR.

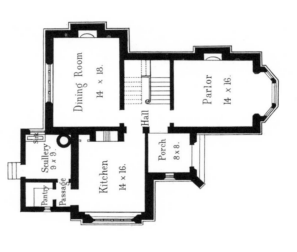

Dining Room
14 × 18.

Scullery
9 × 9.

Pantry

Passage

Kitchen
14 × 16.

Hall

Porch
8 × 8.

Parlor
14 × 16.

FIRST FLOOR.

Scale 16 feet to the inch.

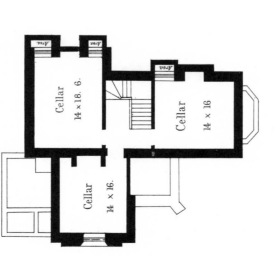

Cellar
14 × 18. 6.

Area

Area

Area

Cellar
14 × 16

Cellar
14 × 16.

CELLAR FLOOR

GROUND PLANS.

Saml Sloan Arch't

P. S. Duval & Co's Steam lith Press Philad.²

Fig. 1.

Fig. 2.

Fig. 3.

Fig. 4.

Fig. 5.

Fig. 6.

Fig. 7.

Fig. 8.

Fig. 9.

Scale ½ inch to the foot.

Sam.ᵗ Sloan Arch.ᵗ   P. S. Duval & Co's Steam lith. Press Philadᵃ.

DETAILS.

Fig. 1.

Fig. 2.

Fig. 3.

Fig. 4.

Scale ½ inch to the foot.

Sam.ᵗ Sloan Arch.ᵗ   P.S.Duval & Co's Steam lith.Press Philadᵃ.

DETAILS.

Flowering Maple which has the curled grain; but owing to the difficulty with which it is worked the Joiner uses it little. The Tulip Poplar, (*Liriodendron tulipifera,*) found every where, is a large tree one hundred feet high and four or five in diameter. The difference in the color of the wood, which is sometimes yellow and sometimes white, results from the soil; the yellow wood is best. It is fine-grained, compact, light, strong, stiff, easily wrought, polishes and takes paint well, but is very liable to shrink and warp. In the West the timber is much used for heavy framing, but is not so durable as other woods mentioned. The Locust is an excellent wood for sleepers, and also the Chestnut, either of which will out-last oak. Mahogany is a native of the West India Isles and the Bay of Honduras. The West India or Spanish Mahogany is most esteemed, and is excellent in joinery of every kind.

We have thus touched upon the most important timber trees of the United States, and refer for further accounts to the Silva Americana, by Michaux, to which we are indebted for many facts not obtained by personal observation. The general subject, Timber, will be continued in the next essay.

AN OLD ENGLISH COTTAGE.
DESIGN TWENTY-FOURTH.

THERE are characteristics about the Gothic cottages of England which entitle them to a rank separate from all others. We do not refer to those erected during the middle ages, but to those which sprang up in a thousand rural spots, suggested by returning good taste, after the mania for Renaissance had somewhat subsided. A cottage of this class comprised the several peculiarities which distinguished the different stages of older Gothic work, sometimes occurring in strong contrast, the whole being fashioned according to the fanciful wish or taste of the builder. These now form marked features in very many of the most beautiful landscapes of England which are unsurpassed in the world for their quiet rural effect. There is no style, perhaps, which better accords with a scene of meadows, streams, and silent woods, variegating a gently undulating surface. There are few such buildings in our land, and though we despise a servile imitation, yet we can but heartily wish that our countrymen would exercise some taste in locating as well as building their houses, and not place, as is often the case, a ghastly Roman palace in a quiet valley, beside a running stream.

We have endeavored to present a design, the side and front elevations of which occur on Plates XCVI. and XCVII. somewhat in the character of those mentioned above. Its decorative points need no mention. The walls are of stone rubble work, having rude quoins on all the corners. The roof is of slate, and the chimney tops of terra cotta ware which can be obtained of any desirable shape or size. The roof of the bay window should properly be of flag-stone.

The Ground Plans, Plate XCVIII. exhibit accommodations for a family of four or five, there being three chambers on the upper floor of ample size. The first floor contains the parlor, dining room and kitchen, with the pantry and scullery attached. The hall is lighted by the window opposite the landing in the second story. There is a fire-place in each apartment. Throughout the base of the building there is a cellar, also exhibited on this plate, having stairs beneath the main stairway.

Plate XCIX. exhibits the Details of the front elevation. Fig. 1, is the cornice and bracket. Fig. 2, a section of the same showing the concealed gutter. Fig. 3, base of the window over the front porch. Fig. 4, front elevation of the porch. Fig. 5, section of the same. Fig. 6, window of the front gable. Fig. 7, section of the same. Fig. 8, front of the bay window. Fig. 9, section of the bay window.

Plate C. consists of the Details of the side elevation. Figs. 1 and 2, are chimney cans. Fig. 3, cornice and gable ornaments, (those of the front elevation are similar.) Fig. 4, gable window.

AN ORNAMENTED COTTAGE.

DESIGN TWENTY-FIFTH.

On Plate CI. is represented a Gothic front applicable to this design. It could not strictly be termed in this case a Gothic building, but by the term we only intend that the principal features are taken from the Gothic style. The walls are of brick or stone, rough cast without pointing. The roof is of slate, and the chimney stacks are of brick, also rough cast. The ornamented front below Plate CII. adapted to the same ground plan, is more in the bracketted style, and a tin roof is substituted for the slate. In this case the angles of the second story rooms are not cut off by the roof, the cornice being more elevated than in the other front.

Plate CIII. presents the Ground Plans of the design. On the second floor are four large chambers and a bed room, furnishing ample room for a family of five or six persons exclusive of the servants. On the first floor if the size of the family required it, the dining room might be used as a back parlor or sitting room, the present kitchen as a dining-room, and the laundry, being removed to an out house, might be used as a kitchen. The hall is to receive additional light by a window in the roof immediately over the well of the stairs. Beneath these stairs is a flight descending to the cellar.

Plate CIV. exhibits the Details of the Gothic front. Fig. 1, chimney stack. Fig. 2, base of the same. Fig. 3, details of the porch. Fig. 4, front door. Fig. 5, cornice and section of the bay-window. Fig. 6, section of the bay-window. Fig. 7, cornice, etc. of the gables. Fig. 8, gable window. Fig. 9, section of the window.

Plate CV. shows the details of the ornamented front. Fig. 1, chimney stack. Fig. 2, 3, and 4, details of the porch. Fig. 5, front balcony, cornice and finial. Fig. 6, section of the same through a, b, showing the bracket. Fig. 7, front window. Fig. 8, base and finish of the bay window.

Sam!. Sloan Arch!.

P.S.Duval & Co's Steam lith.Press,Phil?.

A GOTHIC FRONT.

Sam!. Sloan Arch!.

P.S.Duval & Co's Steam lith.Press,Philad?.

AN ORNAMENTED COTTAGE.

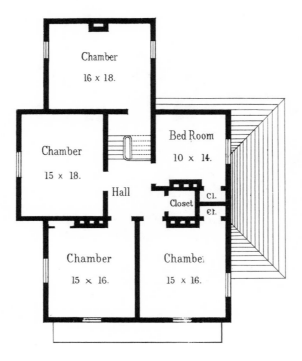

SECOND FLOOR.

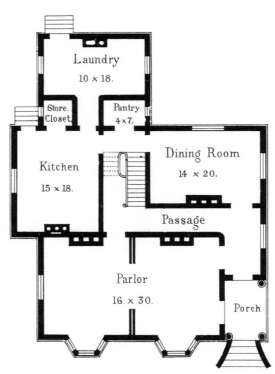

FIRST FLOOR.

Scale 12 feet to the inch.

GROUND PLANS.

Sam.ᵗ Sloan Arch   P.S.Duval & Co.ˢ Steam lith.Press Philad.ᵃ

Fig. 1.

Fig. 2.

Fig. 3.

Fig. 4.

Fig. 5.

Fig. 6.

Fig. 7.

Fig. 8.

Fig. 9.

Scale ½ inch to the foot.

Sam. Sloan Arch.   P.S. Duval & Co's Steam lith. Press Philad.

DETAILS.

Fig. 1.

Fig. 2.

Fig. 3.

Fig. 4.

Fig. 5.

Fig. 6.

Fig. 7.

Fig. 8.

Scale ½ inch to the foot.

Sam.ˡ Sloan Arch.ᵗ   P. S. Duval & Co's Steam lith. Press Philad.ᵃ

DETAILS.

A COUNTRY RESIDENCE.

DESIGN TWENTY-SIXTH.

THERE is no part of the world more beautifully diversified than our own country. It possesses every conceivable variety of scenery formed of mountains, rocks, hills and valleys, of undulating land and plains, of rivers, brooks and groves spread in endless combinations, beneath the cool grey skies of the North, and the warm sunshine of the South. The artist has here no want of studies, and it would be difficult indeed for him to imagine and depict a landscape, whose prototype might not somewhere be found in this vast magazine of natural beauties. To an architect also this affords especial delight, for when called upon to exercise his art in adding a new feature to the scene, he has only to look upon it with an eye that appreciates its excellencies and is at once enabled, as if by inspiration, to design that which will become the centre, irradiating life over the landscape, and receiving from it in return a full measure of nature's softening influence. True art and nature always blend in harmony. There may be contrast, but not discord. To produce this perfect mingling requires a high cast of intellect and sensitiveness seldom found, and hence successful attempts are so rare. This, however, should not deter others from making the effort, for if the highest point is not easily attained, we may approach it in a greater or less degree. It is to be regretted that the many natural advantages which our country affords are not more frequently made use of. We often see buildings designed and placed in utter disregard of the scenery, and sometimes an endeavor is made to force nature into a sort of accordance by terraces, embankments, altering the direction of streams, and other artificial arrangements. These things are repugnant to a refined taste, and it is far less offensive to see an unsuccessful effort to mingle with her charms.

There are other points, however, of greater importance perhaps than these. The comfort and convenience of a household should never be sacrificed to any other object. We love to see enthusiasm for art, but when it sacrifices these points, it steps from its true basis, and is no longer praiseworthy. Few persons are aware how much those essentials to a good dwelling, comfort and convenience, depend upon its locality, and how much may be added to them by laying hold of natural advantages. We have environed our last design in this volume by a landscape intended to illustrate a few of these points. Plate CVI. presents the scene. The building is supposed to face nearly south, in which position its three principal sides receive the sun light, the front being enlivened by it all the day. It is protected in the rear from the cold winds of the north-west and chilling storms of the north-east by a range of hills. These are also supposed to furnish the mansions and gardens with water, which may be easily so collected from the springs into pipes as to play in fountains and be carried into the highest apartment. These are two important matters; to have a fine healthful exposure, and an abundant supply of good pure water. In this perspective view are displayed the various accessories which may be found on a larger scale among the details. The summer house stands in the midst of the grove, and to the right more elevated is the observatory, from which we may readily conceive a fine extensive view.

Plate CVII. shows the front and side elevations of the design. Upon these are displayed the principal ornamental details sufficiently large, in a scale of sixteen feet to the inch. The conservatory, front porch, bay-windows and verandahs are of wood, and also the ornamental cornice. The front porch is designed as a carriage porch, the vehicle passing up the grade beneath it and finding an exit from the other gate. The small attic windows may be seen over the front windows. The circular windows in the gables also light the attic rooms.

Plate CVIII. exhibits the plans of the first and second stories. There is a cellar beneath, in which the furnace will be placed for warming the building. The walls of the cellar are of stone, and those of the superstructure may be of brick rough-cast without pointing. The roof is of tin or galvanized iron. Next the vestibule, on the first floor, is a large ante room, so arranged with sliding doors that on occasion it may be thrown with the drawing-room and dining-room all into one. The kitchen and other offices are to the left. The second floor shows a range of chambers and bed-rooms sufficient for the accommodation of a large family. The front and east windows all reach the floor, giving access to the balconies over the bay-windows and the second story of the verandah. There is an attic story above also containing bed-rooms. The kitchen, bath-room, and all the chambers may be supplied with water from a reservoir on the hills in the rear, or if the location has not such advantages it may be received from a reservoir in the attic supplied by a force pump.

Plate CIX. shows the plan and front elevation of a garden house, the position of which may be found on the plate of the grounds. This building is approached on the sides by a covered arbor, the construction of which is also shown. It may be used for a variety of purposes, either as a gardener's hall, a museum, a billiard room or a place of resort for children. It will be found not only a highly decorative feature, but also really useful in such an extensive dwelling place. On this plate there is also a design for a vase to be placed wherever taste may suggest, and the details of the porch and cornice of the garden house are delineated on a larger scale.

Plate CX. exhibits a view of the observatory such as would occur in our design, which will be evident on examining the plate of the grounds already referred to. It is of wood, and perched on a mass of rough masonry, built against a rock. It is approached from the rear, starting in front where the foot of the hand rail appears, and going around up a flight of steps which land behind. The steps in front of the picture are stone, the rails are wood with stone posts, which furnish pedestals for marble or terra cotta garden figures.

Plate CXI. shows the summer house. This also is approached from the rear. It is composed of wood painted white, or if possible of marble, and is placed upon a mass of smooth masonry, as in the picture. This masonry might be rubble rough-cast, but in such situations the plaster is likely to fall off. This summer house is in the Romanesque style, which is well adapted to such situations, being without the ruggedness of the Tudor or the severe chasteness of the Grecian style.

Plate CXII. presents two designs for a carriage house and stable combined, the one on the left is that exhibited on the plate of the grounds, but the other if desirable may be substituted. Either it is believed will fully answer the purpose, but the one on the left being larger is more complete. The carriage is driven at once into the house, the horses are there unharnessed, and taken through the separating door into their stalls. There is of course a hay loft above.

Plate CXIII. exhibits a vertical projection of the grounds. There is an ascent from the rear of the mansion towards the summer house, which may be seen in the perspective view, though not evident here. The mansion stands front. On the right is a flower garden, and beyond that is the arbor and covered way leading to the garden house. This building faces the large pool, which has a fountain in its centre, in the rear of the dwelling. By winding walks we reach the summer house with its fountain. To the right of this is seen the plan of the observatory, and the position of the steps leading to it. The view on plate CX. is taken from the foot of the steps lying between the observatory and the garden house. On the extreme left is the carriage house, shut off from the rest of the grounds by trees.

Design. XLVI.

Sam.¹ Sloan Arch.ᵗ

P.S. Duval & Co's Steam lith Press Philad.ᵃ

A COUNTRY RESIDENCE.

FRONT ELEVATION

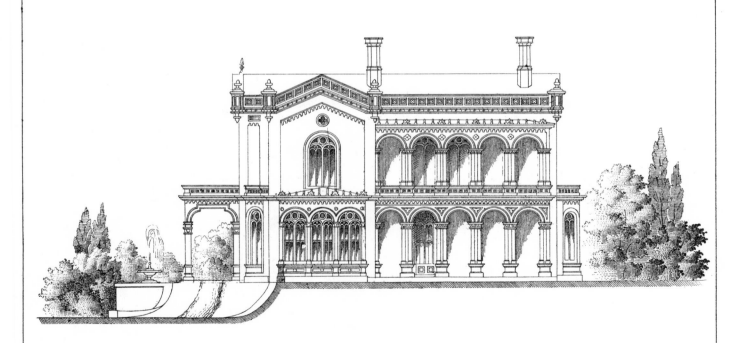

SIDE ELEVATION.

Scale 16 feet to the inch.

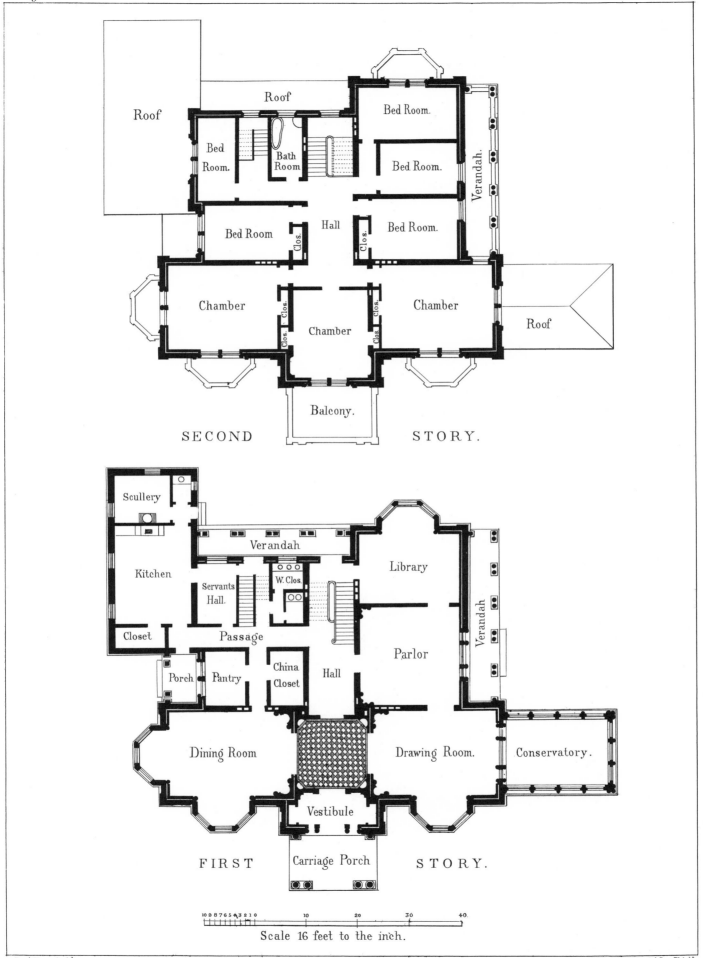

Roof

Roof

Roof

Bed Room.

Bed Room.

Bed Room.

Bed Room.

Bath Room.

Verandah.

Hall

Clos.

Clos.

Bed Room

Chamber

Chamber

Chamber

Clos.

Clos.

Clos.

Clos.

Clos.

Clos.

Roof

Balcony.

SECOND   STORY.

Scullery

Kitchen

Closet

Verandah

Servants Hall.

W. Clos.

Porch

Pantry

Passage

China Closet

Hall

Library

Parlor

Verandah

Dining Room

Drawing Room.

Conservatory.

Vestibule

FIRST   Carriage Porch   STORY.

10 9 8 7 6 5 4 3 2 1 0   10   20   30   40.

Scale 16 feet to the inch.

Sam! Sloan Arch!.   P. S. Duval & Co's Steam lith Press Philad.?

GROUND PLANS.

Pl. CIX.

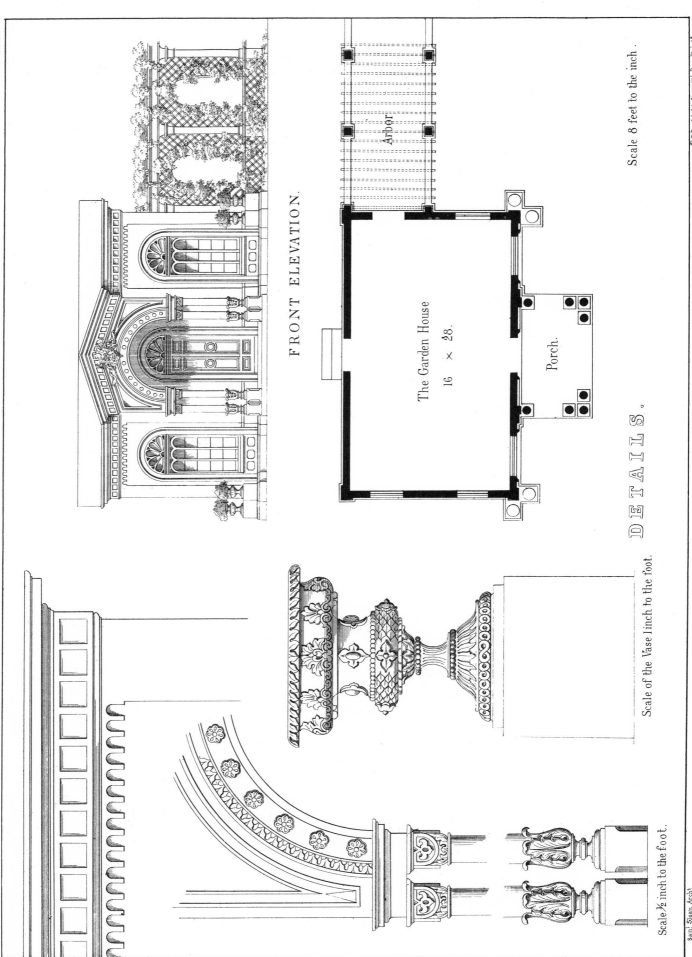

FRONT ELEVATION.

Arbor

The Garden House
16 × 28.

Porch.

DETAILS.

Scale 8 feet to the inch.

Scale of the Vase 1inch to the foot.

Scale ½ inch to the foot.

P. S. Duval & Cos Steam lith Press Philad^a

Sam! Sloan Arch!

Pl. CXI.

Design XXVI.

Saml. Sloan Archt.

P.S.Duval & Co's Steam lith. Press Philad.a

THE SUMMER HOUSE.

Pl. CX.

Design XXVI.

Saml. Sloan Archt.

P.S.Duval & Co's Steam lith Press Philad.a

THE OBSERVATORY.

Pl. CXII.

Harness
Room

9 × 10. 6.

Stable

15 × 20.

Carriage House

15 × 33.

Shed

Stall
6 × 7.

Stable
14 × 29.

Harness
Room
8 × 10.

Closet
5 × 7.6.

Carriage House
12 × 22.

Tool
Room
8 × 12.

Ostler's
Room.
8 × 12

CARRIAGE HOUSES.

Scale 12 feet to the inch.

36   24   12   12   9   1   12

Sam.¹ Sloan Arch.¹

P.S Duval & Co's Steam lith. Press Philad.ª

Scale 40 feet to the inch.

Sam! Sloan Arch!.   P.S.Duval & Co's Steam lith.Press Philad.ᵃ

THE GROUNDS.

A RETROSPECT.

E are now about to close the first volume of this work, and it may not be improper to glance at what has been done before proceeding further. The undertaking was commenced with many misgivings, not only as to our own ability in accomplishing it, but also whether the subject was sufficiently popular to make it successful. In respect to the latter point, the question is answered. The success of the work exceeded our highest hopes, the demand has been constantly increasing, and it is now only a matter of wonder that the interest of the community in the subject could ever have been doubted. There are few persons, even those nursed in the lap of luxury, who have not at some time experienced discomforts arising either from insufficient accommodations or inconvenient arrangements in dwellings. There are many things that money will not buy. It cannot secure comfort in our homes if they be badly arranged, badly lighted, badly heated, or badly ventilated. These points must be secured in the first place, and even with them there is a great diversity of views respecting comfort. No one has greater cognizance of this fact than an architect. A dwelling in which one person would live with the utmost pleasure would render another uncomfortable and unhappy, simply because his education and habits are different. There are but few old homesteads in this country, which descendants take a delight and pride in holding. Our customs are continually changing, and our means improving, and hence what was once considered an elegant mansion is now a second or third rate dwelling. The style of building generally practised here, is by no means the most substantial, and at the same time our population is rapidly increasing. For these reasons every citizen is interested in the art of building, and each expects or hopes at some day to erect a dwelling for himself suited to his peculiar notions of living. He examines architectural works with interest, expecting to glean information from the professional man more extended and practical, than his own observation affords. We have endeavored to direct our work to meet this desire, and intend finally to leave nothing unsaid or undone, so far as we know, which may furnish the wished for information.

In the twenty-six preceding designs, we have confined the variations by those generally conceded ideas of comfort, which place the parlor in front, the domestic offices in the rear, and the sleeping apartments on the second floor. These seem to us by far the most natural arrangements, but they are very different in many other enlightened countries. Within these limits, we have given many various arrangements for apartments, some of which will certainly be adapted to almost any peculiar notions. But this point is by no means yet exhausted, and many other combinations will be contained in the next volume totally distinct from those in this.   We have given to the façades of these designs a considerable variety of style adapted to different tastes and locations.   The greater number of these have been Italian and Gothic, interspersed with occasional Romanesque and fanciful designs, which last lay no claim to any particular style.   Indeed, it is impossible to express in a small building the principles which strictly constitute a style.   We can only make its few details consistent with each other.   The designs are always accompanied by such data as will enable the builder to construct them without difficulty.   In respect to the engraving, no one will hesitate to pronounce a decided improvement.

The letter press has received a full share of attention.   There are short accounts of several of the different styles, giving a description of their rise and progress, and the principles on which they are based. The facts therein stated are collected from various sources, and though perhaps not expressed in the most fluent, graceful manner, are nevertheless reliable.   Besides these, we have begun a series of articles, which are intended to comprise a succinct description of the building art accompanied by numerous collateral facts and reflections.   We have entered but a little way into these subjects, their great extent not being compressible within our limits, but at the same time, we hope that much has been said which will be found useful and new.

The middle point is reached, and but half the labor is done.   As yet there is no feeling of relaxation, but, on the contrary, a strong desire and determination not only to keep up the spirit of the work and render it complete, but to improve it in every practicable way.   We now close the present volume, but at once open the next with the wish and hope of rendering it more valuable to its readers, and more creditable to all concerned in its production.

Finis.

VOLUME TWO

PRESERVATION OF TIMBER.

N the previons article, the general uses and different varieties of timber were discussed. The properties of each, which rendered it available for building purposes, and the quality, dimensions and value of the tree were described. It now remains that we should indicate some more general properties which are in a greater or less degree common to all, and more especially to treat of decay and the many cautions to be observed and methods requisite to retard its final coming. If the cross section of a tree be examined, it will be found to consist of three distinct parts, the pith, the wood, and the bark. The wood in many cases is visibly traversed by thin vertical plates emanating from the central pith, which is the same in substance, and producing, when exposed on the surface of a board, that beautiful appearance called silver flowered grain, so very conspicuous in the oak. The wood itself is composed of minute elongated cells, through which the sap ascends. Between these are the pores, which aid by their capillarity in the ascent of the sap. In the spring the sap, charged with matter dissolved from the soil, is drawn up into the trunk, it passes to the leaves, is there digested, receives additions from the carbonic acid of the air, and then descends through the bark, portions of it, in the form of a viscid gelatinous liquid, being deposited against the wood inside of the bark, and changed into woody fibre. This process continues through the season until the leaves become filled with earthy matter, left by the evaporation of the water which brought it up in solution, and having lost their singular power, die and fall. It is thus that trees grow. Every year a quantity of wood is formed between the bark and trunk, thus slowly increasing the size of the tree, and compressing by contraction the inner portions. This compression often so diminishes the pith as to make it invisible. The wood formed near the close of the season, when this process is somewhat retarded, is much more hard and compact than the other. The difference is distinctly visible in a cross section, of pine in the annual rings, as they are called, by which, each representing a year's growth, the age of the tree may be ascertained.

After a tree has been growing for some years the inner cells gradually become filled with earthy matter in the same manner as the leaves in Fall, and no longer are channels for the ascent of the sap which now must pass through the outer portions of more recent date. This outer part is called the alburnum, or sap wood and the inner portion duramen or heart wood. It is generally known, that this last only is fit for building purposes, since the sap wood is comparatively soft and quickly decays after being hewn. The sap wood is also generally of a light color, often presenting a strong contrast in this respect to the heart. The great variety of color which the different kinds of heart wood present is owing to various foreign matters, the pure woody fibre as in linen being entirely white. The natural secretions, as resin, often color the wood, but variations thus produced are more frequently owing to the character of the soil from whence the depositions before spoken of which fill the cells are derived. The difference in the Spanish and Honduras mahogany is thus caused, and a great variety of colors are produced in woods for fancy articles by allowing them to absorb while growing, different coloring matters.

The age of a tree should be considered before it is felled for timber. The body of a young tree is nearly all of sap wood, and therefore not trustworthy; that of one advanced beyond its prime is affected with incipient decay in the heart, which renders it brittle, and of little value. The best period must be judged of in each, since it varies both with the kind of tree and its locality. We may be more definite, however, regarding the season for felling. The fermentation of the sap is one of the principal causes of rot, and it is desirable to rid the timber of it as much as possible. In spring, the trunk is full of sap, and it is therefore the worst season. Midsummer or autumn is much better, for then the sap is considerably expended; but winter is generally better than either, though some kinds of wood work better, in many respects, when felled in summer. It would be an excellent practice if all trees were first stripped of their bark. This would allow the sap wood to harden considerably, and improve the quality of the whole in many respects. Except in the case of the oak, whose bark is valuable, the improvement thus made seldom justifies the expense of stripping.

Seasoning the timber after it is felled is an important, but very simple process. It is nothing more than to expel the water and fluids of the sap by evaporation or drying. The tree should be allowed to remain in log for some time, at least until the following spring, while seasoning, as the wood is then less liable to warp; but if this time is extended until the wood is entirely dry, it inevitably cracks and splits, because the outside always contracts more than the heart. If the purpose requires a piece of large circumference, as for columns, this liability is avoided to a considerable extent by boring out the centre from end to end. The same cause which cracks large pieces of timber will warp smaller ones, and this may be illustrated by sawing the plank or boards in a particular way. If a plank be taken out so as to contain the centre of the tree, it will not warp, but shrink laterally. If it be taken from one side of the tree, next the slab for instance, the outer surface will shrink more than the inner, and warp the piece. In preparing shingles or clapboards, it being highly important that they neither warp nor crack, they should be split from the centre to the circumference of the log all around. This will not do however for a long piece, since then, the outer edge contracting most, it bends in that direction, or, as the workmen say, it springs. After the log is cut up, place the boards in a dry airy place, not exposed to the sun, but so arranged that warm dry air may have a free circulation between them. If they touch each other, or the circulation be otherwise retarded, the sap ferments, induces the growth of fungi, and the dry rot ensues. Some seem to think that the mere position, whether horizontal or vertical, makes a great difference, but it is of little consequence, so the other point be attained. The process of seasoning should not be a hasty one, as it has been noticed that the timber which has been dried slowly is tough, and lasts better, than that which has been dried quickly. It is an excellent plan to immerse the timber, plank, or boards, immediately after being prepared, in a stream of clear running water for a fortnight. There is much in wood that is soluble, as is evident from the slime that covers a log after lying in water for some time, and it is the soluble portion that mostly forwards decay. By the above means much of this is washed out, and boards thus treated are less liable to shrink, and warp, and will endure far better than those subject to years of dry seasoning. A large portion of our timber is floated down rivers to its destination, and in this case the precaution is unnecessary, but in others it should be adopted. For carpentry, timber should never be used within two years after it is felled, and for joinery a much longer time is necessary to secure good material.

Wood is composed principally of woody fibre or lignin, as it is technically termed. We have an instance of pure woody fibre in linen, but in timber it is mixed with and colored by other bodies. This fibre is in the form of elongated cells, and is essentially the same substance in all kinds of wood, the difference in their properties being caused by the thinness or thickness, the shortness or length, and the compactness of these cells which make the wood either brittle or strong. The cells are in a manner woven together, and contain the various substances which compose the sap. These are starch, juices, resins and earthy salts, all of which are left when the water is driven off in drying. Besides these, they contain a most important substance, known as vegetable albumen, which is entirely similar in its nature to the white of an egg. This albumen is more prone to decomposition than any other part of the wood, and those trees which endure the longest, as the oak, chesnut and locust, are found to contain the least quantity. The porosity of wood, rendering it more or less penetrable, also seriously affects its capability of endurance.

It is a somewhat remarkable fact, but well known to chemists, that the burning and rotting of wood are the same process. As in burning, the products are carbonic acid, water and ash or earthy matter, so in rotting, the final products are also carbonic acid, water and earthy matter. The difference consists only in this; in the first case, the result is produced at once, but in the latter, it is a slow process, and exhibits several intermediate stages. In view of this fact, the German chemist, Liebig, has called slow decay, eremecausis, the derivatives of which word signify, burning by degrees. On the same principle, therefore, that rapid oxidation or burning cannot take place where air, with its oxygen, is excluded, so is it also a complete preservative against decay. Timber will remain sound beneath water, where the air cannot reach, for a thousand years. Pieces have been taken from the bed of the Thames, in excellent preservation, supposed to have been placed there by the Romans. Still, some air is dissolved in the water, and finally by its aid wood in such situations will decay. This decay is remarkably accelerated by the presence of other decomposing organic matter, as in marshy places, in which case the wood putrifies and marsh gas takes the place of carbonic acid, to which, however, it finally changes. In very dry air, the process is also exceedingly slow, and indeed it is believed that the intervention of a certain amount of moisture is essential to decay, though it only acts as a medium between the air and wood. But if the situation of the wood is not exposed, and the circulation about it is free, it will endure for a long time, but if it be confined, fermentation and the dry rot ensue. A fungus or mouldiness, often accompanied by minute insects, now appears, which grows sometimes to the length of several feet, insinuating its delicate fibres throughout the pores of the wood, feeding upon it and promoting disintegration. If wood be exposed to the weather, or the occasional action of water in any way, decay is accelerated, for the water washes away soluble and partially decayed portions, and leaves a new surface exposed. Wood embedded in the earth, especially in that which contains much decaying organic matter, is put to the most severe test. The continual presence of moisture and a sufficiency of air constitute the circumstances most favorable to decomposition. It is also a fact, as before hinted, that the mere contact or presence of fermenting matter, as in the case of yeast, has a great tendency to induce like action, which is the first step in decay. Now, of all these substances, albumen is the most prone to decompose, and by its presence induce decomposition in the woody fibre. Pure woody fibre is very slow to decay, and were it not for the albumen in the wood, we would seldom be troubled with its rotting.

Timber is seasoned with a view as much to its preservation as to secure it from warping and splitting. It is not, however, in all cases sufficient, and many other means have been suggested and tried to prevent decay, but the most of these are too expensive to be adopted in all cases, and very many are entirely useless. It will require but a few words to describe those which are really practicable and valuable. Laying timber in water has already been mentioned. Cold and tepid water slowly dissolve out the albumen, and in this way it may be partially removed. It has been thought well to place the timber in salt water until it is thoroughly impregnated with the salt. This doubtless will give security against worms, and may postpone decay, but is liable chiefly to this objection. The salt is highly hydroscopic, and in wet weather absorbs a great amount of moisture, which in dry weather exudes again, thus keeping the timber always damp. Again it has been suggested to boil or steam the timber. It is often necessary to practise this in order to bend wood in some particular form, and it has been stated that such pieces are less liable to rot. This process removes the soluble portions more rapidly, but instead of dissolving out the albumen merely coagulates it, as the white of an egg is coagulated in boiling. In this a great object is gained, for the coagulated albumen is by no means so prone to decompose. But too much of other soluble matter is removed, as is also the case when timber is washed for a long time by cold water, which considerably impairs its strength.

Many other methods have been successfully tried to preserve wood. Smoking it is an excellent practice, but charring is better where the use of the timber admits it, as in posts. The plan has been in some cases adopted of placing the wood in a large air-tight chamber, and producing a vacuum. This rapidly evaporates the juices of the wood which are condensed in another chamber, but the process is mostly used when the introduction of foreign substances as oil is intended. Tar is an excellent preservative, and for railroad sleepers and the like is advantageously used, but the increase of inflammability renders

Pl. I.

Saml Sloan Archt

P.S.Duval & Co's Steam lith Press.Phil.

T H E   F A R M.

A Scene near Gray's Ferry, Phila. Co. Pa.

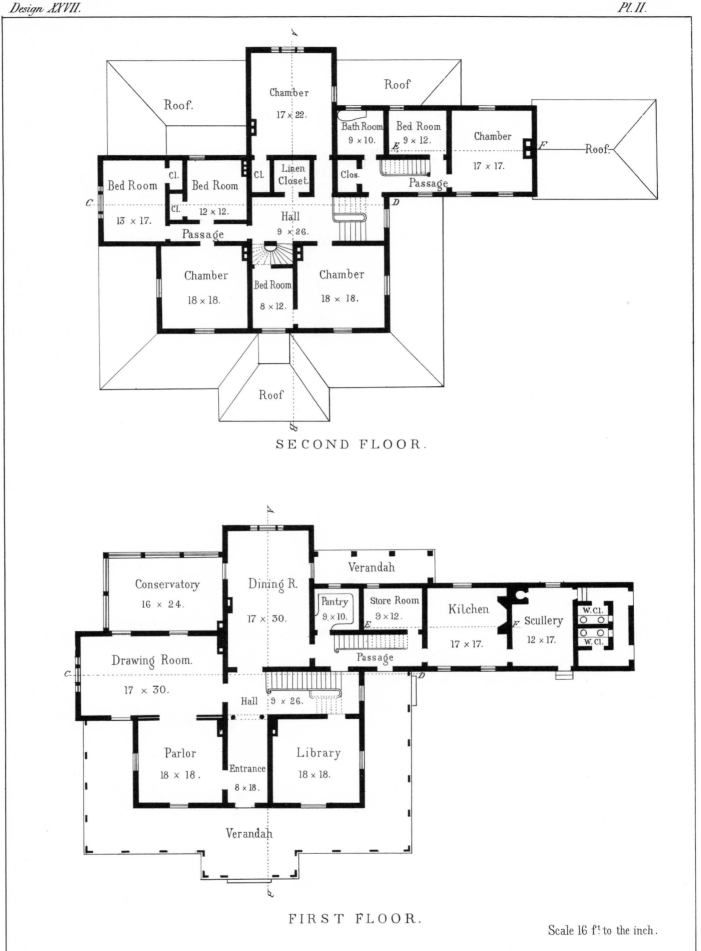

SECOND FLOOR.

FIRST FLOOR.

Scale 16 f.t to the inch.

GROUND PLANS.

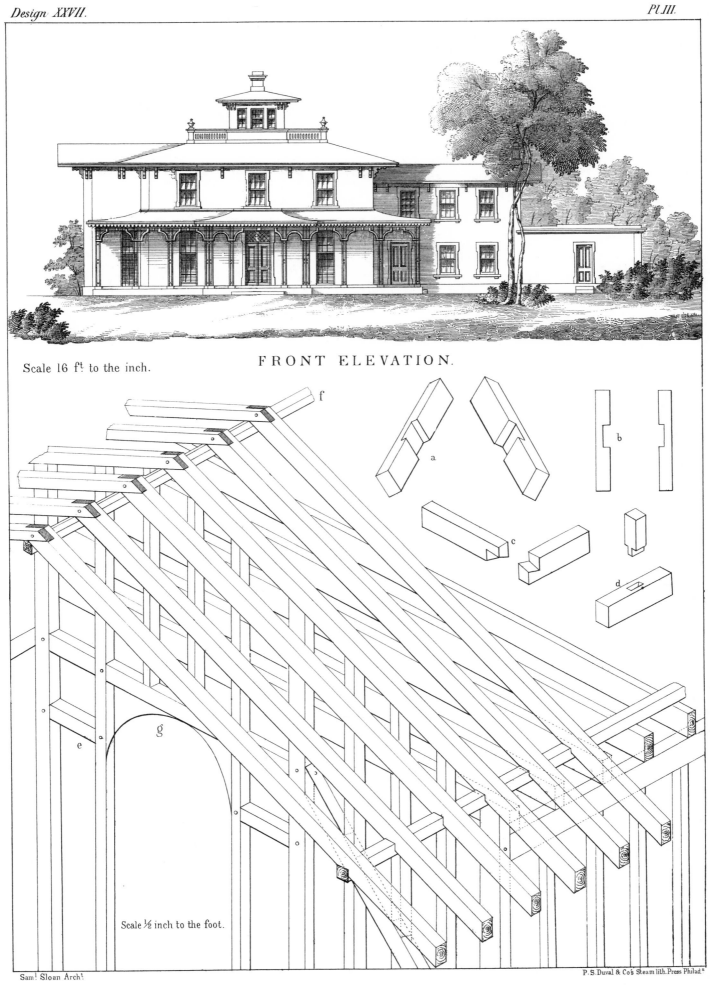

FRONT ELEVATION.

Scale 16 ft. to the inch.

Scale ½ inch to the foot.

Sam! Sloan Arch!   P.S.Duval & Co's Steam lith.Press Philad.ª

D E T A I L S .

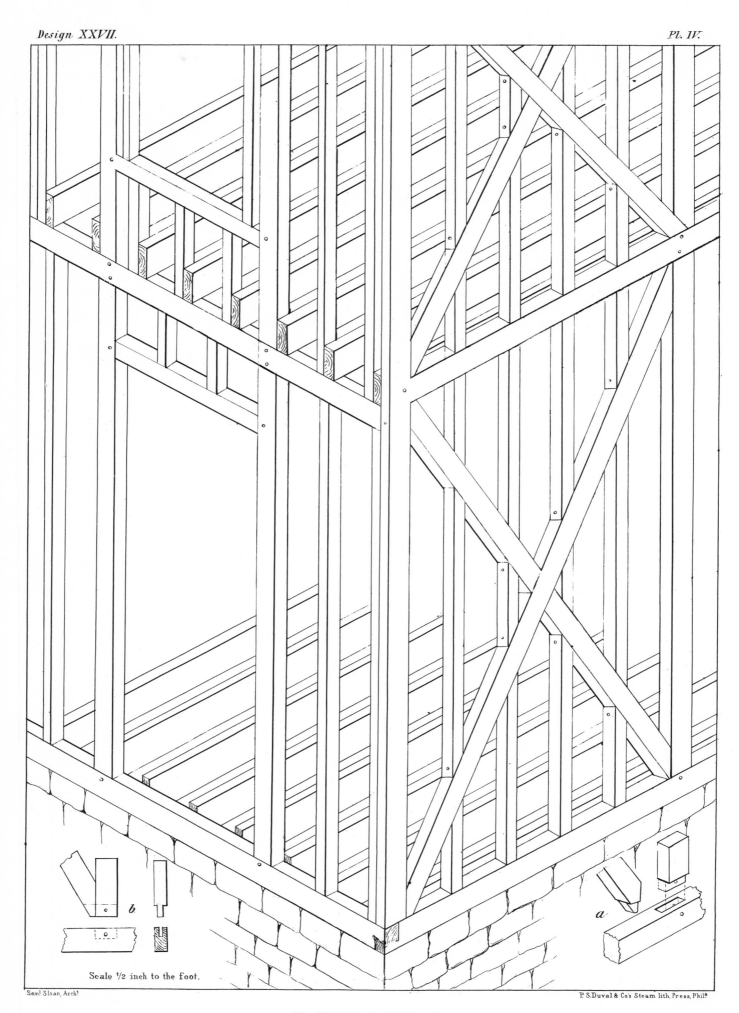

Scale ½ inch to the foot.

Sam.ᵗ Sloan, Arch.ᵗ   P.S.Duval & Co's Steam lith. Press, Phil.ᵃ

DETAILS.

Pl. V.

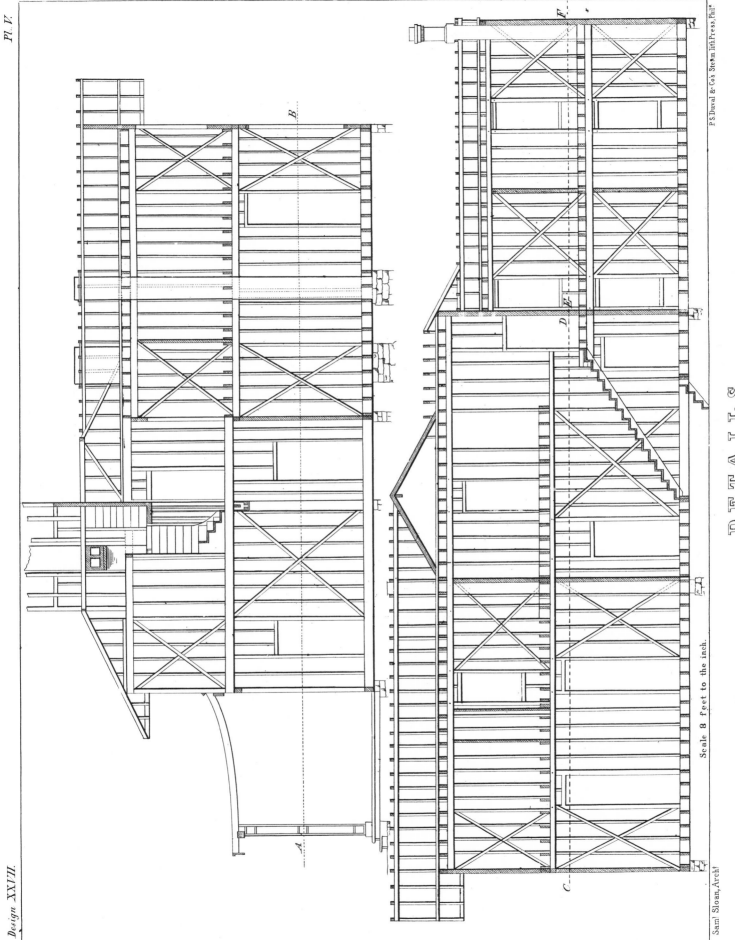

D E T A I L S .

Sam'l Sloan, Arch't

Scale 8 feet to the inch.

P.S.Duval & Co's Steam lith.Press, Phil^a

it objectionable. It acts principally by the creosote coagulating the albumen, and by excluding the air, which last is the chief value of paint as a preservative. Some paints have a tendency also to prevent the burning of wood, but the best means of securing this end is to steep it in a solution of alum. Alum also coagulates the albumen, but it forms with woody fibre a weak chemical compound that rapidly tends to decompose, and detracts much from the value of this process. Wood impregnated with tannin is much increased in durability. Lime has also been considered a preservative, but this is a great mistake, and the powerful action of quick lime should be guarded against in timbers bedded in mortar by tarring them. Whitewash made from hydraulic lime is far better for fences than that made from the ordinary quick lime. The process invented by Mr. Kyan, usually termed Kyanizing, is generally considered the best. The timber is placed in a large tank and secured by cross beams 'to prevent its rising, and a solution of cheap corrosive sublimate is let in. For a time all is quiet, but in the course of ten or twelve hours the water is agitated by the chemical action of the corrosive sublimate in combining with the albumen. This ceases in a short time, and in the course of a week or two the action is complete. Now let it season for two or three weeks more, and it is fit for use. This method has been severely tested. A piece of prepared timber was allowed to remain for five years in the fungus pit at Woolwich dock yard, a place celebrated for producing rapid decomposition, and was taken out as sound as when put in, whereas a precisely similar piece, but unprepared, under the same circumstances was completely rotten. This process deserves the attention of our builders.

The impregnation of the timber with these substances is effected in various ways. The best, but most expensive, is to produce a vacuum, and then let into the chamber the impregnating substance, enough to cover the timber, and on the readmission of air it is forced into the pores of the wood. Ordinary steeping and the practice of placing salts in holes near the base of the tree, before it is felled, in the season of autumn, are generally very effectual. In the latter case, the substance ascends into the tree as the sap descends through the bark. These processes are in general too much neglected.

Timber is usually put together without any other preparation than ordinary seasoning, and even this is too often badly done. Very simple precautions may be taken, that will make a house last long beyond its builder's time. First the timber should be naturally sound, and thoroughly seasoned. Then use white lead in all small joints, and in the larger ones, a preparation like the following. "Take one pound of pitch, a quarter of a pound of grease, and as much powdered chalk as will make the boiling mixture of a proper consistence. The mortice and tenon must be covered with this while hot, and then secured by pins." Lastly, attend to a much neglected point, ventilation. Admit a circulation of air through all the timbers, everywhere, beneath the sleepers, beneath the floors, within the roof, and even, if possible, between the studding. Nothing is so bad for timber as close confinement. It rapidly induces the dry rot, which not only destroys the building, but the health of its inhabitants. Secure these points, and we will seldom see our buildings decay.

THE FARM.

DESIGN TWENTY-SEVENTH.

IN this volume we introduce a new feature. All the principal designs are exhibited in landscapes taken from nature. There are surrounding us in all directions a thousand of beautiful spots, suited in every respect to become delightful places of residence, which are altogether neglected, and by many unnoticed. It is believed that many valuable thoughts will be suggested by locating our designs in the midst of scenery suited to their character, and being engraved in a superior style they will furnish also pictures of various interesting localities.

The view presented on Plate I. is taken from the neighborhood of Gray's Ferry near Philadelphia. This is a spot interesting to every student of American history, and well known also for abounding in beautiful quiet views. In the engraving the building is placed at the intersection of two roads, now occupied by a stone mansion. In front is an orchard, and in the rear is spread out a large tract of excellent farm land. The creek winds its way to the Schuylkill seen in the distance. The road which crosses the bridge is private, and leads to the farm; the other in front of the house is a highway. There is nothing very striking in the view, but for a quiet pleasant farm scene we think it has no superior, though it may have many equals.

Plate II. presents the floor plans of the design. The building is frame work throughout, and we subjoin a comprehensive description and a bill of quantities which render many remarks here unnecessary. The posts of the front verandah may be either of iron or wood, and the apartments on the extreme of the wing may be placed elsewhere. It will be seen at a glance that the building is large and roomy, furnishing sufficient space for the dwelling of ten persons, which is a large number to constitute one family. From the hall of the second floor the winding steps ascend to the observatory. The hall below is separated from the entrance by an arched door-way.

Plate III. exhibits a geometrical projection of the front in a scale of sixteen feet to the inch. Below is an isometric or bird's eye view of the gable over the drawing room, showing the method of framing the roof and double window. The figures a. b. c. and d. are easily understood.

Plate IV. is an isometric view of the framing of a corner, showing the manner of putting together the braces, sills, ties, joists, etc.

Plate V. exhibits two vertical sections of the frame work. The first is made through the line AB on the plate of plans, and second through the lines CD. and E. F. These two sections exhibit all important points in the frame work, and any one on examining them in connection with the other plates, will find no difficulty in understanding the construction of the whole building.

The building is to have a cellar beneath its entire extent, at least six feet six inches deep in the clear of the joists of the first floor, with all necessary trenches for the foundations at least six inches below the cellar floor. All the earth must be graded around the building, as may be directed.

The walls throughout the cellar must be composed of good quarry building stone, laid in the best lime mortar. They are to be sixteen inches thick, and have all facings smoothly dashed and whitewashed. The flues for warm air and gas are

10

to be built of bricks, and so arranged that either stoves or a furnace may be used. They are to be well pargetted and topped out with press bricks, at least four feet above the roof from which they issue. The flues of the main building pass through the observatory. There is to be a well beneath the extreme wing of the building as deep as the water gravel, walled in and provided with a ventilating flue.

The superstructure is to be constructed entirely of framework. The sills are to be six by six inches, the corner posts, four by eight inches, the girts four by eight inches, the plates four by six inches, the door and window studs four by six inches, the braces four by four inches, and the intermediate studding three by four inches. The joists of the first floor are to be three by twelve inches, and all others are to be three by ten inches. They are to be placed sixteen inches between centres, to have three quarters of an inch crown, and each tier must have a course of lattice bridging through the centre. The ceiling joists are to be three by five inches, and also placed sixteen inches between centres. The rafters are to be three by seven inches at the foot, cut in the usual form, placed two feet between centres, and strongly spiked at the plate and ridgepole. The sills are to be of good oak timber, and the frames of the verandahs are to be of oak inferior in quality. All other framing timbers are to be of white pine, except the studds, which are hemlock.

The exterior is to be enclosed with half inch pine siding, well seasoned, planed, jointed, not over three inches wide, and secured, overlapping, by six penny nails. The cornice and observatory are to be constructed according to the drawings. The floors throughout are to be laid with one inch Carolina heart pine of a good quality, well nailed to the joists, and afterwards smoothed off. The roof is to be close sheathed for metal covering.

The windows are all to have a plank face with a large sized moulding. The sash must be one inch and a half thick, and double hung with axle pullies and patent cord. The first story windows are all to have three panneled shutters one inch and a half thick, with fillets and mouldings on the face and bead, and butt on the back. The second story and windows are to have Venitian pivot blinds, one inch and a half thick.

The doors throughout the principal rooms are all to be one inch and three quarters thick, in six panels, with fillets and large moulding on both sides. They are to be hung with four by four inch butts, and secured by four and a half inch upright mortice locks. The closet doors are to be one and a quarter inches thick, with moulding on the outside. The principal doors in the wing are to be one inch and a half thick, in six panels. The entrance doors are to be made in like manner to those first described. Those on the front are to have an eight inch upright rebate lock, and iron plate flush bolts of a suitable length. All other outer doors are to be secured with a knob latch and two bolts to each.

The dressings of the principal rooms on the first floor are to be eight inches, and moulded. The washboard must be ten inches wide, including a three inch base. The moulding on top is two inches and a half high. The dressings in the second story main building are to be five inches wide. The washboards are to be nine inches wide, with a moulding on top.

The stairs are to have a continued rail, and be put up in the best manner, with one and a quarter inch step boards of the best quality. The newel is to be ten inches at the base, and the balusters three inches, neatly turned. The rail and newel are to be of black walnut. The private stairs are to be constructed in the usual manner.

All the walls in the building are to be lathed, plastered and hard finished. The principal rooms are to have cornices in the angles of the ceilings. The roofs are all to be overlaid with the best one cross leaded roofing tin, painted on both sides, the upper receiving two coats. All the exterior and interior must have three coats of pure white lead paint. The newel rail and balusters must have three coats of varnish.

A GENERAL ESTIMATE

OF THE COST IN ERECTING DESIGN TWENTY-SEVENTH.

Excavation, 650 yards @ 20 cts. - - -	$130.00	Weather Boarding, 6,500 ft. @ $30.00 per M. 195.00
Masonry, 500 perches @ $2.00 - -	1,000.00	Assorted Lumber, 10,000 ft. @ $25.00 " 250.00
Bricks and Laying, 20,000 @ $10.00 per. M.	200.00	Window frames, shutters and sash @ $12.00 " 420.00
Plastering, 2,500 yds. @ 20 cts. - - -	500.00	Doors, 1¾ inch, 15 @ $4.25 - - - - 63.75
Joists for floors, 20,000 feet @ $12.50 per M. -	250.00	Doors, 1½ inch and 1¼ inch, 20 @ $2.75 - - 55.00
Joists for ceilings, 3,600 " " " " -	45.00	Workmanship, - - - - - - - 150.00
Ties and Plates, 1,500 " " " " -	18.75	Tinning, - - - - - - - 900.00
Scantling, 6,500 " " " " -	75.00	Furnace and Range, - - - - 300.00
Rafters, 4,000 " " " " -	50.00	Hardware, - - - - - - 450.00
Corner posts, 1,200 " " $18.00 " -	21.60	Painting and Glazing, - - - - - 500.00
Oak sills, 1,000 " " $20.00 " -	20.00	
Sheathing and Scaffolding, 7,000 ft. @ $15.00 per M.	105.00	Total, $6,879.10
Verandah Rafters, (oak,) 2,000 ft. " "	30.00	

WAYSIDE COTTAGE.

DESIGN TWENTY-EIGHTH.

Two elevations represented on Plates VI. and VII. accompany this design. The latter of these is ornamented in a rustic style, and is supposed to face the highway. The first, which is essentially the same design, but with a different façade, looks towards a river, and is termed a Summer Seat. The general appearance of this is well adapted to such a situation. Its walls are of brick, rough-cast, without pointing, and it is covered by a ribbed tin roof.

Plate VIII. presents the floor plans. They are adapted more particularly to the second elevation on plate seventh. There is a cellar beneath the entire building except the laundry, lighted by windows on the sides and rear. Beyond the laundry is a well, sunk to the water gravel, and walled in. The walls of the house are of hammer dressed stone, sixteen inches thick, as high as the level of the second floor. The roof is of slate, laid diamond pattern, and the chimney cans are of terra cotta ware. The roof of the front verandah is of tin, painted in colored stripes. The verandah posts, the rails of the balcony above, and the finial are of unbarked wood, after the fanciful patterns represented. The whole house is intended to be warmed by grates or stoves, but it might easily be arranged for a furnace. It is evident on an inspection of the plans, that the house is quite small and compact, but we think not inconveniently arranged. There are ample accommodations for a family of five or six, including the servants. The laundry may be used as a kitchen, and the scale of the whole enlarged, if it is found desirable.

Plate IX. exhibits the details of the second front, those of the first being simple and similar to many given heretofore. Fig. 1, a design for the verandah post and bracket. Fig. 2, another design for the same. Fig. 3, gable and finial of the front dormer window. Fig. 4, the window. Fig. 5, a section of the window. Fig. 6, rails of the balcony. Fig. 7, the eaves and the side post of the dormer window.

Sam.ᵗ Sloan, Arch.ᵗ   P.S.Duval & Co's Steam lith Press.Phil.ᵃ

A SUMMER SEAT.

Sam.ᵗ Sloan, Arch.ᵗ   P.S.Duval & Co's Steam lith.Press.Phil.ᵃ

WAYSIDE COTTAGE.

Pl. VIII.

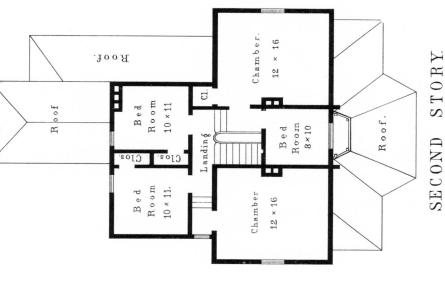

SECOND STORY.

Roof

Roof.

Bed Room 10 × 11

Cl.

Bed Room 10 × 11.

Clos. Clos.

Landing

Chamber. 12 × 16

Bed Room 8 × 10

Roof.

Chamber 12 × 16

FIRST STORY

Laundry 11 × 12

Verandah 7 × 28

Kitchen 12 × 12

Pantry. 5 × 6

Clos.

Passage

Library. 9 × 10

Dining Room 12 × 16

Hall 8 × 16

Parlor 12 × 16

Verandah 7 × 34

GROUND PLANS.

Scale 12 feet to the inch.

12 10 8 6 4 2 0   12   24

P. S. Duval & Co's Steam lith. Press, Phila

Sam'l Sloan, Arch'

Pl. IX.

Fig. 1.

Fig. 2.

Fig. 3.

Fig. 4.

Fig. 7.

Fig. 6.

Fig. 5.

Scale ½ inch to the foot.

Sam! Sloan, Arch!

P.S.Duval & Co's Steam lith Press, Phil.ᵃ

DETAILS.

CARPENTRY.

~~~~~~~~~~~~~~~~~~~~~~~~~~~~

THERE is nothing in the art of building which requires so much mathematical skill as carpentry. The bricklayer and mason regard only the force of gravity, which is the downward tendency, the lateral force exerted by arches, and the resistance to crushing or compression; whereas, the carpenter must study in addition the relative disposition of parts, so as to resist tension, torsion, or whatever strains the structure may be liable to undergo. He must be well acquainted with the strength of materials, both in reference to the amount of weight they can sustain, besides their own, and also in reference to their capability of resisting these forces, to which they may be subjected in various positions. There is a point which it is desirable to find, between a scantiness of material insufficient for the purpose, and a dangerous over-loading of the building, which economy also requires us to avoid. Maximum strength can only be attained by skillful combinations, avoiding both of these extremes.

The chief use of framework is to give support. The great strength of an upright piece, such as a corner post, in resisting perpendicular force is amply sufficient in itself, but when a long horizontal beam has to bear weight in addition to its own, native strength is not enough, and art must be used to prevent not only its breaking but even bending. There is a principle of natural philosophy involved here which ought to be thoroughly understood by every carpenter, not only practically, but theoretically. It is evident that to overcome a force another must be opposed. If it be opposed directly, then the resisting force need only be equal in magnitude to the acting force. It is not always convenient to do this, and indeed if fully carried out it would amount to placing a post under every weight in the building. We must then oppose oblique forces such as occur in all kinds of trussing. A study of the "Composition and Resolution of Forces," will give an understanding of the principles on which oblique forces act, and of the relation between their magnitude and inclination. There are many forces acting upon the framework of a building besides mere gravity, all of which must be provided against. The winds subject it to great strains frequently, and the existence of the oblique forces mentioned argues lateral pressure, though this should be avoided as much as possible by methods hereafter described.

It is not out of place to urge the necessity of mathematical and theoretical study to a carpenter. Often he has to design the framework himself, and without a knowledge of principles he must work clumsily, and in the dark. If he has never done just such a piece of work before, he is totally at a loss how to proceed. His own personal experience does not aid him, and he has no other resource, for the experience of the thousand able men who have studied, practised and written upon the art is unknown to him. Again, it is better for the sake of economy. When he is acquainted with the practical 'lines,' he lays out the work from first to last in his mind, or still better, makes drawings of it, and can proceed at once with celerity and certainty to the task. His pieces are accurately measured and shaped, and are put together for the first and last time in the building, where they fit at once in the best manner. Whereas the ignorant man scribes all his work, fitting it together piece by piece, each tenon being prepared for its particular mortice, and when prepared with a great loss of time and labor and of material the clumsy work is stuck together in the building. Then when in its final resting place, and not until then, is he sure that no fatal mistake has been committed.

A carpenter must exercise skill in the distribution of the weight of his work. He should so arrange it as to have this distribution as equable as possible, so that no part of the building may weigh more heavily on one part of the foundation than another. If the nature of the design is such as necessarily to create inequality, additional support must be provided, just as the mason will build the foundation of a tower heavier than the others. In the carpentry of a stone or brick building this point is of still greater importance. The wall plates for the support of the roof should extend the whole length of the wall, and the ends of the tie beams should always rest over piers and never above an opening. The ends of girders should never be built into the wall, for the timber is apt to shrink and leave the wall. Build into the wall a long flat stone for the end of the girder to rest upon, and another above the hole to support the work above. In all cases it is much the best plan to make the walls entirely independent of the internal framework. They should be attached in no way, but the latter should merely rest upon them. An additional reason for this is that the contraction and expansion of the framework caused by the variations of temperature, or by the shrinking of joints will if attached inevitably exert a thrust upon the walls, or draw them from the perpendicular.

It is no easy matter to furnish good designs to the carpenter. The only way of arriving at excellence in this is by a close study of what has been, and what may be done. It requires a good knowledge of geometrical science, and a thorough practical understanding of the composition and resolution of forces. Besides, there must be an acquaintance with all the usual forms of combination and securing, and also the modern improvements which the experience of ages has at last elicited. To facilitate this study many works have been published, containing all the desirable information, and it is to be regretted that our artizans, in their foolish contempt of theoretic knowledge, do not study them more. It is impossible to attain great skill without, and consequently we have such a superabundant quantity of mere hand laborers. They may be assured it is the only road to eminence, and the only way to become a headman. This is the chief point in which the English mechanics excel ours. Of the works referred to, those by Mr. Peter Nicholson are perhaps the best, though somewhat behind our time, and have furnished matter for numerous compilations bearing other names. His "Carpenter's New Guide" has long been before the American public, in a cheap form, and is now undergoing a thorough revision at our hands. It is intended to be a complete book of lines in carpentry and joinery, and all requisite additions or alterations will be made, in order to render it a full compendium of modern methods of construction.

Many laborious and really useful investigations have been made into the strength of materials, regarding both the varieties of wood, and the resistance which they make to the different forces mentioned. Tabular views of the results of these experiments are to be found in many architectural works, and are valuable for reference, whenever we are at a loss for precedents. But these data are so modified by circumstances, that in the construction of ordinary buildings, where only those combinations occur which have been practised again and again, experience is a sufficient guide, and a good carpenter will judge at once by his eye respecting the native strength of the material in use, without entering each time into those laborious calculations which he should nevertheless understand.

It is proper here to point out the distinction which obtains between carpentry and joinery. The difference may very readily be understood, though it would be difficult to say exactly where the line of separation occurs, since there are many parts of a building which belong no more to one art than to the other, and in this country particularly, it often happens that the whole work is performed by the same person. Notwithstanding, only those parts properly belong to the carpenter, which are essential to the existence of the building, comprising the heavier portions of the wood work, such as the roof, floors and partitions, and if the house be entirely of wood, the framing of the walls and their covering. To the joiner belongs the more ornamental parts of the building, such as are requisite to finish and complete the whole. He puts up the cornices and mouldings throughout, and the doors, windows, mantles, and dressings of every description. The work requires neater manipulation than carpentry, and having no forces to resist, it only requires the knowledge requisite to construct and fit all parts nicely. Owing however to the great variety of work required, the study of geometry and practical lines is quite as necessary and extensive in joinery as in carpentry. Carpenter's work and material is generally measured by the cubic foot, and joinery by its superficial extent.

It is probable that carpentry was one of the first arts ever practised. There is no material but wood within the reach and management of the savage suitable for covering permanent buildings. He might build the walls of stone, but the rude log cabins of the west show us that a tolerably comfortable dwelling may be constructed of timber, with greater ease and very little art. From this beginning we can readily imagine the advances which thought, increased skill and improved tools, would induce. Nevertheless, the most ancient nations on record have left us specimens of architecture which are complete without any wood work whatever. The remains of the Egyptian temples give us every reason to believe that they were constructed entirely of stone, but we may believe that this was only the case in those grand edifices which they wished to be imperishable. The roofs were composed of immense slabs of stone laid horizontally, for rain never falls in that country, and supported beneath by close set rows of columns.

This was certainly a most inconvenient and laborious method of building, and would only be suitable for such purposes, and in such a climate.

In countries where protection from the rain was necessary, we find of course that the roofs have an inclination. It was found easier to cover a large building by having two inclined roofs than one, and this gave rise to that beautiful architectural feature, the pediment. This is first found among the Greeks, though many of their temples were intended to be without covering. It is impossible to tell their attainment in this art, as there are no remains of it, and but slight indications of its existence among them. Among the Romans, however, carpentry attained a very high state of perfection, and there are very few purposes to which it is now applied that were not in use among them. There are some remains still in existence, and some of which we have descriptions. But in the beautiful arches which adorn and support their edifices we have abundant evidence of their skill in carpentry, for these arches must all have required centering, which is one of the most difficult branches of the art.

The carpentry of the middle ages is peculiar to the style of building which then prevailed. Oak timber was principally used, which, owing to its strength, gave great apparent lightness to the work, and admitted of many devices that cannot be practised with other wood. The roof which principally displayed the advances made in carpentry was generally open beneath, and the architect endeavored to produce by it as ornamental an effect as possible. No tie beam was used, but the collar beam and the strength of the walls was depended upon to resist the lateral thrust of the rafters. There are some beautiful specimens, however, in which, although without the tie beam, yet by a judicious system of trussing all lateral pressure is avoided, and the weight of the whole roof rests perpendicularly upon the wall plates. The present system of building differs essentially from this, and except in direct imitation of the style we seldom use an open roof. The high pitch of the Gothic roofs was adopted to throw off the snows of the north, and is a marked feature of the style also in little use at present. The mode of constructing these roofs is consequently of little importance to us, and does not display that skill which the excellence of the masonry might lead us to expect.

In modern times carpentry has probably advanced beyond any point ever heretofore attained. The roofing of some of the enormous edifices in Europe, and the centering of the wide arches now used for bridges, exhibit a constructive skill and an ingenious application of philosophical principles which we cannot believe has ever been excelled. With such great works we are not at present engaged, but the construction of the simplest building requires to do it well, a judicious application of scientific principles; and by such an application the carpenter can perhaps do more to give the building great strength at the least cost than any other one concerned in its erection. There are many, however, who from simple ignorance still hold fast to old clumsy practices. They scribe and fit all their work before putting it together, and from a simple lack of mental energy and the spirit of improvement—remain ignorant, incompetent, and poor.

Pl. X.

THE MANSION.

Saml Sloan Archt

P.S. Duval & Co's Steam lith. Press Philada

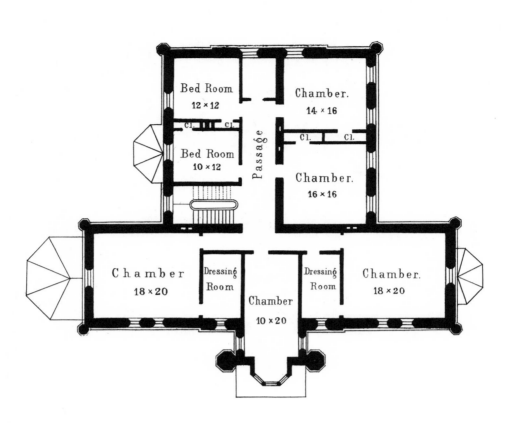

SECOND FLOOR.

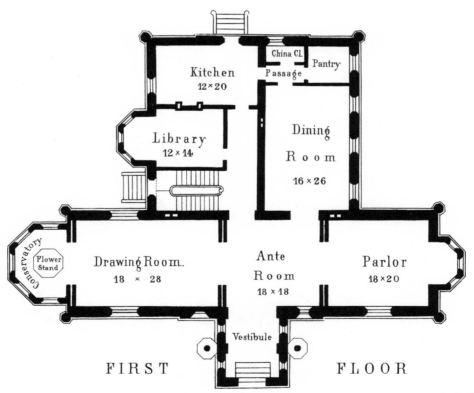

Scale 16 feet to the inch.

FIRST   FLOOR

Sam! Sloan Arch!   P.S.Duval & Co's Steam lith.Press,Philad.ª

GROUND PLANS.

Pl. XII.

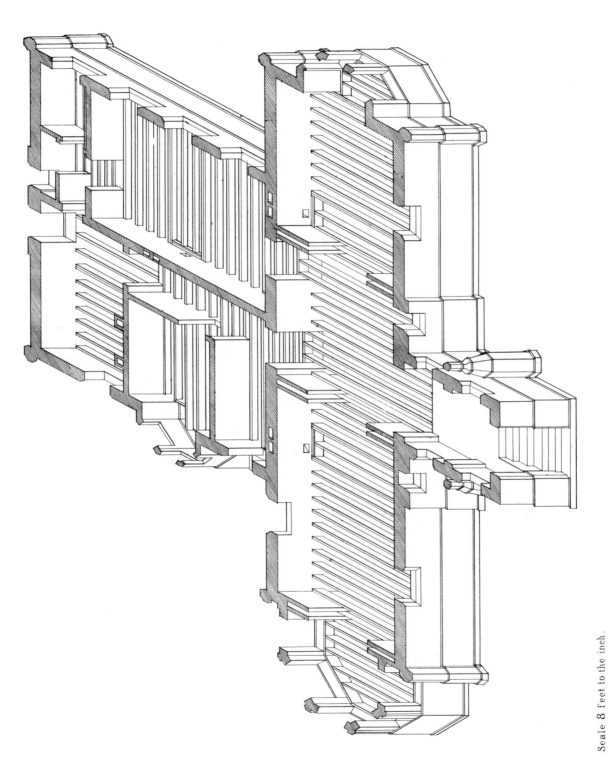

ISOMETRIC VIEW.

Scale 8 feet to the inch.

Saml Sloan Archt.

P.S.Duval & Co's Steam lith Press, Philada

Fig. 1.

Fig. 3.

Fig. 4.

Fig. 5.

Fig. 2.

Fig. 6.

Fig 7.

Scale ½ inch to the foot.

Saml Sloan, Archt.

DETAILS.

FLOWER STAND.

Scale 1 inch to the foot.

Sam⁰ Sloan, Arch⁰   P.S.Duval & Co's Steam lith. Press, Philad⁰

In this country, where timber is so cheap, the great majority of dwellings are entirely of wood. In the old world the remains of the immediate forests are too valuable to be used in this way, and all the timber is transported from great distances, thereby becoming costly. Even in those parts of the houses which are necessarily framework, iron is often substituted for wood. As yet we have an abundance of timber and are not forced into such devices, though indeed by a skillful management of iron the carpenter has much improved his art. Buildings of stone or brick are best on account of their stability, comfort and architectural expression, but where economy is of the first importance, framehouses are preferred. In such there is, of course, the greatest display of carpentry, but every building contains the floors, partitions and roof, each of which involves principles essentially different. The next article will contain a general description of these.

THE MANSION.

DESIGN TWENTY-NINTH.

THE scene before us on Plate X. is not marked by those distinguishing characteristics which would entitle it to rank as a landscape. It is such a view as may be obtained on almost any of our streams skirted by a railway. The idea was originally suggested by an excursion up the Schuylkill, where there are many such scenes. The western bank of the Hudson also abounds in country seats, having spacious lawns in front, gently sloping towards the river. The introduction of the railroad upon the edge of the stream was regarded by the owners of these seats as an intolerable nuisance, not only because of the danger, smoke and noise made by the cars, but also because it destroyed the pretty effect of the lawns gently inclining and passing beneath the rippling surface of the water. This is certainly disagreeable, but the frequent passing of a majestic locomotive with its long train, is decidedly picturesque, to say nothing of the convenience of having the rapid conveyance near. A word may be said of the situation on the banks of a river. If the house is intended simply as a summer residence, then the western bank is far preferable, the building facing the river. This is so chiefly for two reasons. We get a cool shade upon the lawn early in the evening, and avoid the reflection of the afternoon sun upon the water. On the eastern bank we have often experienced very warm afternoons in moderate weather, arising from this cause. Besides the heat, the light is also reflected to the eastern bank in such a manner as to be very disagreeable to the eyes. If the building is intended to be occupied throughout the year, then this objection may be counterbalanced by having on the eastern side a high bank, affording shelter from the eastern winds. The warm reflection, too, at this season would be agreeable. A southern prospect towards a river running east and west would perhaps, in this case, be best.

The present design is in the Tudor style, or as we have before termed it, debased Gothic. It is very similar to many of the old family mansions in England and Germany, somewhat modernized, of course, to suit the wants of our times. The general effect of the building is displayed in the perspective view, and needs no description to make it thoroughly understood. To be entirely true, it should be built of dressed gray stone, but it will answer very well if built of rubble, or brick, and rough-cast. The roof, which contains an attic, is overlaid with slate in diamond pattern. The parapets should be finished either with heavy slate or slabs of stone, to protect them from the action of the weather.

On Plate XI. are delineated the Ground plans. Entering front we pass up the covered steps into the vestibule, which opens into a large Ante room or Hall, lighted by a small stained glass window, having the Parlor on one side and the Drawing room on the other. With these it communicates by sliding doors, so that on occasion the whole may be thrown into one large room. At the end of the parlor is a bay window, and at the corresponding end of the Drawing room is a small Conservatory for the reception of a few choice plants. The Dining room, Library and domestic offices are in the rear. The Library also has a bay window. Passing above stairs we find five large Chambers and two smaller bed rooms, thus exhibiting accommodations for a family of ten or twelve persons, including the servants. It will be remembered that there are two large rooms in the attic above. At the end of the passage there is a small apartment, which may be used either as a linen closet or bath room.

Plate XII. exhibits an isometric view of the first floor naked, the section of the walls being made just above the window sills. The floor is single joisted, there being no necessity for a ceiling to the cellar below. A close examination of this floor will discover many of the principles described in the first part of the article on Framing. The floor of the porch and vestibule is supposed to be paved with tiles. The general effect of a drawing of this description is very false, but, it being isometric, accurate measurements of the bearing of the joists, the thickness of the walls, the height of the windows, &c., &c., may be taken. The flues from the furnace in the cellar are also exhibited.

Plate XIII. presents the details of the outside of the building. Fig. 1 is the tower or buttress which stands at the corner of the vestibule. Fig. 2 is the base of the same. This buttress is constructed of wood, and is merely intended as an ornament. Fig. 3 shows the parapet. A section is also given which exhibits the construction of the inside gutter. Fig. 4, a ball finial. Fig. 5 is a vertical section of the projecting window over the vestibule. Fig. 6 is a part of the bay window of the parlor or the conservatory. Fig. 7 is a horizontal section of the same.

THE FLOWER STAND.

Accompanying the above design, and numbered with it, is a flower stand, exhibited on Plate XIV. It is to be constructed of wood, carved after the Gothic fashion, and is supposed to be placed in the conservatory, at the end of the drawing room. Only a few vases are shown, but places are prepared for placing many others on it. The stand itself is surmounted by a bird cage, which may be made movable, and is thought to be a proper accompaniment to the flowers. It is in the Decorated style.

FRAMING.

THE work of a house carpenter, as mentioned in the previous article, chiefly consists in the framing of the floors, the partitions and the roof. He is frequently called upon to do lighter work, but those particularly belong to his art, and call forth all his abilities. In the march of improvement many different ways have been devised for accomplishing the same object, and variations in the size of work, or the difference of position, require an essentially different style of framing. But let this fact be ever present to the mind. The most simple combinations, provided they be sufficient, are always the best. It is often the case that a vast amount of labor and material are literally thrown away in complicated systems of framing. The roof of the Imperial Riding House at Moscow is one of the most splendid specimens of carpentry in existence. Its principal feature is an arched beam, whose span is two hundred and thirty-five feet, constructed in a curious and scientific manner. But there is no doubt that a large sum of money was unnecessarily expended; for the same thing might have been done more securely in a much more simple manner. Not only are the simplest methods the cheapest, but they are almost always the strongest. All sawing or cutting of timber weakens it, and therefore should be avoided as much as possible. Nothing exhibits this fact more forcibly than the various methods of scarfing timber. This consists in joining two pieces of timber lengthwise, so as to form one long piece. Many methods have been devised for securing the pieces so as to offer resistance either to cross strains, as in a girder, or to a strain in the direction of its length, as in a tie beam. None are so efficient as ordinary splicing, either with a parallel or diagonal joint, and fastening with bolts or bands of iron. These are the most simple methods, and by far the best. The principle should mark all carpentry, and will always produce more strength and durability, with less labor.

The horizontal timbers, which are arranged at different heights in the building, in order to support the flooring boards, are called the naked flooring. The particular arrangement depends, of course, to a great extent upon the form and size of the room, and the amount of weight which they may be required to support; but there are three kinds of floors, each of which is adapted to suit particular circumstances. They are termed single joisted floors, double floors and framed floors. Floors have been and may yet be constructed on entirely different principles from those designated, but we find that they prevail almost universally in civilized countries, and are regarded as the best methods for combining cheapness, strength and durability. There was executed in Amsterdam a singular floor that deserves notice, since it was constructed without the aid of any supporting timbers whatever. "The room is sixty feet square, and surrounded by strong wall plates framed at the angles, and firmly secured by iron straps. The plates are rebated to receive the edges of the flooring. The flooring consists of three thicknesses of one and a half inch boards. The first or lowest thickness is laid diagonally with its edges resting in the rebates of the wall plates, and rising about two inches and a half higher in the middle than at the sides of the room. The second layer of boards is also diagonal, at right angles to the first. The two thicknesses are nailed together. The boards of the third layer are parallel to one of the sides of the room, and form the upper side of the floor, being well nailed to the boards below. All the boards are tongued and grooved together, and form a solid floor four inches and a half thick." This floor is supported by its crown in a manner similar to a vault. It is firm and secure, so long as the weight upon it is tolerably distributed, but it would be endangered by very unequal bearing, since then there would be a liability of its rising in opposite parts.

The first description of floor named, i. e., a single joisted floor, consists of a series of joists supported at either end by walls or partitions. The flooring boards are nailed directly upon these, and the lathing of the ceiling is attached to the under edge. Sometimes every third or fourth joist is made deeper, and ceiling joists fastened to these. This method deafens somewhat, and the ceilings are less apt to crack. The flooring joists should be thin, but deep. Three inches, by about nine or ten, is the best proportion.

It often happens that there are places where the joists cannot have a bearing upon the wall, as in front of flues, in which case the ends have to be framed into cross joists, called trimmers. These trimmers should always be much thicker in proportion to their length than the joists, as is also the case with the trimming joists, which are the two joists which support the ends of the trimmer. They are commonly made by nailing two ordinary joists together.

There is a tendency in the joists when supporting a heavy weight to twist, and if they can do so, the floor will yield much more readily. Wherever the bearing exceeds eight feet, this tendency must be provided against by the use of struts, which add much to the stiffness of the floor. In a bearing of twelve or fourteen feet, two rows of struts should be used, and so on. The struts consist of a row of blocks placed between the lower edges of the joists, the nailed flooring above giving sufficient security to the upper edges. These will effectually prevent any twisting of the joists; but there is another advantage gained by the use of lattice work bridging, or as it is sometimes called, herring bone bridging. By this means, not only are the joists effectually prevented from twisting, but each receives a certain degree of support from the two adjacent ones, and cannot yield without they also do so. Thus the floor is made to possess more uniformity of strength, and is consequently more reliable. The good effects of this arrangement in single joisted floors especially, belong principally to the ceiling attached, which is less apt to crack. It is well to run an iron bar through the middle of the joists close to the bridging, in order to draw them together, then the effect of the shrinkage will be to tighten the whole.

It is highly desirable in constructing a good floor, to use some means to prevent the passage of sound into the room beneath. This process is termed by the carpenters, deafening, and is much more necessary

SIDE ELEVATION.

FRONT ELEVATION.

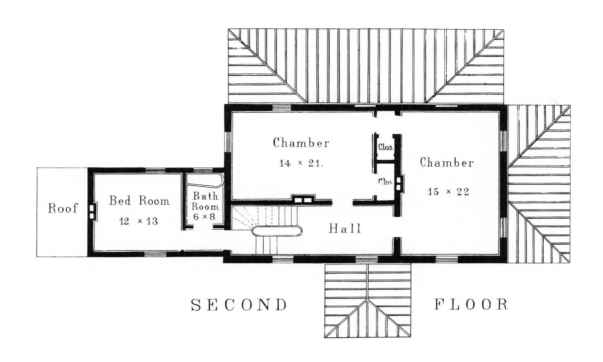

SECOND   FLOOR

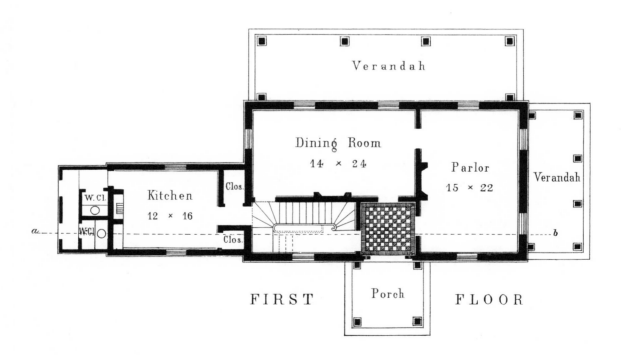

FIRST   Porch   FLOOR

Scale 12 feet to the inch.

GROUND PLANS.

Saml Sloan Arch.^t   P.S. Duval & Co.^s lith. Steam Press, Philad.^a

Pl. XVII.

SECTION.

Sam.l Sloan Arch.t

P. S. Duval & C.o steam lith.press Ph.

in a single joisted than in a double framed floor. The best method of accomplishing it has already been described in the specifications attached to the various designs in this work. It consists in nailing cleats on either side of each joist, about two inches from its upper edge, for the support of an intermediate floor, composed of short boards lying between the joists. Then the space included by this floor and the upper one is to be filled with coarse mortar. The mortar being a very bad conductor of sound, almost entirely prevents its passage, and deadens to a great extent the sonorous vibrations of the timber. It is evident that this arrangement adds greatly to the weight of the floor, but the weight, being so uniformly distributed, gives greater steadiness without endangering it to any considerable extent. If, however, the floor is originally weak, other methods must be resorted to. It is recommended in this case to lay strips of list or thin slices of cork on the upper edge of the joists, before laying the floor.

The floors of a cellar or basement are generally composed of joists resting upon sleepers, bedded in the cellar bottom. Sometimes the joists themselves are bedded in the earth, and the sleepers dispensed with. The joists in these cases need not be so deep as for an ordinary floor. The sleepers should be either of chestnut or of locust; the latter is the best to resist rot. They should be laid in concrete, especially if the ground is damp. The concrete should not come quite as high as the upper edge of the sleepers, so that there may be a passage for air beneath the joists. All the enclosed spaces then communicate with each other, and there should be also some arrangement for them to communicate with the upper air, in order to secure ventilation beneath, thereby hindering rot, and preventing a great source of unhealthiness. If this arrangement cannot be made and the joists only are used, then an inch should be added to their breadth, and the spaces had better be filled entirely flush with the floor. The air is thereby mostly excluded, and the rot retarded. In all cases it is recommended to strew the ground with ashes, which will prevent to a considerable extent the growth of fungi.

The double floor differs from the single joisted floor in having ceiling joists attached to cross beams, called binding joists, which rest upon the wall plates, and also give support in some cases to the flooring or bridging joists. This arrangement throws the whole weight of the floor upon fewer points in the walls where the ends of binding joists are inserted. Since, however, these joists should not be more than six or eight feet apart, we may disregard this matter here. The bridging joists had better not rest entirely upon the binding joists, but may be slightly notched upon them, and ultimately rest upon the wall plates. The binding joists should be about six by twelve inches.

Ceiling joists may be much smaller than the bridging joists. Two inches thick, by eight wide, is sufficiently large. They are attached to the binding joists in various ways, and sometimes very carelessly. The fall of the ceiling, mentioned in the article on school houses, was caused by the joists being simply nailed to the underside of the binding joists. This method, being the easiest and cheapest, is often adopted, but is highly reprehensible, since the joists depend entirely for their support upon the mere tenacity of the nail. We are surprised to find the plan recommended in some works upon carpentry. It is not best to mortice

the joists in, because this is a laborious method, and weakens the binding joists. The best way, as practice has shown, is to nail firmly, continuous strips one inch by three against the sides of the binding joist
flush with its lower edge. Notch the end of the ceiling joist one inch from its lower edge to fit this cleat,
and this will leave four inches of the eight inch ceiling joist above to give support. A strip should be nailed
upon the upper edge of these joists to tie them together. In this way it will be seen that the edges of the
ceiling joists extend one inch below the edge of the binding joist. This is done for the sake of the ceiling.
When the lathing is to be done, a strip is nailed across the underside of the binding joist, connecting the
ends of the ceiling joists, and thus forming a continuous edge to nail the laths against. If we plaster immediately upon the binding joist the ceiling will certainly crack. This can not be avoided in single joisted
floors where a girder is introduced, for it occupies the whole depth. Indeed, the double floor is only used
in order to obtain a perfect ceiling, since it is but little if any stronger than a single joisted floor.

There remains the double framed floor. The difference here consists in the introduction of a girder.
The girder is frequently used in the construction of a single joisted floor where its extent is greater than
the length of the joists. In the double framed floor, proper, the ends of the girders rest upon the wall
plates. The binding joists are framed into them, and the bridging joists also. The best plan for connecting the bridging joist with the girder, is to make a dove-tail notch in the girder to receive the end of the
joist. The double framed floor is only used where the extent is so great as to be beyond the reach of
joists. The single joisted floor with girders may be used in all cases, but the double framed floor secures a
good ceiling, and prevents the passage of sound entirely.

The girder, which is the principal feature in a double framed floor, consists of a long, strong beam, supported at the ends, as before stated, by the walls. The whole weight imposed upon the girder, together
with its own, is therefore transmitted to these two points. Hence it is important that the ends of the girder should always rest over piers, and not over an opening. The bearing should be distributed too by a
wall plate. It is bad to have a girder pass obliquely through a floor, and if this cannot be otherwise
avoided, it may be best to let the end be placed over the opening with an arch and wall plate to throw the
weight on the piers. The size of girders, and their distance apart, depends of course in a great measure
upon their position and service, but they should always be as deep as possible.

The girder spoken of consists of a simple beam. There are methods, however, which have been adopted
for strengthening it, when the length is necessarily great. It is recommended in all cases to saw a girder
down the middle, turn one piece end for end, and bolt them together with the sawn sides outwards. By
this means the stiffness of the beam is much increased, especially if the grain is at all irregular; and if
strips be placed between the pieces so as to allow a free circulation of air, its proneness to decay is lessened.
Some have imagined that the strength of the girder is increased by this operation. It is in fact diminished,
but in so small a degree as to be of no comparative consequence. If there be any difference, the side
having the straitest grain should be turned down. All mortices near the middle of the girder where the strain

is greatest, must be avoided. There are methods, however, by which its strength may be increased. The truss described in the last edition of the Carpenter's New Guide, is good, but is more valuable, as adding to the stiffness of the girder, than to its strength. The plan now in general use, consists in having an iron bar extending from end to end, between the pieces, in such a manner, that the girder hangs upon it. The arrangement is admirable, and should always be adopted. Girders trussed in this manner, will bear weights without sensible deflexion, which otherwise would break them. Therefore, in the same floor we may use a much smaller girder trussed, than one untrussed. In large edifices, whose importance justifies the expense, girders are often made of cast iron. These are of course best, but a description of them would lead us somewhat beyond our present limits.

A crown is sometimes given to floors, by planing the joists, so as to make the floor rise in the middle, about half an inch in ten or twelve feet. This is a good practice, for the best constructed floors will settle to some extent. It is always difficult to make the flooring boards fit tight, for in shrinking, the joints open. A suggestion found in Evelyn's Silva, may not be out of place. "To prevent all possible accidents, when you lay floors, let the joints be shot, fitted and tacked down only the first year, nailing them for good and all the next; and by this means they will lie staunch, close, and without shrinking in the least, as if they were all of one piece: and, on this occasion, I am to add an observation that may prove of no small use to builders, that if one take up deal boards that have lain in the floor one hundred years, and shoot them again, they will certainly shrink (toties quoties,) without the former method."

But few remarks about partitions are necessary. They are generally constructed more carelessly than any other part of the carpenter's work. If it be practicable, they should rest mainly on the walls, and be attached to the floor above, being entirely independent of that below. In this way, the cracking of the cornice may be avoided. It must be remembered, that a partition is, in itself, a very heavy piece of framing, and, therefore, the lightest material should be used, and the whole should be trussed in a secure manner. The doorways often render this a difficult matter, and there are many cases in which it requires much skill to construct one so firm, that the plastering shall not crack at all. It is best to delay the plastering as long as possible, in order to give time for settlement. The next article, will be a continuation of this general subject, and will treat more particularly of roofs.

A PLAIN DWELLING.

DESIGN THIRTIETH.

THE side and front elevations of this design are given on Plate XV. They are engraved in lines, which is a style much preferred by many persons for architectural drawings, to the tinted plates, heretofore given. It requires quite as much labor, and is, therefore, quite as expensive as the other method. The advantage consists in having a sharper outline, from which measurements may be taken, while at the same time the general effect is retained, so as to present a truthful and pleasing picture. Some few buildings in the preceding parts of our work have been delineated in this way, and have met with decided approval, while we must confess that to us it is preferable, as being more in the usual style of the best architectural drawings. The plate before us, as close examination will show, has been lithographed with a pencil instead of a pen, and hence presents more the appearance of a sketch, thus affording the artist an opportunity of producing better effects than can be produced by the engraver's pen.

The building itself is quite plain, and has, according to the proper meaning of the word, a homely appearance. It is two stories and a half high in the body, and two stories in the wing; the rooms not being as high as those in the main building. The fronts are almost destitute of ornament. The walls may be built of stone or of brick rough cast. The roof would be best of tin, painted both above and below, but may be shingled. Indeed the whole house would do very well if built entirely of wood, the walls being closely boarded, painted and sanded. The half story above might be left off, which would bring the eaves down to the string course above the second story windows, but the appearance of the whole would be much injured because of the height of the wing. Beside the front porch there are two verandahs represented, which are to be built of wood. Iron posts, of fanciful patterns, might be substituted. The roofs of these are of tin, drawn over slats. The small flower shelf beneath the gable window, is made of wood, with a wire railing. Beneath the front first story windows are panels. The one to the left is of wood, that to the right is an iron railing, and the sash extend to the floor. This is so arranged to be consistent with the other windows of the parlor which also extend to the floor, so as to lead out to the verandahs.

Plate XVI. presents the ground plans. The vestibule is paved with plain tiles. To the left is the hall, containing the stairway, which extends directly up with a continued rail into the third story. The main building contains two spacious rooms, a parlor and dining room; the back windows of which last also extend to the floor. The end window is panelled below, similar to the window on the left of the front. The wing contains the kitchen and two closets, with a bed and bath room above. The whole house, including the story above, will accommodate a family of six persons, including a servant. The plan of the third story is entirely similar to that of the second story main building.

There are no details accompanying this design, such as we have been accustomed to give. On plate XVII. is represented a section of the building instead, supposed to be made through the line A. B. on the first floor of the ground plans. We have here exhibited in the most advantageous manner, the interior of the building, explaining all the principal constructive features and the style of finishing. The cellar extends only beneath the main building, and is therefore cut off from the well of the water closets. Only a close examination is necessary to comprehend the whole.

Pl. XVIII.

THE VILLA.

P. S. Duval & Co's Steam lith. Press Philad.ᵃ

Samˡ Sloan Archᵗ

DRAWING ROOM.

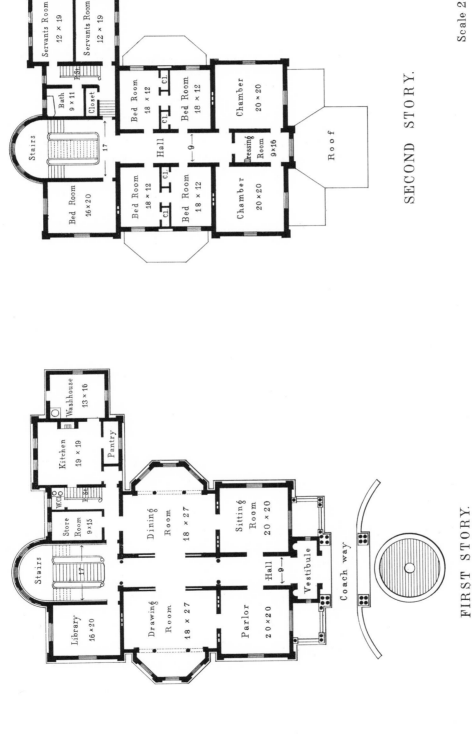

SECOND STORY.

FIRST STORY.

GROUND PLANS.

Scale 24 feet to the inch.

P.S.Duval & Co's Steam lith.Press,Philad?

Sam! Sloan.Arch!

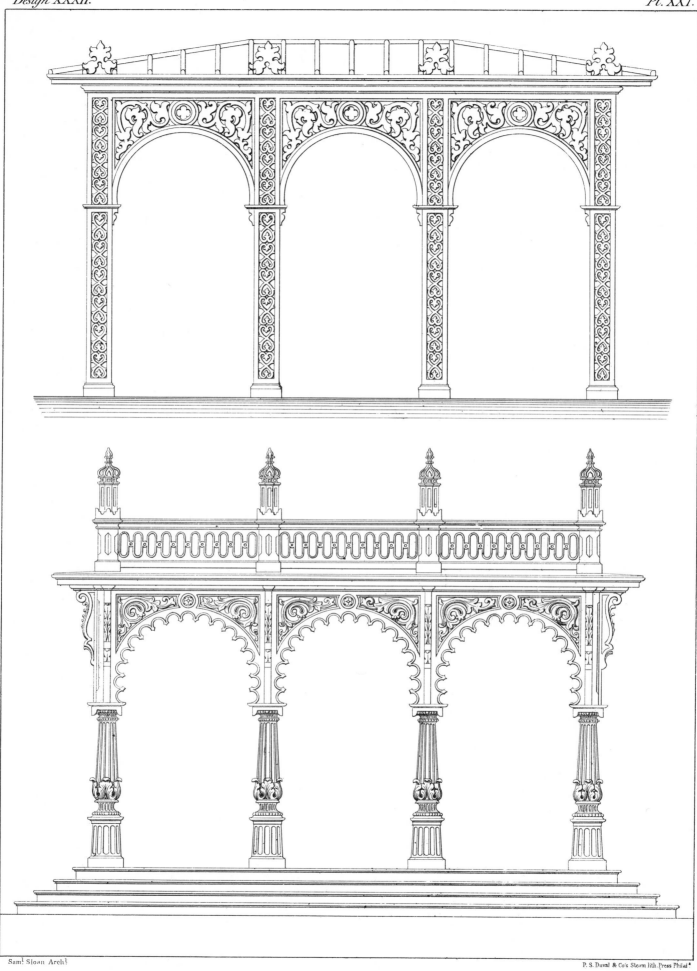

VERANDAHS.

A TABLE

EXHIBITING THE RELATIVE RESISTANCE OF VARIOUS WOODS TO CROSS STRAINS.

Kind of Wood.	Specific gravity.	Length in feet.	Breadth in inches.	Depth in inches.	Deflexion at the time of fracture in inches.	Weight that broke the piece in pounds.	Authorities.
Oak, English, young tree, . . .	·863	2	1	1	1.87	482	By trial.
Ditto, old ship timber, ...	·872	2·5	1	1	1.5	264	Idem.
Ditto, from old tree, ...	·625	2	1	1	1.38	218	Idem.
Ditto, medium quality, ...	·748	2·5	1	1		284	Ebbels.
Ditto, green, ...	·763	2·5	1	1		219	Idem.
Ditto, from Riga, ...	·688	2	1	1	1.25	357	By trial.
Ditto, green, ...	1·063	11·75	8·5	8.5	3.2	25812	Buffon.
Beech, medium quality, . . .	·690	2·5	1	1		271	Ebbels.
Alder, ...	·555	2·5	1	1		212	Idem.
Plane Tree, ...	·648	2·5	1	1		243	Idem.
Sycamore, ...	·590	2·5	1	1		214	Idem.
Chestnut, green	·875	2·5	1	1		180	Idem.
Ash, from young tree, ...	·811	2·5	1	1	2.5	324	By trial.
Ditto, medium quality	·690	2·5	1	1		254	Ebbels.
Ash, ...	·753	2·5	1	1	2·38	314	By trial.
Elm, common	·544	2·5	1	1		216	Ebbels.
Ditto, wych, green	·763	2·5	1	1		192	Idem.
Acacia, green	·820	2·5	1	1		249	Idem.
Mahogany, Spanish, seasoned . .	·853	2·5	1	1		170	By trial.
Ditto, Honduras, seasoned . .	·560	2·5	1	1		255	Idem.
Walnut, green, ...	·920	2·5	1	1		195	Ebbels.
Poplar, Lombardy	·374	2·5	1	1		131	Idem.
Ditto, abele	·511	2·5	1	1	1·5	228	By trial.
Teak	·744	7	2	2	4·00	820	Barlow.
Willow	·405	2·5	1	1	3	146	By trial.
Birch	·720	2·5	1	1		207	Ebbels.
Cedar of Libanus, dry	·486	2·5	1	1	2.75	165	By trial.
Riga fir	·480	2·5	1	1	1.3	212	Idem.
Memel fir	·553	2·5	1	1	1.15	218	Idem.
Norway fir, from Long Sound, .	·639	2	1	1	1.125	396	Idem.
Mar Forest fir, ...	·715	7	2	2	5.5	360	Barlow.
Scotch fir, English growth . .	·529	2·5	1	1	1.75	233	By trial.
Ditto, ditto	·460	2·5	1	1		157	Ebbels.
Christiana white deal	·512	2	1	1	.937	343	By trial.
American white spruce	·465	2	1	1	1.312	285	Idem.
Spruce fir, British growth . .	·555	2·5	1	1		186	Ebbels.
American pine, Weymouth . . .	·460	2	1	1	1·125	329	By trial.
Larch, choice specimen . . .	·640	2·5	1	1	3	253	Idem.
Ditto, medium quality	·622	2·5	1	1		223	Idem.
Ditto, very young wood . . .	·396	2·5	1	1	1·75	129	Idem.
Riga fir	·610	4	3	3		4530	Fincham.
Red pine	·544	4	3	3		3780	Idem.
Yellow pine	·439	4	3	3		2756	Idem.
Cowrie	·579	4	3	3		4110	Idem.
Poona	·632	4	3	3		3990	Idem.

THE VILLA.

DESIGN THIRTY-FIRST.

WE have presented on plate XVIII. a perspective view of this design. The building is in the Italian style, of which we have given various specimens heretofore. As a pretty full description of this design is requisite, we will not delay here to remark upon its different features, or upon the landscape in which it is placed. It was originally designed for Mr. L. A. Godey, the accomplished editor of the Lady's Book, to insert in the pages of that magazine, and has already appeared in its pages. It is, therefore, his property, and by his consent we transfer it to our volume.

Plate XIX. exhibits the interior of the drawing room. It will be seen that the style of finishing is quite elaborate, and adapted in style to the exterior of the building. The ceiling of the room is frescoed in the same general style of the ceiling given in the first volume of this work, though the pattern is entirely different. The cornice and pilasters on the sides of the room, are to be executed in plaster. At the end of the room is an opening, the lintel above which is supported by two columns. Beyond these is a large bay window, finished in the same general style, and admitting light. The view of the room is taken from the main entrance, and there is an additional door upon the left hand, leading into the parlor. The plan may be more readily comprehended by an examination of the next plate.

Plate XX. exhibits the ground plan. In front of the house is a cistern, with a fountain in the middle. Immediately before the vestibule is a coach way covered. The balconies on either side of the vestibule are approached through the front windows of the parlor and sitting room, which reach the floor. The dining room is of the same size and plan as the drawing room, which has just been fully described. They both communicate with the hall by means of sliding doors, directly opposite each other, so that when thrown open the whole will form one large room. Back of these are the stairs, library and domestic offices. The stairway is lighted by the semicircular projecting window. There is also a private stairway near the kitchen, for servants. The second floor of this part of the building, it will be seen, is not so high as the other.

In the second story main building are two large chambers and five good sized bed rooms, containing closets. Between the chambers is a dressing room which may be shut off from either. In the wing are two bed rooms and a bath room.—The whole will comfortably accommodate a family of ten, including servants.

It will be observed that there is a tower on the front of the perspective view. The approach to this tower is by means of a step ladder at the end of the hall. Nothing more was thought necessary, as the ascent is not often made, but if it be preferred the dressing room may be made shorter, and a small permanent stairway built.

GENERAL DESCRIPTION

Of the workmanship and materials, to be used in the erection of this design.

There is to be a cellar throughout the entire extent of the building, including all appendages, at least ten feet deep, below the level of the principal floor. The trenches for the foundations must be at least eight inches below the cellar bottom.

All the exterior walls of the basement are to be of quarry building stone, of the best quality, and they should be flushed in mortar of the best quality, and grouted every two feet, if the material used be of an absorbent quality. These walls must be two feet thick to the level of the first tier of joists. The foundations of the cross walls need not be more than eighteen inches thick. The steps of the front porch, all outer sills, the base course and water table around the building, are to be of the best Connecticut granite, neatly tooled. All the walls of the superstructure are composed of the best burnt bricks. The exterior course should be of hard brick, no soft brick coming within four inches of the face of the wall. The mortar must be removed from all the exterior joints at least a half an inch deep from the surface. The exterior walls of the building are to be fourteen inches thick to the roof, with a hollow space one inch and a half wide in the middle, between the inner course and the body of the wall, the two being tied together by making every fifth a heading course. The division walls in the first and second stories are also to be of good brick work, nine inches thick. The principal openings of the interior must have arched heads to correspond with the apertures in the exterior walls.

The joists of the principal floor are to be of spruce pine, three by twelve inches. Those of the second floor are to be three by ten inches, of hemlock. All are to be placed sixteen inches between centres, to have one course of lattice work, bridging through the centre, and to have three-fourths of an inch crown. The wall plates at the foot of the roof, and those for the gable timbers to rest upon are to be three by nine inches, and are to project two inches from the face of the wall. The rafters are to be of the usual cut, and three by eight inches, those in the vallies being three by ten inches, and those for the flat over the hall three by nine inches. All must be placed sixteen inches between centres, and are to be closely sheathed for a tin or galvanized iron covering.

The floors in the principal story are to be composed of the best Carolina heart pine boards, one inch and a quarter thick. Those of the second story are one inch thick, and this floor must be deafened in the usual manner.

The stairs must be built of one and a quarter inch heart pine, step boards of yellow pine, with one and a quarter inch white pine risers, placed on four three by twelve inch bearers, of hemlock. The newel is to be ten inches at the base, with a richly carved shaft, and the balusters are to be three inches at the base, turned. The rail is to be two and a half by five inches, moulded, and all are to be of black walnut, well varnished. The private stairs are to be constructed in the usual manner.

All the windows in the first story are to have inside shutters, and are to be finished otherwise, together with the doors, in the usual manner, or according to working drawings, furnished for the purpose. All the exterior walls are to be rough cast in the best manner, painted and sanded to represent brown stone. This description will be amply sufficient for a builder, but if more is required a specification must be drawn up.

VERANDAHS.

DESIGN THIRTY-SECOND.

On Plate XXI. are presented two designs for verandahs. They are to be built entirely of wood, with tin roofs. The one below is much the richest, and has the addition of a balcony above. The patterns of the upper one are merely to be sawn out, but that below has carved spandrils, posts and brackets. Verandahs of fanciful patterns are often constructed of iron. These are more lasting, of course, than the wooden ones, but at the same time much more expensive.

A SMALL COTTAGE.
DESIGN THIRTY-THIRD.

THERE is perhaps a much greater demand for small cheap cottages of tasteful designs than for buildings of any other description. The millionares in our country, who wish to retire into a quiet country home, are but few in number, compared with those in moderate circumstances, whose tastes lead them away from the city, at least during the hot summer months. Persons of this class find quite as much comfort and pleasure in a little rural home as they could in a lordly mansion. For such this design, plate XXII., was prepared. It is simple, unostentatious, cheap, and at the same time is not destitute of ornamental effect. The house is framed, and covered upon the outside with vertical weather boarding. The roof may be either of tin, or shingled. The eaves are made very projecting, and are supported by wooden brackets.

On the upper part of Plate XXIV. are the ground plans of the first and second stories of this design. The house is small and simple. There is to be a cellar beneath its entire extent, which has a stairway leading from the kitchen. The cellar walls should be of stone, as high as the first tier of joists. There are four good sized bed rooms in the second story, showing that the house will comfortably accommodate a family of four or five persons. The stairs are enclosed.

LABORER'S HOME.
DESIGN THIRTY-FOURTH.

Plate XXIII. presents a design for including several small dwellings under one roof. The mode of building is cheaper than if each was erected separately, and therefore for the same total sum, more comfortable accommodations can be provided within. It is often the case that a large number of small dwellings are needed near to a large manufactory, for the accommodation of the hands. For such a purpose, a design of this kind is admirably suited. The building represented is to be framed, and closely boarded outside. The roof is to be shingled; and there are small attic rooms, as may be seen by the gable windows.

The floor plan of the design, together with the little gardens in front, are exhibited on Plate XXIV. It will be seen that each dwelling is completely shut off from all others, so that there can be no interference in the families. In each there is a dining room, and a small kitchen back. The stairs ascend into a commodious bed room, which, with the attic room above, is sufficient for a small family. There should be a range of cellars under the buildings, having stairs beneath the main stairway.

In some future number another design of this description will probably be given.

SIDE ELEVATION.

FRONT ELEVATION.

Sam! Sloan Arch. P.S.Duval &C° lith press Ph

SIDE ELEVATION.

FRONT ELEVATION.

Sam Sloan Arch.   P. S. Duval & Cº Steam lith press Ph.

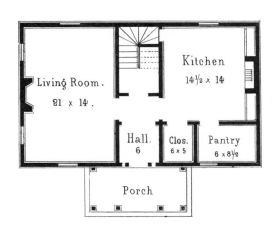

Living Room.
21 × 14.

Kitchen
14½ × 14

Hall.
6

Clos.
6 × 5

Pantry
6 × 8½

Porch

FIRST STORY.

Bed Room
10¼ × 14

Bed Room
10¼ × 14

6

Bed Room
10¼ 14

Clos.

Clos. Clos

Bed Room
10¼ × 14.

SECOND STORY.

Design XXXIV.

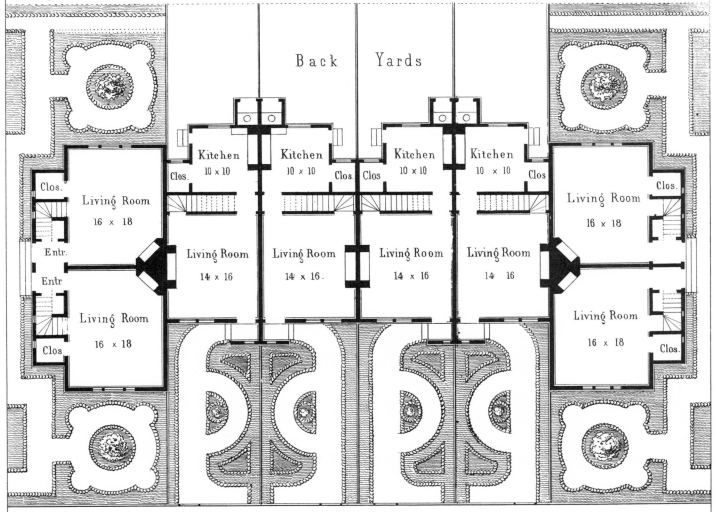

Back   Yards

Clos.

Kitchen
10 × 10

Clos.

Kitchen
10 × 10

Clos

Clos

Kitchen
10 × 10

Kitchen
10 × 10

Clos

Clos.

Living Room
16 × 18

Entr.

Entr

Living Room
16 × 18

Clos.

Living Room
14 × 16

Living Room
14 × 16.

Living Room
14 × 16

Living Room
14 16

Living Room
16 × 18

Clos.

Living Room
16 × 18

Clos.

Scale 12 feet to the inch.

GROUND PLANS

Sam. Sloan Arch.   P. S. Duval & Cº Steam lith press Ph.

FRAMING.

Continued.

OME allusion has already been made, in the article upon Carpentry, to the roofs used by the ancients. The most simple kind were flat, composed of timbers laid from wall to wall.— Such are still used in those countries of the East where rain seldom or never falls. They are covered with metal, tiles or turf, and are pleasant places for evening resort. This is the weakest kind of covering, and can only be used for small buildings. An improvement is the simple inclination, in constant use at the present day. All our small city buildings are covered in this way, which is preferred because there is the least loss of room, and with a metal covering the pitch is sufficient to throw off the rain. In large buildings, where a considerable extent of ceiling is required, other methods must be resorted to, and the roof must be so braced as not to require more than two points of support. The old Gothic roofs always have a high pitch. The outline is a striking feature, and is, in general, gracefully proportioned to the magnitude of the building. The high roofs are in perfect unison with the aspiring character of Gothic architecture, and are best adapted to throw off the northern snows. They were so framed as to resemble an arch resting on the wall as an abutment, which is in principle bad, since the lateral thrust must be provided against. This style of roof has consequently gone entirely out of use, except, as before stated, in direct imitations of the style.

The large roofs of the present day, more closely resemble those of the Greeks and Romans. Of the Grecian roofs we judge only by the pediments, since there are no remains of roofs whatever. The Romans often exhibited wonderful skill in carpentry, and in some respects we are still much behind them. The pediments of the Greek temples vary in their inclination to the horizon from twelve to sixteen degrees; the latter corresponds very nearly with one seventh of the span. The pediments of the Roman buildings vary from twenty-three to twenty-four degrees. Twenty-four degrees is nearly two ninths of the span, and is the angle that Palladio recommends for roofs in Italy. Some of the Roman domes are perhaps the grandest coverings in existence. They are built of entirely stone, and are nothing more than huge circular vaults. The modern domes are mostly constructed of wood, being mere imitations of the other. The building of these, however, has led to the construction of arched roofs where the span is very great, and the successful erection of some of these is among the greatest triumphs of modern carpentry.

The term Roof in carpentry, is applied to the framework which supports the covering of the building. The pitch of the roof is the angle which its inclined side makes with the plane of the horizon, and is varied with us according to the extent of the roof and the nature of the covering. At the present day we are accustomed to roofs much lower than those used formerly under entirely similar circumstances. The whole height need never be above one-third of the span, and it never should be less than one-sixth. The most usual pitch for slate covering is one-fourth, which makes an angle of about twenty-six and a half degrees.

That part of the roof which requires most skill, and on which the whole mainly depends for support, is the frame; usually in the form of an obtuse isosceles triangle. A series of these is ranged across on the wall plates, and give support to the common rafters. The various timbers which are used in this construction have received distinct names, and are entitled to separate consideration. The principal are the Wall Plates, Tie Beams, Collar Beams, King Posts, Queen Posts, Struts, Principal Rafters, Ridge Piece, Pole Plates, Purlins and Common Rafters.

The wall plates are stout pieces laid along on the top of the walls, on which the ends of the tie beams rest. They are intended to distribute the weight of the roof, and to hold the last courses of brick work in their place. Sometimes they are not so wide as the top of the wall, and are laid with the inner edge flush with the face of the wall. Where the walls are very thick this is unavoidable, but it is much the best plan, when the thickness of the walls admit it, to have them, wide enough to cover the whole. Their object plainly shows this. The tie beams are oftentimes cocked down upon them, or otherwise attached. Although it is recommended in many books on carpentry, yet we do not hesitate to say that the plan is a bad one, since any settling of the roof, or shrinkage, must inevitably exert a thrust upon the walls, or draw them from their perpendicular. If this does not result, the wall plate is at least moved from its position, which is bad. Let the tie beams simply rest upon the plates. The mere weight of the roof is amply sufficient to keep it in position.

The tie beam is the piece which extends directly across from wall to wall. The principal rafters are attached to the ends, and the centre is supported by the king post. There is very little strain upon the tie beam, and it is generally made much heavier than there is any necessity for. The thrust of the principal rafters exert a strain in the direction of its length, which, however, is easily resisted. The only cross strain is the weight of the ceiling, but since the tie beam is supported in the middle, and, if it is long, at other points, we can easily see that it does not require much timber to perform its office. If there are rooms within the roof and floors, more strength is, of course, necessary. All morticing into tie beams should be avoided, as it weakens them very much. If a king post is used it should have a very short tennon, just sufficient to keep it in place, and the attachment should be by an iron strap passing beneath the beam. It is a common practice in framing roofs to force the tie beam to a certain degree of camber. This is often done with the notion that then it partakes of the properties of an arch. Were it so, the result would be very disastrous. The only object in this, which is, nevertheless, a good plan, is that the ceiling may have a slight curve, so that in case of settlement it will come to a level, and not sag. The collar beam is a mere modification of the tie beam, and is used in the absence of the latter, being placed above, connecting the principal rafters near their middle. Dovetail joints have been condemned by high authority, but they are the best mode of attachment we have, unless an iron strap be used.

King and Queen posts are going entirely out of use, iron bolts being substituted. They are sustaining pieces. The upper end of the king or crown post fits between the ends of the principal rafters quite similar to the keystone of an arch, the lower end is attached, and gives support to the middle of the tie beam. In some cases the ends of the rafters abut directly against each other, and the king post is attached by means of a strap. In this way the lateral shrinkage of the king post is avoided. Queen posts perform the same office as the king post, and are used when the one central support is not sufficient for a tie beam, owing to its length. Straining beams are placed between the heads of the queen posts to prevent their coming together.

The foot of the principal rafter is framed in to the end of the tie beam, and the head of the king post receives the other end. This is the most important piece in the roof, since it gives support to all the others. The covering rests upon it, and from it are suspended the king post or queen posts, the tie beam and the whole ceiling. The principle on which it gives support, is the same as that of the arch. It is important that these pieces should be strong, and not weakened by mortices. The joint at the foot should be particularly attended to so as to avoid shrinkage, and give it the firmest abutment possible. Between the principal rafter and the tie beam struts are often placed, to prevent its bending in the least beneath the weight of the covering. The proper disposition of these struts often requires much skill.

The ridge piece, as its name indicates, passes along the apex of the frames, thus connecting them together, and giving support to the common rafters. The pole plate lays at the foot of the principal rafters, just above the wall plate, and gives support to the foot of the common rafters. The purlins are intermediate pieces to give additional support to the common rafters. These are notched to the purlins, lying parallel to the principal rafters, and receive the slats or sheathing.

We mentioned that king posts and queen posts were little used at the present time. The introduction of iron into carpentry has worked a great revolution. The great difficulty which carpenters have heretofore encountered, has been the shrinkage of timber and the consequent settlement of their work. This shrinkage is almost altogether in the breadth of timber, that in the direction of its length being insensible. If, then, we can manage to have the points of contact occur only at the ends of the pieces, the settlement will be much reduced. In the roof this is accomplished by having an oaken block placed lengthwise between the ends of the principal rafters, or by allowing them to abut directly against each other, and then having an iron rod passed through this block to support the tie beam in place of the king post. Iron rods, bolts and straps are introduced at many other points with great advantage, but our limits will not permit us to enter into a detailed description of these, and we can only refer the reader again to Nicholson's Carpenter's New Guide, where he will find all parts carefully delineated. Roofs may be constructed on several principles different from those described, such as the lattice work, arch, &c., but they are only used where a great span is requisite, which places them beyond our present limits.

It has been previously stated that in the roof there is more occasion for the exercise of skill than in any other part of carpentry. It is impossible in so short a description as the present to do more than barely glance at general principles. The Carpenter should give to this important branch of his art, close mathematical study, and by no means be satisfied with following in the footsteps of our forefathers. Practice, experience and the use of iron, has developed principles heretofore unknown, and even the best roofs, at the present day, may be looked upon as capable of great improvements.

There are many other offices which the carpenter is called upon to perform, but none of a very important character, in an ordinary building. The arches used in dwellings, are never large, and the centering which they require is simple, and easily managed. Perhaps the most difficult of all works of this nature, is the centering for large stone bridges. They have, for a long time, occupied the attention of our engineers, but the results are still very unsatisfactory, and the works are generally performed at great expense and waste of material. The time is soon coming, we hope, when our carpenters and artizans, will be a body of educated, scientific men. Then, but not until then, may we look for rapid advances in the constructive art.

THE CHURCH.

DESIGN THIRTY-FIFTH.

In all sections of our country, the construction of handsome buildings, for religious worship, is receiving attention. In both town and country the uncouth, uncomfortable structures built fifty years ago, are gradually giving place to neat and commodious edifices—some of them erected at a heavy expense. All who love the beautiful in art must be glad of this, for there is no building in the city or village around which so many associations cluster. Its spire is a prominent object in the landscape, and no building so well repays an expenditure of money, used judiciously, and with correct taste. The design we have given is in the Roman Corinthian style, and may be used in any section of country, and by any denomination. The general features of all specimens of this style are similar. Some variety is allowable in the proportions, as the great masters of the art have seldom agreed in this particular, in the specimens now extant. The form and arrangement of the mouldings and ornaments are arbitrary, and may be varied according to the judgment of the architect.

On Plate XXV. are shown the front and side elevation of the building, and the grave yard that usually surrounds the church, in a country town. The building is intended to be built of undressed stone or brick, and to be rough cast, in imitation of cut stone. The portico is hexastile, and the columns are to be of brick, with capitals of terra cotta, a material cheaper than either wood or stone, and quite as durable. The steeple is of wood, and its whole height, from the basement

Pl. XXV.

Design XXV.

Sam.l Sloan Arch.t

THE CHURCH.

P.S.Duval & Co's Steam lith. Press Philad.a

Pl. XXVI.

Sam.l Sloan Arch.t

INTERIOR.

P.S.Duval & Co's Steam lith.Press.Philad.a

Pl. XXVII.

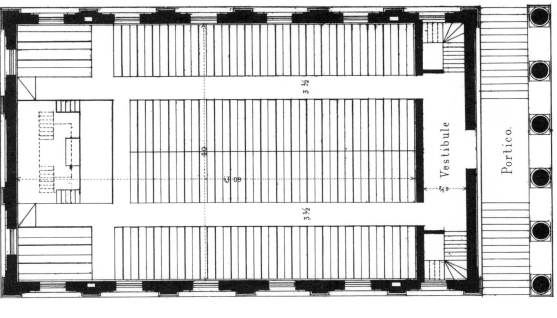

BASEMENT.

Area.

Dressing R.
12 × 13.

Lecture Room.

46 × 40.

Dressing R.
12 × 13.

Furnace

Cellar.

PRINCIPAL FLOOR.

Vestibule

Portico.

3 ½

60 ½ ft.

40

3 ½

6 ½ ft.

G R O U N D   P L A N S .

Scale 12 ft. to the inch.

Sam¹ Sloan Arch.ᵗ

P. S. Duval & Co's Steam lith. Press Philad.ᵃ

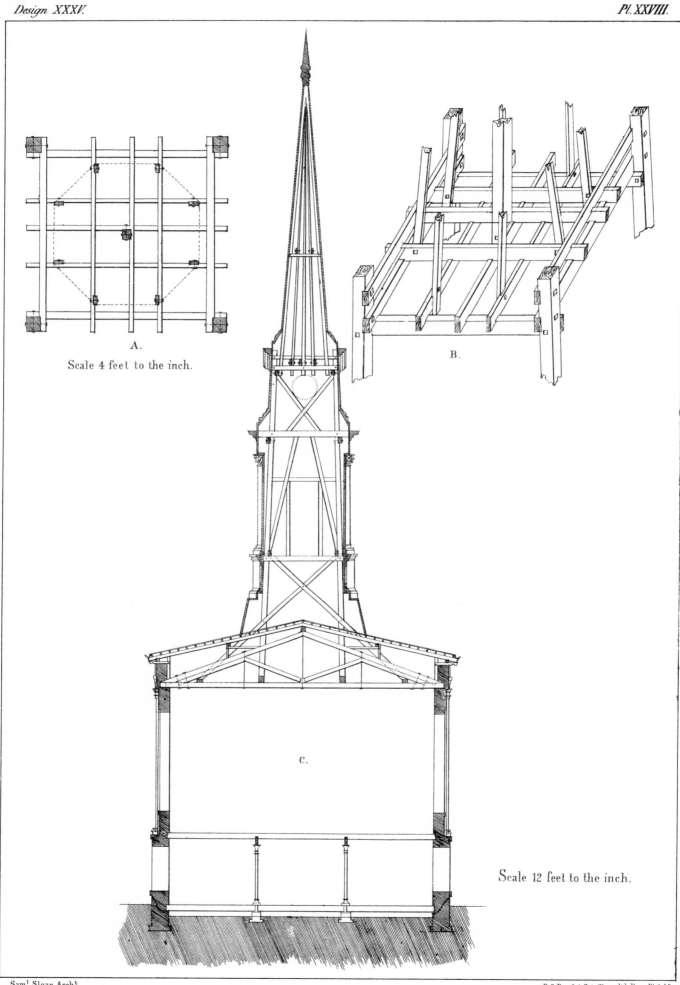

A.

Scale 4 feet to the inch.

B.

C.

Scale 12 feet to the inch.

Saml Sloan Arch.^t   P. S. Duval & Co's Steam lith. Press Philad.^a

VERTICAL SECTION.

floor is one hundred and twenty-five feet. The dimensions of the building are seventy-two feet long by forty-four feet wide. The portico, extending ten feet from the main building, makes the entire length eighty-two feet.

Plate XXVI. shows the interior of the building. In the Cathedrals and Churches of Europe, much expense is lavished upon internal decorations. The walls are covered with monuments of those who have been buried within the church, while the altar is ornamented with paintings of religious subjects, by the ablest masters of art. In our country, custom has not yet sanctioned the erection of monuments, or the use of pictures, to any great extent. Certainly there can be no good reason for neglecting every thing that tends to make the building attractive, and though we may not make our decorations the counterpart of those used on the other side of the Atlantic, the day is not far distant when bare walls and flat ceilings will no longer be thought the only appropriate ornaments of a church. The style of architecture we have chosen for our design does not admit the profusion of ornament that would be appropriate in a Gothic building. The walls may be plain, either papered in panels or painted in fresco. The general effect is heightened by suitable mouldings around the cornice, and by a handsome centre piece. The design we have given includes a view of the pulpit and platform on which it is placed, sometimes called the altar.

Plate XXVII. explains the internal arrangements of the building. The basement story contains a furnace cellar, lecture room, and two robing rooms, with a lobby between them, in which are stairs leading to the pulpit or to the principal floor of the church. In Baptist churches, the Baptistry (represented in the plate by dotted lines,) is constructed in the platform, on which the pulpit is erected. The desk being made moveable, is rolled back to the wall, and the floor of the platform is raised by means of hinges, exposing the Baptistry to view. It is approached from either side by stairs leading down into the water, from the top of the platform, while the bottom of the Baptistry is placed far enough below the floor to give sufficient room for administering the ordinance. The same arrangement, with the exception of the Baptistry, is equally convenient for other denominations. The small rooms below may be used as Vestry Rooms, and the stairs give the minister a private approach to the pulpit. The pews on the principal floor will accommodate about five hundred persons. The vestibule contains two flights of stairs, leading up to the gallery, which extends across the building, and four feet beyond the wall, separating the vestibule from the body of the church. If no organ is placed in it, pews may be arranged in the gallery to seat one hundred persons comfortably. Should more room be desired, side galleries may be added, which will accommodate three hundred more. But the erection of these destroys the beauty of the interior, and renders the house uncomfortable, for both speaker and hearer. Except in those erected upon the most primitive principles, few new churches have these additions. In the country, where space is no object, the expense of increasing the capacity of the body of the building is very little beyond what would be incurred by the erection of side galleries.

On plate XXVIII. is shown, at Figure C., a transverse section of the church and steeple. The two additional figures, marked A. and B., are a vertical and isometrical view of the points where the octagonal part of the steeple is connected with the square. These are all drawn to a scale, and will be found useful to the practical builder.

The whole building may be erected for about nine thousand dollars,—the price varying with the quality of the materials and the nature of the ornaments. Its capacity may be easily increased from seven hundred to nine hundred or one thousand for a slight additional expense. The general effect is much improved by a stone or brick wall around the church yard, with an iron railing of appropriate design, in front of the building. This enclosure is at first more expensive than a wooden fence, but in the end is much more economical.

THE PARSONAGE.

DESIGN THIRTY-SIXTH.

In England, and indeed in all Christian countries, except our own, the Parsonage is always considered a necessary appendage to the church. Regarding present outlay as of more importance than future benefits, we are, in general, content with the erection of a house of worship, as yet acknowledging no obligation or custom which would require an additional building for the use of the future incumbent. It certainly is essential to the comfort of a clergyman, who in many respects is a public servant, that he should be provided with a house suitable to his station and calling. In some sections of our country, houses have been erected in connexion with the church, but generally, the minister is compelled to shelter his family in any house he may find to rent on his coming into a village. The design we have given, may be appropriately joined to that of the church just described. It is a neat and commodious building, in the Ionic order, one of the simplest forms of Grecian Architecture, with internal arrangements adapted to the purposes for which it is intended. It will accommodate a family of five or six persons, with servants, and may be erected for about three thousand dollars. A location near the church is desirable, both for the sake of architectural effect and the comfort and convenience of the occupants; but in making the selection of a site, the proper authorities will be governed by the circumstances of each case.

Plates XXIX. and XXX., represent a perspective view and elevation of the building. The front is two stories high, with an attic, and the rear three stories high. The first landing place of the stairway leads into the second floor of the back part of the building, the second into the second floor of the front part. This arrangement decreases the height of the ceilings of the back rooms, but with nearly the same materials gives two additional chambers. The walls are intended to be of brick or stone, rough cast, and laid off in squares, to imitate cut stone. The columns of the portico are to be of wood, with wooden caps and base: and the windows of the second story open on the Roof of the Portico, which is surrounded by a Parapet, on the eave. The dimensions of the main building are thirty-five feet front, by thirty deep: the wings each extend sixteen feet in front, by fifteen in depth. The whole is to be roofed with tin.

Plate XXXI. shows the ground plan of the building. The first floor contains a large drawing room, divided into equal parts by columns or folding doors; a hall seven feet wide, with a stairway in the back part; a sitting or family room, a dining room; study or library, kitchen and pantry, with doorway into the dining room. On the second floor are four large chambers. The portion cut off by the hall may be made into closets, or one small chamber. The third floor in the rear contains two large chambers, corresponding to those below, and the attic in the front of the building, two large bed rooms, for servants, and a large closet.

Pl. XXIX.

P. S. Duval & Co's Steam lith. Press Philad.ª

THE PARSONAGE.

Sam. Sloan Arch.ᵗ

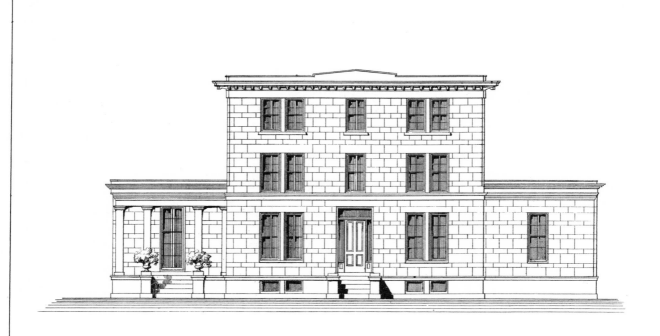

REAR ELEVATION.

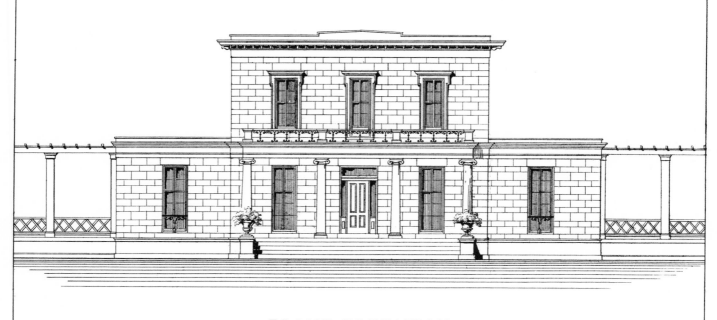

FRONT ELEVATION.

Sam.ʳ Sloan Arch.ᵗ   P. S. Duval & Co's Steam lith. Press Philad.ᵃ

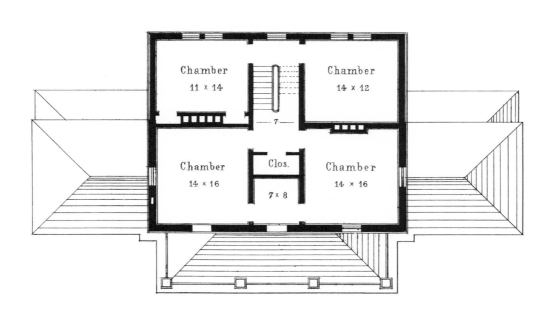

SECOND FLOOR.

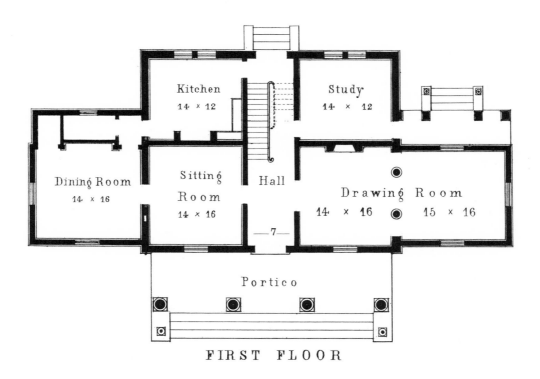

FIRST FLOOR

GROUND PLANS.

Scale 12 feet to the inch.

GRECIAN ARCHITECTURE.

THE origin of Grecian Architecture is hid in remote antiquity. From our little knowledge of the history of nations, we surmise that the Greeks must have received the rudiments of the art from Egypt, but it is evident that they must soon have abandoned their prototypes, since we have no remains in Greece, bearing the least resemblance to the architecture of Egypt. One great cause of admiration is, that the art, as practised by the Grecians, began, and was perfected, among them; the mechanical rudiments only having been brought from abroad. When we remember that all the boasted skill of modern times has been expended in the attempt to produce mere imitations of the ancient temples, without success, and that they still stand in their grandeur, unapproachable, surely the enthusiastic and seemingly extravagant admiration, which has been lavished upon them, does not seem without reason.

Shelter was certainly the first object for which buildings were erected. We can readily believe that a desire for security prompted the first important additions and alterations. Hence arose the disproportionate and astonishing exertions bestowed on those walls, the remains of which are common in different parts of Greece, and which by their polished posterity were regarded as the work of supernatural power, performed by gigantic Cyclopeans. Of these remains Tiryus and Mycenæ are among the most ancient and most celebrated. It is supposed that in Greece, treasuries were built next, for the retention and preservation of the rich spoils gathered in conquest. The exquisite appreciation of the beautiful in form, which seemed inherent in the Greek nation, soon rid their edifices of clumsiness and superficial weight, and began to establish graceful proportion, and elegant decoration. As early as six hundred and fifty years before our era, traces of distinct orders begin to be evident. These soon grew to a richness and perfection unsurpassed. This growth was not luxuriant, but was rather the result of the pruning, which gives strength. The beauty of the Grecian orders does not consist in the abundance of ornament, but in their truth or purity, and their proportions. The few decorations admitted are quite simple, but so wonderfully expressive, that no addition or alteration since made has been considered an improvement. The pure Grecian style has been called severe, but it is that severity which results from uncompromising truthfulness. If, at the present day, our architects would adopt the principles of these, their ancient predecessors, depend but little on the ornamenting chisel, study grace in proportion, truth and the expression of member, we would at once behold, with astonishment, great and unprecedented advances in the art. Until they do, we can expect no advance but in extent.

The treasuries of the Greeks were soon dignified into temples, and then their religious feeling urged them to still greater exertions.   One of the oldest is the temple of Jupiter, at Ægina, which is said to have been built before the Trojan war.   The temple of Jupiter, at Olympia, is supposed to have been built as early as six hundred years before the Christian era; and the remains of the Doric temple, at Corinth, prove it to have been a work of remote antiquity.   Next in order of time, we may class the Grecian cities in Italy, which were built by colonies from the several Grecian states.   The remains of these cities contain some of the finest early specimens of the art.   Next to these, in relation of time, come the Athenian temples. Here we may pause on the full perfection of the art.   After this period nothing was added, but in a few years the decline commenced.

The Orders of Grecian Architecture are three in number,—the Doric, the Ionic, and the Corinthian. They are distinguished from each other, principally by the columns which front or surround the building, though in many minor points the differences are characteristic.

The Doric order is the oldest and most original of the three.   Mr. E. Aiken, who has thoroughly studied and written elaborate essays on this subject, says:—" In considering the buildings of antiquity, and particularly of Greece, the first circumstance that strikes us is their extreme simplicity, and even uniformity. The temples of Greece were invariably quadrilateral buildings, differing only in size and the disposition of their porticos, which either ornamented the front alone, or surrounded every side with their beautiful shady avenue.   The system of Grecian architecture is founded on the simple principles of wooden construction. A quadrangular area is surrounded with trunks of trees, placed perpendicularly, with regular intervals. These support lintels, upon which rest the beams of the ceiling, and an enclosed roof covers the whole. Such was the model.   When touched by the hand of taste, the post and lintel were transmuted into the column and entablature, and the wooden hut into the temple.   It appears probable that the earliest Greek temples were really of wood, since so many of them were consumed during the invasion of Xerxes; and that large and magnificent edifices were principally of this material, is rendered evident by the example of the temple at Jerusalem, which was surrounded by columns of cedar.   But builders soon adopted the more noble and durable material, stone; and though the general system of architecture was already established, its forms received some modifications by being thus translated into a new language.****** These alterations led to the perfection of the Grecian style.   The original model secured simplicity of form and construction, while the superior material preserved it from the meagreness attendant upon wooden buildings.   Thus arose the Doric, or as it might be emphatically called, the *Grecian* order,—the first-born of architecture, a composition which bears the authentic and characteristic marks of its legitimate origin in wooden construction transformed into stone.

In contemplating a capital example of this order, as for instance, the Parthenon, at Athens, how is our admiration excited at the noblest as well as earliest invention of the building art!   What robust solidity in the column!   What massy grandeur in the entablature!   What harmony in its simplicity!   Not destitute of ornament, but possessing that ornament alone which dignifies and refines the conception of vigorous genius. No foliage adds a vain and meretricious decoration, but the frieze bears the achievements of heroes, while every part, consistent in itself, and bearing a just relation to every other member, contributed to that harmonious effect which maintains the power of harmonious impressions, and excites increasing admiration in the intelligent observer. Other orders have elegance, have magnificence, but sublimity is the characteristic of the Doric alone."

The account here given, of the origin of this order, is undoubtedly the true one, but many others, more fanciful, have been invented. That given by Vitruvius is interesting, from its antiquity, but is believed to be entirely fabulous. He says:—"Dorus, the son of Helenus, and of the nymph Optice, King of Achaia and all Peloponnesus, having once caused a temple to be built to Juno, in the ancient city of Argos, this temple was of the style we call Doric. Afterwards, this order was employed in all the other cities of Achaia, without having, as yet, any established rule for the proportions of its architecture. But as the Greeks were unacquainted with the proportion it was necessary to give to columns, they sought means to make them sufficiently strong to sustain the weight of the edifice, and to make them agreeable to the view. For that end they took the measure of the foot of a man, which is a sixth part of his height, after which they formed their columns, in such a manner that in proportion to this measure, which they gave to the foot of the column, they made it six times that height, including the capital. Thus, the Doric column which was first employed in the edifices, had the proportion, force and beauty of the body of a man." This is a very absurd, but amusing story, amusing to think that Vitruvius should calculate so largely on the credulity of his readers.

The Doric order is heavy, and expresses great strength. The column has no base, not even tori or fillets. The shaft is sometimes fluted, and sometimes plain. Authors, who are fond of telling wonderful stories, have endeavored to account for the flutings in various ways. Some say that they are in imitation of the bark of an oak. Others say that they were made to lean spears in, and that the Greek armies stacked their arms in this way, when they went to sacrifice. The origin of this surmise may be found in the first book of Homer's Odyssey, where Telemachus, receiving Minerva in the form of Mentes, takes from her a spear, and places it within a spear holder, against a column. We can readily imagine this to have been merely a channel.

It cannot be expected, in a work like the present, that any allusion should be made to the drawing of the orders. Mr. Nicholson's work on the five orders, including the two Roman orders, Tuscan and Composite, is, or ought to be, in the hands of every student of architecture. It may be useful, nevertheless, to give, in a tabular form, the details of one or two of the best specimens of each order.

		TEMPLE OF THESEUS, AT ATHENS. Height of the Members.			TEMPLE OF MINERVA, AT ATHENS. Height of the Members.		
		MODULES.	PARTS.	FRACTIONS.	MODULES.	PARTS.	FRACTIONS.
Entablature,	Cornice,	—	25	½	—	26	—
	Frieze,	1	25	—	1	19	—
	Architrave,	1	20	—	1	14	¹⁄₅
Column,	Capital,	1	—	—	—	28	—
	Shaft,	10	—	—	10	2	—
Height of the Column,		15	11	—	—	15	—

The Ionic is a lighter and more elegant order than the Doric. It differs from it in many essential respects and although richer in ornament, is not, by any means, so true and unexceptionable as the Doric. The volutes of the capital may be considered the distinguishing feature of this order, and it is written that they were made to imitate the curling hair of a woman, and, also, that the proportions of the column were taken from the perfect female form. Others have thought that the whole were invented to express elasticity and consequent lightness; this is a much better opinion. The Ionic order appears to be quite as old as the Doric, though usually regarded as its successor. It was at first chiefly confined to the Asiatic states, and the earliest specimen of it, which has yet been found, is the temple of Juno, at Samos. Two of the best specimens are the temple of Minerva Polias, which was erected during the Peloponnesian war, and the temple of Ilissus, at Athens. The proportions of these are here given.

		TEMPLE OF ILISSUS, AT ATHENS. Height of the Members.			TEMPLE OF MINERVA POLIAS, AT ATHENS. Height of the Members.		
		MODULES.	PARTS.	FRACTIONS.	MODULES.	PARTS.	FRACTIONS.
Entablature,	Cornice,	1	2	—	1	7	¼ ½ ½
	Frieze,	1	19	—	1	18	½
	Architrave,	1	25	—	1	21	—
Column,	Capital,	—	27	¼	1	13	—
	Shaft,	14	2	¾	16	22	½ ½ ½
	Base,	1	—		—	24	½ ½ ⅔
Height of the Column,		20	16	—	23	17	
Volute,		1	6	—	1	5	

The Corinthian order, an after invention, is the richest in ornament of the three, and is considered the most beautiful. All the members are enriched to a greater or less degree by mouldings and sculptured foliage, and the design of the column is of the most elaborate character. Vitruvius tells quite a romantic story about the origin of the capital, which is ornamented with acanthus leaves. It is this:—" A young lady at Corinth fell ill and died. After her burial, her nurse collected together sundry ornaments, with which she used to be pleased, and putting them together in a basket, placed them near her tomb, and lest they should be injured by the weather, she covered the basket with a tile. It happened that the basket was placed on the root of an acanthus, which in growing shot forth its leaves. These, running up the side of the basket, naturally formed a kind of volute, in the turn given to the leaves by the projecting tile. Happily, Callimachus, a most ingenious sculptor, passing that way, was struck with the beauty, elegance and novelty of the basket, surrounded by acanthus leaves; and, according to this idea, or example, he afterwards made columns for the Corinthians, ordaining the proportions such as constitute the Corinthian order." Whether this story be true or not, it is certain that the Corinthian capital is a most remarkable and happy invention, and was probably the first introduction of foliage as an architectural ornament

The first examples of this style, in Greece, appear to have been produced during the last few years of the Peloponnesian war. Many of the ornamental theatres, so numerous in Asia Minor, may, perhaps, be referred to a period considerably before the Roman conquest. This conquest spread the Corinthian order throughout Greece, almost to the exclusion of every other; and although the buildings of the period which followed, are often more splendid and costly, they are deficient in the pure taste and correct design of the preceding ages. The proportions of two principal specimens are given below.

		CHORAGIC MONUMENT OF LYSICRATES. Height of the Members.			TEMPLE OF JUPITER OLYMPUS, AT ATHENS. Height of the Members.		
		MODULES.	PARTS.	FRACTIONS.	MODULES.	PARTS.	FRACTIONS.
Entablature,	Cornice, . .	1	20	—	1	18	—
	Frieze, . .	1	9	$\frac{1}{2}$	—	21	$\frac{1}{2}$
	Architrave, . .	1	21	—	1	11	$\frac{2}{5}$
Column,	Capital, . . .	2	23	—	2	7	—
	Shaft, . . .	16	16	—	16	7	—
	Base, . . .	21	21	—	1	1	—

The proportions and arrangements of the parts of these orders are so perfect, that any innovation is received with little intolerance. Hence arises the great difficulty in adapting them to modern buildings. Nevertheless, we have many modern buildings, which so far as measurements and form of ornaments are concerned, are excellent imitations of their originals, but they always lack the beautiful material, the pure white and almost translucent Grecian and Italian marbles. But indeed, latterly, the architectural world has been startled and astonished by the discovery of the fact that the Greeks painted their temples. How and in what colors, we know not, but the fact sadly interferes with the usually received notions of the purity of Grecian architecture. Another thing which the moderns lack, is that skill in sculpture which gave the marble leaf a vital grace. In short, we lack the refined taste requisite even to throroughly appreciate the thousand beauties that lurk in every part of a Grecian temple. To properly understand them, one must study within the very shadow of the great originals.

For the use of the builder, proportions of other models are added:

		TEMPLE OF THESEUS, AT ATHENS. Projection from the Axis of the Column.			TEMPLE OF MINERVA, AT ATHENS. Projection from the Axis of the Column.		
		MODULES.	PARTS.	FRACTIONS.	MODULES.	PARTS.	FRACTIONS.
Entablature.	Cornice, . .	2	4	$\frac{1}{2}$	1	26	$\frac{1}{2}$
	Frieze, . .	—	29	$\frac{1}{2}$	—	28	$\frac{1}{2}$
	Architrave, . .	1	2	$\frac{1}{4}$	1	—	$\frac{1}{2}$
Column,	Capital, . .	1	4	$\frac{1}{2}$	1	2	—
	Shaft, . .	$\frac{-}{1}$	$\frac{23}{-}$	$\frac{1}{2}$	$\frac{-}{1}$	$\frac{23}{-}$	$\frac{3}{4}$
Intercolumniation from axis to axis, .		5	6	—	4	20	—

TEMPLE OF ILISSUS, AT ATHENS.

Projection from the Axis of the Column.

		MODULES.	PARTS.	FRACTIONS.
Entablature,	Cornice,	2	11	—
	Frieze,	—	28	$\frac{3}{4}$
	Architrave,	1	2	$\frac{1}{2}$
Column,	Capital,	1	1	—
	Shaft,	1	25	$\frac{1}{2}$
	Base,	1	11	$\frac{1}{2}$
Pedestal,	Cornices,	—	—	—
	Die,	—	—	—
	Base,	—	—	—
Volute,		1	15	$\frac{3}{4}$
Intercolumniations from axis to axis,		6	15	—

TEMPLE OF MINERVA POLIAS, AT ATHENS.

Projection from the Axis of the Column.

		MODULES.	PARTS.	FRACTIONS.
Entablature,	Cornice,	2	7	$\frac{1}{2}$
	Frieze,	—	—	—
	Architrave,	1	7	—
Column,	Capital,	1	—	—
	Shaft,	1	25	—
	Base,	1	15	—
Pedestal,	Cornices,	—	—	—
	Die,	—	—	—
	Base,	—	—	—
Volute,		1	15	$\frac{1}{4}$
Intercolumniations from axis to axis,		8	—	—

CHORAGIC MONUMENT OF LYSICRATES.

Projection from the Axis of the Column.

		MODULES.	PARTS.	FRACTIONS.
Entablature,	Cornice,	2	15	—
	Frieze,	—	29	$\frac{1}{4}$
	Architrave,	1	3	$\frac{1}{2}$
Column,	Capital,	1	17	—
	Shaft,	1	25	—
	Base,	1	15	—
Pedestal,	Cornice,	—	—	—
	Die,	—	—	—
	Base,	—	—	—
Intercolumniation from axis to axis,		—	6	—

TEMPLE OF JUPITER OLYMPUS, AT ATHENS.

Projection from the Axis of the Column.

		MODULES.	PARTS.	FRACTIONS.
Entablature,	Cornice,	2	19	—
	Frieze,	1	2	$\frac{1}{2}$
	Architrave,	1	9	$\frac{1}{2}$
Column,	Capital,	1	25	—
	Shaft,	1	26	$\frac{1}{2}$
	Base,	1	12	—
Pedestal,	Cornice,	1	13	—
	Die,	1	5	$\frac{1}{2}$
	Base,	1	14	$\frac{1}{2}$
Intercolumniation from axis to axis,		—	—	—

GATE OR ENTRANCE LODGES.

DESIGNS THIRTY-SEVENTH, EIGHTH AND NINTH.

In Europe, where the law of primogeniture passes estates undivided from generation to generation, and where the example of prodigal royalty is constantly exciting aristocratic emulation, embellishments are necessary to complete the grandeur and magnificence of the designs adopted by many of the landed proprietors. The entrance lodge, the park lodge, the mansion lodge, the game-keeper's lodge and hunting lodges are often found upon the same estate, all properly disposed, and so constructed as to give architectural effect to the landscape. The varied scenery which nature, assisted by skilful art, has grouped together upon the grounds of the same proprietor, has each its appropriate style. In one place may be found a building after the Grecian style, in another, among rocks and ravines, a Swiss cottage. A Gothic design meets you at one turn, while some distance beyond is an Italian villa. Nothing is lost of which the taste and ingenuity of the artist, or the skill of the builder can take advantage.

SIDE ELEVATION.

Saml Sloan Arch^t. P. S. Duval & Co's Steam lith Press Philad^a

A GATE LODGE.

Pl. XXVIII.

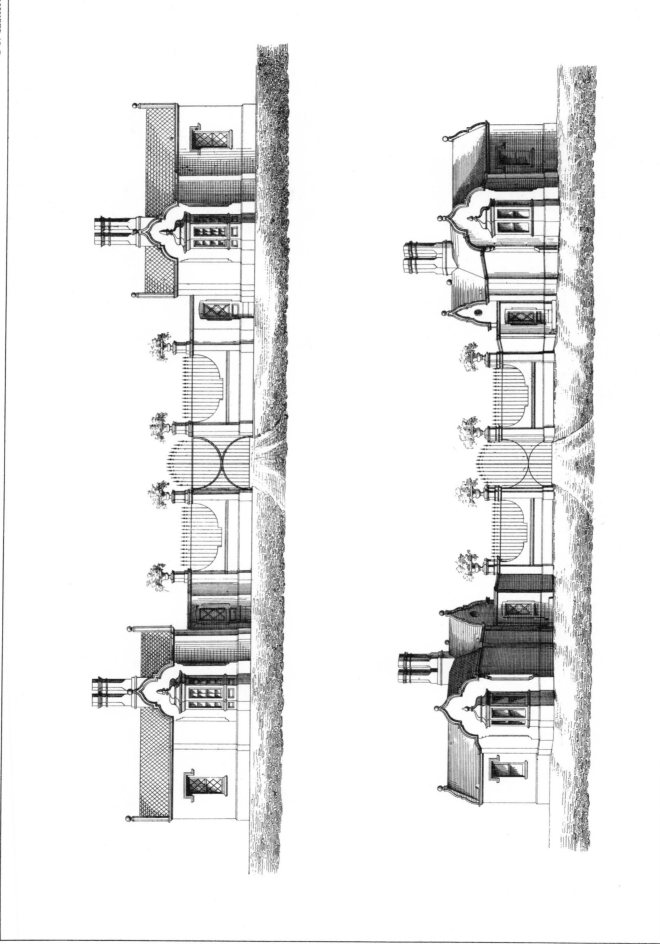

Saml Sloan Arch.^t

P. S. Duval &Co's Steam lith. Press Philad.^a

GATE LODGES.

FRONT ELEVATION.

SIDE ELEVATION.

Sam.l Sloan, Arch.t   P.S.Duval & Co's Steam lith. Press, Philad.a

GATE LODGES.

Pl. XXIV.

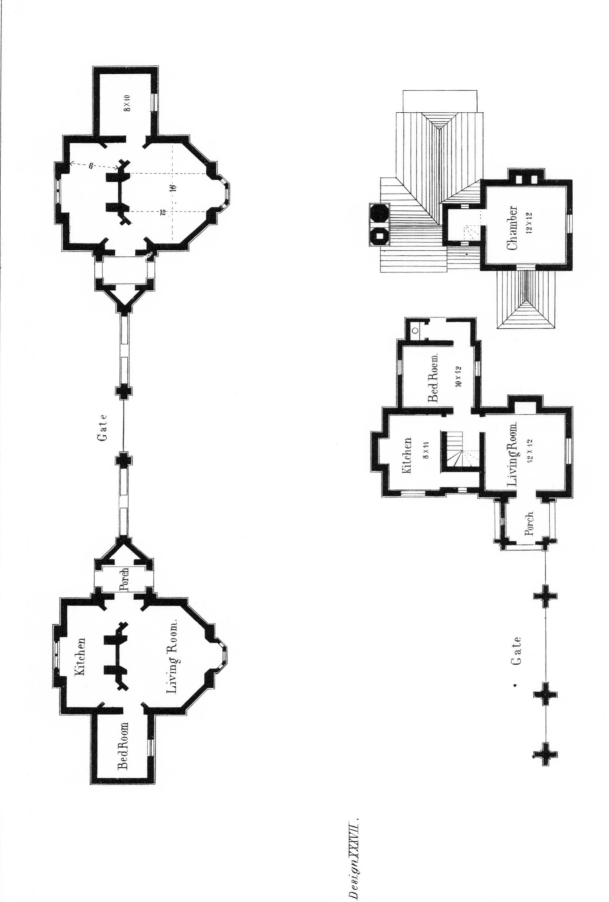

Design XXVIII.

Design XXVII.

8 X 10

8

16

12

Gate

Porch

Kitchen

Living Room.

Bed Room

Chamber
12 X 12

Bed Room.
10 X 12

Kitchen
8 X 11

Living Room.
12 X 12

Porch

Gate

GROUND PLANS.

P. S. Duval & Sons Steam lith. Press, Philad.ª

Samᴸ Sloan, Archᵗ

In this country, unfortunately for the architect of magnificent views, but fortunately for the people, the effect of our peculiar institutions is such as to prevent the indulgence of similar tastes. A hundred farms, with commodious and comfortable homes for their owners, take the place of one vast estate. The eye searches in vain for densely wooded parks, ancient manor-lands, of four or five thousand acres, and hunting grounds, stocked with every variety of game. In their stead, are fields of standing grain, and well watered meadows. To a certain extent, however, the ability and inclination of many permit them to add to their country seats more than is requisite for the mere purposes of habitation, but as yet the idea of utility has not been separated from that of ornament. Whatever has been done in this "ballad-making of architectural poetry," as some one has fancifully termed it, includes only such embellishments as may be made to serve a useful purpose.

Plate XXXIII. represents a design of this kind. It is a Gate Lodge, constructed in the old English style. The first engraving represents the side elevation of the house, and the carriage way, over which the gate extends. The lower engraving presents a front view of the Lodge and Gate. The gate is a Gothic pattern, and to be constructed of wood or iron, hung between stone pillars. It is a simple and pleasing design, appropriate to the style of the Lodge. This should be of brick or stone, rough cast, to represent hewn stone. The roof is shingled or covered with slate, cut into diamond shape. The chimney-tops are of terra-cotta.

On Plate XXXV. are seen the ground plans. The first floor contains a living room, bed room and kitchen, with spaces that may be made into convenient closets. The second floor contains only a square chamber. The house is intended for a small family, and may be erected for about twelve hundred dollars.

On Plate XXIII. are a front and perspective view of another Gate Lodge, having a tenement on each side of the carriage way. Some architects have objected to this arrangement because "it has an air of too great formality, and unless there be some kind of an arched Gateway between the cottages, they have withal a solitary look." By far a more reasonable objection is that "two buildings, each of which have the appearance of being fit for a dwelling, render the elevation by far too extensive, unless the mansion itself be on a very large scale." We leave our reader to exercise his own taste in making a choice between the two.

The ground plan of the structure is shown on Plate XXXV. Each building contains a living room, kitchen and bedroom. The shape of the body of the building is hexagonal. One may be occupied by the gate keeper; the other by the head gardener.

We have, on Plate XXXVI., a third design for a Gate Lodge, consisting, like the first, of a single building, on one side of the gateway. A front and side elevation are given. The shape, dimensions and ground plans are the same as those of that first described. It may be erected for about one thousand dollars.

FENCING.

DESIGN FORTIETH.

NONE of the appendages to a country seat, better repays an expenditure of taste and money than the fencing. Whatever the size of the grounds attached, the enclosure is an important feature in the landscape. On large estates, both in this country and England, hedges have been used for many years, and when properly disposed, add greatly to the effect of the view. Lately, in some sections, wire fencing has found favor, but more for the sake of economy than ornament. Immediately around the dwelling house, an enclosure more expensive and more ornamental than either of these, has generally been thought desirable. It may be of stone, brick, iron or wood. The two latter admitting greater variety of pattern, are more suitable than a wall of either stone or brick.

Plates XXXVI. and XXXVII. represent some specimens of fencing, and among these will be found one at least, suitable for any style of building. It is difficult to classify them, or to give a name to any of the individual specimens. The architect, in their composition, is guided more by his own taste and the rules of proportion, than by any models he may have studied. The builder, in selecting any one for use, must consider the shape and size of the grounds, the building to be enclosed, and the material to be used.

No. 1., on Plate XXXVI. might be appropriately used around a large villa. The gate is a fine specimen of the Elizabethan style. It might be erected for about two dollars per foot. No. 2. is suitable for a Gothic cottage, and would cost about one dollar and a quarter per foot. No. 3. is somewhat similar in style to the last, and would suit a cheaper building. Its cost should not exceed one dollar per foot.

No. 1., on Plate XXXVII. represents fine specimens of rustic patterns, and might be erected around any ornamental villa for the same price as No. 3. on the last plate. No. 2. costs about one dollar and a half, and is suitable for an extensive building. At No. 3. are neat patterns for enclosures around Cottages and Farm Houses. They can be erected for about seventy-five cents per foot.

ORNAMENTAL OUT-HOUSES.

DESIGN FORTY-FIRST.

WE have already given ornamental designs for a fountain, flower stand, bird cage, summer-houses, &c. These all contribute to the comfort, cheerfulness and beauty of the grounds around the dwelling, and could not be properly omitted in the progress of our work. Plate XXXVIII. contains three designs of small structures, partly useful and partly ornamental. The first is a Squirrel House, made of wood, and wired like a bird cage. The openings for feeding and cleansing are in the rear.

The second is a Fountain, somewhat peculiar in its style and construction. The water issues from the mouth of the figure. If placed in a small pool, it might be made to bear the semblance of utility, and a very slight descent from a natural artificial reservoir would be needed to make it operate constantly. The best material would be stone, iron or terracotta, painted and sanded. The last is but little more expensive than wood.

The third is an ornament for a small Lake, the object of which is explained by the engraving. It is novel in design and would be a very pleasant object in such a location. In Europe, these miniature palaces are very common, and when skilfully arranged, contribute very much to the beauty of the landscape.

Scale ½ inch to the Foot.

FENCING.

FENCING.

SQUIRREL HOUSE.

FOUNTAIN.

POULTRY HOUSE.

Saml Sloan, Arch.^t P.S.Duval & Co's Steam lith.Press,Philad.^a

OUT-HOUSES.

JOINERY.

HIS branch of the building art relates more to the ornamental than the useful parts of the edifice. The distinction which obtains between joinery and carpentry has already been fully pointed out, so that no further remarks upon this are necessary. The joiner requires a neat manipulation, in order that his work may please the eye. The beauty of a design can have but little effect if it be executed in a bungling or careless manner. But the joiner must possess more than this. In that beautiful but difficult part of his art, stair building, it is absolutely necessary to have thoroughly studied geometrical lines, such as are given in a former part of this work. To understand these well, much thought and practice is necessary, and the joiner cannot claim to have advanced far in his avocation until this be accomplished. The nature of the present work precludes the possibility of our giving more than some general instructions of this subject. The little work of Mr. Smeaton contains an article which gives so much valuable information respecting joinery, that we cannot refrain from following his method, and quoting him in many places verbatim, in connexion with our own observations.

There is not much that is new in joinery, but there are many joiners who might much improve their work by giving attention to a few general facts. One of the most important agents in joinery is glue, and as its quality is of great importance to the joiner, we must speak of the tests by which to ascertain its adhesive properties, that the workmen may know how to select that which is best, and to reject that which has not the requisite adhesive property. Glue is made from the skins and sinewy parts of animals, or from the skins and cartilage of fishes. The glue that is made from animal substances is considered to be better than that made from fishes; though isinglass, which is made from the air-bladders of a large fish found in the Russian seas, is one of the strongest with which we are acquainted; but its price in the market prevents the joiner from employing it. From the chemical experiments which have been made, it appears that the glue manufactured from the skins of animals is superior to that which is made from the sinewy or horny parts, as well as that which is made from the skins of fishes, not being so readily affected by the moisture of the atmosphere. The workman, therefore, always prefers animal-glue to that which is called fish-glue, though the latter is often sold as glue of the best quality. Some directions may be given to enable the joiner to choose this necessary cement, and to judge of its adhesive qualities. All glue, in the cake, is subject to the effects of dryness or moisture, which, in the atmosphere, are constantly changing, becoming soft in damp weather, and brittle in dry. But the different kinds are differently affected. Glue should be purchased in dry weather, for that which is then soft is not of so good a quality as that which is crisp Some opinion of the quality may be formed by its transparency, for that which is most transparent is best. If it be possible to make an experiment with a sample of the article before a quantity is purchased, a cake may be immersed in water, in which it should remain two or three days, and, if the glue be good, it will not dissolve, but swell; but if it be of inferior quality, it will partly, if not wholly, dissolve in water; from which it will follow that that which is least dissolved in cold water is the best, or possesses superior qualities of adhesion, and will be least affected by moisture or damp. Another test is that, being dissolved in water by heat, the glue is best which is the most cohesive, or may be drawn into the thinnest filaments, and does not drop from the glue-brush as water or oil, but extends itself in threads when falling from the brush or stick; and this it will always do if the glue possesses the requisite properties. These tests will enable even the inexperienced workman to judge of the quality of the material offered to him for sale; and, in a very short time, he will find no difficulty in selecting that which will give firmness and solidity to his work. It may be worthy remark that the glue made from the skin of old animals is much stronger than that of young ones.

In general, nothing more is necessary to glue a joint, after the joint is made perfectly straight, or, in technical terms, out of winding, than to glue both edges while the glue is quite hot, and rub them lengthwise until it has nearly set. When the wood is spongy, or sucks up the glue, another method must be adopted, one which strengthens the joint, while it does away with the necessity of using the glue too thick, which should always be avoided; for the less glue there is in contact with the joints, provided they touch, the better; and when the glue is thick, it chills quickly, and cannot be well rubbed out from between the joints. The method to which we refer is, to rub the joints on the edge with a piece of soft chalk, and, wiping it so as to take off any lumps, glue it in the usual manner; and it will be found, when the wood is porous, to hold much faster than if used without chalking.

In bending and glueing-up stuff for sweep-work, much judgment is necessary, and, as the methods are various, we shall mention a few which the workman may apply, as occasion may require, one method being preferable to another, according to the nature of the work in hand.

The first and most simple method is that of sawing kerfs or notches on one side of the board, thereby giving it liberty to bend in that direction; but this method, though very ready and useful for many purposes, weakens the work, and may cause it to break when strains are thrown on the piece. But a tolerably strong sweep may be made in this manner, if, after sawing the kerfs (particular care being taken to make them regular and even, and to saw them at regular depths,) some strong glue be rubbed into each kerf. When bent into the required sweep, a piece of strong canvass should be glued over the kerfs themselves, and the glue be left to harden in the position to which the stuff is bent.

Another method is to glue up the stuff in thin thicknesses, in a cawl or mould, made with two pieces of thick wood cut into the required sweep. This method, if done with care, that is, making the several pieces, of equal thickness throughout, of wood free from knots, is perhaps the best that can be devised for strength and accuracy. It is also a practice sometimes to glue up a sweep in three thicknesses, making the middle piece the contrary way of the grain to the outside and inside pieces, which run lengthwise. This method, though frequently used for expedition, is much inferior to the above, as the different pieces cannot shrink together, and consequently the joint between them is apt to give way.

A solid piece, if not too thick, may be sometimes bent into the form required. If a piece of timber be well soaked upon the intended outside of the curve, it may be bent into position, and if kept in that position till cold will retain the curvature that is given to it.

The only other method of forming a curve, necessary for us to mention, is that of cutting out solid pieces to the required sweep, and gluing them upon one another till they have the thickness required, taking care that the joints are alternately in the centre of each piece below it, something in the manner of courses of bricks one above the other. In this case, it will be necessary, if the work be not painted, to veneer the whole with a thin piece, after it has been thoroughly dried and planed level, and then made somewhat rough with either a rasp or toothing-plane. But the joiner must adopt one plan or another, according to circumstances.

Scribing is the operation by which a piece of wood-work is made to fit against an irregular surface. Thus, for instance, the plinth of a room is made to meet or correspond with the unevenness of the floor. To determine the portion which is to be cut off from a partition, or any wood-work where a floor or ceiling is irregular, it is only necessary to open the compasses to a width equal to the greatest distance between the plinth and the floor; and, passing one leg over the uneven surface, the other leg will leave a mark on the plinth. If the wood be cut away on that line, a surface will be obtained which will make a good joint with the floor or ceiling. But the chief use of the art of scribing is to enable the joiner so to connect the moulding of panels or cornices, that, when placed together, they shall seem to form a regular mitre-joint. This method has certainly one advantage over the common method of mitring, for, if the stuff should shrink, little or no alteration will be made in the appearance, but, under the same circumstances, a mitre would open, and the joint would be shown. The method adopted is this. To cut one piece of the moulding to the required mitre, and then, instead of cutting the other to correspond with it, cut away the parts of the first piece to the edge of the first moulding, which will then fit to the other moulding, and appear as a regular mitre.

As joiner's work is generally intended to increase the beauty of a building, and as the appearance much depends upon the manner in which it is finished, we shall mention a few principles which must be attended to; for, however well the work may be executed, so far as regards the strength and accuracy of the several joints, if the finishing be disregarded, whether the wood be intended to have its natural appearance or to be varnished or painted, the elegance required cannot be obtained if the joiner does not properly finish his work. When a joiner works in wainscot, oak, or mahogany, his chief object must be to obtain a surface perfectly smooth and even.   When the framing is glued together, the glue which oozes out, and may be spilt upon the work, must be allowed to remain a few minutes and chill, and may then be carefully scraped off with a chisel, and the parts which cannot be thus cleaned may be washed with a sponge dipped in hot water and squeezed nearly dry.   This not only saves trouble in operations which follow, but prevents staining, always produced when glue is suffered to remain till quite hard, particularly on wainscot, which turns black in every joint or place where the glue is suffered to remain.   After this operation, which, though it may appear tedious to some workmen, will be found a saving of time, the work should remain till perfectly dry; and, when the joints and other parts have been leveled with a smoothing plane, the whole surface may be passed under a smooth scraper, and finished with fine glass-paper.   It will be sometimes necessary, when the grain is particularly cross, to dampen the entire surface with a sponge " to raise the grain," and then again to apply the glass-paper.   The work will then be ready for polishing with wax, or for oiling or varnishing, and the good appearance of the work will be in proportion to the time and trouble expended in the process.

In cleaning deal, the same precautions must be taken for the removal of glue left upon the joints, or spilt upon the work, as already described.   This being done, the work may be cleaned off with a piece of glass-paper that has been rubbed with chalk, or, in some cases, with a piece of hearthstone.   The work is then ready for the painter; but, as there are knots and other places where the turpentine contained in the wood is apt to ooze out, either with or without the increase of heat, and thus spoil the appearance of the finishing, those parts are done over with a composition, and the process is called priming.   This is properly the painter's business; but it must sometimes be done by the joiner for the sake of saving his work.   The composition used for this purpose is made with red lead, size, and turpentine, to which is sometimes added a small quantity of linseed oil.   Priming has also the advantage of preventing the knots from being seen through the paint.   Some workmen omit, in this composition, the oil and the turpentine, but the size of itself is apt to peel off, and does not thoroughly unite itself with the wood.

Another method of cleaning off deal is sometimes adopted.   When the surface has been made quite smooth with the plane, it is rubbed with a piece of chalk, and the whole is cleaned with a piece of fine pumice-stone, as in the former process it was done with glass-paper; but, if the grain should be still rough, the work may be damped with a sponge, and the operation repeated when dry.

As, in finishing interior work, it is now customary to imitate the graining of different kinds of wood, it is necessary that the joiner's work should be well finished; for, if a good, even surface be not provided, it will be impossible for the painter to produce the effect he desires.   Every defect in the ground will, in fact, be more visible under a delicate graining than when the surface is covered with successive coats of color; but, even in the latter case, work well prepared will not only look better, but the color will not be so apt to chip and peel off as when the surface is not properly leveled.

ITALIAN HOUSES.

DESIGN FORTY-SECOND.

THE Plates of this Design represent the plans and elevations of two suburban dwellings in the Italian style. This is a style admitting of much ornament, and has heretofore found much favor in our country. Originally adapted to the wants of social life in a climate nearly corresponding to that of the middle and southern sections of the Union, it requires less alteration than any other style to adapt it to our tastes and habits. In our oppressive summers, the broad roofs, ample verandahs and arcades, are especially agreeable, and though not strictly Northern, there are many of its features that will always render it a favorite in the Middle and Western States. The prominent features of the style are flattened roofs, projecting upon brackets or cantilevers: windows varied in form, with massive dressings, frequently merging into the round arch, and always permitting the use of the Venetian blinds: arcades, supported on arches or verandahs, with simple columns: and chimney-tops of tasteful and characteristic forms. Above all, when the composition is irregular, rises the *campanile*, or Italian tower, bringing all into unity, and giving an expression of power and elevation to the whole composition. One of the greatest merits of the style, is, that it permits additions, wings, &c., &c., with the greatest facility, and always with increased effect. As a rural style, it is inferior to the pointed and high roofed modes. Expressing, rather, the elegant culture and variety of accomplishment of the retired citizen, or man of the world, it will ever be, as it were, a medium between the spirit of the town and country life.

The plan selected, the elevations of which are shown upon Plate XXXIX. comprises two houses. To give it proper effect the lot should be a hundred feet front, allowing fifty for each building, thirty for the house, and twenty for the yard. The entrance door is in the side, and the front and rear of each house are ornamented by bay windows, with a small balcony above. The houses should be constructed of stone or brick, and rough cast, to represent cut stone. The ornaments of the exterior are of carved wood or terra cotta, a cheaper material, and one answering the same purpose. The window and door frames are of wood: the front steps of cut stone: and the roof is to be covered with tin.

The ground plans are shown on Plate XL. The basement contains a large kitchen, a cellar for fuel, store room, furnaces; and convenient closets connected by well lighted passages. On the first floor are a parlor and dining room, each twenty feet by seventeen, and sitting room. A hall six feet wide, into which the front door opens, extends the width of the house. At right angles with this, is another hall, containing a commodious stairway. Connected with the dining room, are a large fire-proof and china closet. The chambers on the second floor correspond to the rooms on the first, except that a bath room is constructed over the fire-proof. The third floor can be made to contain two additional bed-rooms, by reducing their size, and making use of the space over the halls. Thus each building might accommodate a family of ten persons with servants.

Plates XLI., XLII., and XLIII. are details of the external ornaments. They are drawn to a scale of half an inch to the foot, and measurements may be taken directly from them. Figure 1 is a view of the front door-way. Figure 2 is a section of the same, showing the side of the bracket. Figure 3 the front of the window directly over the front door. Figure 4 a section of the same showing the side of the bracket and the projection of the balcony.

Figure 5 is a view of the side windows in the first story.   Figure 6 the windows directly above these, and a section showing the side of the bracket.   Figure 7 shows two of the pillars of the piazza, and the adjoining wall of the building.   Figure 8 the twin window over the Bay.   Figure 9 the attic windows in the side, and a portion of the panel, with the enrichments extending along that story.

Figure 10 is a full drawing of the Bay windows.   Figure 11 the attic window in the front, and enrichments of the gable. Figure 12 exhibits the face of the raking cornice, and side view of the level.   Figure 13 the front of the level, and the side of the raking.

Each building should not cost above five thousand dollars.   This, however, would be determined by the amount of ornament used, and the materials of which the ornaments are composed.   In the estimates given below, all the items are rated at the market cash price in this city.

Excavation, 275 yds. @ 20 cts. per yd. - - $55.00	Doors, 6 @ $5.00 each, - - - - 30.00
Stone, 65 perch, @ $2.00 per perch, - - 130.00	" 6 @ $3.50 each, - - - - 21.00
Bricks, 100,000 @ 10.00 per M. - - - 1000.00	" 15 @ $2.50 each, - - - - 37.50
Rough Casting, 400 yds. @ 40 cts. per yd. - 160.00	Cut stone, - - - - - - 100.00
Plastering, 1800 yds. @ 20 cts. per yd. - - 360.00	Hardware and nails, - - - - - 150.00
Plaster Cornice, 400 feet Lineal, @ 18 cts per ft. 72.00	Smith work, including fire-proof doors, - - 100.00
Hemlock for joists and scantling, 20,000 ft. @	Painting and glazing, - - - - 250.00
$12.50, per M. - - - - - - 250.00	Roofing, 250 ft. @ 10 cts. per ft. - - 250.00
Flooring, 7000 ft. @ $30.00 per M. - - 210.00	Mantles, 4 @ $37.50 each, - - - 150.00
Sheathing and scaffolding, 4000 ft. @ $15.00 per M. 60.00	Furnace and registers, - - - - 200.00
Assorted lumber, 8000 ft. @ $27.00 per M. - 216.00	Terra cotta ornaments, - - - - 75.00
Window frames, inside shutters and sash, 18 @	Carpenter work, - - - - - 600.00
$20.00 each, - - - - - - 360.00	Turning, - - - - - - 25.00
Window frames and sash inside shutters, 6 @	Bells, 6 @ $3.50 each, - - - - 19.50
$12,00 each, - - - - - - 72.00	———
Window frames and sash, 6 @ $6 each, - - 36.00	4889.00

A SCHOOL-HOUSE.

DESIGN FORTY-THIRD.

IN Vol. I. of this work, Design XVII. will be found the plan of a school-house, which, as there mentioned, had been adopted by the Board of Controllers of the Public Schools in the city and county of Philadelphia.   This was accompanied by full details of the internal arrangements, and lengthy specifications.   Since the publication of that number of the work, the authorities have been using every means in their power to perfect the plans that had been adopted, and have paid especial attention to the warming and ventilation.   To profit as much as possible by the experience of others, suitable persons have been sent to other cities to examine the different modes in use, and report to the Board.   The result of their labors and investigations is presented to our readers in the accompanying Design.   In external appearance, it is similar to a building for a Normal school, now in the course of erection in Philadelphia, under the superintendence of the author, and will accommodate about seven hundred and twenty pupils.   Plate XLIV. shows the front and side elevation.   The

Saml Sloan Arch.^t   P. S. Duval & Co's Steam lith. Press Philad.^a

ENTRANCE FRONT.

Saml Sloan Arch.^t   P. S. Duval & Co's Steam lith. Press Philad.^a

LAWN FRONT.

ITALIAN HOUSES.   Scale 12 feet to the inch.

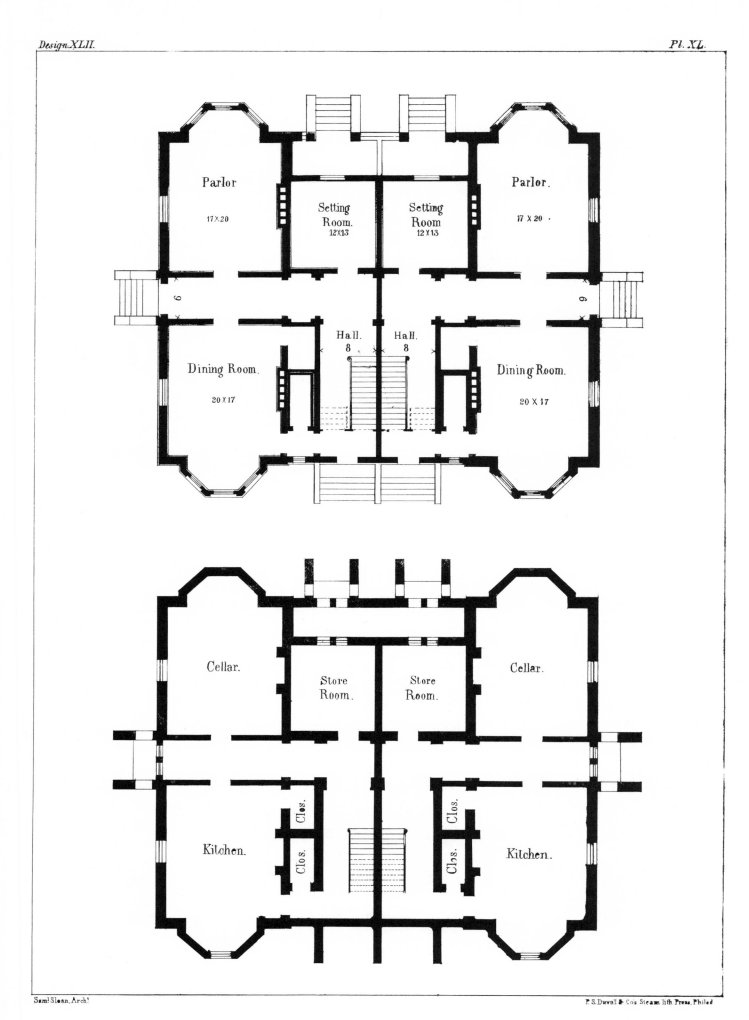

Parlor

17 × 20

Setting
Room.
12 × 13

Setting
Room
12 × 13

Parlor.

17 × 20

6

6

Dining Room.

20 × 17

Hall.
8

Hall.
8

Dining Room.

20 × 17

Cellar.

Store
Room.

Store
Room.

Cellar.

Kitchen.

Clos.

Clos.

Clos.

Clos.

Kitchen.

Sam! Sloan, Arch!

P. S. Duval & Co's Steam lith Press, Philad

GROUND PLANS.

Fig. 3.

Fig 4.

Fig. 1.

Fig. 2.

DETAILS.

Fig. 9.

Fig. 6.

Fig. 8.

Fig. 5.

Fig 7.

Sam! Sloan, Arch!　　　　　　　　　　　　　　　　P.S.Duval & Co's Steam lith.Press.Philad?

DETAILS.

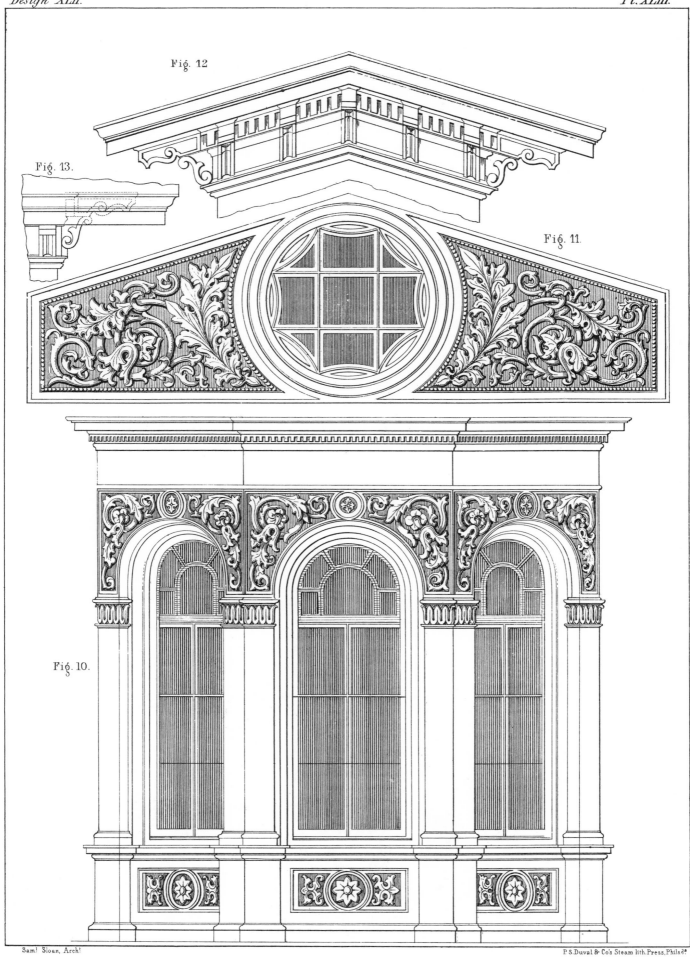

Fig. 12

Fig. 13.

Fig. 11.

Fig. 10.

Sam! Sloan, Arch!.

P. S. Duval & Co's Steam lith. Press, Philad?

DETAILS.

Sam.ˡ Sloan Arch.ᵗ

P. S. Duval & Co's Steam lith. Press Philad.ᵃ

S C H O O L   H O U S E .

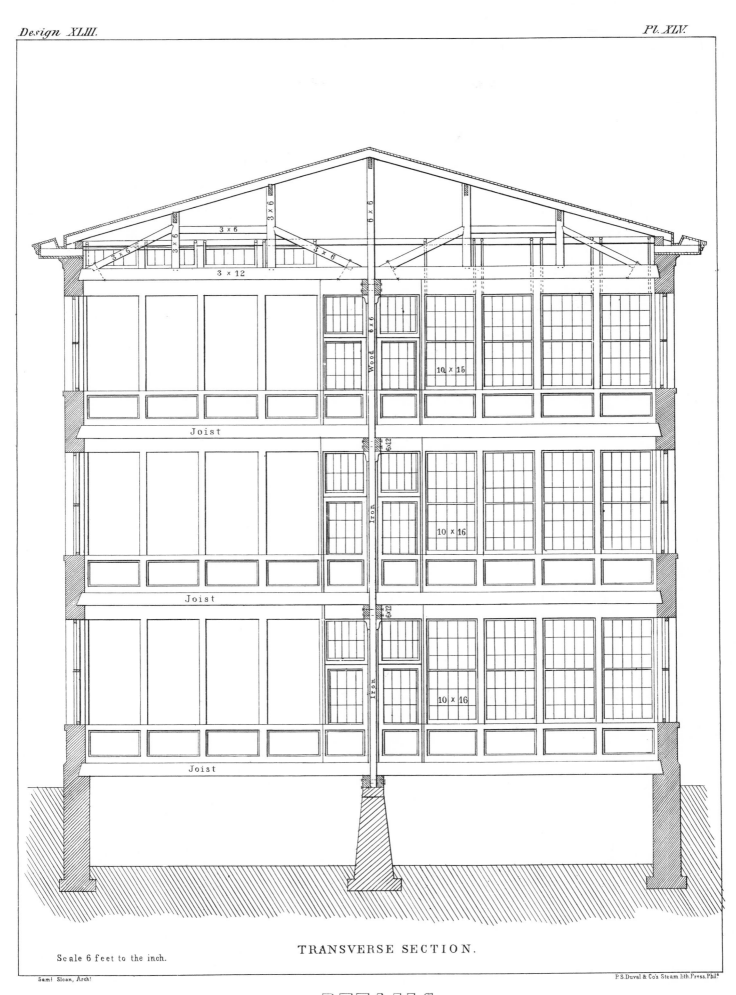

3 × 6

3 × 6

6 × 6

3 × 6

3 × 6

3 × 6

3 × 12

Wood 6 × 6

10 × 15

Joist

6×12

Iron

10 × 16

Joist

6×12

Iron

10 × 16

Joist

Scale 6 feet to the inch.

TRANSVERSE SECTION.

Sam! Sloan, Arch!   P.S.Duval & Co's Steam lith Press.Phil*

DETAILS.

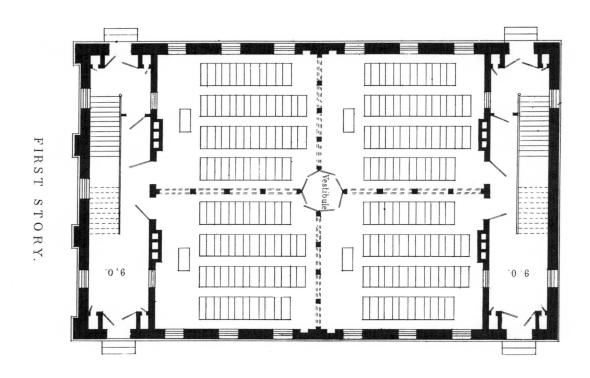

FIRST STORY.

9' 0.

Vestibule

9' 0.

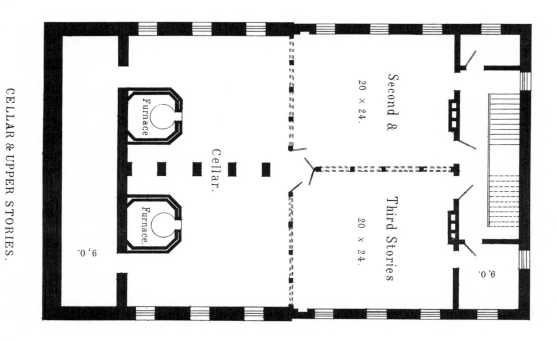

CELLAR & UPPER STORIES.

Scale 12 feet to the inch.

Cellar.

Furnace

Furnace.

9' 0.

Second &

20 × 24.

Third Stories

20 × 24.

9' 0.

Sam.ᴵ Sloan Archᵗ.   P. S. Duval & Coˢ Steam lith. Press Philadᵃ.

GROUND PLANS.

most suitable material for such a building, and that generally used in this city, is pressed brick.   The base and belt courses are formed of moulded brick, as are the corbal courses.   The heads and sills of the doors and windows, and the outside steps are of cut or dressed stone, the cornice of wood.   The shutters should be on the inside, and in such buildings they are hung to open against the jamb, without boxes, a plan not more expensive than the usual cost of outside shutters.

The internal arrangements, as regards partitions, &c., are the same as those recommended in Design XVII., already alluded to.   Plate XLV. is a transverse section of the interior, exhibiting the manner of framing, the roof, and hanging the sash.

Plate XLVI. exhibits the first story complete.   There are four entrances, with the doors opening outwards, the platforms extending to the lines of the doors: and two vestibules, each containing a commodious stairway, with landing or resting places about two-thirds the height.   These are enclosed with plank partitions, dressed and grooved together.   The other Diagram exhibits one-half the Basement, showing the location, &c., of two of the furnaces: and one-half of the second and third floors, which are alike in their construction.   The same system of ventilation is pursued in this building as in the school house shown in the first volume.   For the general principles of this subject, we refer the reader to the remarks in the essay on warming and ventilation.

BUILDING HARDWARE.

We subjoin a list of many articles of Hardware indispensable in the erection of almost every building, with the prices annexed.   The value of such items is apparent to every one who has ever engaged in building practically, and our only regret is that want of room does not permit an enumeration of any except the most important articles.   The list was furnished by Messrs. Wm. McClure & Brother, 287, Market street, who have for years devoted their attention to this branch of the Hardware business.

Sash Pulleys.—Of these there are two kinds, the axle pulley, which are the best, and the sham axle pulley; of these two kinds there are many sizes and prices.   The axle pulleys.   Sizes, $1\frac{1}{2}$ in. to $2\frac{1}{2}$ in.; prices 40 cts. to \$1.50 per doz.   The $1\frac{3}{4}$ and 2 in. are most used.   The sham axle pulleys.   Sizes, $1\frac{1}{2}$ to 2 in.; prices 20 cts. to 50 cts. per doz.   The $1\frac{1}{2}$ and $1\frac{1}{4}$ in. are most used.

Shutter hinges,—Two kinds, the reveal, for fronts of houses, and the strap shutter hinges, for back fronts, made of wrought iron, though some are made of cast iron, they, however, are very poor, and the material is not adapted for this use.   Wrought iron reveal hinges.   Sizes, 14 to 24 in. long, prices \$1.50 to \$2.00 per sett, complete, which comprizes the rivets and turnbuckles, and rings and staples necessary for 1 pair of shutters.   Wrought iron strap hinges.   Sizes, 12 in. to 22 in.; prices $62\frac{1}{2}$ to \$1.25 per sett, complete as above.

Sash weights,—Made of cast iron.   Sizes 2 lb. to 30 lb. each; price $1\frac{1}{2}$ to 2 cts. per lb.   Sash cord, two kinds, the patent and the common; is sold in pieces of 12, 24 and 36 yards length, or by the lb.   Patent cord per lb. 30 to 33 cts. according to the quality.   Common cord per lb. 20 to 25 cts. according to the quality.

Cast iron butt Hinges, for doors.—In this article, there is a great variety of sizes and qualities.   Those made by Baldwin are the best, although some very excellent ones of other makers are sold.   Sizes, narrow butts, for thin doors, 1¼ to 5 in.; prices, 31 cts. to $1.25 per doz. pairs.   Sizes, broad or wide butts, edge or zigzag holes, 2 by 2 in. to 6 by 6 in.; prices, 40 cts. to $5.00 per doz. pairs.

Screws.—Iron, some five hundred sizes, ⅜ to 5 in.; prices 12 cts. to $3.00 per gross.

Locks and Latches.—Of these articles, the variety is immense, there being no less than four or five hundred different sorts. They are, however, divided into two kinds, mortice and rim, the mortice being set into the edge of the door, and the rim upon the outside of the wood.   These, some twenty years ago, were all imported from England, but at present are almost exclusively manufactured in this country, in the eastern States principally, where immense capital and manufactories are employed in this branch of industry, and by the introduction of machinery, they are produced at almost incredibly low prices.   To attempt to describe the many kinds of locks and latches, would be impossible; we shall, however, give a description of a few kinds, and the range of prices, commencing with those used for front doors.   When the door is thick enough, the mortice lock is generally preferred, with the night latch attached.   If it is a single door, the plain faced lock is used, but if a double door, opening in the centre, then the rabbetted lock is used.   These locks are put up with many kinds of knobs, such as the silver plated, the white porcelain, dark mineral and brass.   In cities, the silver plated is most prefered.   Sizes, 6 in. to 9 in. upright, prices $3.00 to $15.00 each; without the night furniture attached $2.00 to $7.00 each.   Rim front door locks, with the night furniture attached, and the same variety of knobs, &c.   Sizes, 6 in. to 8 in. upright; prices $1.50 to $9.00 each; without night furniture, prices, $1.00 to $4.00 each.   Vestibule mortice latch, for vestibule doors, with keys to match the night keys of front door, can always be opened by the knob from the inside, and can be opened with the knob from the outside or not, and make it necessary to use the night key, according to the pleasure of the occupants. Sizes, 4½ to 6 in. upright; prices, $3.00 to $6.00 each.   Mortice locks, for inside doors, are the most numerous in variety. The builder or owner will, however, invariably find that a good article is the cheapest, for if a common lock is put on, and afterwards a better one is required, as is frequently the case, it cannot be changed without spoiling the door.   The knobs used for this description of locks, are very numerous.   Beside the silver plated knobs, the porcelain, plain white or decorated are at present the most preferred.   Some of the decorated are very beautiful, in both design and finish, and of these there are some hundreds of patterns, with the knobs for the closets, inside shutters, sash knobs, bell levers and finger plates, to match. Sizes of mortice locks, 3 in. to 6 in. upright; prices, with knobs, &c., complete, 35 cts. to $5.00 each.   Mortice latches, for doors, where keys are not required; sizes 2½ in. to 5 in.; prices, with knobs, as above, 25 cts. to $2.00 each.   Closet locks, mortice or rim, as the thickness of doors will permit.   Sizes, 2½ to 4 in.; prices 15 cts. to 50 cts. each.   Rural rim locks and latches, with or without a slide bolt, for thin doors, with knobs as above; sizes, 3 in. to 5 in.; prices, 25 cts. to $1.25 each.

Shutter Bolts.—Wrought and cast iron, the first being preferable.   Sizes, 6 in. to 18 in.; prices $1.25 to $7.00 per doz.   Round bolts, wrought or cast iron.   Sizes 4 in. to 10 in.; prices, 75 cts. to $3.00 per doz.

Silver plated Hinges,—For front and parlor doors, are much used in good houses, and present a handsome appearance. Sizes, 3 by 3 in. to 7 by 7 in.; prices $4.00 to $6.50 per pair.   Sliding door locks and latches, mortice, with the usual variety of knobs or flush knobs, where the doors are required to be entirely within the casing, complete, with sheaves and rail; prices, $3.00 to $20.00 per sett.

French Window Fastenings.—The Espagnlette bolts, an article used altogether in France, is the most complete fastening, for drawing the sash close, both top and bottom, with every style of knobs to match the other furniture, $3.00 to $5.00 each for one pair sash.

WARMING AND VENTILATION.

N fulfilment of a promise made in the first volume of this work, we propose to offer our readers some practical suggestions upon the proper ventilation of houses. Its importance need not be urged, yet there is, perhaps, no subject connected with domestic life, about which there prevails so much ignorance, among all classes. To Dr. Franklin belongs the honor of first calling public attention to it, and discovering principles whose value will be felt so long as men inhabit artificial dwellings. Count Rumford and Dr. Arnott, of London, also made it a study, and to them the public are indebted for many valuable improvements. Lately, it has, in the hands of scientific and professional men of known ability, become almost a science, and a distinct and important branch of the builder's art. We cannot, of course, in the space allotted to us, do more than give some of the results of their investigations. For details, and the process by which these results were reached, we must refer the builder to standard works on the subject, in which he will find its different branches treated at length.

A few facts will demonstrate the necessity of a constant supply of fresh air, not only for the purposes of health, but to sustain life itself. The atmosphere, when pure, is composed of about seventy-eight parts of nitrogen, twenty-one of oxygen, and one of carbonic acid. Oxygen is the vital portion, and when absorbed, as in a close room, in which charcoal has been burned, life becomes extinct. After the air has been used for the purposes of respiration, its proportions are changed by the action of the blood and lungs, and when exhaled, the same quantity of air contains eight parts less of oxygen and eight more of carbonic acid. This last is deadly hostile to animal life, and air is unfit to enter the lungs in proportion as it is impregnated with this gas. A healthy man takes in about forty cubic inches of air at each breath. He thus *poisons* every hour nearly two and a half hogsheads. Though we are often unconscious of the presence of this vitiated air, because invisible, yet the oppression of the lungs and the enervating feeling experienced from confinement in a crowded and poorly ventilated room, for which many are unable to account, are unerring detectors of its presence. Familiar illustrations of the remark are also seen in the haggard and sickly countenances of children confined to the nursery, or to the close air of towns and cities, or in the delicate frames and colorless cheeks of the majority of American women, who voluntarily, for almost five months in the twelve, subject themselves to imprisonment, in close and badly ventilated apartments.

The object of the builder should then be to construct edifices in such a manner that this constant destruction of the vital principle of atmosphere be compensated for by a never failing supply of pure and fresh air, for the purposes of respiration ; and the removal of all impurities, generated by combustion or other causes. In climates where fire is never needed for comfort, this is easily done, and houses are so arranged that there is but little difference in this respect, between being under the roof and in the open air. But in our climate, every precaution is adopted to exclude every particle of air, for the purpose of obtaining proper warmth during the winter months. Windows are often made double, and door frames air tight, to keep out the bleak winds. Heretofore, the evil consequences of such construction have been remedied by the plans devised for warming. The common fire-place and chimney secure the escape of the vitiated air from within, and the introduction of pure air from without, for there is always a strong current of air from the floor towards the fire, to support combustion and supply the partial vacuum in the chimney, occasioned by the ascending column of smoke and rarified air. But these are now, for economical and other reasons, yearly going out of use, and their places supplied by furnaces and flues, or in large buildings by pipes for heating by steam or hot water. These supply warm but not fresh air. The loss of the chimney as a ventilator, must be supplied by some arrangement that will produce the same results.

The means provided for ventilation, must be sufficient to secure the object, independent of windows and doors, and other lateral openings, which are intended, primarily, for the admission of light, passage to and from the apartments, and similar purposes. Any dependence on the opening of doors and windows, except in summer, subjects the occupants of the room to currents of cold air, and extreme and rapid changes of temperature. There should be in every living room one or more openings, both at the top and bottom, of not less than a foot square, capable of being closed wholly or partially by a slide of wood or metal, to regulate the quantity of air passing through them, and placed at such points, and at such distances from the openings for the admission of pure warm air, that a portion of the heated air will traverse every point of the room, and impart as much warmth as possible, before it becomes vitiated and escapes from the apartment. These should be connected with flues of a capacity equal to at least eighteen inches in diameter, air tight, smooth, (if of boards, they should be seasoned, matched and planed; if of bricks, the inside must be finished round and clean,) and carried up on the inside of the room, or in the inner wall, with as few angles and deviations from a direct ascent as possible, above the highest portion of the room. All such flues, even when properly constructed and placed, and even when acting in concert with a current of warm air, flowing into the room, should be supplied with some simple, reliable, exhaustive power, acting at all seasons of the year, and with a force varying with the demands of the season, and the condition of the air in the apartment. The most simple, economical, available and reliable power is heat, or the same process by which the natural upward movements of air, are induced and sustained. This can be applied to the column in a ventilating flue, by carrying it up close behind, or even within the smoke flue, which is used in connection with the heating apparatus, or by carrying the smoke pipe within the ventilating flue, either the whole length, or in the upper portion only. When several apartments are to be ventilated, the most effectual and economical way of securing this power, is to construct an upright brick column or shaft, in which is the smoke pipe of the stove or furnace, and then to discharge the ventilating flues from the top and bottom of each room, into this upright shaft. Then the flues may be lateral, and the openings into them inserted near the floor. At the roof of the building, the shaft should be terminated, by an ejecting ventilator, like that invented by Mr. Emerson, of Boston, or any other that will answer the same purpose. By the use of some arrangement of the kind, downward blasts are avoided, and no matter how light, or from what quarter the wind may be, there is always an active, upward current of air. For a house or room intended for twenty-five persons, the diameter of the shaft or principal ventilating flue should be ten inches. If two are used, each should be at least seven inches. For larger houses or rooms, intended for the accommodation of a greater number of persons, the size of the flues must be increased in the ratio of one to one-third. The area of flues for the admission of fresh air should exceed those for the discharge of vitiated air by about twenty-five per cent.

One advantage gained by the use of such ventilators, is that they exhaust the bad air at all times, and their action is increased by the difference in the temperature of the air, within and without the house. For this reason they ventilate equally well in summer and winter, and serve to cool an apartment in the oppressive days of July, as well as to supply pure air in December, when doors and windows are kept shut. The difference between a house ventilated in this manner, and one in which no such means are used, is not trifling, whether considered in respect to permanent health, or the mere pleasurable sensations at the moment. The lassitude, the debility, the blanched complexions, which invariably result from the pernicious habit of heating by furnaces or stoves, with the fire-places all closed, and no means of ventilation, would no longer exist, and the inmates of such houses, after the introduction of a proper ventilating apparatus, would be surprised by the elasticity, freshness, and purity of the air, always changing, yet always of an agreeable temperature. Many persons have been at great pains and expense to warm their houses comfortably, yet, when all is done, they find there is something oppressive and distressing about the very comfort they have thus procured. This is wholly owing to the want of fresh air, from the total neglect of all means of ventilation. The house itself must *breathe* by means of some plan that will rid it of vitiated air and supply in its place, air fit for the purposes of respiration. Those who are in delicate health, and fear to sleep with windows raised, even in summer, would find their slumbers sounder and more refreshing, without the least danger of taking cold from draughts of air passing over them, if their rooms were provided with a simple chimney valve, or the houses with a proper ventilating apparatus. The former may be fixed in any room for a few shillings. The latter can be constructed at a less cost than the price of some article of furniture purchased more for show than use.

After ventilation, the most desirable mode of warming dwellings, demands the attention of the builder. It is, to a certain extent, only ventilation reversed, and is governed by the same general principles. Two ends are to be accomplished, the production of a uniform temperature, in all weather, and to do this by the most economical and least troublesome method. The antiquated fire-place, with its capacious chimney, as has already been intimated, serves for the purposes of both warming and ventilation. But it is computed that only about one fiftieth of the heat generated in this manner, becomes of actual use in the room, an objection that at once proves the necessity of adopting some other plan, without stopping to consider the constant care and attention to the fire, devolving upon the housekeeper, who is desirous of having comfortable apartments. In the northern portions of Europe, where the intensity of the cold has compelled the inhabitants to greater activity in seeking the means of relief, much has been done to obtain warmth, consistent with that economy of fuel so necessary in countries where wood alone is burned. By the proper construction of their buildings to this end, the warmth of one fire is diffused through several rooms and passages. Although this is done on the pernicious principle of impregnating air with heat, by close stoves, composed of masses of iron or brick work, such means are better calculated to procure comfort and preserve health, than those often resorted to among us. Here the effect of a single fire in a room is counteracted by cold vestibules, passages and sleeping apartments, and the extremes of heat and cold to which the inmates are constantly subjected, cannot fail to be prejudicial to the most robust. The system of warming houses by close and unwholesome stoves, that in many instances have supplanted fire-places, cannot, therefore, be regarded as an improvement, when its effects upon health are considered. Economy of fuel, is the only advantage many of them can claim. Yet such a mode involves the necessity of conveying fuel to second and third stories, and a perpetual supervision of a number of fires.

Heating by steam or hot water, is a plan that is not likely to meet with general favor, except in public buildings, manufactories, &c., or in the most expensive and luxurious mansions. The necessary pipes and apparatus are expensive, and need more care and attention than it is practicable to give them in ordinary dwellings. The best mode is by pure heated air, from a properly constructed furnace, placed in the cellar, with flues attached, by which its effects may be felt in any part of the house. Among the many inventions for this purpose, that will claim the builder's attention, we cannot confidently pronounce any to be the best. In making a selection, circumstances and a number of contingencies, it is impossible now to consider, must have due weight. Reference has been made, in other parts of this work, to those of Mr. Chilson, of Boston, and the experience of the author has so fully tested their merits, that it is believed they will be found to answer every desired purpose. Before advising the use of any, the builder should satisfy himself that the fire in them can be maintained without noise, and without throwing dust or smoke into the rooms. The offensive odors and impurities of burnt air, or rather, of particles of vegetable or animal matter, floating in the air, should not be experienced, and the heat should be so conducted into the house, at different points, and diffused throughout the rooms and halls as to secure a uniform temperature, whose height can be regulated by a mere arrangement of the flues and registers, without increasing or decreasing the quantity of fire. No furnace is fit for use in which the air is warmed by coming in contact with plates of iron heated to a high temperature, often red hot. When this is the case, the air is deoxygenized as soon as it comes in contact with the metal, and thus robbed of its vital element before passing to the room where it is to be breathed. Besides this objection, cast iron always contains some carbon, sulphur, and even arsenic itself, and the air that passes over it when in an incandescent state, becomes saturated with these gases, not only offensive to the smell, but destructive to the organs of respiration.

In conclusion, we would enjoin upon the builder the consideration, necessarily involved in our opening remarks, that no system of producing artificial heat, is advisable or even endurable, unless connected with some arrangement for securing ventilation. The use of any furnace and flues in a new building, or their erection in an old one, is a fruitful source of disease and death, when not accompanied by means for supplying pure and fresh air. That apparatus, therefore, which throws into an apartment the greatest amount of air, which warms it sufficiently, without a red hot surface, which diffuses it rapidly and effectually throughout the room, which furnishes the means of removing the foul and poisoned air, and which yields a never failing supply of fresh and untainted air, is alone entitled to the favorable consideration of the builder, or any one contemplating the erection of a healthy and habitable dwelling.

A SOUTHERN MANSION.
DESIGN FORTY-FOURTH.

THE most of the designs already furnished for our work, have been prepared with reference to the habits and manners of the inhabitants of the Middle or Eastern States. That now offered is of a dwelling suitable for the southern sections of the Union. There are many reasons why the principal features of the buildings North and South are and will be essentially different. Here, land is an object, and the architect is compelled to compress his plans into the smallest possible space; our climate requires a house that will prove equally habitable in the sultry days of June and July, and during the severe weather of December and January: and our habits need but one tenement,—kitchen, servants apartments and dwelling all being under the same roof. On the contrary, the southern gentleman is not circumscribed in the construction of his house, or the laying out of gardens and lawns, by the walls or fences of his neighbors, and the number of laborers at his command, the entire year, render him less chary in the indulgence of his taste in these particulars, than he would be, if, to keep them in order, required a constant drain upon his purse. Instead of building upward, he prefers increasing the area of his ground floor, and having fewer stories to ascend. The climate of the Carolinas or of Louisiana, does not demand, for the comfort of the inmates, windows with double sashes, and doors set in air-tight frames, and those houses are most suitable whose openings are so constructed as to permit, at pleasure, such an union of rooms and verandahs as to make them almost one and the same apartment. The laws of hospitality, observed there, require a larger number of sleeping apartments, for a family of the same number of persons, since, at many seasons of the year, the southern householder takes a pride in converting his mansion into a sort of honorary hotel. The kitchen, which is there the dwelling for the house servants, is rarely under the roof of the mansion, but is made a separate tenement, so connected with the main building as to furnish ready communication in all weathers, and is often furnished with bed rooms on the second floor.

The design we have chosen, the elevations of which are seen on Plate XLVII. will, on inspection of its details, be found to combine all the features desirable for a southern residence.   It is of Italian origin, though it cannot properly be classed in any distinct style.   The roof is Tuscan, and projects considerably beyond the face of the walls, protecting them from the heavy rains and shielding the bed room windows from the rays of the sun.   The porch or verandah extends entirely around the building, sheltering the entrance doors and bay window, besides affording an agreeable place of retreat during the cool of the day.   The value of these wide-spreading roofs, is two fold; they keep the walls or sides of the house cool, protecting them from the direct rays of the sun, and by the strong contrasts of light and shade, made by such projections, produce a fine architectural effect.   The windows of the first floor extend to the floor, and all open on the verandah. Those in the second story are all to be furnished with green venetian shutters, designed more for protection from the sun than for security, this being a feature seldom observed by a southern builder.   The kitchen is detached from the main building, and approached from the Dining Room and Hall, by an enclosed passage.   The building is designed to be forty-eight feet square, and three stories in height.   The first story and verandah is twelve feet four inches high in the clear, the second, ten feet four inches, and the third seven feet.

Plate XLVIII. is a plan of the grounds around the house, and of the first floor of the mansion and out houses.   The kitchen yard and vegetable garden, are hidden from view by an arbor, separating them from the rest of the grounds.   The space on both sides of the house from the front line of the porch back to the arbor is appropriated to flower gardens.   This arrangement gives a pleasing effect to the view, both from the parlor, and the library and dining room windows.   In front of the house is an extended lawn, ornamented with clumps of trees, a fountain, serpentine walks, and a carriage way leading to the steps of the front porch.   In the first story are a parlor or drawing room, seventeen feet by forty-five, a hall, twelve by forty-five, containing a commodious stair-way, and affording a free passage of air, the entire length of the house, a dining room, seventeen by fifteen, with a water closet and lobby in the rear.   On the right of the house, and in the rear of the flower garden, is a small edifice, intended as a play house for children.

Plate XLIX. exhibits the plans of the cellar and second and attic stories.   The second story contains four chambers seventeen feet by eighteen, one twelve by twelve, two bathing or dressing rooms, each nine by twelve, and four wardrobe closets.   In the third story are the same general arrangements as in the second, except that the space appropriated for dressing rooms may be used for bed rooms. The observatory is approached by steps leading from the hall of this story. The cellar should be seven feet deep, and divided on each side the hall into three divisions.   The centre divisions are for the furnaces and fuel.   The others, for wine, vegetable, provision and storing cellars.   The cellar walls are designed to be of stone, twenty-one inches thick to the level of the first floor.   Those above of rough brick, thirteen inches thick, and coated with rough casting.   The roof is to be covered with leaded roofing tin, and the porches are of cast iron.

On Plate L. are the building details drawn to a scale of half an inch to the foot.   Figure 1, is an elevation of the observatory.   Figure 2, an upright and bracket of the porch.   Figure 3, a view of the eave and bracket supporting the roof. Figure 4, the upper part of a window in the second story.

We annex a bill of quantities, with the cost of each, including labor and materials.   Every item has been carefully calculated and may be relied upon.   The prices marked are those prevailing in and near Philadelphia.

Excavation, 700 yds. @ 15 cts. per yd. - -	$105.00	Laying them, @ $2.00 per M. - - -	460.00
Stone for foundation wall, 190 perches @ 90 cts.	171.00	Lime, 345 bu. @ 19 cts. per bu. - - -	65.55
Laying stone, 217 perches @ 55 cts. - -	119.35	Sand, 230 loads @ 50 cts. per load, - - -	115.00
Lime for masonry, 200 bu. @ 19 cts. per bu. -	38.00	Rough casting, 900 sq. yds. @ 45 cts. per yd.,	
Screened gravel, 200 loads @ 30 cts. per load, -	60.00	including materials, - - - -	405.00
Bricks, 230,000 @ $6 per M. - - - -	1380.00	Plastering, 2980 sq. yds. @ 25 cts. per yd., do.	745.00

FRONT ELEVATION.

Sam.ˡ Sloan, Arch.ᵗ   P.S.Duval & Co's Steam lith. Press, Philad.ᵃ

SIDE ELEVATION.

SOUTHERN MANSION.

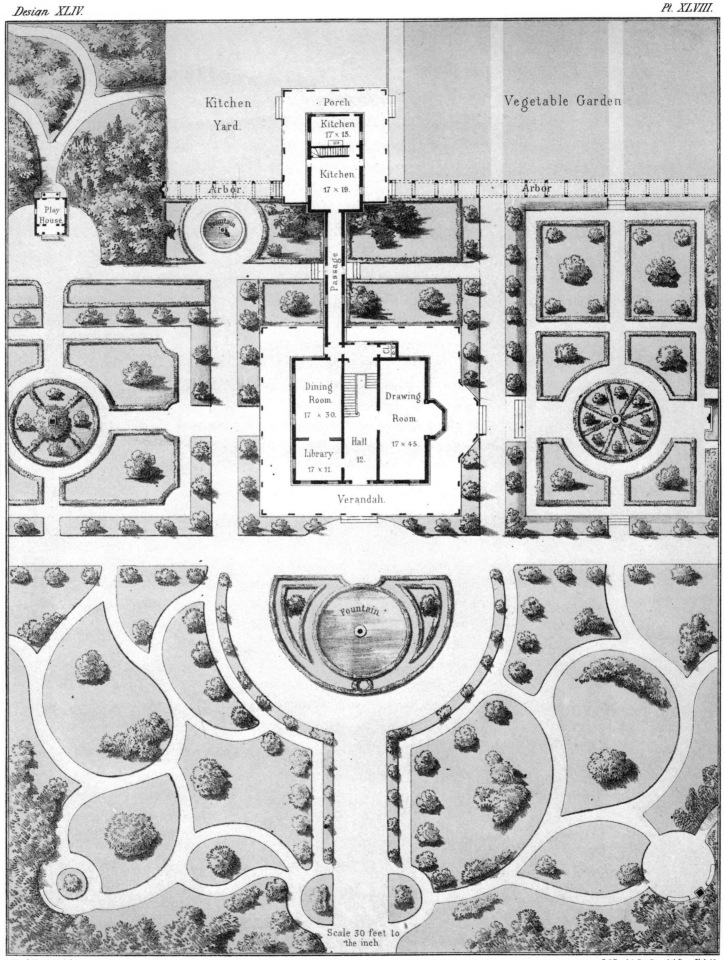

Kitchen Yard.

Vegetable Garden

Porch

Kitchen
17 × 15.

Kitchen
17 × 19.

Play House

Fountain

Arbor

Arbor

Passage

Dining Room.
17 × 30.

CL.

Drawing Room.
17 × 45.

Library
17 × 11.

Hall
12.

Verandah.

Fountain.

Scale 30 feet to the inch.

Sam.ⁱ Sloan Arch.ᵗ   P. S. Duval & Co's Steam lith.Press Philad.ᵃ

GARDENS & GROUND PLAN.

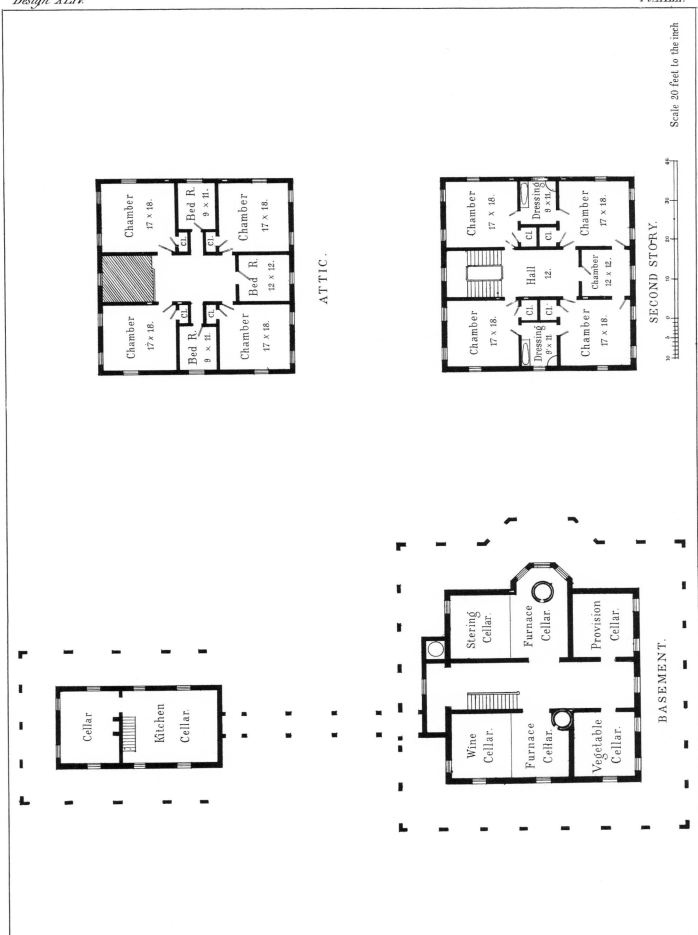

Scale 20 feet to the inch

ATTIC.

Chamber
17 x 18.

Bed R.
9 x 11.

Chamber
17 x 18.

Cl.

Cl.

Bed R.
12 x 12.

Chamber
17 x 18.

Bed R.
9 x 11.

Chamber
17 x 18.

Cl.

Cl.

SECOND STORY.

Chamber
17 x 18.

Dressing
9 x 11.

Chamber
17 x 18.

Cl.

Cl.

Hall
12.

Chamber
12 x 12.

Chamber
17 x 18.

Dressing
9 x 11.

Chamber
17 x 18.

Cl.

Cl.

BASEMENT.

Cellar

Kitchen
Cellar.

Stering
Cellar.

Furnace
Cellar.

Provision
Cellar.

Wine
Cellar.

Furnace
Cellar.

Vegetable
Cellar.

Sam!. Sloan Arch!.

P. S. Duval & Co's Steam lith. Press Philad.ª

PLANS.

Fig. 3.

Fig. 2.

Fig. 4.

Fig. 1.

Saml Sloan Arch.^t   P. S. Duval & Co's Steam lith. Press Philad.^a

DETAILS.

Tin roofing, 7834 ft. @ 10 cts. per ft. - -	783.40
Stucco cornice, in Drawing Room, 132 ft. @ 80 cts. per lineal ft. - - - - - -	105.60
One centre ornament for do. - - - - -	20.00
Cornice in Hall, 120 ft. @ 35 cts. per ft. lineal,	42.00
Cornice in Dining Room, 98 ft. @ 30 cts. per ft. lineal,	29.40
Cornice in Library, 68 ft. @ 20 cts. per ft. lineal,	13.60
Centre ornament for Hall, - - - - -	12.00
" " " Dining room, - - -	10.00
" " " Library, - - -	8.00
Hemlock flooring joists, 3 by 12 in. and 18 ft. long, 12,960 ft. @ $12.50 per M. - -	162.00
Do. for Hall, 3 by 10 in. and 12 ft. long, 1200 ft. @ $12.50 per M. - - - - - -	15.00
Do. for ceiling over the room, 2 by 10 in. and 18 ft. long, 2400 ft. at $12.50 per M. - -	30.00
Do. over Hall, 2 by 12 in. and 12 ft. long, 800 ft. @ $12.50 per M. - - - - - -	10.00
Wall plate, 2 by 9 in. double, 1176 ft. @ $12.50 per M.	14.70
Rafters for framing observatory, 3100 ft. - -	38.75
Joists for porch floor, 4200 ft. @ $12.50 per M.	52.50
" " ceiling, 1800 ft. @ $12.50 per M.	22.50
Rafters for do. 1650 ft. @ $12.50 per M. -	20.62
Plate around porches, 600 ft. @ $20 per M. -	12.00
Joists for kitchen, 3 by 12 in. and 18 ft. long, 1512 ft. @ $12.50 per M. - - - - -	18.90
Ceiling joists, 2 by 10 in. and 18 ft. long, 600 ft. @ 12.50 per M. - - - - - -	7.50
Rafters for do. 1300 ft. @ $12.50 per M. -	16.25
Sheathing boards, on main roof, 4200 ft. @ $15 per M.	63.00
Do. for porches, 2850 ft. @ $15 per M. - -	42.75
Do. for kitchen, 2070 ft. @ " per M. - -	31.05
Flooring boards, 8084 ft. @ $30 per M. - -	242.52
Do. for porch, 2950 ft. @ $30 per M. - -	88.50
Do. for kitchen, 1870 ft. @ $28 per M. - -	52.36
Window frames in first story, 12 @ $4.50 each,	54.00
do. second story, 16 @ $3.75 each,	60.00
do. attic story, 16 @ $2.25 each,	36.00
Front door frame, with side and head lights, -	5.00
Back " do. - - - -	4.50
Window frames for kitchen passage, 10 @ $3.25 each,	32.50
Door frames for kitchen passage 4 @ $2.50 each,	10.00
Shutters, 9 pair, 10 ft. high @ 50 cts. per ft. -	45.00
Inside shutters, to Bay window, - - -	15.00
Blinds, 16 pair, 7 ft. long, @ 50 cts. per ft. -	56.00
Lights, $1\frac{3}{4}$ sash, 296 @ 12 cts. each, - -	35.52
" $1\frac{1}{2}$ " 108 @ 6 cts. each, - - -	6.48
Stairs, 36 steps @ $5.50 per step, (including all materials,) - - - - . - - -	182.50
Doors, double framed, $1\frac{3}{4}$ in. thick, 23 @ $4 each,	92.00
do. $1\frac{1}{2}$ " 18 @ $3 each,	54.00
Scaffolding, 4000 ft. @ $15 per M. - - -	60.00
Lumber for inside dressings, 6400 ft. @ $35 per M.	224.00
Carpenter's work, 630 days, at $1.75 per day, -	1102.50
Water closets complete, - - - - - -	125.00
Two bath tubs, leaded complete, - - -	40.00
Two permanent wash basins, with spigot, draw cock, &c., complete, in walnut stands, - -	75.00

Plumber's bill, - - - - - - - -	175.00
Iron verandah, - - - - - - - -	650.00
Cellar window bars, 350 lbs. @ $4\frac{1}{2}$ cts. per lb.	15.75
Nails, 1200 lbs. @ $4 per hundred, - -	48.00
Nine sett shutter hinges, for first story, @ $3 per sett,	27.00
Do. for second story, 16 sett @ $2 per sett, -	32.00
Do. " kitchen and passage, 10 sett @ 1.12\frac{1}{2}$,	11.25
Axle pullies, 12 doz. @ $1.00 per doz. - -	12.00
Sham do. $3\frac{1}{2}$ doz. @ 50 cts. per doz. - -	1.75
Patent sash cord, 16 lbs. @ 33 cts. per lb. -	5.28
Sash weights, 1840 lbs. @ 2 cts. - - - -	36.80
Butts, 4 by 4 in., 23 pair @ 20 cts. per pair, -	4.60
" $3\frac{1}{2}$ by $3\frac{1}{2}$ in. 18 " @ 16 cts. per pair, -	2.88
" $2\frac{1}{2}$ by 2 in. 15 " @ 7 cts per pair, -	1.05
Two sett sheaves to brass, 6 in. wings, - -	12.00
Two 10 in. frame plate flush bolts, - - -	1.25
Two 2 ft. 6 in. do. - - -	2.00
Back flaps, 10 pair @ 5 cts. per pair, - -	50
One 8 in. front door mortice rebet lock, with night key and porcelain furniture, - -	12.00
One 7 in. do. for back door, - - - - -	7.00
Fifteen $4\frac{1}{2}$ in. do. @ $2.00, - - - - -	30.00
Thirteen, $3\frac{1}{2}$ in. do. @ $1.75, - - - - -	22.75
Five 3 in. knob mortice latches @ $1.25, - -	6.25
Brass clothes hooks, 4 doz. @ $1.50, - -	6.00
Sash lifts, 28 sett @ 25 cts. per sett. - -	7.00
" fastenings, 28 sett @ 25 cts. per sett, -	7.00
Nine 12 in. shutter bolts @ $37\frac{1}{2}$ cts. - -	3.37
Sixteen 10 in. do. @ 25 cts. - - - -	4.00
Screws, 2 gross, $1\frac{1}{2}$ in. @ 30 cts. - - - -	60
" 6 " 1 in. @ 20 cts. - - - -	1.20
" 2 " $\frac{3}{4}$ in. @ 19 cts. - - - -	38
Lightning Rod, with platinum point, - -	30.00
White lead, 650 lbs. @ 8 cts. per lb. - -	52.00
Oil, 36 gallons @ 75 cts. per gallon, - -	27.00
Turpentine, 8 gallons @ 60 cts. per gallon, -	4.80
Litherage, 10 lbs. @ 8 cts. per lb. - -	80
Varnish, 1 gallon, - - - - - - -	3.00
Sand paper, 4 quires, 20 cts. per quire, - -	80
Lights, 160 14 by 18 in. @ 12 cts. - - -	19.20
" 120 14 by 20 in. @ 15 cts. - - -	18.00
" 132 10 by 15 in. @ 6 cts. - - -	7.92
" 28 12 by 28 in. @ 18 cts. - - -	5.04
Putty, 83 lbs. @ 4 cts. per lb. - - -	3.32
Painter's bill, 125 days @ $1.75 per day, -	218.75
Italian marble mantle, for drawing room, -	60.00
One Chilson's No. 6 furnace, - - - - -	125.00
Setting the same and materials, - - -	50.00
Two silver plated registers, for parlor, - -	12.50
One do. for hall, - -	9.00
One do. for dining room, -	5.00
One do. for library, - -	4.50
Four do. for second story chambers @ $3.50 -	14.00
" do. for third " @ $1.00 -	4.00
Kitchen range, - - - - - - - -	40.00
	9805.49

GOTHIC VILLA.
DESIGN FORTY-FIFTH

Is that of a Gothic Villa, in the Elizabethan style, about to be erected in the vicinity of this city. Plate LI. is a perspective view, showing the effect of the design when surrounded by shrubbery. Plate LII. is a geometrical elevation of the entrance front, drawn to a scale of thirteen feet to the inch. The outer walls are intended to be of quarry building stone, and in the cellar, are twenty inches in thickness, up to the line of the first floor; thence to the square, sixteen inches; and the gables and dormers, fourteen. A projection of two inches on the level of the first floor, extends entirely around the building. The division walls are to be of brick, and nine inches thick. There is a furnace in the cellar, under the division wall of the dining room and hall, near the dining room wall, by which all the rooms in the main building are warmed. The nursery over the kitchen, is warmed by a flue from the range below. The exterior is to be finished with rubble work, and ridge pointed with mortar. The windows have all inside shutters; those of the bay windows in the dining and drawing rooms, parting in the centre and folding into soffits constructed in the side jambs. They are all double hung with weights and cord. Those under the verandah, extend to the floor. The head mouldings and corbels on the exterior are of wood, and also the balconies, porches, and the carriage drive at the entrance door. The corner piers of the porch, supporting the library, are of brick, rough cast, and sanded. The roof is covered with slate, cut in diamond form, and laid on sheathing boards, secured by two nails in each piece. All the cornices, barges, window frames and sash, balconies and verandahs are to be painted in imitation of old oak. The head mouldings, corbels, porch supporting the library, and the carriage drive, should be painted and sanded to represent stone.

On Plate LIII. are the ground plans of the first and second stories. The first floor contains a drawing room, a hall, a dining room, sitting room, a kitchen and wash house in the rear, a large store room, a carriage drive, porch and verandah. The second floor, three chambers and dressing rooms, library, nursery, bath room, closets and a water closet approached by a gallery on the outside. The attic may be made to contain five bed rooms, with a passage extending from the library to the private stairway, by which arrangement, each room may be approached from the passage. The cellar extends under the whole of the main building, including the private stairway and store room. It should be at least seven feet deep, in the clear, below the joists, and have a window under each of the windows in the first story, extending, at least, eighteen inches below the surface of the ground. These should be protected by the segment of a circular nine inch brick wall, laid in cement, and the top course placed upon the edge. By this means, the whole is made secure, and protected against the action of the frost. Each window should have square or round one inch iron bars, with the ends flattened, and set in the jambs, not more than five inches apart, with cast iron or wire guards, on the outside: and glazed windows hinged to a casing on the inside, as a protection from the winter's cold. The door is under the window of the store room, and to facilitate the storing of fuel, there is an iron gate between the carriage drive and the angle of the dining room wall. The floor should be coated with a bed of concrete, at least six inches thick, composed of stone chips, and well filled with liquid cement. This must be applied at intervals of at least three days, till the whole becomes flush, and when dry, coated with mortar, to produce a smooth surface. The expense of such a plan would be merely nominal, as the whole can be done

Pl. LI.

Design XLV.

Sam.l Sloan, Arch.t

P.S.Duval & Co.s Steam lith. Press, Phila.d

GOTHIC VILLA.

Pl. LII.

ENTRANCE FRONT.

Scale 12 feet to the inch.

GOTHIC VILLA.

Sam! Sloan Arch!

P.S. Duval & Co's Steam lith. Press Philad.ᵃ

Pl. LIII.

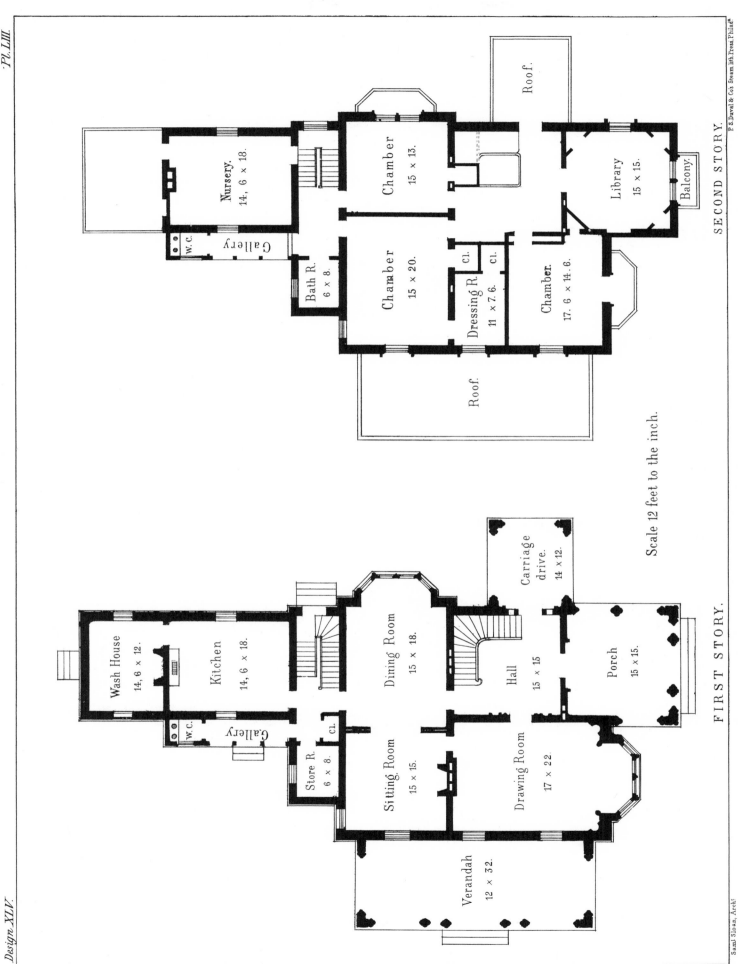

SECOND STORY.

Nursery. 14, 6 × 18.

Gallery

w.c.

Bath R. 6 × 8.

Chamber 15 × 13.

Chamber 15 × 20.

Roof.

Dressing R. 11 × 7. 6.

Cl. Cl.

Chamber. 17. 6 × 14. 6.

Library 15 × 15.

Balcony.

Roof.

P L A N S .

Scale 12 feet to the inch.

FIRST STORY.

Wash House 14, 6 × 12.

Kitchen 14, 6 × 18.

Gallery

w.c.

Store R. 6 × 8.

Cl.

Sitting Room 15 × 15.

Dining Room 15 × 18.

Drawing Room 17 × 22

Hall 15 × 15

Carriage drive. 14 × 12.

Porch 15 × 15.

Verandah 12 × 32.

Sam⁏ Sloan, Arch⁏

P.S.Duval & Cos Steam lith.Press.Philad⁏

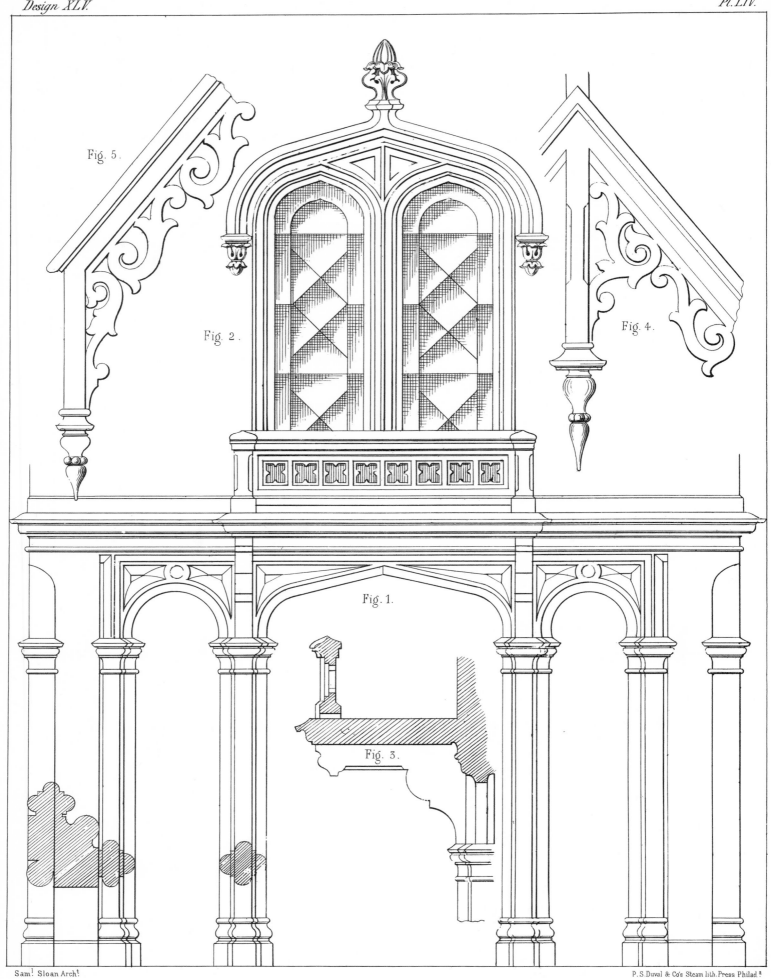

Fig. 5.

Fig. 2.

Fig. 4.

Fig. 1.

Fig. 3.

Sam.! Sloan Arch.!.   P. S. Duval & Co's Steam lith. Press Philad.ᵃ

DETAILS.

during the erection of the building, by any laboring man who understands the mixing of mortar. By its use, dryness, cleanliness, and a protection from rats and vermin are secured. A well ventilated and properly constructed cellar, is an important appendage to any building, and one which neither pains nor expense should be spared to secure, even though it be necessary to diminish the expense of another part of the house. In too many instances, the custom prevails of making the cellar the depository of vegetable and animal matter. Its decay, especially in the summer time, is ever a prolific source of disease, for its effects must be felt throughout the entire building. All such articles of food should be stored in vaults or apartments detached from the main building. The practice of depositing in the cellar refuse matter of any kind, is too manifestly pernicious to need remark here.

Plate LIV. contains building details. Figure 1 represents the porch, under the library. Figure 2, the library window, over the centre arch of the porch, with a projecting balcony. Figure 3, a section of the balcony. Figure 4, an ornamental barge and its connection with the pendant, at the apex. Figure 5, the barge, and its connection with the pendant at the eave.

The above description of the principal features, with the aid of one of the general specifications already given, would enable any one acquainted with the builder's art, to prepare complete specifications for the erection of this design. Its entire cost in a vicinity where proper stone could be delivered at the rate of ninety cents per perch, and other materials at a proportionate rate, would not exceed nine thousand dollars.

BELLS AND SPEAKING TUBES.

FORMERLY, bells were only found in the most expensive houses. Lately, they have been introduced in nearly every dwelling constructed with a proper regard to the convenience of the inmates. The most approved method of hanging, is to have the tubes for the wires introduced before the house is plastered. These tubes are of either copper or tin. The first is preferable, but the latter lasts nearly as well, and can be procured for about one-fifth the cost of the copper. Annealed iron wire is used in dry places, but where there is much dampness or exposure to the water, copper wire should be substituted. The best cranks, springs and other apparatus, are the same as those that have been in use for many years, but the styles of levers, pulls, &c., have been much changed. Formerly, they were made of lacquered brass, bronze, &c., but now they are made more ornamental. Those with silver plated caps and knobs are the most expensive; those of plain white, or decorated porcelain, can be had for a less price, and make a neat finish.

Speaking tubes are found of great convenience to a housekeeper, and may be introduced without incurring much expense. They are made of copper, tin, or gutta-percha. Tin is, perhaps, the best article for the purpose, and most mechanics, who attend to this branch of house-finishing, give it the preference over either the copper or gutta-percha. Mouth pieces are to be had of almost every material, and at all prices. Those to be preferred are of silver plate, ivory or porcelain.

JOINERY.

Continued.

T is designed, in the succeeding article, to particularize those parts of the building which properly belong to the joiner's art. We have already described his work to be of a more ornamental character than the carpenter's, being intended to give finish to the building, and therefore requiring neater manipulation. The carpentry of dwellings, is always covered and hidden from sight by the joiner and plasterer, and hence requires only strength, endurance and firmness, but the joinery, in addition to these qualities, must please the eye, and conduce to comfort. Not only is the joiner required to be skillful in handling tools, in gluing, and in polishing, but a very considerable knowledge of practical mathematics is requisite, for him to attain the higher branches of the art. Any one who examines " Nicholson's Guide for the Carpenter and Joiner," will find propositions there, many of which would trouble a good mathematician to demonstrate, yet it is necessary for the mechanic to understand and put into practical operation all these, before he can be called a good workman. This branch alone of the mechanic's art, requires more intellectual exercise than many occupations whose votaries affect to despise all manual employment.

The work which principally calls forth the joiner's skill, is the Stair Casing. The general design and position of the stair case is left to the architect, but the minutiæ of the general plan constitute the difficulties. The old Italian architect, Palladio, to whom reference has before been made, has some quaint but sensible remarks on this point. He says:—" Stair cases will be commendable if they are clear, ample and commodious to ascend, inviting, as it were, people to go up; they will be clear if they have a bright and equally diffused light; they will be sufficiently ample if they do not seem too scanty and narrow for the size and quality of the fabric, but they should never be less than four feet in width, so that two persons may pass each other; they will be convenient with respect to the whole building, if the arches beneath can be used for domestic purposes, and with respect to persons if their ascent is not too steep and difficult, to avoid which the steps should be twice as broad as high." The stairway should occupy a central point in the building, for the convenience of the different apartments. The front hall is the best place, because it is not used as a sitting room, hence the draught of air, created by the open well, does not subject the inmates of the dwelling to inconvenience, nor are the stairs in the way of the furniture, both which would be the case if they were placed in an occupied apartment. The effect on entering the house, is pleasing, if the stairs are well planned and executed. It connects the upper and the lower floors, and makes the visitor understand the building, and feel that he is introduced at the principal point.

There are various kinds of stairs, one of which is termed by the workman, indifferently, half-pace, half place, and half-space. There are also the doglegged stairs, the fliers and French fliers, besides others. It is unnecessary to define the different kinds. The winding stairs, whether describing a part or the whole of a circle, can generally be made more elegant than any other kind, but they are really far more inconvenient to ascend than the straight stairs. For public buildings the elliptical stairway is most handsome. The most convenient is the half-place stairway, where the landing is about two-thirds or three-fifths of the way up. They not only conduct a person in a straight line, but give him an opportunity for rest.

The height and breadth of the step is a matter of some considerable importance. They should never be higher than seven inches nor more than one foot in breadth. They are sometimes made lower and broader, but the measurements given will most generally be found best in appearance and easy in ascent. The construction of the hand-rail is the most difficult work about the stair casing. Frequently, in cheap half-place stairs, newel posts are fixed at each turn, connected by a straight hand rail. Here there is no great difficulty. The continued rail is far more beautiful than this, and at the same time, more difficult to execute. It begins with a scroll at the foot, and whether the stairs be half-place, winding or circular, it continues up without another newel, and finally passes into the well. The newel properly is the long upright post of close winding stairs, but the word is commonly used in referring to the posts at the ends of the hand rail. The cutting out of a continued rail is no easy matter. The well of the stairs is regarded as a cylinder around which the rail winds, following in each quarter revolution the line of an inclined section, which is part of an ellipse. When we add to this the twist requisite to give the proper position, we may understand something of the difficulty. In order to comprehend and execute such work, a close study of mathematics, and the practical lines is necessary. The lines for one kind of stairs, is given in the first volume. A machine has been invented for cutting out hand railing, that produces very perfect work.

It is always very convenient in a private dwelling of ordinary size, to have a private stairway for the use of domestics. If the half-place stairs are used, it is the most convenient plan to have the private stairs land on the half-place, whereby we prevent the passing up and down in the front of the house, and also economize room as well as expense. If there are back buildings, the second floor may be one riser higher than the half-place of the main stairs, and the private stairs may be placed any where in the rear, with a passage approaching the half-place. Various conveniences of this description are extensively illustrated by the plans contained in this work.

There is nothing more ornamental about the interior of a building than a handsome flight of stairs. Above all other points let them be roomy, of easy ascent, and well lighted. The light should be equally diffused, and the best way of accomplishing it is by means of a sky light. This throws the light perpendicularly and equally on the steps, and by it we avoid dark shadows. The general objection to this sort of light is its tendency to leak, and the trouble of repair. If it be constructed in the first instance as it should be, there is no sort of excuse for its leaking, and it only wants protection from hail. Skylights, besides affording the most pleasant and best diffused light for a stairway, can be made otherwise highly ornamental, and hence add to the finish of the building. Numerous designs for skylights, may be found in the books of practical lines. Another good and more usual method for lighting stairs, is by means of a window on the half-place or landing. This throws a body of light down the stairway, and if the window be of stained glass, has a very fine effect. Side lights, though sometimes unavoidable, seldom appear well.

The window, at the present day, is a very prominent feature. We say at the present day, because, in former times, among the Greeks and Romans, it was little regarded. How the Greeks managed in their private dwellings, we do not know, but the remains of their temples do not exhibit any traces of apertures for the admission of light. Strange as it may seem, these temples were mostly intended to have no roofs, and therefore did not need windows. The apartments of the Romans were lighted by means of small apertures, which were sometimes closed, to exclude the weather, by oiled paper or alabaster. Among the relics in Herculaneum, however, glass has been found, but doubtless was too expensive to have been extensively used. Not until the latter part of the middle ages, did the window form a marked feature, and then it seemed to affect the whole character of the architecture. To us, the window is of the greatest importance, and has been the object of much study, not for the sake of its appearance and position merely, but in its construction. In general, it is placed too high from the floor, and is made too small. Two windows, of a good size, are amply sufficient to light any apartment of ordinary size, and they should both be placed, if possible, on one side of the room, to avoid the bad effect of cross lights and shadows. The original aperture in the wall should always, in the first story, extend to the level of the floor, and the lower part of the inserted frame should be panelled as high as the sash sill. By far the best plan is to make the frames with pullies and boxes for weights, such as may be seen in many sections of windows given in the detail plates. This arrangement, although somewhat more expensive than the old plan of lifting sash, has proved after years of trial, to be much the best, and no well finished house is now built otherwise. The French casements have unquestionably a better architectural effect than the poised sash, but are objectionable on many accounts, chiefly because it is almost impossible to make them weather tight. The ventilation of a room in summer is much more readily managed with poised sash, where the one also moves, than with any other. The sash themselves, are now almost always made by machinery, and therefore require no further comment.

AN ITALIAN VILLA.
DESIGN FORTY-SIXTH.

WE have already remarked upon the popularity of the Italian style. Nearly one-half of the suburban dwellings that have been erected in this country within the last ten years, are in this style, modified to suit tastes and climate. The facilities it offers for alteration and addition of any kind, recommend its use in almost every section. The details, shown on Plate LV. are less elaborate than those of many designs already given. Should more ornaments be desirable, they can easily be added from buildings of the same style, already furnished in other parts of this work. The principal floor of this design is elevated five feet above the surface of the ground, and is approached by a flight of eight steps, leading to the base of the campanile, which is open the height of the first story, affording a kind of lobby at the main entrance. By this arrangement, a commodious basement is obtained for domestic purposes, and a better light and freer circulation of air are secured for the upper stories. The outer walls should be of building stone, and rough cast, to imitate cut stone, sanded and tinted the desired color. Those of the cellar are to be twenty inches thick: those of the first story, eighteen; of the second, sixteen. The tower walls are eighteen inches in thickness to the third floor, and sixteen thence to the square. The partition walls are of brick. In the cellar, those supporting partitions above, should be thirteen inches thick; all others, nine. Those of the first and second floors are also nine. The roof is to be covered with leaded tin, painted on both sides. The eave projects three feet ten inches, showing the ends of the supporting rafters. The steps on the exterior, and the dressings of the doors and windows are all of wood. The conservatory is to be enclosed with sash in the usual manner, and finished throughout in accordance with the design.

Plate LVI. contains two line drawings, of the front and side elevations, drawn to the scale of sixteen feet to the inch. As has been before remarked, the value of this style of engraving consists in the fact that the lines are all so distinctly brought out as to admit of measurements being taken correctly from them.

On Plate LVII. are the plans of the first and second floors. On the first are a drawing room, eighteen feet by twenty-eight, parlor thirteen by twenty-three, library fourteen by seventeen, dining room eighteen by thirty, a vestibule, eighteen by eighteen, fire proof, large closets, lobby, verandah, and porch. The second floor contains seven sleeping apartments, including the tower, which in this story may, if desired, be converted into a small bed room, a bath room, wardrobe closets, water closets, a gallery over the vestibule, and a stairway to the upper stories of the tower.

The basement floor, and roof are shown on Plate LVIII. The first extends four feet below the surface of the ground, and contains the kitchen, with dumb waiters, closet and pantry, servants' hall, laundry, store room, pump room, apartments for the storing of fuel and two furnaces. The plan of the roof shows the sky light over the vestibule and gallery.

Plate LIX. contains building details. Figure 1 is the circular and upper window, and part of the roof of the tower. Figure 2 is a vertical section of the same. Figure 3 is a section of the roof. Figure 4 is a section of the balcony, and drawing room window.

The cost of the entire building would not exceed four thousand eight hundred dollars, when materials can be procured at prices prevailing near this city.

A BUILDING IN THE CASTELLATED STYLE.
DESIGN FORTY-SEVENTH.

THIS novel style will doubtless meet with favor among those in search of a plan at once beautiful, yet differing in general effect from the magority of buildings. It might properly be called a Romanesque Villa, yet by the use of the term we would wish to be understood only as indicating the style from which certain ideas of composition have been obtained. There are, properly speaking, no Romanesque villas in the whole of Southern Europe, but the architecture which bears this name, and which flourished before the origin and prevalence of the Gothic styles, offers a rich field of study to the architect, who would work out of the materials of the past, a new construction, suited to the wants of the present age. The distinguishing features of the plan we have drawn, are the projecting bastions at the four corners and centre of the flanks. These and the semi octagonal vestibule or entrance, are sufficient to break the monotony and regularity of the plain square of the body of the building, and by varying the outline, redeem the elevation from the charge of tameness and poverty.

Plate LX. shows the front elevation and a perspective view of the building. It is fifty feet in front by forty in depth, and constructed entirely of timber. In many sections of our country, wood is the only available material for building purposes, and there is no prospect for years to come of any perceptible diminution of the abundance that nature has afforded. This fact has given rise to a style of architecture, that though rude enough in many particulars, may almost be considered as national. It becomes the duty then of the architect to suit his designs to the peculiarities of the district for which they may be intended, and to endeavor to extract beauty from the materials thus thrown in his way. Attempts to produce in wood bold and striking effects that properly belong to stone or other material, may, for a time, please an uneducated eye, but cannot fail ultimately, to be condemned as they deserve. Were it not for the consideration that all such paltry imitations and ridiculous pretences, cannot, in their frailty, last long enough to outlive the attacks that improving taste and maturer experience are preparing for them, some comments might seem necessary upon the entire unfitness of the material and the failures that many recently erected wooden structures exhibit. The material itself is a beautiful and manageable one, and examples are not wanting to show in how attractive a manner it may be used by a skillful artist. While we condemn any attempt at imitation, which by its magnitude and want of good taste, would prove a failure, we would not be understood as condemning, entirely, every imitation of stone, but would rather recommend it as giving more solidity in appearance, and more durability in fact. In this instance, the style of the building would warrant painting and sanding the whole exterior. In our design, the boards are nailed on vertically, are all of an uniform width, and terminate under the string course, above the first floor, and at the eave, with Gothic heads, connecting one with the other, and extending around the whole building. All the joints are to be carefully ribbed. The semi octagonal vestibule is one story high, and its crowning mouldings terminate and connect with the string course. A break, both front and rear, projecting one foot, extends to the eave, and on this is placed the gable, surmounted by a battlement, corresponding to the crownings of the bastions. The chimneys are also ornamented in a style corresponding to the principal features of the building. The cellar extends under the entire building, with division walls under the partitions above. These may be of stone, sixteen inches thick, or of hard burnt brick, nine inches, with the necessary communicating doors. The outer walls should be of stone

Pl. LV.

P.S.Duval & Co's Steam lith.Press, Philad^a

Sam! Sloan Arch!

I T A L I A N   V I L L A .

FRONT ELEVATION .

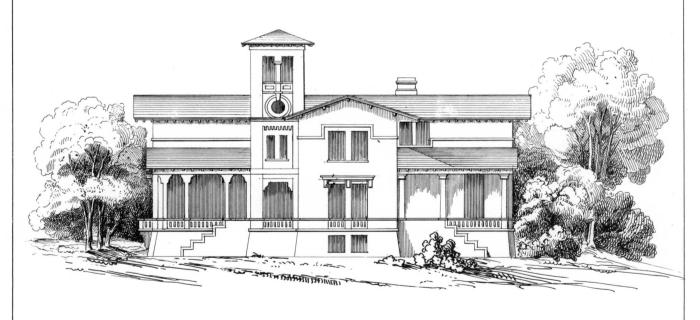

SIDE ELEVATION.

Scale 16 feet to the inch.

Sam. Sloan Arch.ᵗ   P. S Duval & Cᵒ Steam lith. press Phil.

ITALIAN VILLA.

SECOND STORY.

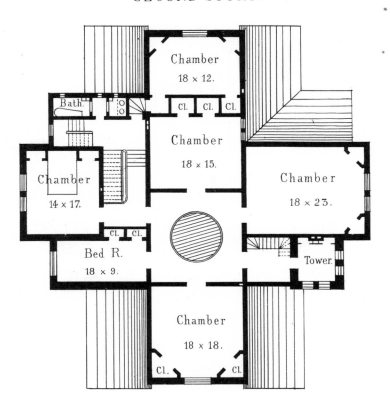

FIRST STORY.

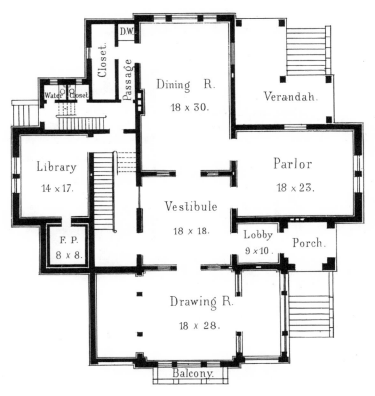

Scale 16 feet to the inch.

Saml Sloan Archt.   P.S. Duval & Co's Steam lith. Press Philadª

PLANS.

DIAGRAM OF THE ROOF.

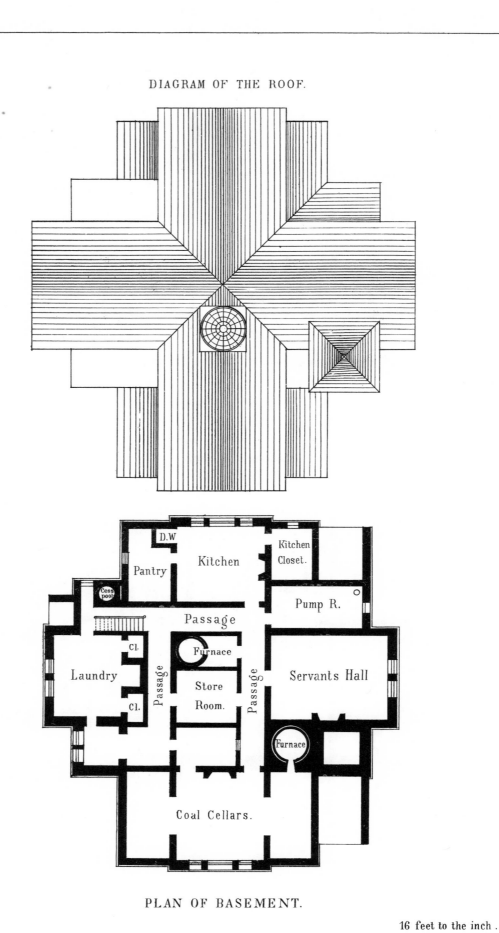

PLAN OF BASEMENT.

16 feet to the inch.

Sam! Sloan. Arch!.   P. S. Duval & Co's Steam lith. Press Philad a.

ROOF & CELLAR PLAN.

Pl. LIX.

Fig. 3.

Fig. 4.

Fig. 2.

Fig. 1.

Scale ½ inch to the foot.

Sam.ᵈ Sloan Arch.ᵗ

P. S. Duval & Co's Steam lith. Press Philad.ᵃ

BUILDING DETAILS.

and sixteen inches in thickness, projecting three inches beyond the line of the heavy timbers of the main building. Above the surface of the ground, their exterior is to be coated with cement, and jointed in blocks, of a color corresponding to that of the wooden part of the elevation.

On Plate LXII. are the plans of the first and second stories, showing accommodations for a family of eight persons. On the first floor are a parlor, dining room, library, kitchen, vestibule and hall. On the second, are five chambers. The closets on both floors, are constructed in the bastions on the corners and centres of the flanks.

A FULL ESTIMATE

OF THE COST OF ERECTING DESIGN FORTY-SEVENTH.

The whole cost of erecting this design of timber, should not exceed four thousand four hundred dollars. If stone is used, and rough cast, four thousand nine hundred: if brick, five thousand two hundred. An estimate and bill of quantities is added. The prices marked, are those prevailing in the vicinity of Philadelphia.

Excavation for cellar and foundation, 420 yds. @ 15 cts. per yd.	$44.10
One hundred perch of stone for cellar walls, @ 60 cts. per perch,	60.00
Laying 135 do., including lime and sand, @ 90 cts. per perch,	121.50
Brick, for cellar and partition walls, and chimneys, 15,000 @ $6 per M.	90.00
Laying do., including lime, sand and materials, @ $4 per M.	60.00
Norway sills, 6 by 8 inches square, 1140 feet @ $18 per M.	20.52
White pine do., 1500 feet @ $20 per M.	30.00
Scantling 3 by 4 in., 8000 feet @ $12 per M.	96.00
Joists and rafters, 12600 ft. @ $12 per M.	151.20
Flooring boards, 5500 ft. @ $27 per M.	148.50
Weather boarding, 4800 ft. @ $22.50 per M.	108.00
Sheathing boards, 2600 ft. @ 15 per M.	39.00
Tin for roofing, 2900 feet @ 10 cts. per ft.	290.00
Lumber for ribs and exterior, 1100 ft. @ $20 per M.	22.00
Eight windows in first story, including inside shutters, sash and frames delivered @ $12 each,	96.00
	1376,32

Ten windows, including sash and frames for second story, delivered @ $10.50 each,	105.00
Twenty-two small windows and frames, delivered @ $4 each,	88.00
Nine doors, for first story @ $4,	36.00
Six doors for closets, @ $3,	18.00
Five do. for second story rooms, @ $3.50,	17.50
Eight do. for closets, @ $3 each,	24.00
Stair way, including materials,	160.00
Lumber, for inside dressing, 4300 ft. @ $30 per M.	129.00
Carpenter's bill for finishing, exclusive of articles here mentioned,	635.00
Plasterer's bill, including materials,	460.00
Painting and glazing, including materials,	275.00
Hardware bill, including locks,	210.00
Sanding the exterior with an extra coat,	115.00
Cooking range,	45.00
Furnace in cellar, and registers for rooms, all complete,	175.00
	2494.50
	1376.32
	3870.82

A PLAIN DWELLING.

DESIGN FORTY-EIGHTH.

Our work is intended, if possible, to convey valuable hints upon the subject of building, as well to the man of slender means as to those who can afford to disregard economy in the construction of their dwellings. Every one, it is true, cannot possess extensive domains, or erect with the most expensive materials, large and showy houses, but all can alike exercise correct taste, and by a judicious use of the means in their power, collect around their dwellings, however humble, those attractions that contribute to make home happy. There are thousands of working men in this country who wish to give something of beauty and interest to the simple forms of cottage life. The author has, in the selection of these and similar plans heretofore given, avoided all useless and unsuitable ornaments, and chosen cheap materials, so that not a dollar more would be expended in the execution of his designs than the same accommodaticn would cost in the usual plain modes of building.

On Plate LXI. are designs of cottages of this kind, drawn to the scale of sixteen feet to the inch. The upper one is a double cottage, whose ground plans are seen on Plate LXII. On the first floors, are a living room and kitchen, and on the second, two chambers. The cost of erecting the two, would not exceed eighteen hundred dollars. The other is that of a single cottage. On the first floor, also shown on Plate LXII. are a living room, bed room, kitchen, pantry and vestibule. On the second, are two chambers, over the bed and living rooms of the first floor. If of timber, this structure can be erected for twelve hundred dollars. If of stone, and rough cast, the cost would be increased a hundred dollars.

(66)

Sam! Sloan, Arch!.   P. S. Duval & Co's Steam lith Press, Philad!

A BUILDING IN THE CASTELLATED STYLE.

Scale 16 feet to the inch.

Sam.! Sloan Arch.

P.S.Duval&C.? Steam lith.press Phil.

CHEAP COTTAGES.

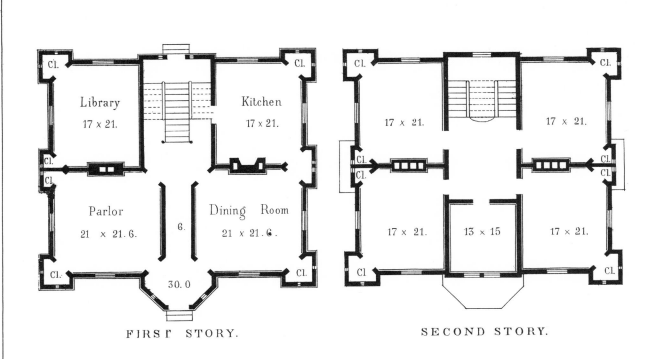

FIRST STORY.   SECOND STORY.

Design XLVIII.

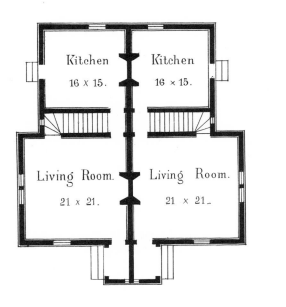

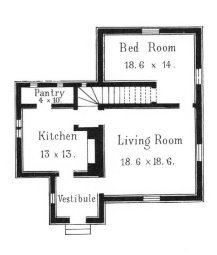

GROUND PLAN OF DOUBLE COTTAGE.   GROUND PLAN OF SINGLE COTTAGE.

Scale 16 feet to the inch.

PLANS.

JOINERY.

Continued.

N no art has greater advances been made than in the manufacture of glass. When we remember the expedients to which the ancients were compelled to resort, we cannot appreciate too highly this beautifully transparent and durable material. It seems that no improvement is possible, unless we could take away its frangibility, and give it instead malleability. As it is, our comforts are increased a thousand fold by this simple material. We cannot remark here, at length, upon its use in windows, as the subject is out of place, but a word about stained glass may not be amiss. The Egyptians were the greatest artists in stained glass that have ever been known to exist, and there were valuable processes, known to them, which have been lost. The Gothic architects well knew the effect of stained glass, and employed it in all their churches. For dwellings, at the present day, it is coming somewhat into use, and by its aid we can much improve the internal appearance of the building. The head and side lights of the front door may be of stained glass, and any other windows which the hall may contain, especially that which lights the stairway. Besides the beautiful appearance within, in this last case, the stained glass also shuts out, to a great extent, the view of the back premises, which is often very desirable. This obstruction to the view, constitutes the great objection to the use of such windows, in the sitting apartments. This may be obviated, in some degree, by using diamond sash, and having the colored glass alternate with purely transparent glass. By this arrangement, a beautiful effect is produced, which, in rural cottages especially, is admirable. The patterns for the windows are composed by the architect, but frequently are left to the artist, who puts it together. To do it skillfully, requires not only great taste, but a considerable knowledge of the properties of light. This may be illustrated by one example. The effect of the colored light upon the eyes is objected to the use of stained glass in private apartments, such as the sitting room or library. But the artist knows that if he combines his colors in the same proportion in the window, that they exist in the spectrum, a clear white light will be diffused through the room, although there be no white glass in the window, and hence the eyes are no more affected than by the light without, except when looking directly at the glass. To maintain this proportion in each, and at the same time produce various patterns, must evidently require skill.

The window shutters, whether internal or external, come properly within joinery. The ordinary Venitian blind is now generally made by machinery, and we would only urge that the pivot blind be always used. Outside shutters, in large buildings, destroy much of their architectural effect, and hence are never represented in architectural drawings.   They are nevertheless often preferable, since they combine security with but a partial exclusion of light, and may be used for either. The panelled outside and inside shutters only are used for security, and in their case the light must be excluded by curtains or drawing Venitian blinds.   Still we much prefer the inside shutters, that fold into the jamb.   They afford sufficient security, they can be managed without opening the sash, which, in rainy weather, is unpleasant, and no injury is done to the architectural effect of the building without.   The construction of these inside shutters may be more readily and satisfactorily ascertained by an examination of the various sections of them, given in the detail drawings, than by any description.

In the construction of doors there is great variation, and indeed, they too are most frequently made by machinery.   More attention than is usual should be paid to the door dressings.   They and the window dressings are frequently so meager that no sort of furnishing can make a room look well.   The architrave should be broad and bold, with simple but rich mouldings.   It is sometimes well to surmount the whole with a cornice, in correspondence with the style, but never place a pediment over this.   The door itself, to look well, should be of some rich wood, as mahogany or oak, or if these be too expensive, it should be painted in some color to accord with the object of the apartment.   We have seen an elegant drawing room, with a frescoed ceiling, with crimson velvet paper on the walls, furnished with a rich Turkey carpet, and handsome rosewood furniture, the whole effect of which was marred by a huge, white, badly designed door, on one side of the room.   This is very bad taste.   It is no longer customary to use large folding doors between apartments.   Sliding doors are substituted, and are much more convenient, since they slide into the partition and are out of the way.   Heretofore, these have been placed on sheaves moving on iron ways set into the floor.   It is much better, as recent practice has proved, to have them suspended on sheaves.   We then can dispense with the ways below, and the doors move more easily.

A vast number of contrivances have been patented for fastening doors and windows, but for ordinary doors there is no better lock than the mortice, frequently referred to in our specifications.   It is essential to a well hung door that it should shut itself tightly, and that it should clear the carpet of the apartment into which it opens.   There are various means by which these may be accomplished at the same time. There is an excellent method, not now much in use, of having hinges made on the principle of a spiral, so that when the door opens, it generally raises and closes again by its own weight.   A carpet sill is generally laid, however, and if the door be well hung, there is no necessity for its rising.   In this case, it closes with a spring.   The springs generally used are very clumsy, but there is one recently invented, we believe, which consists of a small rod three feet long, placed between the hinges and having one end fastened to the door and the other to the jamb.   Now when the door is opened, the simple torsion of the rod acts as spring, and shuts it again.   The contrivance is excellent, because it performs admirably, and may be entirely hidden.

There are many parts of the exterior of a building which properly come within the province of the joiner's art, much of the exterior wood work, though not altogether superfluous, being of an ornamental character. The crowning feature of the exterior is the cornice. Properly, a cornice is part of the Grecian entablature, supported by columns, which consist, in addition, of the frieze and architrave. The term is used quite loosely, however, and serves to describe any mouldings which run along the upper edge of a wall or lintel. Each of the Grecian orders has an accompanying entablature of definite proportions, which should not be deviated from in strict imitations of the style. The Romans were not so definite, and in modern Renaissance, any cornice is used that the individual taste of the architect may suggest. The best specimens of the Gothic style are without cornices, and not until latterly has the parapet been used. The cornices of small buildings, are almost always of wood, and for this reason require the skill of the joiner. Their construction is simple, but judgment must be exercised in the arrangement of the profile. It should be remembered that they are to be placed at a considerable elevation, and hence the effect of small members will be lost. Again, we look up to the cornice, and it should present the best appearance to a spectator when looking at an angle of about 30°. The members or different mouldings of which the cornice is composed, should, of course, be proportioned to its depth, but in general they should be simpler and bolder than is customary. The projections should be distinct, and the depressions should be very deep, so as to make a decided shadow. The size of the cornice is also, in general, too small in proportion to the size of the building. There is nothing which has the effect of giving weight and richness to the building more than a deep, well designed cornice.

The Grecians seem to have understood all branches of architecture better than the Romans, and in no respect is it more strikingly exhibited than in their mouldings. Sections of all the Grecian mouldings discover the curves of the cornice sections, mostly elliptical and parabolic. These curves are very expressive, and their management requires refined taste. For instance, the echinus, which forms the principal part of the Doric capital, immediately beneath the abacus, expresses, with great emphasis, vast upheaving might; the abacus is the point of repose, and the entablature is the weight. The Romans seem not to have appreciated this, or they did not understand the making of the curves. All their mouldings are formed of parts of circles, which express nothing, mean nothing, and their meagerness could only be disguised by profusion, just as we say " he that thinks least, talks most." The mouldings of the Gothic architects were also taken from the circle, but in this style they were comparatively unimportant members, and so much was expressed by other means, that we can excuse the seeming want of force in this. From these statements, it may be inferred that the joiner should always, except in direct imitations of other styles, use the Grecian mouldings, for the eye never wearies with their beautiful combinations.

In sunny climes, it is highly desirable that the walls of dwellings, especially, should be protected, as much as possible, from direct rays. This fact has given rise, in Italy, to a style in which the eaves of the building project considerably. This projection is often so great, that unless there be some apparent support for the eaves, the eye is offended by a sense of insecurity. The defect is remedied by the use of can tilevers and brackets; whence the name bracketed style, in use among some authors. The style is growing among us, and deserves high commendation, for country residences especially, since, in addition to cooling shade, it gives many other pleasing effects. The simplest form of a bracket is a straight piece, one end of which is fastened to the outer edge of the soffit, and the other to the wall. From this we may pass to an almost endless variety of forms, affording scope for the display of taste. Many designs are given in this work, in all of which we have endeavored to express the principle of yielding support. Sometimes beautiful brackets are made of terra cotta; and these are well fitted to support heads and sills to doors and windows.

In order that a bracket should look well, its base, or the part against the wall, should be longer than its upper edge. In cantilevers, the base is much shorter than the upper edge, and hence they must be understood to give support on a different principle. They represent, or are supposed to be the ends of joists, extending out to give support to the eaves. These ends left naked and shaped into some ornamental form, present cantilevers. Hence, the cantilever should never be placed where this principle cannot be expressed. We may place it, however, on the gable, and then it represents the end of a purlin.

The growing taste for porches and verandahs, indicates that their many merits are beginning to be appreciated. We speak of them as used in country buildings, where they play an important part in effecting the embellishment of the exterior. They tell of fresh air and shelter, they give deep masses of shade, protect the walls from the weather, and serve to break up the rectangular outline of the building. A porch is any covered platform before the main entrance, which affords an opportunity for rest and shelter before crossing the threshold. It varies in size according to that of the building, and admits a vast number of modifications, to suit different styles. The Grecian portico was generally a magnificent colonade, extending across the entire breadth of the edifice, and is by far the most elaborate part of the building. The Romans endeavored to give still greater grandeur to their porticoes, and failed in every thing except massiveness and multitudinous detail. The Gothic architects used small porches, but made them a most graceful and highly finished member. At the present day, considerable taste is exercised in this matter, the principal faults being a meagerness in size. The verandah differs from the porch principally in being of lighter construction, and in having greater length. The piazza is properly an inner court, such as are common in oriental countries, but the word is frequently used to indicate a sort of two storied verandah, the floors corresponding to the first and second floor of the building. These are in constant use at the south. For country houses, the verandahs with open work, supports, and curved, tent-like roofs are the prettiest, though much depends on the size of the building. The supports are often of iron, and these are much the best. These parts of the building being comparatively light and ornamental, are referred to the joiner. We will only remark that as the work is exposed, he should be careful to use white lead in every joint, otherwise, decay speedily begins.

Here close our somewhat lengthy remarks upon this subject. It necessarily introduces a variety of points, and we are conscious that in speaking of them we have not in each, confined our remarks to the *work*, but it must be remembered that we write not so much for particular instruction as for general information. No abstract rules can teach a man to perform his labor well. Practice, and a close study of "the lines" alone can give him skill. Had space permitted, it would have been well to have spoken of carving as closely allied to joinery, and perhaps we will yet remark upon it. The art, in consequence of its great cost, has been in little use recently, but it deserves more serious attention, and is rapidly growing into much favor.

AN ORIENTAL VILLA.

DESIGN FORTY-NINTH.

THE style of architecture chosen for this design is little known in this country. It has never, we believe, been chosen for any public building, and there are few instances in which private individuals have selected it for their houses. There are, probably, good reasons why it is not desirable that it should be generally adopted. A large edifice is necessary to give it proper force and expression. When adopted in one of slender pretensions, it loses its characteristic richness, and soon degenerates into absurdity and insignificance. The necessity of ornaments, that are mere ornaments, to render it at all pleasing, will prove another obstacle to its obtaining general popularity; for these increase the expense, without adding to the comfort or convenience of the edifice.

There are, however, some cases where these objections are of little force; and many persons, contemplating building, seek for a design, at once original, striking, appropriate and picturesque. Our work would be incomplete without such an one; and that now offered, cannot fail to meet the approbation of many of our readers. The origin of its style, it would be difficult to trace. The Arabians, from whom it is derived, were originally a simple, frugal people; but when they extended their conquests over more luxurious nations, they acquired a taste for the fine arts, and began to adorn their cities with edifices built with magnificence and splendor. Many of these soon became celebrated for their imposing and original effects. The great mosque at Damascus, then the seat of empire, was the first instance in which the lofty minaret was admitted. This innovation has since become a characteristic of that style of architecture. The effect produced by its proper use, is light and graceful, and its marked outline, the pointed arch, was subsequently used, with great prodigality, in the Gothic style, that had its rise in Europe, centuries afterwards. When the seat of empire was removed from Damascus to Bagdad, neither labor nor expense was spared to make the new capital eclipse the old, and the magnificence of the architecture of this city, so luxuriously described by the author of the Arabian Nights' Entertainments, might be thought an Eastern fable, were it not amply attested by cotemporary authority. Some of the buildings erected by the caliphs of Spain, yet remain to attest the genius and liberality of those who constructed them. The mosque at Cordova, and the Alhambra, described by Irving, are still in existence,—the latter, a perfect model of pure Spanish-Arabian Architecture. Probably one of the finest specimens of this style, is found in the mosque of St. Sophia, at Constantinople, rebuilt by the emperor Justinian, and which, to use the words of Gibbon, "remains, after twelve centuries, a monument of his fame. The architecture of this church, now converted into the principal mosque of the city, has been imitated by the Turkish sultans, and that venerable pile continues to excite the fond admiration of the Greeks, and the more rational of European travellers." The same author closes a polished description of the building with the remark that "a magnificent temple is a laudable monument of national taste and religion, and the enthusiast who entered the dome of St. Sophia might be tempted to suppose that it was the residence, or even the workmanship of the Deity."

Plate LXIII. is, we think, a proof of the fact, that the important features and characteristics of this style may be judiciously, and with much effect, made subservient to the uses of domestic life. The facade of the building is sufficiently modest for a private dwelling, yet striking in conception, and bold in outline. The design is octagonal and the elevation of each side is alike. The second story recedes from the first, and the whole is surmounted by a magnificent Persian dome. The cornice of each floor, is a parapet whose angles are flanked with turrets, from which spring the minarets, the peculiar feature of this style. The walls are intended to be of cut stone, or brick roughcast. The piers, and entrance steps should be of stone. The columns, arches, and ornamented friezes of the verandahs are of iron, and the floors laid with tiles upon iron joists. The parapets, minarets, turrets, and dome are all of wood, and should be well painted and sanded.

Plate LXIV. shows the plans of the first and second floors. On the first, are four porches or verandahs, a drawing-room, parlor, dining-room, and entrance hall, containing the stairway, each seventeen feet by thirty-six, a conservatory, sitting-room, library, and boudoir, each fifteen feet by twenty-two, and an inner hall immediately under the dome with the floor laid in tiles, as represented in the plate. The second floor contains five chambers, each seventeen feet by twenty, one, seventeen by eighteen, a bath-room, water-closets, and gallery under the dome.

On Plate LXV. are plans of the roof and basement. The latter contains the kitchen, laundry, wash-room, house-keeper's or steward's room, servants' hall and bedrooms, with apartments for the stowing of wine, provisions and fuel. The entire building is to be heated with furnaces.

Plate LXVI. is a vertical section of the main building from dome to foundation drawn to a scale, and will be found of great value to the builder. It shows the end of the vestibule, parlor and hall on the first floor, and, on the second, the gallery and entrance doors to the chambers, with the stairway leading out on the roof. One-half the dome is also repre-sented, showing the ceiling and enrichments of the interior. For these it is not intended to employ the jeweller or lapidary, as was the custom in ornamenting dwellings in the East. We would recommend painting in frescoe, as being at once both chaste and economical. By the exercise of skill and good taste, the most pleasing and striking effects may be produced, at a moderate expense. The use of plate glass, ground into appropriate designs, or stained glass, may be recom-mended in such a building; while the effect of well selected pieces of statuary, judiciously placed, should not be overlooked.

Pl. LXIII.

Design XLIX.

P. S. Duval & Co's Steam lith Press Philada

ORIENTAL VILLA.

Scale 12 feet to the inch.

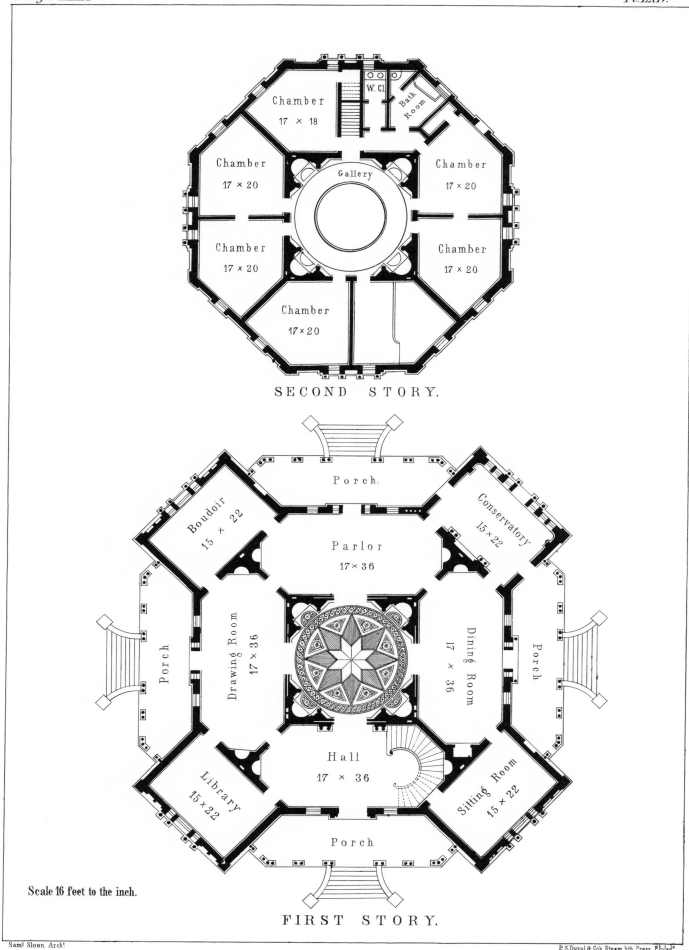

SECOND STORY.

Chamber
17 × 18

Chamber
17 × 20

Chamber
17 × 20

Gallery

Chamber
17 × 20

Chamber
17 × 20

Chamber
17 × 20

W. Cl.

Bath
Room

FIRST STORY.

Porch.

Boudoir
15 × 22

Conservatory
15 × 22

Parlor
17 × 36

Porch

Drawing Room
17 × 36

Dining Room
17 × 36

Porch

Library
15 × 22

Hall
17 × 36

Sitting Room
15 × 22

Porch

Scale 16 feet to the inch.

Saml. Sloan Archt.   P. S. Duval & Co's Steam lith. Press, Philada.

PLANS.

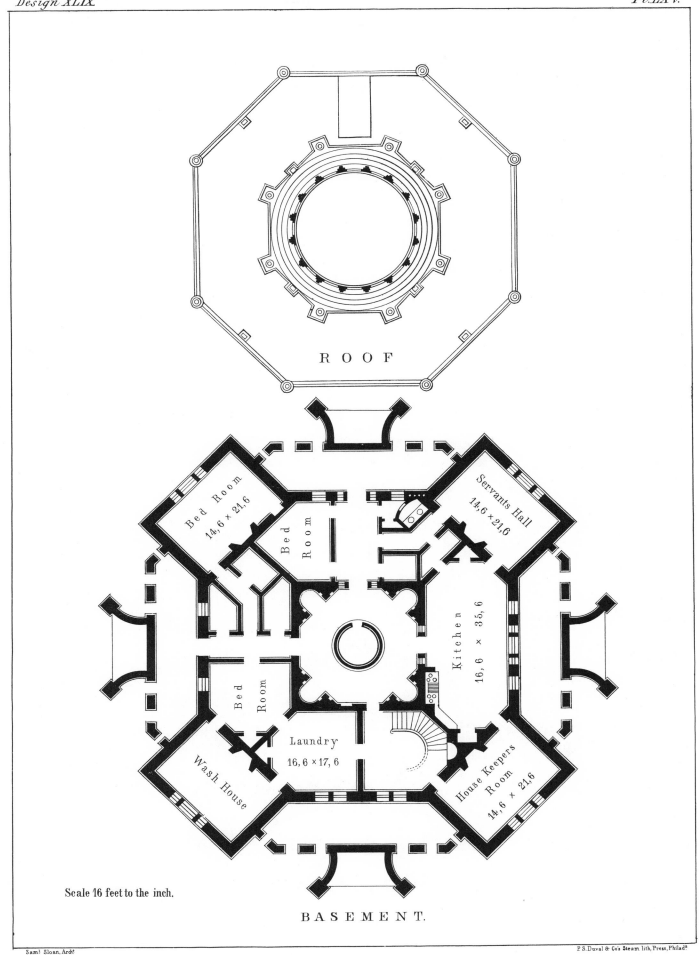

ROOF

Bed Room
14,6 × 21,6

Bed
Room

Servants Hall
14,6 × 21,6

Bed
Room

Kitchen
16, 6 × 35, 6

Wash House

Laundry
16, 6 × 17, 6

House Keepers
Room
14,6 × 21,6

Scale 16 feet to the inch.

BASEMENT.

Sam.ᵈ Sloan, Arch.ᵗ   P.S. Duval & Co's Steam lith. Press, Philad.ᵃ

PLANS.

Scale 8 feet to the inch.

Sam! Sloan Arch!.   P.S.Duval & Co's Steam lith.Press Philad.ª

VERTICAL SECTION.

Pl. LXVII.

Fig. 1.

Fig. 2.

Sam. Sloan Arch.ᵗ

P. S. Duval & Cº Steam lith. press Ph.

DETAILS.

Fig. 3.

Fig. 4.

Sam. Sloan Arch^t.

P.S.Duval & Co Steam lith.press Ph.

DETAILS.

The building details are represented on Plates LXVII. and LXVIII.   Figure 1 is a front view of the windows over the verandahs drawn to the scale of half an inch to the foot.   Fig. 2 is a sectional view of the same.   The ornaments should be either of wood or iron.   The windows of the library, boudoir, and conservatory are seen in Fig. 3, showing the whole end, with the parapet on the top, and the termination of the turret on the angle of the parapet.   Fig. 4 is a ground plan of the same windows, showing the base of the columns and the base of the urn.

The entire cost of this building may be seen in the following bill of items.   The estimates are, as heretofore, at the prices of labor and materials prevailing in and near this city.

Excavation 1000 yds., at 25 cts. per yd. - - $250.00	Sliding doors, 4 pair, @ $35 - - - - 140.00
Stone, 800 perches, at $2.00 per perch, - - 160.00	Carpenters' work, - - - - - - 3000.00
Brick, 275,000, at $10 per M. - - - - 2750.00	Carving and Turning, - - - - - 1500.00
Plastering, 5000 yds. @ 20 cts. per yd. - - 1000.00	Cut stone, - - - - - - - 3000.00
Roughcasting, 1000 yds. @ 50 cts. per yd. - 500.00	Tiles, and laying them, - - - - 1600.00
Plastic enrichments, - - - - - - 500.00	Roofing 7000 ft. at $10 per M. - - - 700.00
Joist and scantling, 65,000 ft. @ $13 per. M. - 845.00	Lead, 1000 sq. ft., 3 lb. lead, 3000 lb. - 1800.00
Sheathing, 10,000 ft. @ $15 per M. . - 150.00	Iron Verandahs - - - - - 2500.00
Flooring lumber, 17,000 ft. @ $32 per M. - 544.00	Hardware, and smith work, - - - 1200.00
Best common lumber, 10,000 ft. @ $30 per M. - 300.00	Painting and glazing, - - - - 3000.00
Second best do. 10,000 ft. @ $25 " - 250.00	Plumbing, - - - - - - 500.00
Third best do. 10,000 ft. @ $17.50 " 175.00	Furnaces and registers, - - - - 1000.00
Fourth best do. 5,000 ft. @ $20 " 100.00	————
Scaffolding, 8000 ft. @ $13 per M. - - 104.00	19940.00
Doors, 75, average each, of $4 - - - 300.00	7928.00
————	————
7928.00	27868.00

CHEAP DOUBLE HOUSES.

DESIGN FIFTIETH.

On Plate LXIX. are front and side elevations of double houses intended for small families.   By erecting houses in the same block the cost of each is lessened, and the expense incurred for fuel when they are heated by furnaces is greatly diminished.   The entrance to one of these houses is in the side, to the other, in front.   By this arrangement, economy of room is gained, and for the plan presented a location on the corner of a street or road would be desirable.

Plate LXX. shows the plans of the basement and three stories drawn to a scale.   On inspection, they will be found to contain accommodations for a family of six persons.   The two could be built of smooth brick or stone roughcast for $2400.00.

PLASTERING.

IN a previous article, we mentioned the principles to be observed in the composition of mortar. They were there applied directly to its preparation when used as a cement, and directions were given, necessary to enable any one, not only to understand the principles of its action, but to prepare the material and perform the work. Since the mortar used in plastering is essentially the same in its composition, and acts in the same way, it is unnecessary to repeat those principles, and the inquirer is accordingly referred to the article headed, Mortar. There are, however, some slight variations in the proportions of the ingredients of plaster according to its use and position, as it is intended for the floor or walls, the first, second, or third coat. These variations are of such a nature that they can be learned only from actual practice, and are, therefore, much better understood by the plasterer than by any theorist. A few general directions, however, may not be out of place.

The plaster for the first coat should be of harder setting material than that intended for the others, because it has more weight to bear, and is supported only by the space between the laths. This, however, is not the case where the plaster is laid upon a brick wall. Then it has the firmest hold possible. It is always desirable that this coat should set quickly and become firm before the second is applied. The second coat should be composed of finer material than the first, in about the same proportion, though it is not so essential that the mortar should be hard setting. With these two first coats it is customary to mix a quantity of hair in order to bind the parts together more strongly. Usually for economy's sake, too little hair is used, and that not sufficiently disseminated through the mass by long continued working. The third coat is composed almost entirely of lime, and is called the hard finish. If it is desired to make a floor of mortar, as is often the case in a basement or on hearths, hydraulic lime laid on a brick pavement should always be used. Whenever a floor of this kind is wanted, it should be made so as to reject moisture entirely; and in order to improve the qualities of hydraulic mortar in this respect, it is well to intermix a quantity of asphaltum. Some such composition should always be used on the walls of a basement for the same reason. Sometimes small pebbles are mixed with floor mortar that it may better resist wear. This is a good plan, but small stone chips are preferable, for the mortar does not cling to the pebbles as firmly as to stone chips, and they besides are found to wear with the floor.

The laths upon which the plastering is spread, are usually of hemlock, cut out by machinery. In the South and West they are often split from blocks, and these when well made are the best, because they are stronger and rougher, giving the mortar a better hold. In nailing them on it is a very common fault to

SIDE ELEVATION.

Sam! Sloan Arch!   P. S. Duval & Co's Steam lith. Press Philad?

FRONT ELEVATION

Scale 16 feet to the inch.

DOUBLE DWELLINGS.

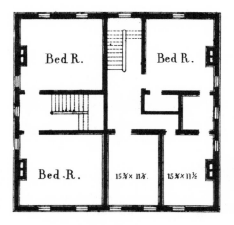

THIRD STORY.

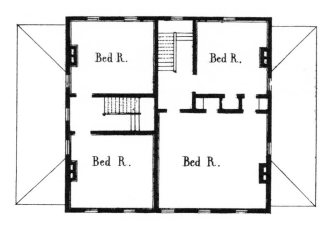

SECOND STORY.

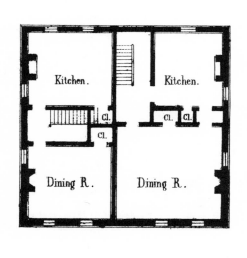

BASEMENT.

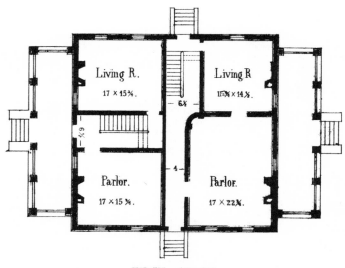

FIRST STORY.

Sam! Sloan Arch!   P. S. Duval & Co's Steam lith Press Philad?

PLANS.

place them too close together. The plasterer often uses his mortar too much diluted, because it is thus easier to manage; and then, if the laths are at the proper distances, it falls from between them, and gives him trouble. To avoid this, he has them placed near each other, and the consequence is, that the mortar cannot get sufficient hold, and when the wall receives a heavy jar, the plasterer's work falls bodily. How often do we hear of half a ceiling tumbling down, endangering the life of those beneath. Another cause of such mishaps is, that the mortar is generally laid on too thick, thereby giving too much weight to the mass. The first coat should be just thick enough to remain in its position, the second, just thick enough to give an even surface for the hard finish, which should be as thin as possible. There is a limit to this, however, for by diminishing the thickness we greatly increase the liability to crack. The cracks in plastering are most frequently caused by the shrinking and saging or springing of the timbers. The first is in a measure unavoidable, but the second when it occurs, displays bad carpentry.

The finishing of plastering is very nice work. One chief aim must be to make a perfectly smooth and level surface. The latter is attained by frequent applications of the straight edge in all possible directions. If the wall is to be papered, there is no necessity for the third coat, since the paper may be laid directly on the second. The third coat is often superseded in cheap buildings by white wash, which besides its roughness is objectionable, since paper cannot afterwards, if desired, be put on the wall. The paste takes hold only on the wash, and both peel off together.

Some of the most elegant ornaments in modern buildings are made of plaster. We refer to the cornices placed in the angles of the wall and ceilings, and to the centre pieces. When the pattern of these is simple, they are frequently made by the workman who does the plain plastering; but when they are more elaborate, an artist must be employed. He prepares the design in moulds, and puts it in place after the other work is completed. The material is generally plaster of Paris, which is nothing more than calcined gypsum or sulphate of lime. Such work is costly, but nothing adds more to the elegant appearance of an apartment. The correct name for this kind of work is stucco. The term is frequently applied to the plaster on the exterior of a building, but we now use it in its strict sense. The material is sometimes varied by mixing pulverized marble with plaster of Paris, the whole sifted and wrought up together. Architectural and sculptural ornaments, such as fruits, flowers, garlands and festoons, are made with this composition. When the stucco is mixed, it forms a very soft and ductile paste, which soon hardens, and then the desired form is given to it, either by moulds or by a little spatula of iron. During this operation it continues to harden. It may even be cut, and those ornaments may be executed which require a nice finish. In time, it becomes as hard as stone, and takes a beautiful polish. Vitruvius makes mention of stucco, and the art of preparing architectural ornaments in this way, was well known to the Romans.

It now seems conceded on all hands that brick buildings are out of place in the country. Wooden buildings are too perishable to satisfy most proprietors, and stone is difficult to obtain. How then can we erect a handsome and permanent dwelling? The walls must be built of brick, and the exterior roughcast or stuccoed as the word is commonly used. The greatest objection to this style of finishing has been, that after a few years' exposure to the weather, the plaster falls off; but a careful attention to a few important points will obviate this difficulty. In the first place, the mortar must be removed from between the bricks to the depth of half an inch from the face of the wall. These interstices will afford a strong hold for the plaster. Then when the work is about to be commenced, the whole wall should be well swept with a stiff dry brush to remove all loose mortar from the brick work and all particles of dust which interfere much with the adhering of the plaster. Again, as the work proceeds, the wall should be well soaked or washed with water, in order that the mortar of the plaster may have full time to set and become hard. Otherwise the dry wall will rapidly absorb the moisture of the mortar, before the setting process is complete, and leave a crumbling mass that will soon yield to to the weather. If the precautions mentioned be taken, and good hair mortar used, the coating of plaster will stand as long as the wall.

After the mortar is laid on, several methods are used to give it a finished appearance. In roughcasting, a pricking up coat of hair mortar is first put on; upon this, when tolerably dry, a smooth coat of the same mixture is laid, and a second workman follows with a vessel full of a thinner mixture which he throws over the work as fast as it is finished. This last produces uniformity of color and the rough appearance, whence its name. Many have thought to introduce an improvement here by pointing the surface in imitation of stone. If a design for a stone building is executed in rough cast, then this artifice must be resorted to; but if the building be for roughcast, such an imitation destroys the original effect. The present tastes and economical views of the times, demand such imitations; but if architects were allowed to exercise their own taste, they would exclude all such absurdities. In stucco work, as it is called, the surface is smoother, and is often painted and sanded for the purpose of preserving it, of giving uniformity of color, and to take away the gloss arising from a smooth surface, which, though sometimes allowed to remain, has generally a bad effect.

Another, and better method of producing a desired color, is to imbue the whole mass of the mortar, when making it, with some substance that will produce the tint throughout the whole. This is a comparatively cheap method, and is preferable for other reasons which are bringing it into constant use. A patent has been taken by Mr. Silver of Philadelphia, for a method of forming this mortar, which we think superior to any other. We have no interest in this invention, but unhesitatingly recommend it, simply because we are convinced of its excellence. Not only are the most delicate and uniform colors produced, but the plaster is also made impervious to moisture by a mixture of oleaginous matter, and hence, walls coated with it are kept perfectly dry in every condition of the weather, while this admixture does not interfere in the slightest degree with the firm attachment of the plaster to the wall.

P A I N T I N G .

T is unnecessary to descend into the details of this familiar subject. In the space we have devoted to its consideration, it is of course impossible to do more than state a few important facts, and lay down some very general rules and suggestions, for the information of all interested in such matters. When we reflect that painting is itself the chief ornament of a building. and serves to finish or adorn nearly all other ornaments, and that in addition to this, it is a great preservative against decay, its importance becomes strongly apparent.

For many years past, white lead has constituted the principal ingredient and body of almost all paints. This substance is a carbonate of lead, obtained from the metal by various processes, and its manufacture has become of national importance in those countries where it is practised on a large scale. The Dutch process, one of the most common, and quite ancient, is this. "A great number of earthen jars are prepared, into each of which are poured a few ounces of crude vinegar; a roll of sheet lead is then introduced in such a manner that it shall neither touch the vinegar nor project above the top of the jar. The vessels are then arranged in a large building side by side upon a layer of stable manure, or, still better, spent tan, and closely covered by boards. A second layer of tan is spread upon the top of the latter, and then a second series of pots; these are in turn covered with boards and decomposing bark, and in this manner a pile of many alternations is constructed. After the lapse of a considerable time, the pile is taken down, the sheets of lead removed, and carefully unrolled. They are then found in great part to be covered by a carbonate which merely requires washing and grinding to be fit for use."

Several other substances have been used, but not so extensively, as the basis of paints. Lamp black, which is simply a form of nearly pure carbon, is used for black paint, and when mixed with white lead forms lead color. Latterly many changes have been introduced into this art. Zinc has been substituted for lead with admirable effect, and extensive manufactories for zinc paints are now in operation. Many mineral substances have been found native, in a state to be worked up into excellent pigments. Patents have been taken out for the preparation of these, some of which are valuable and others worthless. Among them is one for the preparation of paint from Parker's cement, which is remarkable, and has proved valuable. Most of the mineral paints are represented as imparting the property of resisting the action of heat, and hence are termed fire proof. If, however, we can obtain a basis for paint that is cheaper than white lead, that will resist the action of weather, and will retain its body longer, and more effectually preserve wood work from decay, it is all we can expect.

The bases of paints, when unmixed, are fine dry powders. It is necessary that some ingredient be added which will render them plastic. Sometimes water is used, and paints of this class are termed water-colors. They are but little used about buildings, as they do not endure exposure. For ages, linseed oil has been preferred to any other substance, principally because of its extraordinary fitness for resisting moisture. When the paint has become dry, a thin transparent pellicle from the oil will be found to cover the whole surface. It is this which renders it impervious to moisture. There is also a gloss formed over the entire work which it is desirable to remove. This is done by mixing turpentine with the last coat, causing it to dry quickly, and leaving a clear soft white surface. Sometimes turpentine is mixed with every coat, but this is a practice that should be avoided. Varieties in color are obtained by intermixing with the basis used different substances that impart the desired hue.

On entering some of our villages, the only color which meets the eye is white. Everything is white; the houses, the fences, the stables, the dog kennel, aud sometimes even the trees cannot escape, but get a coat of white wash. There are in our opinion only two excuses for this. It gives a neat and cleanly appearance, and when the house is embowered by trees and overrun with vines, the effect, by way of variety, is not unpleasant. On entering the house, everything except the carpets and furniture is found to be of the same color, save perhaps an unlucky mantle, which mourns its exclusion in deep black. Is this taste? Whether it be or not, one thing is certain, that a great change is coming over our people in this respect. They are beginning to see that there are beauties in color as well as form. Many of the attempts to improve in this matter are ridiculous enough we know, and the result is often some absurd combination of color. But this cannot last, and improvement is certain. It will soon be attained by observation and a cultivation of taste, but one thing must be remembered always, that there is to the eye harmony and discord among colors, just as the ear detects harmony or discord in the notes of the musical scale. Whenever colors are to be combined, attention must be given to general effect as well as to the tint, tone, and shade of each. They may be beautiful separately, but excessively disagreeable to look upon when blended together. In architectural painting, strong or even positive colors are always to be avoided. Soft neutral tints are only proper to be used. For the exterior of a dwelling, nothing is more beautiful than the soft delicate tint of the Connecticut brown stone. The depth of the shade must be varied to suit circumstances. In truth, it is a safe rule, to adopt, for artificial purposes, the colors of natural objects. These seldom fail to suggest the most beautiful tints.

There is one species of decoration, however, to which we would more particularly allude. Fresco painting is of great antiquity, having been practiced to some extent by the Egyptians, and afterwards perfected by the Greeks. Some of the ceilings made by their artists, were considered so beautiful and so difficult to reproduce, that their vain and not over scrupulous conquerors, the Romans, cut them bodily from the walls and had them transported entire to their own capitol. During the middle ages, the art of Fresco painting having been lost, tapestry was substituted, and the walls were hung with representations of hunting scenes and military achievements. The discoveries at Pompeii and Herculaneum have contributed not a little to revive a taste for this kind of decoration. Our method of papering was doubtless originally an imitation of it, but has now become a distinct and might be made a legitimate and separate branch of the decorative art.

In the first volume of this work a design for a ceiling is presented. As there stated, it might be executed either in stucco or fresco, or both, since it is entirely allowable to paint the carved stucco ornaments. The painting is done in water colors and requires skill and experience, though we believe there are some who practise the art injudiciously upon any wall, satisfied if the work look well on pay day, but totally regardless of its durability. The true and tested plan is as follows. Two operators are engaged, the painter with the plasterer in constant attendance. To prepare the work for the painter, a rendering and a finishing coat are required, and the colors are prepared only with water. No alteration or amendment can be made, and the artist must possess great ability and judgment, with quickness of execution. This is the ancient method. An improvement has been introduced by the Germans. While fresco paintings of the former kind are not very durable, except in a few cases, as at Pompeii, where their preservation is due to the entire exclusion of light and air, and artists have reason to mourn over the destruction of the greatest master pieces; those obtained upon the new principle are capable, not only of withstanding the action of water, weak acids and alkalis, but also the great changes of climate during a severe German winter, without injury to the freshness of the coloring. The colors are so firmly attached to their ground that they exhibit no tendency to separate from it, nor can they be removed by mechanical agency. The particulars of the process have not been made known, but it is probable that it consists in the silification of the lime mortar. Though this branch is one of the most difficult as well as most expensive of architectural decoration, the day is not far distant when it will be fully revived.

THE GRAPERY.

DESIGN FIFTY-FIRST.

WE have already furnished many designs of ornamental buildings intended for the embellishment of the grounds around the mansion house. In fact no work of the kind would be complete without them. The elevations of a dwelling may be conceived and executed in the best taste, the interior may be commodious, and admirably adapted to the wants of its inmates, the shrubbery may be planted with care, and at a heavy cost to the owner, but the effect of all these is often destroyed by the erection of out houses in a style totally at variance with the requisitions of beauty and fitness of design or location. It is not now our purpose to lay down any rules to be observed by those who are in quest of such ornaments for their grounds. The principles that must guide them are in a measure arbitrary, and dependent upon the particular circumstances of each case. Climate, the nature, size, and location of the grounds, the shrubbery, the elevation of the dwelling house, must all be taken into consideration in making selections. Those who would pursue the subject further are referred to the essay on Landscape Gardening, of which beautiful art it is an important and legitimate branch.

The uses of the Grapery need not be discussed here. We have only to remark upon the design presented on Plate LXXI., which on inspection, will be found to answer every purpose for which such a building is intended. It is to be constructed of glass and iron, or if wood is used, the ornaments may be made of terra cotta. It is drawn to the scale of eight feet to the inch, but the scale may be enlarged or diminished, to suit the taste and wants of the projector.

On Plate LXXIII. is the ground plan, drawn to the same scale. The heavy lines show the position of the walls, doors and windows. The shape of the foundation, the steps, the position of the vases on the exterior, and the racks for pots within the building, are indicated by the lighter lines.

OBSERVATORY.

DESIGN FIFTY-SECOND.

As an accompanying design to the last, Plate LXXII. is the elevation of an observatory. The object of such an edifice is obvious. It is intended to be one hundred feet high, and to contain five stories. A spiral stair case extends from bottom to top. Forty feet from the ground there is a gallery, projecting four feet, reached by a door in each side of the building, and serving as a landing place during the ascent.

On Plate LXXIII. is the plan of the gallery floor, showing the walls of the tower, and the doors, drawn to a scale of sixteen feet to the inch.

If constructed of timber, boarded and sanded, the cost would not exceed $3.800 : if of brick, and rough cast, $5.000.

Pl. LXXI.

Saml. Sloan, Archt.

T. Sinclair & Co's Steam lith Press Philada.

GRAPERY

Sam! Sloan Arch^t   P.S.Duval & Co s.Steam lith. Press Philad^a

OBSERVATORY.

Pl. LXVIII.

Design LII.

Design LI.

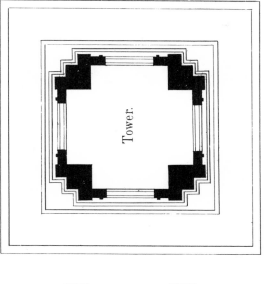

Tower.

Scale 16 feet to the inch.

Scale 8 feet to the inch.

PLANS.

Samˡ. Sloan Archᵗ.

P.S.Duval & Co's Steam lith Press Philadᵃ.

A SOUTHERN HOUSE.

DESIGN FIFTY-THIRD.

To meet the wishes of many of our correspondents, we present another design of a building intended for the south and south-west. We have already spoken at some length of the objects to be attained in the erection of a dwelling in warm climates, and of the peculiarities of construction required by the social and domestic habits prevailing in those sections of the country. The detachment of the kitchen from the main building, the size of the ground floor, the necessity for large windows, wide doors and ample verandahs, the difference in the number of stories, and many other considerations all tend to render a design prepared for a northern mansion totally unfit for the wants and convenience of a southern family.

A perspective view of the building, is given on plate LXXIV. It is in the Italian style, and the campanile or tower is a marked feature of the elevation. The entire design is similar in most of its features to plans prepared by the author for J. S. Winters, Esq., of Montgomery, Alabama. The site most suitable for such a dwelling is a broken or rolling country, and may be on a plantation with the same propriety as in the vicinity of a town or city. For a section unbroken by hills, we would recommend, as more appropriate, the elevation of Design XLIV. of this volume.

The front and side elevations are on Plate LXXV. drawn to a scale, and will be found of great value to the practical builder, as measurements may be taken directly from them. The first floor is elevated six feet from the surface of the ground. The walls are to be built hollow, or with a space of two inches from the foundation course upwards, between the inner and the outer wall. By this arrangement, the house is kept perfectly dry, and the rooms of the basement are as effectually protected from dampness as those of the upper stories. In buildings of every class we would recommend the construction of the walls on this principle. It can be effected with the least difficulty when brick are used. In ordinary buildings, the walls should be one and a half bricks or thirteen inches thick, and by adding two inches for the desired space, we have a wall of fifteen inches. The inner course should be a single thickness, and bonded to the outer with alternate headers, in the heading courses, which should always be laid every fifth course. In smaller buildings, where the walls are only one brick, or eight and a half inches thick, the two inch space gives a wall of ten and a half inches. The outer and inner courses are then of a single thickness, and should be bonded in the same way. In such cases, the timbers or flooring joists bear upon the inner course four inches, this support being sufficient for ordinary purposes. In buildings of a larger class, where the size of the timbers and the thickness of the walls are increased, a larger bearing, of from six to seven inches, is required. In walls from nineteen to twenty-three inches thick, that is constructed of two bricks and a half with the space of two inches, the inner courses should be an entire brick, or eight and a half inches. In stone walls the same object can be effected by making the stone or outer wall of the required thickness to sustain the whole, and constructing an inner wall of one course of four inch brick, two inches from the stone, the two to be braced together by iron clamps. Though this is more expensive than the common mode of erecting cleats and lathing for the plastering, it is much more durable, and more likely to secure the object desired. The moisture penetrates the outer wall, and the wood work and plastering must soon decay, but when the other plan is adopted, we have never known an instance, even in the most exposed localities where the slightest dampness has been detected in the dwelling. The walls of the main building, represented in the design, are intended to be nineteen inches thick, from the foundation to the level of the first floor; those of the wings, will also be nineteen inches thick from the foundation to the surface of the ground to obtain sufficient strength for resisting the pressure of the earth against them, and then reduced to fifteen inches from the surface of the ground to the level of the first floor by a break of four inches on the outside. The walls of the main building from the first floor to the roof, are fifteen inches thick; those of the wings, eleven inches. The walls of the tower are to the first floor, twenty-seven inches; to the second floor, twenty two; to the fourth, eighteen; and thence to the roof thirteen. The roof is of tin, cross leaded, and painted on both sides, the top with two coats.

The verandahs, the window heads, sills and all the large ornaments are to be of iron. Plate LXXVII. shows at Figure 1 the enrichments and projection of the windows of the first story. Figure 2 is the base of the windows of the second story, the upper part being similar to those of the first. Figure 3 is the main entrance and base of the second story window in the tower. The upper part of the same window is seen in the elevations on Plate LXXV. Figure 4 on Plate LXXVIII. shows the windows of the basement and first floor, with a section of the verandah.

On Plate LXXVI., are the ground plans. The basement contains two cellars, two store rooms, a housekeeper's apartment, the dining room and furnaces. The first floor contains the parlors, two chambers, a bed room, library or sitting room, entrance through the tower, lobby and hall. The second floor, two chambers, a dressing room, a room in the tower, closets and hall. The kitchen is constructed apart from the main building. The accommodations are intended for a family of ten persons.

The cost of the entire building, in a section where materials and workmanship could be obtained at the prices prevailing in the neighborhood of Philadelphia, would not exceed seven thousand five hundred dollars.

Pl. LXXIV.

SOUTHERN HOUSE.

P.S. Duval & Co's Steam lith. Press Philad.

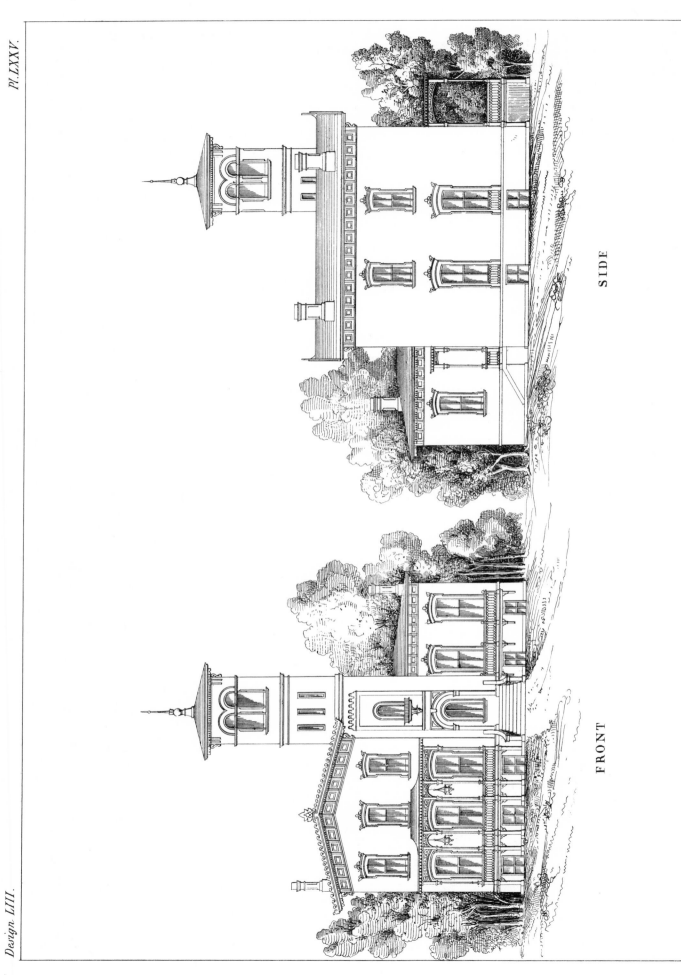

SIDE

FRONT

ELEVATIONS.

P.S.Duval & C? Steam lith press Ph.

Sam Sloan Arch?

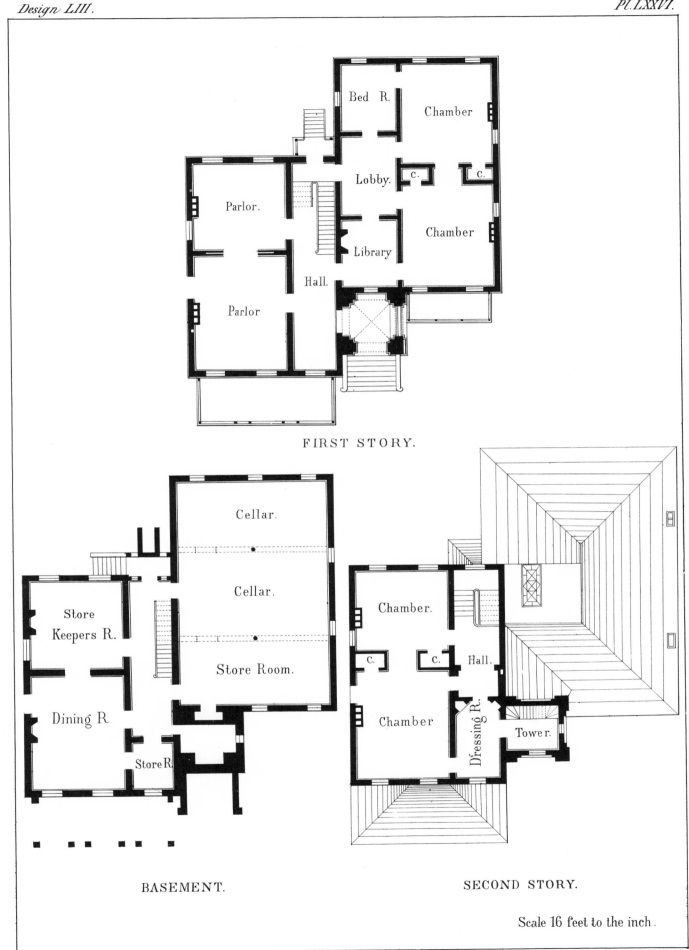

FIRST STORY.

BASEMENT.

SECOND STORY.

Scale 16 feet to the inch.

PLANS.

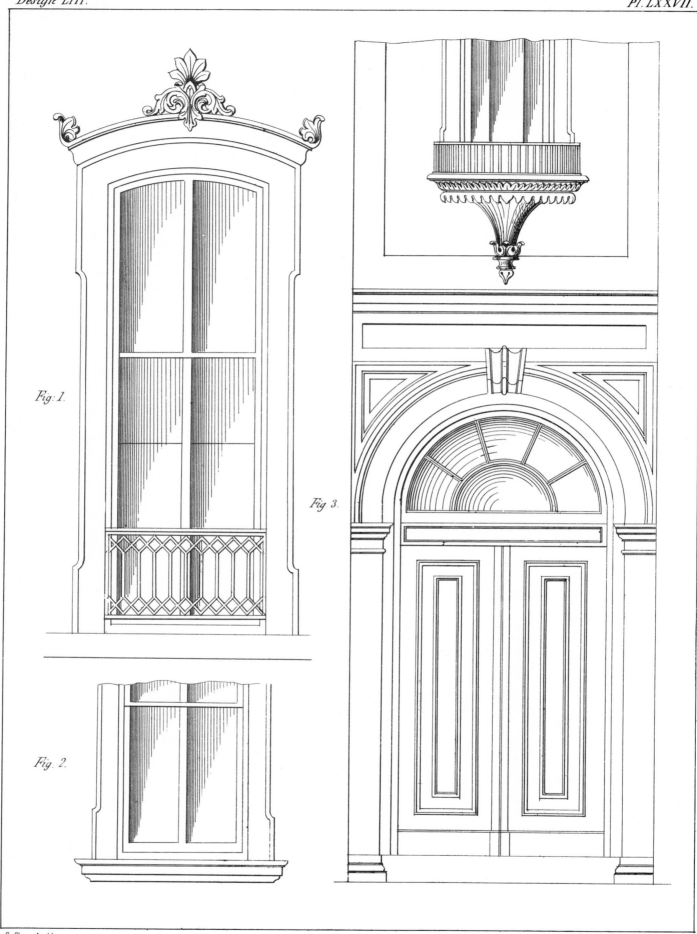

Fig: 1.

Fig. 2.

Fig. 3.

S. Sloan Arch.t

P. S. Duval & Co Steam lith press Phil

DETAILS.

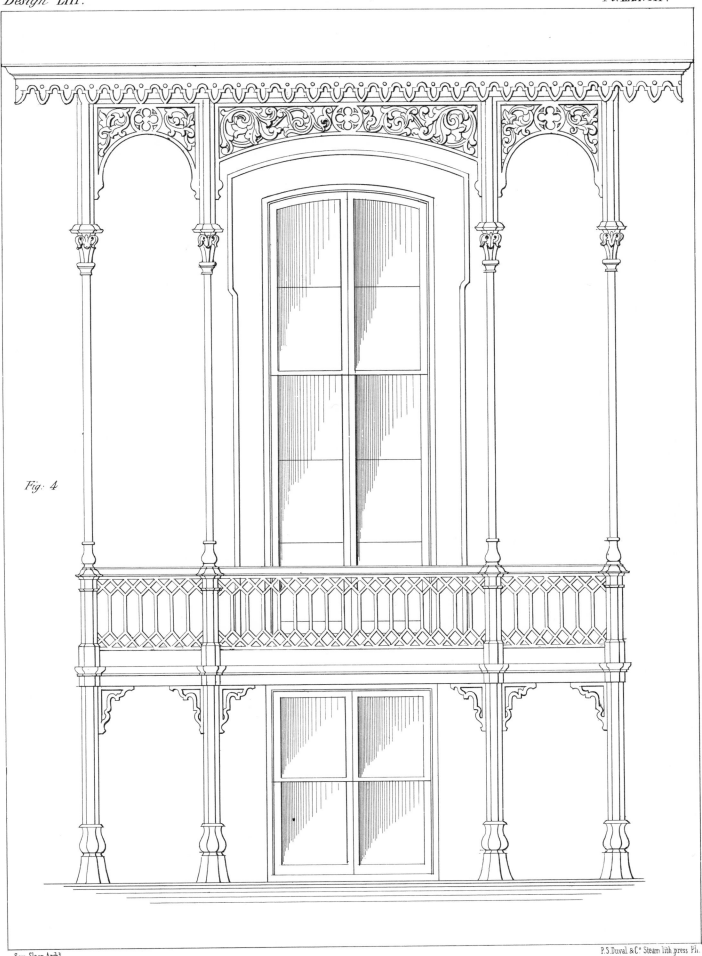

Fig: 4

Sam. Sloan Arch^t.   P.S.Duval &C^o Steam lith.press Ph.

DETAILS.

FINISH OF ROOFS.

A DWELLING affords protection to its inmates, by means of its roof as well as by its walls and floor. Indeed, regarding the weather alone, this is a far more important part than either of the others, and it is probable that in many climates, walls were originally erected for no other purpose than to support the roof. As no rain ever fell in Egypt, the people only wanted protection from the sun, and all the roofs were constructed of large stone slabs, laid horizontally. Flat roofs are still found in oriental countries, and may be regarded as nothing more than upper floors, especially as the top of the house is often used as a sleeping apartment. Wherever it became necessary to provide protection from the rain, it was accomplished by giving inclination to the roof. On large buildings it is easier to fix two inclined planes than one. The use of these gave rise to the pediment which first appears among the Greeks, though strange to say, many of their buildings having this feature were never intended to be covered at all. Then came the magnificent Roman dome rising above stupendous piles, and giving unity and grandeur to the whole. Of these three forms, we have endless modifications. Roofs have been built at every angle beyond thirty degrees according to their requirements. In all countries north of the line of occasional snow, they have a high pitch, in order that the snow may slide off readily, and not weigh upon the structure. The pitch of a roof is the angle which an inclined side makes with the plane of the horizon, and the angle of the roof is that which the inclined sides make in meeting.

Latterly, roofs have been made with much less pitch than formerly, the use of metal covering having introduced great changes in this respect. When they have sufficient pitch to be visible from the ground, they should be so constructed as not only to prevent their marring, but as to cause them to increase architectural effect. The high pitch of the Gothic roof made it a prominent feature in the building, and much pains was often spent in making it highly ornamental; as in the instance of the roof of Westminster Hall. Always, when using shingle or slate, the roof is necessarily high. It is only by the use of metallic covering that we can in our climate make it nearly flat. In long buildings, a roof hipped at the ends has a good effect. This arrangement is most suitable for a wing or a lean-to, but should always be avoided in short buildings. It gives the edifice a pyramidical and peaked contour that tends to destroy the general effect.

The cheapest covering for a permanent building is of shingles, or perhaps it should be said they involve less expense at the outset. Whether they are or not more expensive in the end is a matter for inquiry. When cypress shingles can be obtained, they are much to be preferred, since they will last for nearly forty years, while white pine shingles must be renewed every fifteen or twenty years. A roof of this description cannot be made very ornamental, though some relief from excessive plainness may be obtained by pointing the end of each shingle. The durability of the roof is not however increased by this means. The pitch of a shingle roof should be about twenty-six and a half degrees, making the height about one fourth the span.

A slate covering is for many reasons much better than one of wood. The slates differ in quality, and the excellence of the roof depends much upon this. The best are from Westmoreland, England, but a much greater quantity of the Welsh slates are imported, and are considered the next in quality. There is no doubt that we posess in this country beds of slate fully equal to those of the old world, that only want developement. The purple slate presents the best appearance, though the blue and green are equally durable. The coarser varieties are not so good, and generally are lighter in color; the fine grained being dark, and splitting into thinner plates. All are originally separated from their beds like other stones, by gunpowder, after which the masses are divided into plates through the planes of cleaveage. These plates are then shaped by various means.

Oaken slats, one by two inches, are nailed across the common rafters at proper distances. To these the slates are attached by means of nails passing through two small holes in each, made by sharp strokes from a pointed instrument called the pick. Copper nails are often used; and though expensive, are the best for the purpose. Small iron nails, boiled in linseed oil to preserve them from rust, are substituted. All vallies and gutters must be lined with leaded tin, painted of a sombre color, to resemble the slate. If nothing more than this is done, a pelting rain will beat up between the slates, and drip upon the ceiling. To prevent this, the lower side of the slating is plastered with strong hair mortar, or if the plates are very large, simple pointing will be sufficient. For common slate, the pitch of the roof should not be much if any less than that for shingles; for large slate it may be about twenty-nine and a half degrees, or one fifth of the span. The weight of common slates on the square yard of roofing is from five to nine hundred pounds; that of the larger slate may be as much as twelve hundred. The appearance of the roof is often enhanced by laying the slate in the lozenge, or some other fanciful pattern. Sometimes a good effect is produced by mingling several patterns together on the same roof. These modes shown are in several of the preceding designs.

In many countries of Europe, and on some of our own buildings, erected many years ago, we find tiles used as a covering. They are nothing more than baked earth, of various shapes. There are some objections to their use which have caused them to fall into disrepute. They are the heaviest covering known, if we except the slabs of marble which are sometimes placed on expensive public buildings, and are liable to be cracked in frosty weather if unglazed. They nevertheless may be made to form a most excellent fire proof roof, if properly managed. The pan-tiles are often met with in Italy, and give a picturesque finish to the buildings, forming a feature in the style which with us is badly imitated by placing round slats under metal. The pitch of a tile roof should be about the same as for those of common slates.

Metal coverings are now supplanting all others. We have been long accustomed to tin and leaden roofs. The only difference now observable is in the quality of the material used, which has been vastly improved in the manufacture. Lead, owing to its expense, has gone much into disuse, but the use of tin has increased. Zinc is in many instances taking the place of both lead and tin, in the useful arts; and has been found much more lasting upon roofs, than either of the other metals, from the fact, that it resists corrosion better. The preparation of zinc, corresponding to that of tin, is called galvanized iron, and has of late years attracted the attention of architects and engineers, on account of its many valuable qualities. Simple sheet iron is sometimes used, but is expensive, and rusts easily, unless protected by heavy coats of paint. All metal coverings, however, should be painted, since the thin pellicle of linseed oil, as well as the metallic substance contained in the paint, tends greatly to retard oxidation. In the specifications prepared for this work, we have always directed two coats of paint above, and one beneath.

If the metal roof is so inclined as to be seen from the ground, it is necessary that its smooth and dead appearance be relieved by some means. This is frequently well and effectually done by nailing slats at short intervals on the sheathing, parallel to the rafters, and about as far apart as the width of the plates used. The metal is bent carefully close over these, and the roof then presents somewhat the appearance of being covered with pan-tiles. Though the effect is not what could be desired, it is better than that produced by leaving the roof plain. One of the greatest advantages resulting from the use of metallic covering is, that the roofs may be made almost flat, and yet exclude the damp as effectually as those of a greater pitch. It is customary now, in all cities, to give the roof so little inclination that it is not only altogether invisible, but affords a platform on which one can walk with safety. This plan is far preferable to the old peaked roof, and economizes room, for instead of having garrets with sloping sides, we may have in their place, without increasing the cost of the building, square, airy rooms. For country dwellings, we cannot so highly recommend flat roofs, since the usually received styles of rural architecture require a display of the roof. The floors of observatories and balconies however, should be overlaid with metal, and their inclination should always be sufficient to permit the rain to fall off readily. The curved, tent-like roofs for verandahs and bay windows have been mentioned in other places of our work. They are necessarily of metal, and are usually painted in colored stripes, to relieve the monotonous effect of the uniform surface.

The arrangement of gutters and pipes for conveying off the water, at the eaves, is a matter worthy of some consideration. Usually plain tin gutters are hung just beneath the eaves, leading to long tin tubes that reach the ground. These last are often placed in the middle of some front pier, or perhaps, pass down the angle formed by a pilaster and the wall. They are most generally left unpainted, and the white tin glistens in glory, being the most prominent object about the house. Is this taste? If the building has any architectural pretensions whatever, this practice is certainly enough to enrage its designer. The appearance of the cornice, if there be any, and of the piers or pilasters, is spoiled. It is a much better plan to conceal the gutter entirely, and thus obviate this objection. Various explanatory sections are given here and there among our details. But this expedient does not do away with the pipe. If there must be pipe on the exterior of the building, by all means place it in the rear or at the ends, or in some place less prominent than the front, and for the sake of appearances, as well as for its preservation, paint it the color of its back ground. Pipes made of terra cotta ware are now to be had, the ends of which fit into each other with the inner surface glazed. These can be built within the body of the wall for the purpose of conveying the water from the roof to the ground. The time will come when these, and the iron pipes, will be universally used in all buildings that aim at something more than barren utility. While speaking of terra cotta ware, it may be well to mention the chimney cans, various representations of which have been given in different places. These are not only highly ornamental, but resist the action of the weather and of the escaping gases much better than a plain brick finish. They generally have sufficient weight to make them firm, when well set in strong mortar.

Lastly, the lightning rod should receive a due share of attention. We have seen hundreds so arranged, through neglect or ignorance, as to be an injury instead of a protection. Should a heavily charged cloud chance to come within their influence, they would be most surely the means of bringing certain destruction to the building and its inmates. For carelessness in this particular, we can suggest no remedy. To those who may not be aware of the reasons why a lightning rod is at any time a protection, a word or two may be invaluable. Most people seem to think that its object is to attract the fluid. This is not the case. "The finest needle, held in the hand towards the knob of one of the jars of a highly charged electric battery will silently discharge it in a few seconds." Herein we have the principle. The sharp points of the lightning rod rapidly conduct to the earth the electricity of the surcharged cloud, and when within striking distance, it is discharged by the rod and rendered harmless. The rods are sometimes struck, nevertheless, and then also protect the building, but this is not their chief original purpose. The following remarks, unabridged, will be acceptable. " Lightning rods are at present usually constructed of wrought iron, about three-fourths of an inch in diameter. The parts may be made separate, but, when the rod is in its place they should be screwed together, so as to fit closely, and to make a continuous surface, since the fluid experiences much resistance in passing through links, and other interrupted joints. At the bottom, the rod should terminate in two or three branches, going off in a direction from the building. The depth to which it enters the earth should not be less than five feet; but the necessary depth will depend somewhat upon the nature of the soil; wet soils require a less, and dry soils a greater depth. In dry sand, it must not be less than ten feet, and in such situations it would be better still to connect by some convenient conductor, the lower end of the rod with a well or spring of water. It is useful to fill up the space around the part of the rod that enters the ground with coarsely powdered charcoal, which at once furnishes a good conductor, and preserves the metal from corrosion. The rod should ascend above the ridge of the building to a height determined by the following principle: that it will protect a space in every direction around it, whose radius is equal to twice the height of the rod. It is best, when practicable, to attach it to the chimney, which needs peculiar protection, both on account of its prominence and because the products of combustion, smoke, watery vapor, &c., are conductors of electricity. For a similar reason the kitchen chimney, being that in which fire is kept during the season of thunder storms, requires to be especially protected. The rod is terminated above in three forks, each of which ends in a sharp point. As these points are liable to have their conducting power impaired by rust, they are protected from corrosion by being covered by gold leaf, or they may be made of solid silver or platinum. Black paint, made of charcoal, forms a better coating for the rod than paints of other colors, the bases of which are worse conductors. The rod may be attached to the building by wooden stays. Iron stays are sometimes employed, and in most cases they would be safe, since electricity produces the most direct route; but in case of an extraordinary charge there is danger that it will divide itself, a part passing into the building through the bolt, especially if this terminates in a point. Buildings furnished with lightning rods, have occasionally been struck with lightning; but on examination, it has generally, if not always, been found that the structure of the rod was defective; or that too much space was allotted for it to protect. When the foregoing rules are observed, the most entire confidence may be reposed in this method of providing for safety during thunder storms."

A GOTHIC CHURCH.

DESIGN FIFTY-FOURTH.

ARCHITECTS have differed on no subject more than in the erection of edifices for Divine worship. The models of the great masters of all ages and nations have been the temples of the ancients. For a long period, simplicity and uniformity were the only objects sought to be obtained. After Italy had been overrun by the fury of the Visi-Goths, the structures that had been the pride of Rome, were buried in the dust. All the edifices afterwards constructed, were from the precious remains that ignorance or avarice had gathered from the ruins. The inappropriate application of these fragments resulted in a confusion, and unnatural perversion of the principles of architecture. The art fell into a real chaos; and from the ruin rose what is called the Gothic style. Subsequently, when the state of society permitted a return to the arts of peace, and patronage was afforded to those men whose genius still lives in their works, the wants of Christianity opened to them an extensive field. The fitness of their construction for the new form of worship, had suggested the use of the *basilica* of ancient Rome, for the early churches. Many of these edifices were altered to suit the purposes of the worshippers, and others were erected after them as models. Modifications and additions were made from time to time, and in the twelfth century, the Gothic was the prevailing order of church architecture. The facility it offers for producing appropriate effects with the use of almost every material, has gained for it popularity in this country, and some of the most expensive and elaborate structures we can boast, serve as authority for its adoption.

The plates of the design represented, contain full details of all matters necessary to be known by any competent builder, to enable him to erect an edifice of the kind. Plate LXXIX. is a perspective view. The size is forty-eight feet front by seventy in depth, measuring from the outside of the walls. The tower projects five feet, and the vestry rooms two, from the body of the building. The basement is ten feet in the clear, and its floor is four feet below the level of the pavement. The principal story or audience room is twenty-five feet in the clear, and a gallery sixteen feet wide extends over the vestibule. The walls are to be of hard burnt brick, and in the basement are twenty-three inches in thickness; from the main floor to the roof, nineteen inches, the outer wall thirteen inches, the inner four, with a space of two inches between them. The buttresses are eighteen inches on the face.

The tower is one hundred and twenty-five feet high, eighty from the ground to the base of the spire, and thence forty-five to the summit. Its walls are two feet seven inches thick to the main floor, two feet, three inches to the gallery joists, twenty-two inches to the battlement course, and eighteen inches to the base of the spire.

The exterior is to be roughcast in the best manner, with a coat of fresh wood burnt lime and clean sharp, sand mixed with a preparation of tallow. This coat and the whole of the wood work on the exterior, should be well painted and sanded.

The finials, brackets, corbels, the head mouldings over the windows, and the crochets over the entrance door, are of wood or terra cotta. The spire is of wood, and covered with the best narrow purple Welsh slate. The roof is also covered with the same kind of slate cut into diamond form. The floors are of one and a quarter inch Carolina heart pine, of uniform width, and smoothed over after they are laid. The sash are alike in their construction, double hung, with two and a half inch patent axle pullies, and the best Italian hemp cord. The pullies of the windows in the basement are one and three quarters inch axles. The front doors are three inches thick, double, hung with five by five inch butts, and fastened, one by an eight inch mortice rabbit lock, the other by two iron plate flush bolts. The inner doors are one and three quarters inches thick, moulded on both sides, hung with four by four inch butts, and fastened by four inch mortice locks. The pews all have panelled ends and doors. The ends have scroll tops, and the backs are moulded with black walnut. The rostrum is elevated one foot from the floor. The pedestals for the pulpit and reading desk are made of black walnut, and panelled. The chancel has a railing of five inch hexagonal balusters, capped with eight inch moulded rail, also of walnut. The chancel windows are of stained glass, and may contain any appropriate device. The others are of the best American clear glass. The effect produced by a good quality of stained glass, for all the windows, should not be overlooked. The plain plate glass, however, is preferable to an article poorly stained, whether with or without devices. The interior, throughout, is to be plastered, floated and laid off in blocks, to represent stone. The ceiling is curved, ribbed and tinted. This is sometimes made of wood, and when well finished, has a good effect, but increases the expense of the building. The organ loft is within the tower, in the gallery.

Plate LXXX. is a front elevation of the building, representing the ornaments over the door, and the effect of the tower and spire.

Plate LXXXI. is the side elevation, done in lines. The cornice, turrets and window mouldings, are accurately displayed. The whole is drawn to the scale of twelve feet to the inch, and measurements may be taken directly from the engraving.

Saml Sloan Archt   P. S. Duval & Co's Steam lith Press Philad.

GOTHIC CHURCH.

FRONT ELEVATION.

GOTHIC CHURCH.

Scale 12 feet to the inch.

S. Sloan Arch.t   P. S. Duval & C.° Steam lith. Press Ph.

SIDE ELEVATION.

Pl. LXXXII.

Altar
17 × 10.

Lobby

MAIN FLOOR.

Robing Room
10 × 17.

Lobby
8 ft.

Vestry Room.
10 × 17.

Platform.

Furnace
below.

BASEMENT.

Scale 12 feet to the inch.

P L A N S .

Sam.! Sloan Arch.t

P. S. Duval & Co's Steam lith. Press Philad.

Pl. LXXXIII.

Fig. 1.

Sam.ᵗ Sloan Arch.ᵗ

P. S. Duval & Co's Steam lith Press Phila.ᵈ

DETAILS.

Fig. 4.

Fig. 2.

Scale ¼ inch to the foot.

Fig. 3.

Scale ½ inch to the foot.

DETAILS.

On Plate LXXXII. are the plans of the first floor, and the basement. The first is approached by steps leading to the front doors, or by two stairways, leading from the basement to the vestibule. These give access to the body of the church from the lower floor without leaving the building, and are much used in inclement weather. The rostrum is approached by a stairway leading from the robing or vestry room, which are intended for the use of the officiating minister, or if the building is erected for the Baptist denomination, give access to the Baptistry, usually placed under a moveable pulpit.

The basement floor contains a lecture room, and two rooms in the rear, that may be used for a library, robing or vestry room, a study, or for Sunday School purposes, according to the wants of the congregation. The furnaces are within the walls of the tower, and require an excavation eight feet deeper than that of the body of the building. They are to be reached by steps under one of the stairways, leading to the vestibule above. The position of the registers is indicated in the engraving, showing two for each floor. The warm air is conducted from the chambers of the furnace by tin flues, those extending to the main floor being in the walls of the tower. To warm the building comfortably, a Chilson's No. 6 furnace, or one of other makers, of similar power, will be required. Ventilating flues should be constructed in the walls, opposite the buttresses, with ventilating registers placed below the cornice and near the floor. For the reasons why this mode of ventilation is preferable to any other in use, the reader is referred to the essay on that subject. An additional reason why it is of value in a church or hall, is that the acoustic qualities of the room are always injured by the ordinary ceiling ventilators.

On Plates LXXXIII. and LXXXIV. are shown the building details. Figure 1 represents the front door and buttress, the finial, crochets and corbel course, with its cornice, drawn to the scale of one quarter of an inch to the foot. Figure 2 is a side window, with two buttresses, finials and corbel course, with its cornice. Figure 3 is a section of the tower, showing the corbels, the battlement course and belting cornice. Figure 4 is the top of the spire. The scale of the three last is half an inch to the foot.

BILL OF QUANTITIES,

SHOWING THE NATURE AND COST OF MATERIALS, USED IN THE ERECTION OF DESIGN FIFTY-FOURTH.

THE prices marked in the following bill of quantities, are those prevailing in and near this city.

Bricks laid in the wall, including all materials, 260.000 @ $10 per M. - - - - -	2600.00
Stone, including all materials, 250 perches, quarry measurement, @ $2 per perch, - - -	500.00
Excavation, for foundation and basement, 540 yds. @ 20 cts. per yd. - - - - - -	108.00
Brown stone, 750 ft. @ 95 cts. per ft. - -	712.50
Plastering, including materials, 2100 yds. @ 20 cts. per yd. - - - - - - -	420.00
Roughcasting, 2500 yds. @ 40 cts. per yd. -	1000.00
Framing timber, 35000 ft. @ $20 per M. - -	700.00
Slating, 5000 ft. @ 8 cts. per ft. - - -	400.00
Flooring boards, 1¼ inch, 10800 ft. @ $35 per M.	378.00
Sheathing boards, for roof, 6000 ft. @ $15 per M.	90.00
Joists and scantling, 23000 ft. @ $15 per M. -	345.00
Assorted lumber, 18000 ft. @ $3 per M. - -	340.00
Scaffolding, 6000 ft. @ $12 per M. - -	72.00
Tin gutters, 800 ft. at 12 cts. per ft. - - -	96.00
Conductors, 120 ft. @ 16 cts. per ft. - - -	19.20
Painting and glazing, and sanding exterior, -	760.00
Carving for exterior, - - - - - -	275.00
" interior, - - - - - -	110.00
Hardware, including locks, - - - -	170.00
Smith work, - - - - - - -	190.00
Iron posts to support basement floor, - - -	36.00
Chilson's No. 6 furnace, and setting it, - -	210.00
	9531.70

MODEL COTTAGE.

DESIGN FIFTY-FIFTH.

THE line engravings, on Plate LXXXV. represent the front and side elevations of a cottage. Its external appearance renders it peculiarly suitable for a suburban residence. The internal arrangements are intended for both summer and winter. The material used for its construction is timber of the best quality and thoroughly seasoned. The sills are of oak or heart pine, six by eight inches, and securely imbedded in mortar on the wall. The corner posts, girts and plates, are of white pine, four by eight inches. The frames are four inches square, and the intermediate studding three by four inches, with sixteen inches between the centres. The studding of the doors and windows is four by six inches. The rafters are tapering, eight inches at the foot, with two feet between the centres, and well secured to the plates and ridge-pieces. The joists are three by eleven inches, with sixteen inches between the centres, bridged, backed, &c. The floors are of one inch second quality Carolina heart pine, mill worked, well laid, and then smoothed off. On the exterior, the boards are placed vertically, of uniform width, grooved together, with joints cleated with three and a half inch moulded cleats, all finished for painting. The interior is also boarded with grooved hemlock boards, laid horizontally, and firmly nailed to the studding. The boarding is afterwards cleated with one and a quarter by three inch hemlock cleats, one to each stud, thus measuring sixteen inches between centres, being the proper distances for lathing. By this means, the frame work of the building is much more firm, and the cold winds are prevented from penetrating, as is the case when the lathing and plastering is put on the frame work in the usual way.

The roof is to be overlaid with the best leaded roofing tin, and furnished with the usual gutters, pipes, conductors, &c. The windows are furnished with inside shutters. Those in the gables have brackets, and are inclosed with a balcony. The room doors are all one and a half inches thick, those of the closets, one and a quarter. The whole is to be plastered with three coats. The parlor, hall, library and dining room, have a neat cornice and centre flowers. All the wood work, on the exterior and interior, has three coats of white lead, or one of zinc paint. The glass is the best American.

The cellar is seven feet deep in the clear, below the joists, and extends under the entire building. The wall is of quarry building stone, sixteen inches thick. The division walls are fourteen to the same level. The furnace flues are so arranged as to warm all the rooms of the main building, including the bath room, which is furnished with an iron tub. A No. 3 Chilson range is placed in the kitchen, with a twenty-five gallon boiler, and an iron sink attached.

Plate LXXXVI. shows the ground plans, drawn to the scale of twelve feet to the inch. The first floor contains the parlor, dining room, library, kitchen and store room, with a shed or wash house in the rear. The second, four large chambers, servants' bed room, bath room and closets, and the third, four bed rooms. The accommodations are ample for a family of ten persons.

The entire cost of the building would not exceed four thousand three hundred dollars, where work and materials can be had for the prices prevailing in and near this city.

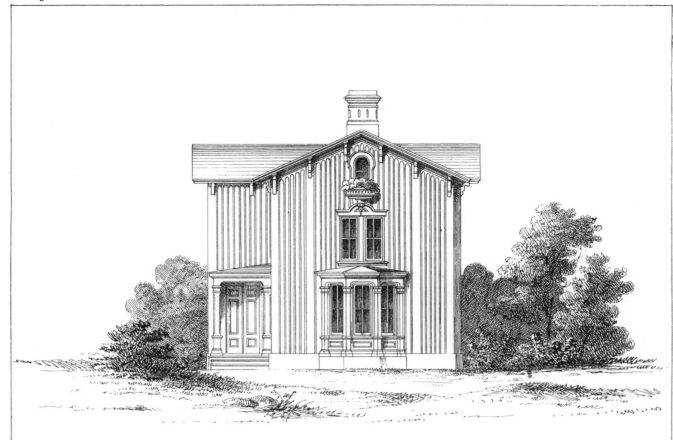

FRONT ELEVATION.

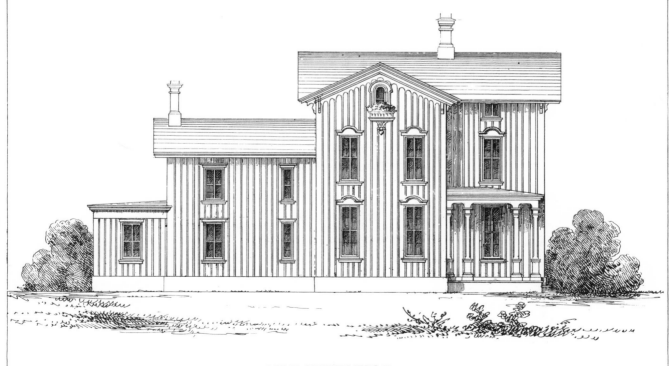

SIDE ELEVATION.

Scale 12 feet to the inch.

Sam.¹ Sloan Arch.ᵗ   P. S. Duval & C.ᵒ Steam lith press Phil.

COTTAGES.

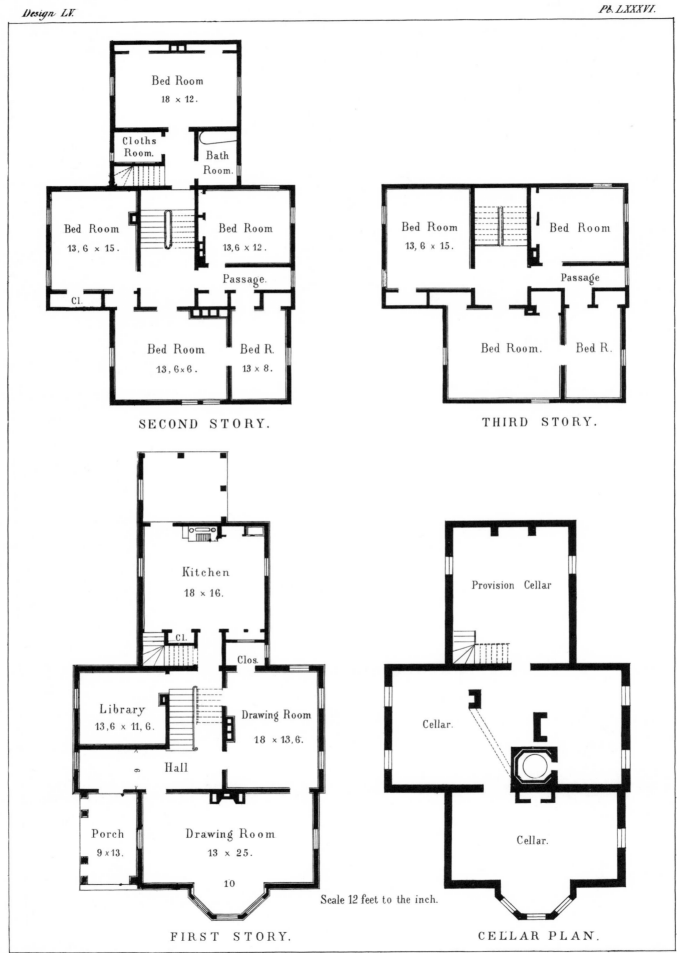

SECOND STORY.

Bed Room
18 × 12.

Cloths
Room.

Bath
Room.

Bed Room
13, 6 × 15.

Bed Room
13, 6 × 12.

Passage.

Cl.

Bed Room
13, 6 × 6.

Bed R.
13 × 8.

THIRD STORY.

Bed Room
13, 6 × 15.

Bed Room

Passage

Bed Room.

Bed R.

FIRST STORY.

Kitchen
18 × 16.

Cl.

Clos.

Library
13, 6 × 11, 6.

Drawing Room
18 × 13, 6.

Hall

Porch
9 × 13.

Drawing Room
13 × 25.

10

Scale 12 feet to the inch.

CELLAR PLAN.

Provision Cellar

Cellar.

Cellar.

Sam! Sloan Arch!　　　　　　　　　　　　　　　　　P. S. Duval & Co's Steam lith. Press Philad.

PLANS.

LANDSCAPE GARDENING.

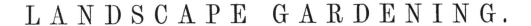

ERETOFORE our remarks have been confined to the construction of the building, and its different parts. In treating of the grounds adjacent to it, and their embellishments, it is not pretended to offer a full discussion of the subject. Many volumes have been written upon it, and the reader desirous of making it an especial study, must be referred to them. The art is not a new one. The magnificent hanging gardens of Babylon, rising in a series of terraces, one above the other, three hundred feet in height, were thought worthy of being styled one of the seven wonders of the world. The gardens of Versailles, the Villa Ludovisi, the Villa Albani, and the Villa Borghese, at Rome, are familiar to the European traveler. Our own country too, furnishes instances of a successful application of the principles of the art. As early as 1805, Woodlands, near Philadelphia, then the seat of the Hamilton family, now used as a cemetery, was highly celebrated for its beauties. The Bartram gardens, now the property of a private gentleman who is rescuing them from the decay into which they had fallen, the country seat of the late Judge Peters, and Lemon Hill, now owned by the corporation of Philadelphia, were all known to those who had studied the condition and prospects of the art in America; while New York and the Eastern States contain many models of this beautiful art.

The style and pretensions of the garden, by which term we mean to include all the ground belonging to a building, should be determined by the general aspect of edifice to which it is attached. For a town residence, the regular and confined surface employed, the importance of the building, and the influence it should naturally have over the limited space attached to it, render a symmetrical distribution necessary. Neatness and order ought to constitute the ruling features around villas and country residences. As the grounds immediately adjacent to the residence may be considered a part of the site, they may be distributed with regularity, governed by the general plan of the seat. Yet it should be the object of the amateur or artist to avoid the mathematical precision and exactness that, for many years, prevailed in England, known as the productions of the Dutch School. In these, the elements of both grace and beauty were wanting. They pained the eye with their unerring uniformity, and the constantly recurring geometrical figures, in which the shrubbery, or trees, were trained and clipped.

By Landscape Gardening is not meant merely an imitation of the agreeable forms of nature, but an expressive, harmonious and refined imitation. It should be the aim to separate the accidental and extraneous, and preserve only the spirit or essence of those beauties that pervade every part of nature. Where circumstances compel the cultivation of the Beautiful, rather than the Picturesque, it should be strictly adhered to, for blending the two styles, as is often the case, on a diminutive scale, is productive of effects more ludicrous than pleasing. In the shape of the ground, there should be no abrupt elevations or depressions, but changes are rather to be effected by a series of gentle undulations. The trees chosen should be those with smooth stems, full, round and regular heads of foliage, and luxuriant branches, often drooping to the ground, an effect attained by planting and grouping, so as to permit free developement of form, and by selecting trees of suitable character, as the elm, the ash, the silver leaf poplar, and the like. In the use of roads and walks, they should be made to proceed by easy flowing curves, following natural shapes of the surface, with no sharp angles or abrupt turns. Where water may be permitted to enter into the scene, it should be in a smooth lake, with curved margin, embellished with flowing outlines of trees, and full masses of flowering shrubs, or in the gentle winding curves of a brook. The additions to such an effect, are grass mown into a velvet-like softness, and gravel walks kept perfectly hard, dry and clean. Among the trees and shrubs should be conspicuous, the finest foreign sorts, distinguished by beauty of form, foliage and blossom.

The Picturesque aims to produce outlines of a spirited irregularity, surfaces comparatively abrupt and broken, and growth of a bolder and wilder character. The smoothness of the ground may be broken by sudden variations, and occasionally run into rocky groups, ravines and broken banks. The trees may be old and irregular, cut out, as it were, from their native wilds, and grouped in every variety of form. In water, all the wildness of romantic spots in nature is to be imitated or preserved, and the lake or stream with bold shore and rocky margin, or the bold cascade may be a characteristic feature. Though firm gravel walks near the mansion are indispensable for comfort and fitness in all modes, the lawn may be less frequently mown, and the edges of remote walks less carefully trimmed. For such grounds, the Gothic, old English, or Swiss style, should be chosen for the main building.

In the selection of trees, the advice of an experienced gardener should be procured. There is no branch of the art of ornamenting that requires greater care and attention. The round and full species, of which the oak and horse chesnut are familiar examples, are always preferable, where but few are to be planted. When young, they are generally beautiful, from the smoothness and elegance of their forms. They harmonize with almost all scenes, buildings, and natural or artificial objects, uniting well with other forms, and offering no violence to the general effect. In all grounds where the surface is abruptly varied by steep banks, or rocky precipices, trees with spiral tops, as the pine and fir, have a pleasing effect. From their sameness and uniformity, when planted in large bodies, the eye soon becomes weary. Their chief value on level grounds, is the pleasing variety produced by planting them with trees of a different species to relieve or break into large masses of foliage. They are mostly evergreens, but are seldom of much value as shade trees. Conical trees, of which the Lombardy poplar is a well known example, have been frequently used by proprietors in different sections of the country, to destroy the beauty of many a fine building and its surrounding prospect. If indiscriminately planted, by their tall and formal growth, they invariably diminish the apparent magnitude as well as the elegance of the house. Like the spiral topped species, they should be used sparingly, and only to increase the effect produced by large bodies of round headed trees, forming pyramidal centres to groups, where there was only a swelling and flowing outline. The prominent characteristics of drooping trees, as the weeping willow, or the drooping elm, are grace and elegance, and they are unfit to be employed to any extent in scenes where it is desirable to keep up a wild or picturesque expression. They show to the best advantage on the borders of groups, or the boundaries of plantations. All strongly marked trees, like bright colors in pictures, only admit of occasional employment, and the very object aimed at in introducing them is defeated, if they are brought into the lawn or park in masses, and heedlessly distributed on every side.

The management of the walks and roads, connected with the mansion, must be determined by the circumstances of each case, and constitute a branch of the subject concerning which it is impossible to do more than offer a few general remarks. They serve as the means of displaying the finest points of prospect, and the most attractive beauties of an estate. Since the rejection of the rectangular style, many act upon the impression that nature has a horror of straight lines, and invariably run into the other extreme, filling their grounds with zigzag and regular serpentine walks and roads. A safe rule to adopt is, that a curve should never be constructed without some reason, real or apparent. The most natural method, when the ground gently undulates, is to follow, in some degree, the depressions of the surface, and to construct curves around eminences. In the straight walk of half a mile, the whole view is seen at a glance, and the eye soon becomes wearied with the monotony. By a judicious use of the curve leading the walk to agreeable retreats or pleasing points of view, every new turn opens a new prospect, and "leads the eye a kind of wanton chase," continually affording novelty and variety.

Fencing and hedging must not be overlooked. The detail plates of our work contain many suitable designs for enclosures, immediately around the mansion. The prevailing practice of subdividing ground of a limited or even a great extent into a vast number of lots or small fields, is reprehensible. It destroys the general effect of the prospect, and gives unnecessarily the idea of contraction. Where divisions are requisite for agricultural purposes, they may be made with wire fencing, or skilfully placed hedges. Though the latter have heretofore been but little used, their value, permanence and beauty will one day recommend them to general favor. Five or six years are, in our climate, under ordinary circumstances, amply sufficient to produce ornamental hedges, forming barriers secure from all attacks to which they are liable, and lasting for many generations. The common Arbor Vitae, found in great abundance in many districts, and the New Castle or Washington Thorn, are much better adapted to this climate than the English Hawthorn. The Buckthorn is rapid in its growth, is not liable to be infected by insects, and makes an efficient screen sooner than most other plants. In all cases where hedges are employed in the natural style of landscape, a pleasing effect is produced by allowing them to grow somewhat irregular in form, or varying the outline by planting near them small trees or flowering shrubs. For cottage residences, a pretty enclosure may be formed of rustic work, made of stout rods of any of our native forest trees, with the bark on. These are sharpened and driven into the ground in the form of a lattice, or wrought into any figure of trellis work. When covered with luxuriant vines, or climbing plants, such a barrier adds much to the general appearance of a small building.

In the management of bodies of water, good taste forbids the attempt of any thing beyond graceful or picturesque imitations of natural lakes or ponds, brooks, rivulets or streams. In this way alone, can they be made to harmonize, agreeably with natural scenery. There can be no apology made for the introduction of straight canals, round or oblong sheets of water, or any of the forms of the geometric mode. All appearance of constraint and formality should be avoided, and however used, it should be permitted to take its own flowing and graceful forms. In architectural or flower gardens, where a more artificial arrangement prevails, a departure from these principles may be allowed. More regular shapes, with various jets, fountains, &c., are admissible, since they combine well with the other accessories of such places. Fountains are highly elegant decorations, but are rarely seen, not so much from the cost incurred by their erection, as from the fact that so few of our artizans have made their construction a study. Designs for these ornaments may be found in great numbers in the works of rural embellishment. A single jet is one of the simplest and most pleasing. Weeping or Tazza fountains require a very moderate supply of water. The conduit pipe rises through and fills a vase so constructed as to permit the water to flow over its margin. A species of rustic fountain is made by introducing the pipe or pipes among groups of rock work, and the water issues either in the form of a cascade, a weeping fountain or a single jet.

The employment of statues in the embellishments of villas and country seats, may considerably increase their beauty. They ought not only to present all the perfection of art, but likewise possess the power of exciting those sentiments suitable to the situation. The statues of Jupiter, Mars and Hercules, should not be placed where we expect to find those of Ceres, Bacchus, Pomona and Flora. With these ornaments might be classed vases, and their pedestals, arches, sundials, &c. Those made of marble or granite are too costly to obtain general favor. Terra cotta, or artificial stone of any kind, and cast iron, are much less expensive, and are manufactured with great skill and taste. When well painted, they will endure exposure for a long time, and contribute to the animation of the scene.

Among the designs prepared for our work, are many of decorative out buildings. These are erected for every purpose, and in all grounds, of any pretensions, are necessary to complete the effect. The conservatory, grapery, gate-lodge, arbor, ornamental bridges, aviary, bath and boat house, have all their appropriate places and uses. No one can fail to remark the impression on the landscape that fabrics of this kind spread around them. They not only determine the character of the grounds, but produce in them as it were, a new energy, and augment the degree of pleasure, gaiety, gravity or melancholy of the scenes of which they form a part. An open rotunda, situated on an eminence, will increase the aerial aspect produced by the tall and thinly planted shrubs that surround it on all sides. A temple imparts a solemn, a hermitage, a melancholy, and a thatched arbor, a rural character. If, instead of making these buildings accord with the character of each scene, a pavilion of a noble style be raised on a wild site, if ruins be erected on one that is level and carefully cultivated, a cabinet for study, adjacent to a principal walk or promenade, or a bath on the summit of an eminence, the laws of fitness would be outraged. When a number of these structures are introduced into grounds, they should be distinguished by the diversity of their forms and appearance, and all symmetry and equality of position should be avoided. Though a single architectural production requires in its construction an exact observance of the laws of symmetry, this rule cannot be extended to the situation, distance and position of a number of rural buildings, each of which has an insulated being and governs the particular portion of the grounds belonging to it. A capricious medley of the architecture of different ages and nations should be carefully avoided. There ought not to be, in the same perspective, an Egyptian obelisk, a Grecian temple, a Roman arch, a Gothic tower, and a Chinese pavilion. This absurd assemblage and confusion of productions, differing both in time and space, that so ill accords with the charms of nature, and the simplicity of pleasure grounds, can only be the result of a perverted taste, and an inordinate mania for imitation.

SUBURBAN VILLA.

DESIGN FIFTY-SIXTH.

THE elevation on Plate LXXXVII. is that of a residence in the Italian style, lately erected near Philadelphia. It is simple, and free from ornament, but commodious, and constructed with all modern appliances.

On Plate LXXXVIII. are the plans of the different stories. The cellar contains apartments for stowing away fuel and provisions, and the furnace. The first floor, a parlor, dining room, library and kitchen, with a large hall and closets. The second, two chambers, two bed rooms, a nursery, bath and closets. The private stairway is represented on the plate. In the attic, are sleeping apartments for servants. The accommodations are ample for a family of ten persons.

Complete specifications of the workmanship and materials are annexed. These are usually prepared by architects for the erection of buildings of even moderate pretensions, and constitute part of the contract made with the builder. They are his guide, and, when carefully prepared, often prevent misunderstanding between him and the owner.

CONDITIONS.—The contractors severally, are to provide such material, set forth under their respective heads, as may be necessary for the erection and completion of the building, in all its parts, to the full intent and spirit of the design and specifications, either expressed or implied. They must bear all loss from accident, or neglect during the progress of their respective divisions of the work, and hold the owner free from all responsibility, until the building shall be fully completed, according to agreement. The materials thus required to be furnished, are all to be of the best quality, and it is hereby fully understood that the owner or his superintendent shall have full power, at all times during the progress of the work, to reject any materials either may consider unfit to be used, or different from those described, also the power to cause any defective work to be taken down, or altered, at the contractor's expense. Either of them shall also have the privilege of making any alterations or additions they may deem proper, without in any way interfering with, or lessening the agreements and contracts made upon said plans, and without additional expense, unless such alterations or additions cost more than is here specified or contracted for, the additional expense in such case to be agreed upon in writing, between the parties, in all particulars.

GENERAL DIMENSIONS.—The whole extent of the porch is to be thirty-six feet by fifty-two feet deep, and two stories high, with attic. The first story is twelve feet six inches from floor to floor. The second story, eleven feet three inches from floor to floor. The attic, five feet at the wall and seven feet six inches in the centre. The kitchen and store rooms ten feet eight inches from floor to floor. The nursery and bath room, ten feet nine inches from floor to floor, and the attic over them is seven feet four inches in the clear. These heights will bring the cornice of all on the same level. For the divisions and general arrangements, reference must be had to the plans upon which they are all figured.

EXCAVATIONS.—The cellar extends throughout the entire extent of the building, and six feet below the intended level of the surface of the ground, being seven feet in the clear of joists. The first floor is elevated twenty-eight inches, being three risers of seven inches each. The foundations for the porches, &c., are of sufficient depth to ensure them against frost; the top soil from the excavations to be removed to the rear end of the lot, and remain for the owner. All surplus earth not required in grading the yard, must be removed from the grounds.

MASONRY.—The walls of the cellar must be of good quarry building stone, laid in a proper manner, upon their broadest beds. The walls are all sixteen inches thick up to the top of the first floor of joists, and project two inches out from the face of the brickwork, forming a base course around the building. All windows and cellar doors to be formed as shown upon the ground plans; said masonry to be laid in mortar composed of fresh wood burnt lime, and sharp gravel.

BRICK WORK.—All the outer walls from the aforesaid stone walls are to be of brick, nine inches thick; the outside to be faced with good dark stretchers, with joists made flush for painting. No soft brick are to be used, in any part of the outside face. The two division walls in the cellar are also of hard brick, and nine inches thick. Construct all flues, &c., for warm air and gas, as marked upon the plans, and topped out above the roof with rough hard bricks, as per elevation, and afterwards roughcast. The flues are all to be smoothly pargetted on the inside. The mortar for said brick work must be composed of fresh wood burnt lime, one half river sand, and one half grey gravel, in such proportions as will ensure an approved cement.

CARPENTER'S WORK.—The joists of all the floors front, from the flues are to be three by eleven inches, and all in the rear, three by twelve inches, of good sound hemlock boards, back with one course of bridging, through the centre of each tier, and all to be placed sixteen inches between centres. The partitions on each side of the parlor, and upwards, to be constructed with three by six inch scantling, set the size each way, framed sufficient to support the tiers of joists. All other partitions are to be three by four inch, set three inches, very strongly nailed at the floors and ceilings; all placed sixteen inches between centres. The roof has four gables and valley rafters, with ridge pole. The ridge pole to be three by twelve inches, the valley rafters three by ten inches and the wall plate three by eight inches, crossed at the end and well nailed together. The common rafters to be the usual rafter cuts, all to be fitted up, and firmly nailed to the ends, and to be closely boarded and prepared for metal. The floors are of the second best quality Carolina Heart Pine, well worked, well seasoned and well nailed to the joists, and afterwards smoothed off.

STAIRS.—The main stairs are constructed in the hall, from the first to the second floor, with a closet beneath. The steps are one and a quarter inches, with inch risers glued and blocked together, and secured by four strong carriages. The rail is four and a half inch moulded, the newel will be eight inches, turned cap and base, with a clogon shaft, all of mahogany. The balusters are curl maple, two inches hexagonal. The private stairs are constructed in the usual manner, and extend from the cellar to the attic story, with a door at the head of the private stairs, and also at the foot of the second story stairs.

WINDOWS.—These are all alike in their construction, with a six inch face and mouldings; the sills to be heart pine; the second story front, and each of the wings, to have heads as per elevation. The sash are all double hung, those of the first stories, one and three quarter inches thick, and all the others one and a half inches thick; the front and ends of the wings, each to have a circular window in the gable. The rear has two windows in the attic room, also double hung. The front windows, first story, are two lights wide, five lights high, twenty-two and a half by fifteen inch glass. The store room and kitchen windows, and second story front wings, and those over the dining room to be two lights wide, four lights high, nineteen and a half by fifteen inch glass. The front window, first story, to have side lights. The three dining room windows also to be two lights wide, and four lights high, twenty-two and a half by fifteen inches glass. Those in the nursery, bath room and private stairs to be in like manner, with glass eighteen by fifteen inches, and those in the rear of the attic will be twelve lights, ten by fourteen inch glass. The circular windows to be hung with three inch butts, and secured by a six inch bolt. The cellar windows will all have sash hung with two and a half butts, to a narrow casing, and secured by small bolts.

DOORS.—The front entrance doors to be one and three quarter inches thick; six panels with mouldings on the one face, and bead and butt on the other, hung with four by four inch butts, and secured by an inch upright rabbet mortice

Pl. LXXVII.

Sam.l Sloan Arch.t

SUBURBAN VILLA.

P.S.Duval & Co's Steam lith Press Phila.d

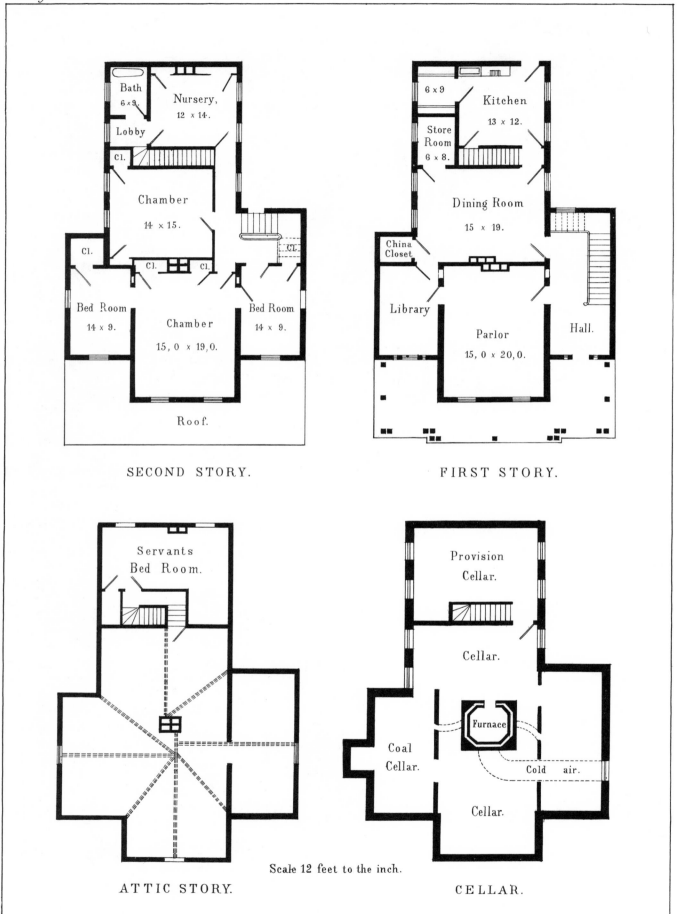

Bath
6 x 9.

Nursery,
12 x 14.

Lobby

Cl.

Chamber
14 x 15.

Cl.

Cl.

Cl.   Cl.

Bed Room
14 x 9.

Chamber
15, 0 x 19, 0.

Bed Room
14 x 9.

Roof.

SECOND STORY.

6 x 9

Kitchen
13 x 12.

Store
Room
6 x 8.

Dining Room
15 x 19.

China
Closet

Library

Parlor
15, 0 x 20, 0.

Hall.

FIRST STORY.

Servants
Bed Room.

ATTIC STORY.

Provision
Cellar.

Cellar.

Furnace

Coal
Cellar.

Cold   air.

Cellar.

CELLAR.

Scale 12 feet to the inch.

Sam! Sloan Arch!   P. S. Duval & Co's Steam lith. Press Philad?

PLANS.

lock, with night latch. The frame to be made with side and head lights. The entrance doors, from the hall to parlor and dining room, and the one from parlor to library, to be one and three quarter inches thick; six panels, with mouldings on both sides, hung with four by four inch butts, and secured by four inch mortice locks. All the other room doors, including bath room, store room and china closet to be one and a half inches thick, six panels, with mouldings on both sides, hung with three and a half inch butts, and secured by three inch mortice locks. The back door of the hall and kitchen each to have two iron plate flush bolts. The closet doors all to be one and a quarter inch thick, six panels mouldings on one side and raised panels on the other, hung with three and a half by two inch butts, and secured by the best closet locks, with knobs corresponding with those on the other room doors. The closets and store rooms are all to be fitted up and fully shelved, and clothes hooks where desired. Kitchen dressers are to be fit up on both sides of the kitchen store room, with panel doors top and bottom, and drawers in the centre. The washboard in the parlor, dining room, library and hall will be twelve inches wide, including two and a half inch sub., and two inch mouldings. In the chamber above, they are to be ten inches wide, including two inch sub. and one and a half inch moulding. Those in the kitchen and room above will be seven inches wide, with one and a half inch moulding, planted on the top and in the closets and store rooms, they are to be four inch, with one inch bead, planted on the top, the attic from the private stairs front to have no washboard. The dressings of the doors and windows in parlor, dining room, library and hall will be architrave and mouldings, eight inches wide. The rooms over, including the nursery, to be five inch moulding. The store room, bath room, and servants' attic all to be three and a half inches. The cellar door to be made on the west wing, four feet wide by three and a half feet, in two parts, of one inch white pine grooved boards, firmly put together, with wrought nails, with white lead in the joints, hung with wrought hooks and straps, and secured by a swinging on the centre. The cheeks to be five by six inch heart pine, with four by eight inch sill of the same material. A shed also to be constructed across the rear eight feet out, supported by four pine posts, four by four inch, planed, cornered and laid down within seven feet of the pavement, with pitch outwards, and boarded over for tin. The front porch to be constructed according to the drawings. The floor will be one inch white pine grooved boards, of a good quality, not over four inch wide, and laid with white lead in the joists. The sleepers will be hemlock, three by seven inch, and bear upon a cross beam four by eight inches, all firmly secured. The dimensions can all be measured from the drawings. The cornice of the building to be constructed according to the drawings. The brackets to be required to all sides.

SHUTTERS.—The first story windows are all to have outside shutters, one and a half inches thick. Those on the front will be four panels each, or eight panels to the window, and the others to be three panels each, hung with hooks and straps, and secured by ten shutter bolts. All the above shutters will be moulded on one side, and bead and butt on the other. All the second story windows to have inside shutters, one inch thick with three folds to the window, four to each, with mouldings, hung and secured in the usual manner. The windows of the dining room are to have panels back, and of the principal chamber doors, are to have Venitian pivots that serve for ventilation. Provide also trap door in the roof, hung and secured as usual, with a step ladder to approach the same.

PLASTERING.—All the walls and ceiling including that of the front porch to have two coats of brown mortar, and one of a hard white finish. The ceiling of the parlor to have a cornice in the angle to girt fourteen inches, one in the dining room to girt twelve inches, one in the library and hall, to girt ten inches. The parlor to have a centre flower to be three feet six inches in diameter. One in the dining room, to girt two feet six inches, and a small flower in the library and hall. The mortar for said plastering must be composed of river sand, and wood burnt lime, in such proportions as will ensure the most approved mortar. All laths to be sound and free from bark.

PAINTING AND GLAZING.—All the wood work that is usual to paint interior and exterior, to have three coats of prime white lead, and best linseed oil. The brick walls are all to be coated four coats, and sanded in the best manner, and also the wood of the interior and exterior in such tints as the owner may desire. The sash all to be glazed with the best quality American glass, well bradded, leaded and back puttied.

PLUMBING.—The water to be introduced to bath room, hot and cold, and to the water closet, and to the sink in the kitchen, also hot and cold. The bath tub to be made in the usual manner, panelled front and neatly crossed, the tub to be lined with lead. The water closet to be fitted up in the best manner, self-acting, with china hopper, and incased. The seat to be made walnut with hinged lids, &c. The sink in the kitchen to be iron, large size, fitted up with a closet beneath, all pipes to be extra strong, with all necessary stops and draw cocks, to make the whole complete. Also, with all necessary waste pipe. The said pipe from the water closet, to be five inch iron, and to extend to a well at least twenty feet from the building. The supply pipe will extend to the outer wall, below the surface of the ground, at the nearest accessible point, to connect with the main in the street, from that point to the street to be provided by the owner.

GAS.—The Gas is to be introduced from the main in the street, and arranged through the building for burners, in the ceiling of the parlor, the dining room, kitchen, and in chamber over library, two over parlor, one hall, two over dining room, one in the passage, one in bath room and one in the nursery, all of which are marked on the plans.

BELLS.—A bell from the front door to the kitchen, one from the dining room, and one from front chamber to the servants' room, and also one from front chamber to the kitchen.

HARDWARE.—All the hardware to be of good quality. The locks to be American, with patent silvered glass knobs, to all the first story, except the kitchen, and porcelain to the second story chambers. All the others to be mineral. The cellar windows are to have cast iron ornamental guards. The pullies to be patent axle, and the sash cord to be of the best patent hemp made cord. The bell pull to correspond with front door knob. The posts of the front porch to be set with cast iron boxes.

TIN WORK.—All the roofs are to be overlaid with the best quality leaded roofing tin, painted on both sides, the top side to have two coats. All gutters to be properly formed to convey water to four eave pipes. Provide also, four three inch conductors, to convey the water to the ground, with three spouts.

FURNACE AND RANGE.—The iron work of the furnace, including the register and tin work, to be purchased and set by the owner. The brick and mortar to be provided by the contractor. The range and boiler also to be purchased by the owner. The brick and mortar to be furnished by the contractor.

COUNTRY HOUSES.

DESIGN FIFTY-SEVENTH.

ON Plate LXXXIX. are two elevations. The upper one is that of a building suitable for a farm house, two stories high, and with ample accommodations for a family of twelve persons. The plans of the two stories, with the position of the verandah and porches are seen on Plate XC. A hall ten feet wide, extends through the building. On one side is a drawing room, on the other a sitting room, dining room and stairway. Two kitchens and a large store room are in the rear. The second story contains six chambers and a bath, with a sufficient number of closets.

The lower elevation is that of a cottage, with more pretensions to comfort and convenience than beauty. Its plans are shown on the right of Plate LIX. of Vol. I. The first story contains a parlor, hall, dining room and kitchen, the second four chambers, and the attic, two chambers suitable for servants' apartments.

DOORS AND CEILING.

DESIGNS FIFTY-EIGHTH, FIFTY-NINTH, AND SIXTIETH.

PLATES CXI., CXII., and CXIII., are drawings that will prove of great practical value to the builder. The two doors are on the scale of one inch to the foot. The ceiling ornaments are two inches to the foot. A section of the cornice is displayed.

FARM HOUSE.

Sam.l Sloan Arch.t   P. S. Duval & Co's Steamlith. Press Philad.a

ITALIAN STYLE,
COUNTRY HOUSES.

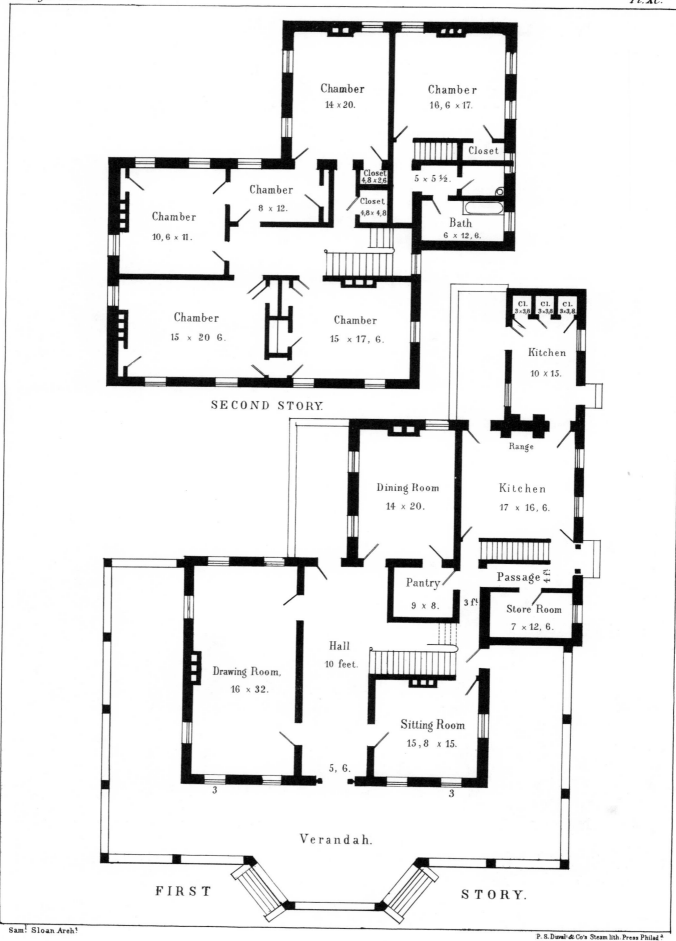

SECOND STORY.

Chamber
14 x 20.

Chamber
16, 6 x 17.

Chamber
8 x 12.

Closet
4,8 x 2,6

Closet

5 x 5 ½.

Chamber
10, 6 x 11.

Closet
4,8 x 4,8

Bath
6 x 12, 6.

Chamber
15 x 20 6.

Chamber
15 x 17, 6.

Cl.
3 x 3,8

Cl.
3 x 3,8

Cl.
3 x 3,8

Kitchen
10 x 15.

Range

Dining Room
14 x 20.

Kitchen
17 x 16, 6.

Pantry
9 x 8.

3 f.t

Passage   4 f.t

Store Room
7 x 12, 6.

Drawing Room,
16 x 32.

Hall
10 feet.

Sitting Room
15, 8 x 15.

5, 6.

3

3

Verandah.

FIRST   STORY.

Sam.l Sloan Arch.t

P. S. Duval.l & Co's Steam lith. Press Philad.a

PLANS.

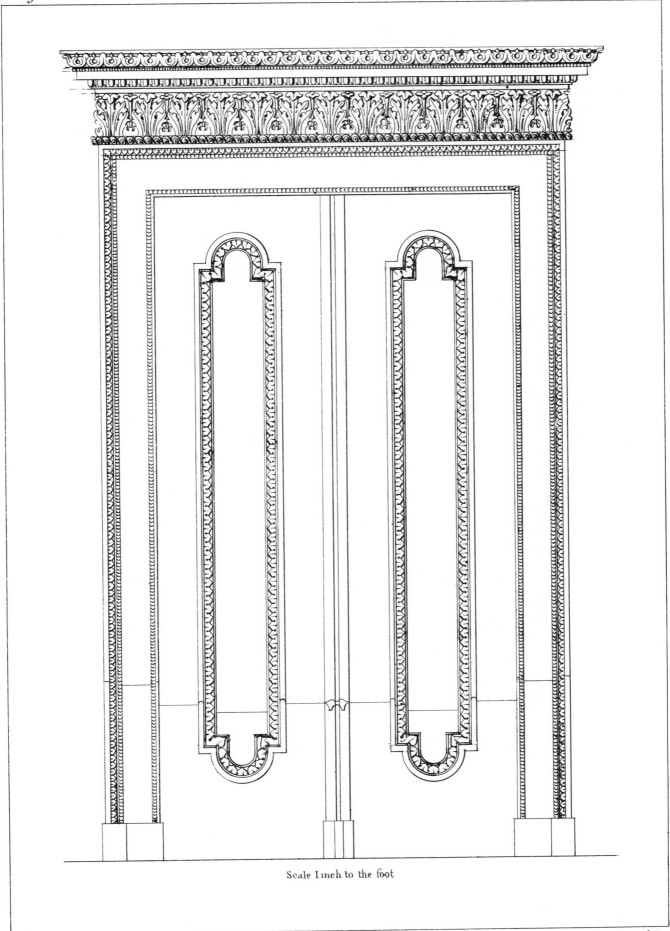

Scale 1 inch to the foot

DOOR & ENRICHMENTS.

Scale 1 inch to the foot.

Sam. Sloan Archt.   P.S.Duval & Co. Steam lith press Phil.

DOOR IN THE NORMAN STYLE.

Scale ½ foot to the inch

Sam.ᵈ Sloan Arch.

P. S Duval & Cᵒ steam lith press Phil.ᵈ

STUCCO CENTER PIECE & CORNICE.

CONCLUDING REMARKS.

THE twenty-fourth number of our work is at last completed. For two years, the author has spared no pains to collect and prepare for publication such matter as he thought would be of practical value to all who are interested in the progress of the building art in our country. His object has been to furnish useful and valuable designs, regarding beauty and ornament as matters of secondary importance. The plates of details and ground plans, though perhaps, the least attractive, have not been the least valuable part of the book. In their preparation, originality has not so much been his aim as practical and suggestive drawings, that by the aid of a competent mechanic would contribute to the comfort and happiness of those who cared to make application of the hints they afford. The approval many have bestowed upon this portion of his labor, has not been to him the least gratifying portion of the pleasure he has derived from the preparation of the work. As was said in the opening remarks, in the first volume, his desire was to produce a "matter of fact, business like book." He has attempted to let this idea govern the preparation of every page. How far the attempt has succeeded, others will judge.

A difficulty encountered during the entire progress of the work, has been the fact that the author was without precedents to guide him. American works on architecture are few in number, and no works on American architecture have yet been written. Yet there is no country in the world where more houses are projected and built in the course of a year, than in our own. Towns and cities spring into existence, south and west, almost daily. In the eastern cities, the frail fabrics erected but a few years since, are constantly giving place to substantial and magnificent edifices. Throughout the length and breadth of the land, the idea seems to pervade all classes that at some period of his life, every man must build his own house and homestead. The erections of others are invariably regarded as temporary dwellings, soon to be vacated for more congenial and convenient residences. All these causes conspire to create a demand for the services of professional architects, and for a building literature adapted to our wants and condition. Yet, strange to say, it is only within a few years that such a profession has been recognized in our large cities, and in the country at large, carpenters, master masons and others are made to perform its duties, while we have been, and still are dependent upon foreign publications for hints and suggestions upon the subject. As works of art and literature, many of these are perfect in themselves, but are not adapted to American tastes and American habits. Our buildings are necessarily, and, in some respects to our loss, unlike those erected in European countries. We are unwilling to expend either the time or the money

(99)

required to erect similar edifices. The American architect therefore, often to his regret, is compelled to arrange his plans and project his designs accordingly. By the circulation of works upon the subject adapted to our tastes and wants, this spirit must inevitably undergo a change, and every architect owes it to himself and his profession to hasten such a time by every means in his power. It was to supply, in some measure, this deficiency in our national literature, as well as to lend his influence to correcting the prevailing abuses in the noble art, that the author has ventured to turn aside from the daily routine of his profession. It may be that others will follow the example, and we shall soon possess valuable American works on the art of building in our own country.

The sale of the present work has already far exceeded the expectations formed at the outset, thus fully attesting the interest of the public in the subject of which it treats. This fact, and the belief that such a work is much needed by artizans throughout the country, has induced the author to prepare a work on Street Architecture, or the erection of public and private buildings in towns and cities. In its execution and principal features, it will be similar to the work just concluded. The first part will make its appearance at no distant day.

FINIS.

CIRCULAR STAIR BUILDING.

THE accompanying plates of stair lines were prepared by Robert Riddell, Esq., well known as one of the most accomplished stair builders of this city. They form a part of the mode which he proposes making public in a work soon to be issued. Those who have paid attention to this branch of art will at once see the value and meaning of the diagrams. Those desirous of making a practical use of the plates will be able to understand their meaning from the following explanations.

Fig. 1, ground plan on the line A W; lay off one half the number of steps that is required in the cylinder; in this there is five; the half pace is considered equal to one; the manner of doing this is shown in Fig. 2; from the line of the string draw C P at right angles to C S; from C to T half a step; the distance from T to P equals two steps; with a radius from b k make an intersection, the line V O; from the point of intersection, draw lines T o P, and where these lines cut the cylinder at d N, t gives the position of the risers. We will now return to Fig. 1. Draw the tangent L N through the centre of the rail; make L R equal to the height of two and a half risers; make the line R S T equal to the common plane or pitch board, cutting the tangent at N; from N draw the intersection N S, extended to e; draw e o B through the centre of rail and at right angles to intersection; draw H o and P B parallel to N f; extend P B both ways; make B A equal to P S; draw A F, extended to C, cutting the intersection at e. This gives the required plane, also the semi-major axis, and the plumb bevel, which is shown at A, and also at Fig. 6, Plate 3. To obtain the bevel for the joint, draw f W, and where it intersects at V, draw V k P. The line that intersects at M is at right angles to V P; and with M for a centre, draw the quadrant; with the same centre extended to N, draw the quadrant N W; then M X W is the bevel for the end of the joint and is shown at Fig. 5, Plate 3. For the spring bevel at the intersection at T, draw m n at right angles to P S; at n as a centre draw the quadrant, from which the line extended to draw P is the required bevel. This will not be required if a tip is taken off each end of the mould, and slide the mould on the square edge of the plank according to the plumb bevel, shown on Fig. 6, Plate 3; draw the centre of rail G C, Plate 3, Fig. 4, equal to P f, Fig. 1, Plate 1. The chord P g, Fig. 1, Plate 1, transfer to G L, Fig. 4, Plate 3; draw the line A L K extended, and at right angles draw A B, which gives the quadrant of the rail; draw L H and c a at right angles to A G; on the major axis, with a radius of A E, with A for a centre, make an intersection on the lines A K, A B; draw the lines L H c a at right angles to A G or parallel to the major axis; at the points of intersection drop perpendiculars to cut these lines. This at once gives the exact quantity of the ellipses for the rail. Draw the lines A H and A C, at G, shows the centre of rail, with half the width in the compasses, with L and C for a centre; mark the width of rail on the line A K A B; these lines extended, cutting A H and A C, give the points that the trammel will pass through. Any quantity of straight wood may be added and is drawn, parallel to the line A C. In order to determine the width of the mould on the major axis, and also to set the trammel, a new and beautiful principle is shown. Draw the diagonal G E, extended with one half the width of rail, on each side of the major axis; cutting the diagonal line G E let fall perpendiculars, then M N is the given width of mould. In its application, the stuff may be cut square through or vertical, at the discretion of the workman. Either way produces the same results, the edge of the plank perfectly square. The manner of sliding the mould is shown at Fig. 6, Plate 3, half the distance that the plumb bevel makes through the plank with the centre line marked on the edge of the mould, which is shown at *b a*; this equally divides the plank from its centre; the thickness of plank is shown at *d c*.

Fig. 2, Plate 2, the half twist. The drawings are so near alike that a brief description will be sufficient. The only difference is that the height of both wreaths is taken together on the line X Z; the height, which is equal to two and a half risers at the intersection of tangents at Y, make Y K equal to the whole diameter; extend Y both ways to F C; draw F K where P *i* is intersected; at P draw P E parallel to *j i* D *c*, extended to B. To the tangent Y K draw D E, at right angles to Y X; from D through the centre of the rail at C, draw the intersection; the remainder of the drawing is the same as plate 1, Fig. 1; make *o* L equal to P I; the distance A B is the semi-diameter of the rakeing mould, Fig. 3, Plate 3; the distance F P is the semi-diameter of the mould for the level part; the right line E H is the joint; all the centre joints are at right angles from the face of the plank; the bevel, as applied to the level, is shown at A B C D, Fig. 3, Plate 3; and its application the same as Fig. 6; the position of the rail landing is shown in plate 2; the line R *h* is the last riser; *g h* extended is the common plane or pitch board; *f e* half a riser. This makes the balusters on the level, the same height as the long balusters on the steps.

In drawing the moulds, the centre of the rail is first laid down, and from this, as a basis, the moulds are constructed. The wreaths, when sawed out, at once give an outline of the required curve; and as we have adopted a centre line for its formation, the centre on each end of the wreath piece is taken as a point to square from, which is all that any workman wants. Falling moulds we discard, from the fact that their application to cylindrical surfaces, in nine cases out of ten, produces a deformed and crippled curve.

FINIS.

Plate 1.

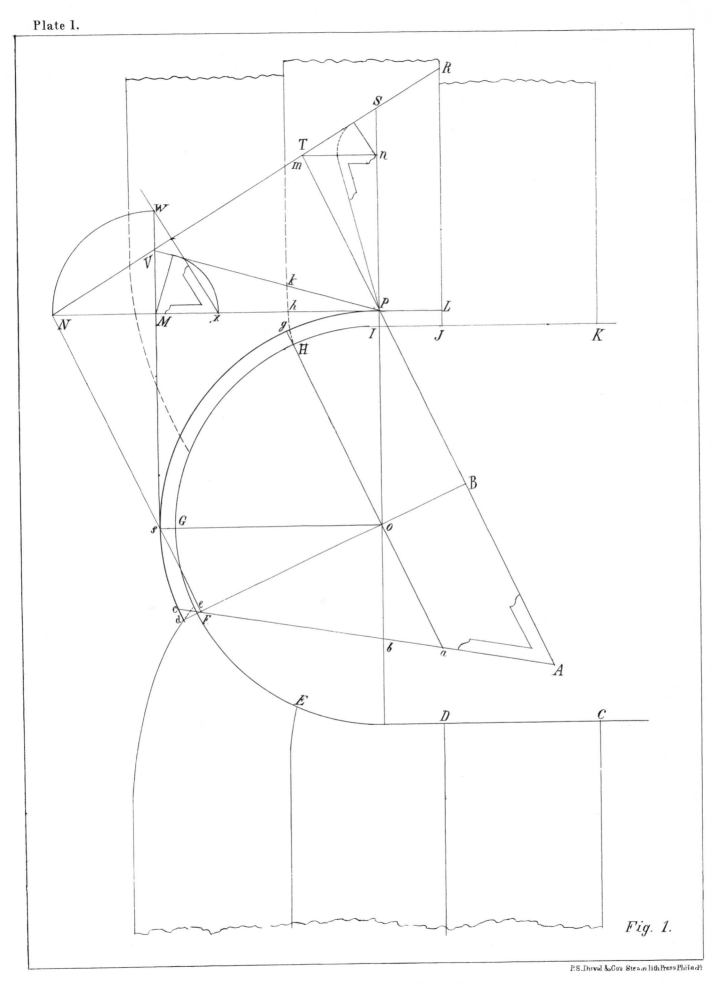

P.S. Duval & Co's Steam lith Press Phila d̃a

DIAGRAM OF STAIR LINES.

Fig. 1.

Plate 2.

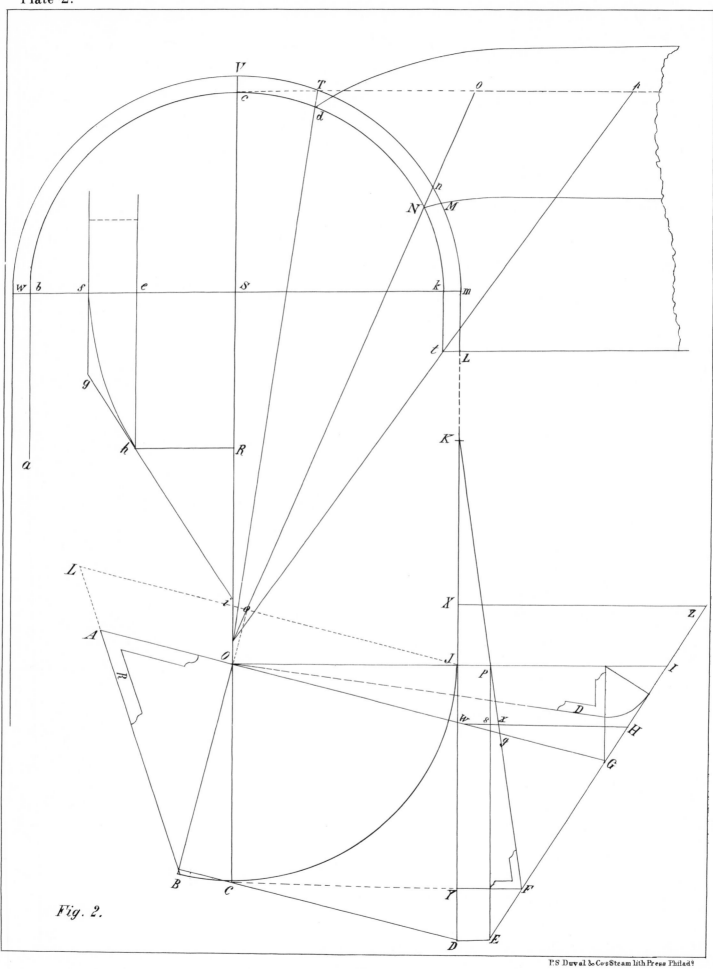

Fig. 2.

P.S Duval & Co⋅Steam lith Press Philadᵃ

DIAGRAM OF STAIR LINES.

Plate 3.

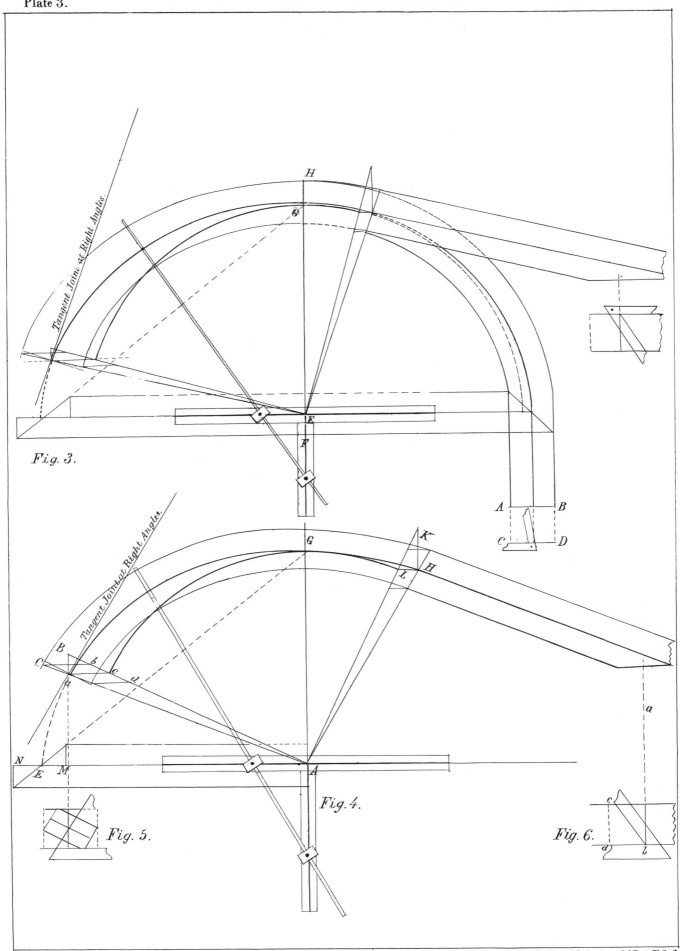

Fig. 3.

Tangent Joint at Right Angles.

H

e

E

F

A   B

C   D

G

K

Tangent Joint at Right Angles.

B   L   H

C   b

a   c   d

N

E   M   A

a

Fig. 4.

Fig. 5.

Fig. 6.

c

d   l

DIAGRAM OF STAIR LINES.

TERRA COTTA ORNAMENTS
for Cottages, Villas, Pleasure Grounds &c.

Such as Chimney Tops, Vases, Flower Pots and Pedestals,
Fountains, Statuary &c.&c. From the Garnkirk Works.

Imported and for Sale at Moderate Prices by

J. E. MITCHELL   14 York Avenue, Philadelphia.